D1827533

POSTCONFLICT ECONOMICS IN SUB-SAHARAN AFRICA

Lessons from the Democratic Republic of the Congo

Editor Jean A.P. Clément

International Monetary Fund

Production: Grammarians, Inc.
Cover design: Luisa Menjivar
Cover photograph: Marco Longari/AFP/Getty Images

Cataloging-in-Publication Data

Postconflict economics in Sub-Saharan Africa : lessons from the Democratic
   Republic of the Congo / Jean A. P. Clément, editor — Washington, D.C. :
International Monetary Fund [2004].
      p. cm.

   ISBN 1-58906-252-3

   1. Postwar reconstruction — Economic aspects — Congo (Democratic
Republic) 2. Congo (Democratic Republic) — Economic policy. 3. Congo
(Democratic Republic) — Economic conditions. 4. International Monetary
Fund — Congo (Democratic Republic) 5. Civil war — Economic aspects
— Africa, sub-Saharan. I. Clément, Jean A. P. II. International Monetary
Fund.

HC955.P67 2004

Price: $28.00

Address orders to:
External Relations Department, Publication Services
International Monetary Fund, Washington, D.C. 20431
Telephone: (202) 623-7430; Telefax: (202) 623-7201
E-mail: publications@imf.org
Internet: http://www.imf.org

Contents

Page

Foreword v

Acknowledgments vii

1. Introduction and Overview
    Jean A.P. Clément 1

2. The Democratic Republic of the Congo:
    Lessons and Challenges for a Country Emerging From War
    Jean A.P. Clément 6

3. The Economics of Postconflict Countries:
    A Survey of the Literature
    Ragnar Gudmundsson 62

4. The Economics of Civil War in Sub-Saharan Africa
    Charles Amo Yartey 87

5. Economic Performance over the Conflict Cycle
    Nicholas Staines 129

6. Sources of Growth in the Democratic Republic of the Congo:
    An Econometric Approach
    Bernardin Akitoby and Matthias Cinyabuguma 177

7. Political Instability and Growth in the Central African
    Republic, a Neighbor of the Democratic Republic
    of the Congo
    Dhaneshwar Ghura and Benoît Mercereau 205

8. Empirical Evidence of the Sources of Hyperinflation
and Falling Currency
Bernardin Akitoby 226

9. Challenges to Financial Intermediation in the Democratic
Republic of the Congo
Bernard Laurens and Wim Fonteyne 236

10. Rebuilding Fiscal Institutions
Nicolas Calcoen 263

11. Structural and Sectoral Policies and Their Sequencing
Jacob Gons 281

12. The Long Road to Demilitarization: 1997–2003
Markus Kostner, Ely Dieng, and Adriaan Verheul 303

The following symbols have been used throughout this volume:

. . .   to indicate that data are not available;

—   to indicate that the figure is zero or less than half the final digit shown, or that the item does not exist;

–   between years or months (e.g., 2003–04 or January–June) to indicate the years or months covered, including the beginning and ending years or months;

/   between years (e.g., 2003/04) to indicate a fiscal (financial) year.

"n.a." means not applicable.

"Billion" means a thousand million.

Minor discrepancies between constituent figures and totals are due to rounding. The term "country," as used in this volume, does not in all cases refer to a territorial entity that is a state as understood by international law and practice; the term also covers some territorial entities that are not states, but for which statistical data are maintained and provided internationally on a separate and independent basis.

Foreword

The Democratic Republic of the Congo (DRC), the third-largest country in Africa, is making significant strides at both the political and economic fronts to extricate itself from one of the bloodiest wars in African history (resulting in 3 million deaths) and decades of economic mismanagement. The DRC has succeeded in breaking the vicious circle of hyperinflation, falling currency, and collapsing output. This remarkable turnaround offers interesting lessons for countries coping with conflict and for the international community in its efforts not only to prevent conflict but also to provide adequate and timely support to postconflict countries. One important lesson is that the early involvement of the International Monetary Fund was key in catalyzing support for the reformers inside the country and fostering the goodwill of the international community to help buttress the peace process.

The DRC still faces many challenges ahead, in particular, the demobilization and reintegration of all ex-combatants, the creation of a unified army, the holding of free elections, and the reunification of the country, while, at the same time, it needs to consolidate the remarkable progress achieved so far in creating a macroeconomic environment conducive to sustainable growth and the reduction of poverty. If the DRC succeeds in addressing these challenges, it could become one of the main engines of growth in Africa. However, this achievement will only be possible if the international community intensifies its efforts to strengthen the peace process in the Great Lakes region, hopefully with the genuine participation of all countries concerned. Creating a durable peace in the heart of Africa would alleviate the suffering of millions of Africans, while contributing to a more stable world.

This book looks at the lessons and challenges from conflict to reconstruction, providing a summary of the most recent research on conflict, an analysis of the causes of conflicts in Africa, and their key economic characteristics. It reviews the remarkable turnaround in the DRC and its efforts to cope with the many challenges in its path from conflict to stabilization and to reconstruction. These issues have been at the center of the IMF staff's work on the DRC in recent years.

The book brings together material and analysis prepared during late 2000 to mid-2004 by the IMF team working on the DRC under the supervision of Jean A.P. Clément, and includes an insightful article from our colleagues from the World Bank on the demilitarization and reintegration of ex-combatants in the DRC. The team of authors was led by Jean A.P. Clément and included Bernardin Akitoby, Nicolas Calcoen, Matthias Cinyabuguma, Ely Dieng, Wim Fonteyne, Daneshwar Ghura, Jacob Gons, Ragnar Gudmundsson, Markus Kostner, Bernard Laurens, Benoît Mercereau, Nicholas Staines, Adriaan Verheul, and Charles Yartey.

Abdoulaye Bio-Tchané
Director
African Department

Acknowledgments

The authors acknowledge the valuable support, input, and comments provided by a number of current and former colleagues at the International Monetary Fund, including Olivier D'Ambrières, Christian Bremeersch, Dominique Bouley, Alain Catalan, François Corfmat, Noël Guetat, Brett House, Jérôme Fournel, Arend Kouwenaar, Stéphane Schlotterbeck, and Prosper Youm. Stéphanie Denis and Ngoc Le provided excellent research assistance, and we are indebted to Marie-Jeannette Ng Choy Hing, Marthe Malouf-Hardesty, and Moira Sucharov for assisting with numerous drafts. The authors are grateful to Thomas Walter and Thea Clarke for their skillful editing of the book and Jeffrey Hayden and Gail Berre of the External Relations Department, who coordinated its production. The IMF team working on the Democratic Republic of the Congo (DRC) has enjoyed the support and close collaboration of colleagues from the World Bank, including, in particular, Emmanuel Mbi (former country director for South Central Africa and the Great Lakes department), Xavier Devictor, Brendan Horton, Helena Ramos, Yvan Rossignol, and Onno Ruhl. This book would not have been possible without the unrelenting support of the management and staff of the Central Bank of the DRC, the ministry of budget, the ministry of finance, the ministry of planning, and the fruitful discussions with the representatives of the international community and the DRC's civil society. The DRC team would like to extend its warmest thanks to the Congolese authorities for their hospitality and openness in discussing the many challenges facing their country.

The opinions expressed here, as well as any errors, are the sole responsibility of the authors and do not necessarily reflect the views of the Congolese authorities, the Executive Directors of the IMF, or other members of the IMF staff.

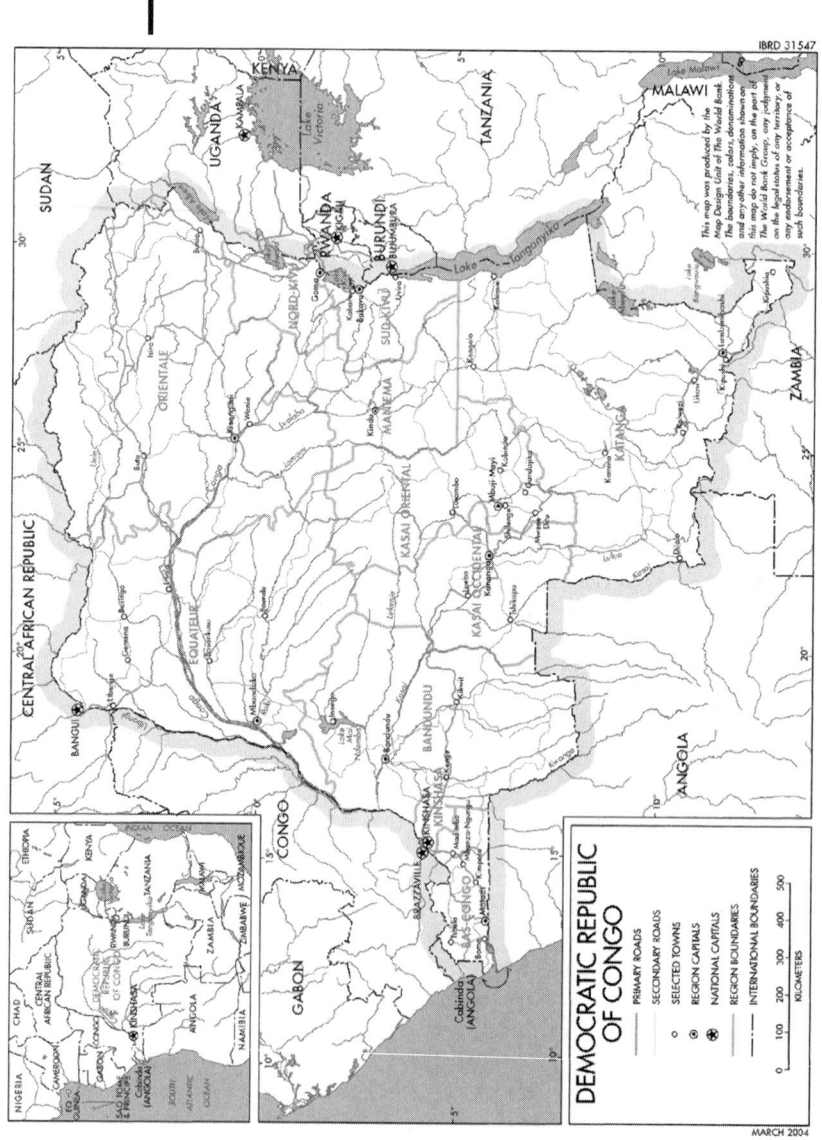

DEMOCRATIC REPUBLIC
OF CONGO

PRIMARY ROADS
SECONDARY ROADS
SELECTED TOWNS
REGION CAPITALS
NATIONAL CAPITALS
REGION BOUNDARIES
INTERNATIONAL BOUNDARIES

KILOMETERS

0   100   200   300   400   500

IBRD 31547

This map was produced by the
Map Design Unit of The World Bank.
The boundaries, colors, denominations
and any other information shown on
this map do not imply, on the part of
The World Bank Group, any judgment
on the legal status of any territory, or
any endorsement or acceptance of
such boundaries.

MARCH 2004

viii

1

Introduction and Overview

JEAN A.P. CLÉMENT

Internal conflict and wars have seriously affected Africa's development and caused immense suffering to its population. One of the bloodiest wars since World War II took place in the Great Lakes region. The Democratic Republic of the Congo (DRC), the third-largest country in Africa, had the sad privilege to be the main battlefield of the conflicts, which involved seven neighboring countries. This war, which some labeled as the "Third World War," directly or indirectly affected about 100 million people. However, since early 2001, under the leadership of its new president, Joseph Kabila, the DRC has made remarkable progress in moving from conflict to reconstruction.

This turnaround on both the political and the economic front, while fragile, offers lessons and challenges not only for other postconflict countries but also for the international community, in particular the International Monetary Fund. One key lesson is that an early, proactive, and coordinated approach of the international community and the IMF and World Bank is critical for taking advantage of windows of opportunity opened by the willingness of country officials (even if they are few) to extricate their country from war. This early involvement is not without risks, but is essential to create a momentum and catalyze support inside and outside the country involved in a conflict. Another key lesson is that a lasting peace process must include an economic pillar that duly takes into account the particular characteristics of a country (or region) exiting from war. This is crucial to buttress the peace dividends that will gradually benefit the entire population and, therefore, its support of the peace process. Authorities must early on reach a common diagnosis of the economic situation and share it with representatives of civil society and the international community. A common diagnostic helps in forging the ownership of a well-sequenced road map of measures to address the economic situation as well as in ensuring the timely support of the international community, including the early buttressing of administrative capacity. The new Transitional Constitution of the DRC foresees the holding of free and transparent elections after a two-year interim period. The holding of elections now scheduled for 2005 will be facilitated by a steadfast implementation of the regional demobilization and reintegration program of armed forces. Notably, the United Nations and European Union will help the DRC prepare for the elections, which represent the hopes and aspirations of millions of people for the installation of a major democracy in the heart of Africa.

This book addresses the different lessons and challenges that a post-conflict country faces in its path from conflict to reconstruction, focusing particularly on the case of the DRC and the Great Lakes region. It also offers a summary of the most recent research on conflict and its implications for postconflict assistance. The book investigates the causes of the civil wars in sub-Saharan Africa, including in the Great Lakes region. In particular it analyzes the sources of growth in the DRC and the impact of the conflict on the Central African Republic (C.A.R.), a neighboring country. It reviews the issues of financial disintermediation and sources of the vicious circle of hyperinflation and falling currency in the DRC. The book analyzes the challenges of rebuilding institutions, addressing structural bottlenecks, and coping with debt overhang. Finally, the book reviews the demobilization and reintegration of armed forces, with particular emphasis on its regional implications.

Lessons and challenges for a country exiting from war

Chapter 2 attempts to show how the early, proactive approach of the IMF and the ensuing timely support of the international community have been critical in strengthening the DRC's peace process and its remarkable economic turnaround. It shows that the mutually reinforcing support of the IMF and the actions of proreformers in the DRC government, despite the risks involved, were essential in putting in place a courageous, bold, and front-loaded economic agenda that helped stabilize the macroeconomic situation and led to the normalization of financial relations with the international community while addressing the debt overhang. The chapter reviews the dire situation facing the country in early 2001, and the content and results of the enhanced interim program monitored by the IMF, as well as results achieved thus far under the economic program of the government supported by the Poverty Reduction and Growth Facility of the IMF, the design of which was consistent with the DRC government's poverty reduction strategy.

The economics of civil war and sources of growth

Chapter 3 summarizes the most recent research on conflict, with a focus on its economic, rather than social or political, dimensions. It offers a number of recommendations regarding the main areas in which to concentrate efforts to assist countries emerging from conflicts. Chapter 4 recalls the experience of about 20 countries in sub-Saharan Africa that have undergone at least one period of civil war since 1960. It investigates econometrically (the Collier-Hoeffler model) the causes of civil wars by determining which factors are more important in explaining the risk of civil war, including in the Great Lakes region. More specifically, it examines the extent to which economic growth and the development of good-quality institutions can help prevent civil wars in sub-Saharan Africa. Chapter 5 takes a detailed look at the profile of economic growth in 24 conflicts since 1970. It argues that there was a significant shift in the key economic characteristics of these conflicts during the 1990s, including shorter conflicts, deeper economic contractions, and a stronger rebound in growth after conflict. It explores the role of macroeconomic policy and changes in aid flows since the end of the cold war in causing this shift, in particular regarding the DRC. Chapter 6 investigates econometrically the sources of growth in the DRC, using the Johansen and Juselius (1990) and Johansen (1988 and 1991) methodology of cointegration, interpreted as representing a long-run equilibrium relationship. It evaluates the relative importance of productivity growth and factor accumulation. Unlike most studies on sources of growth, the analysis is extended to key sectors of the economy: agriculture, mining, and transport. Chapter 6 also assesses the DRC's medium-term growth prospects. Based on the econometric findings, the analysis suggests a simple methodology for projecting the real GDP growth rate. Chapter 7 addresses the causes of political instability and growth in the C.A.R. It finds, among other things, that successful efforts on the part of neighboring countries (including the DRC) to resolve conflicts and achieve sustained growth would be beneficial to the C.A.R.'s economic performance.

Financial intermediation

Chapter 8 describes how the Central Bank of the Congo is facing the challenges of addressing financial disintermediation and dollarization and discusses the recent experience of nonfungibility between cash and bank deposits. It draws lessons for other postconflict countries in the conduct of monetary policy and the need for early technical assistance. Chapter 9 analyzes the causes and consequences of the hyperinflation and falling currency rates that the DRC experienced until it succeeded in breaking this vicious circle with the implementation of a bold program monitored by the IMF.

Rebuilding institutions

Chapter 10 underlines the message that rebuilding macroeconomic management capacity was key in the recent economic turnaround in the DRC. Compared with a few other examples in which a number of international donors provided technical assistance from the outset (e.g., in Afghanistan), this rebuilding was made possible only because the IMF provided early and comprehensive technical assistance while a full peace agreement was still being negotiated. The chapter highlights the importance of an early strengthening of budget control and tracking of expenditure (including budget formulation and execution and reform of the civil service), as well as the enhancement of revenue mobilization. It offers important lessons for other postconflict countries on the sequencing of policies and the provision of international support and notes that the reunification of a country poses particular challenges. Chapter 11 describes how assistance from the World Bank, followed subsequently by other international partners, was also key in progressively removing major structural bottlenecks to growth. It notes, in line with Chapter 10, that the sequencing of measures was not fortuitous in helping to create a link early on between the macroeconomic and microeconomic reforms through the creation of an overall legal framework conducive to private-sector-led growth (notably through the adoption of new mining, forestry, labor, and communication codes). The strengthening of good governance and transparency in public affairs is also a key aspect of the Congolese authorities' new economic strategy, as illustrated particularly by the adoption of a new code of ethics for the civil service and the creation of a new institution, Bureau Central de Coordination, which ensures, with the help of the World Bank, a transparent procurement and bidding process.

The long road to demilitarization

Chapter 12 reviews efforts regarding the demobilization and reintegration of ex-combatants in the DRC between 1997 and 2003. Shortly after coming to power in May 1997, the new Congolese authorities requested assistance for the preparation and implementation of a demobilization and reintegration program for members of the army of the ousted regime. The renewed outbreak of war in August 1998 put these activities on hold but, with the signing of the Lusaka cease-fire agreement in July 1999, the international community was able to launch several small-scale initiatives. A reinvigorated, concerted effort was begun in mid-2002. These activities were increasingly brought under a new regional framework, the Multi-Country Demobilization and Reintegration Program. International coordination and capacities improved significantly during 2003, and the DRC government has started to assume a leadership role with the creation of a national institutional structure in December 2003.

2

The Democratic Republic of the Congo: Lessons and Challenges for a Country Emerging From War

Jean A.P. Clément

The Democratic Republic of the Congo (DRC) has made remarkable progress in the past three years to extricate itself from one of the bloodiest wars since World War II. The war had devastating effects on the population, which had already suffered from the plundering of the country's vast natural resources during the colonial period and under the corrupt regime of President Mobutu. The DRC is rated today as one of the poorest countries in the world, a tragic irony and infamous episode in human history, characterized by the globalization of greed.

This chapter attempts to show how the early, proactive approach of the International Monetary Fund and the ensuing timely support of the international community have been critical in strengthening the DRC's peace process and its remarkable economic turnaround. It shows that the mutually reinforcing support of the IMF and the actions of the proreformers in the DRC government, despite the risks involved, were essential in buttressing the peace process and putting in place a courageous, bold, and front-loaded economic agenda. It also highlights the fact that in addition to the usual political and security pillars, a lasting peace agreement must include an economic pillar.

Section I provides a background to the dire economic and social situation that led the country into a full-fledged war. Section II describes the critical role of the proactive approach adopted by the IMF staff. It also suggests that intense and timely discussions with a broad spectrum of representatives of civil society and the international community are crucial to forge ownership of the economic reform agenda. This section points out the need for early technical assistance in addressing macroeconomic structural bottlenecks in a sequenced manner. Section III describes the content of the interim program, which was monitored by IMF staff, and of the mutually reinforcing actions in the political, security, and economic areas that helped move the country forward. Section IV discusses the period from macroeconomic stabilization to reconstruction and from conflict to reunification. Section V concludes the chapter, drawing lessons and presenting challenges for the DRC, both of which could be of interest to other postconflict countries.

Section I. A Dire Economic and Social Situation

The DRC is the third-largest country in Africa, with an area of 2.3 million square kilometers (about the size of western Europe). The DRC is potentially one of Africa's richest countries. It is endowed with fertile land, vast mineral reserves (copper, cobalt, coltan, diamonds, and gold), huge hydroelectric potential, and one of the largest rain forests in the world, containing numerous species of precious wood. Its population, estimated at about 56 million (comprising more than 350 ethnic groups) is growing at a rate of 3 percent a year and ranks fourth largest in Africa. The country occupies the basin of the 4,300-kilometer-long Congo River, with 11 highly diverse provinces stretching from the Great Lakes region to the Atlantic Ocean. Its regional importance, with internal waterways and land links to nine states, makes the DRC a potential engine for regional growth as significant as South Africa.

This unique endowment, however, has been more of a curse to the Congolese than a source of development.[1] A succession of predator governments sustained by powerful—local and international—vested interests have not been able or willing to translate this potential in a virtuous circle of growth and poverty alleviation. The regime of "Maréchal" President Mobutu Sese Seko (1965–97), which was supported by the West during the cold war period, was marked by widespread corruption and the plundering of natural resources to the benefit of only a few.[2] The collapse of the state and the misguided policies were punctuated by frequent riots and arson by an unpaid military and civil service, which led to the destruction of infrastruc-

---

[1]Notwithstanding the fact that the country in the 1960s enjoyed one of the best education systems in Africa as well as a strong civil service and dyamnic entrepreneurship.

[2]A political background is included in Appendix 2.1.

ture and plunged the population into abject poverty. In the early 1990s, most western countries and multilateral institutions—including the IMF and World Bank—which had been indulgent toward what was then Zaïre during the cold war and until the fall of the Berlin Wall, suspended their economic assistance.[3]

The overthrow of the Mobutu regime by the forces of Laurent Kabila in 1997 was greeted with hope, but a devastating war broke out shortly thereafter, in August 1998. The war, which lasted until the end of 2002, involved seven neighboring countries that sent troops to the DRC; four (Angola, Namibia, Zimbabwe and (initially) Chad) sided with the DRC government and three (Burundi, Rwanda, and Uganda) sided with the rebel groups, mainly in the eastern DRC. About half of the national territory was occupied. This war led to "a silent human genocide" that was hardly mentioned in the international press until late 2000. It resulted in 3 million deaths (2,500 deaths per day); millions of displaced people; a growing number of refugees, disabled people, widows, and orphans; the systematic rape and enslavement of young girls and women; enrollment of child soldiers; total isolation of large parts of the territory; the closure of the Congo River; and the destruction of infrastructure, including hospitals and schools. Pandemics, such as human immunodeficiency virus/acquired immunodeficiency syndrome (HIV/AIDS), malaria, cholera, and malnutrition increased dramatically, and life expectancy plunged (see Box 2.1). In addition, according to successive United Nations (UN) reports,[4] foreign as well as local forces systematically plundered the natural resources of the country. The formal economy shrank dramatically through the reckless abuse of an unlawful situation by a number of corrupt international and local companies, as well as private individuals, pushing the population into an even more dire state of poverty. Today, more than 80 percent of the population lives on much less than US$1 per day.

In July 1999, the DRC government and five of the seven foreign countries taking part in the conflict signed an accord at a conference in Lusaka, Zambia, while the two main rebel groups signed in August. The accord called for a cease-fire, a troop standstill, the disarmament of the militias by the de facto administration in each region, and the initiation of an inter-Congolese dialogue leading to reunification and a political solution to the

[3]The financial arrangements with the IMF before the war in 1998 included a medium-term program supported by the IMF's Structural Adjustment Facility approved on May 15, 1987, and a Stand-By Arrangement supporting a one-year program approved on June 9, 1989. Both programs encountered difficulties early on and were eventually suspended.
[4]See Appendix 2.2 for a list of UN resolutions on the DRC since 1990.

Box 2.1. Key Social Indicators in the Democratic Republic of the Congo

- Life expectancy. The rates are 51 years for men and 47 years for women (down from 54 years and 51 years, respectively, in 1966).
- Infant mortality. The rates are 101 deaths per 1,000 in the cities, and 161 deaths per 1,000 in rural areas.
- Maternal mortality. The rate is 1,850 deaths per 100,000 live births (the highest in Africa).
- HIV/AIDS. The prevalence rate is high: in Kinshasa, 15 percent of infants under 5 years old are reported to be infected. The situation is much worse in the eastern provinces.
- Illiteracy. The rate has increased to 41 percent from 26 percent in 1992.
- School enrollment. The rates are 75 percent at the primary level and 25 percent at the secondary level (the Roman Catholic Church is managing 80 percent of primary and 60 percent of secondary education).
- Water. Eighty percent of the population (45 million people) has no access to safe water.
- Electricity. Only 6 percent of the population has access to electrical power.

---

conflict.[5] The Lusaka Accord, which was quickly and widely violated by all of the concerned parties, represented nevertheless a milestone in what would be a slow and difficult peace process. About 60 percent of the country (with a population of more than 30 million) was then under the control of the government. Highly tentative estimates indicated that the Congolese army or FAC (Forces Armées Congolaises) numbered about 185,000 soldiers, of whom about one-third were combat capable. The FAC was backed by about 30,000 soldiers from allied forces. The rebel groups, including several Congolese militias, comprised about 100,000 combatants (see Box 2.2 for a list of the factions involved in the conflict).

---

[5]The main provisions of the Lusaka Accord of July 10, 1999, included (1) the creation of a joint military commission comprising representatives of all parties to the conflict and responsible for monitoring the peace agreement in conjunction with the UN; (2) the deployment of a UN peacekeeping force; (3) the withdrawal of all foreign troops within nine months of the signing of a cease-fire; (4) the disarmament and repatriation of all armed groups operating in the DRC; (5) the holding of an inter-Congolese dialogue between the Congolese government and the armed and unarmed opposition; and (6) the granting of amnesty for all rebel groups, excluding those implicated in acts of genocide. In the 18-month period following the accord, little progress was made, and

---

Box 2.2. Key Actors in the Great Lakes Region Conflict

Between 1996 and 2001, armed forces of seven countries, rebels groups, and militias fought a terrible war in the DRC.

Of the foreign countries involved in the conflict, four were on the government's side—Angola, Namibia, Zimbabwe, and (initially) Chad—while three were on the rebel side—Burundi, Rwanda, and Uganda.

Key former rebel movements included the following:

- Rassemblement Congolais pour la Démocratie (RCD-GOMA), supported by Rwanda and headed by Azarias Ruberwa, in control of large parts of eastern provinces;
- Mouvement pour la libération du Congo (MLC), supported by Uganda and headed by Jean-Pierre Bemba, in control of the northern regions; and
- Breakaway factions of the original RCD, in control of stretches of territory in the eastern and northeastern parts of the country.

Several Congolese militias (including Mayi-Mayi and Banyamulenge groups) were also active in the eastern part of the country.

Section II. Seizing a Window of Opportunity (Late 2000–Early 2001)

Initiating Contacts with Proreform Officials in Late 2000

During 2000, the Congolese authorities showed an interest in strengthening cooperation with the IMF staff. Following a private visit by Mr. Camdessus in May 2000[6] to Kinshasa at the invitation of President Laurent Kabila, a DRC delegation, including Mr. Masangu, Governor of the Central Bank of the Congo or BCC (Banque Centrale du Congo), who participated in the Annual Meetings of the IMF and the World Bank in Prague in September 2000, expressed to management the Congolese authorities' desire to renew discussions with the IMF staff. Subsequently, IMF management decided that a small staff team would take advantage of its participation in October 2000 in a Forum on Public-Private Partnership in Kinshasa, organized by the United States

---

fighting continued, more or less continuously, despite periodic cease-fires and intense diplomatic activity. For more details, see "Peace Agreements Digital Collection: Democratic Republic of the Congo." Available via the Internet: http://www.usip.org/library/pa/drc/drc_07101999.html

[6]Mr. Camdessus left the IMF in February 2000. He was succeeded by Mr. Köhler as Managing Director of the IMF in May 2000.

Agency for International Development to initiate contact with the Congolese authorities and discuss plans for future policy discussions. The World Bank staff would also be participating in the discussions, enabling a close collaboration between the two institutions.

At that time, the DRC was still at war, and the security situation in Kinshasa was rated as phase 4 by the United Nations.[7] The team found that a window of opportunity was opening in the DRC, as a small group of key officials inside the government were advocating a change in the economic policy stance to address the rapidly deteriorating economic situation. Several members of the international community in Kinshasa, though fully supportive of the resumption of a policy dialogue between the Bretton Woods institutions and the DRC, were skeptical of the DRC government's willingness to change its course of action. Nevertheless, most of the community welcomed the IMF's initiative, noting that the Lusaka peace agreement did not include an important pillar: the economic aspect of the process. In contrast, a few believed that beginning a dialogue and possibly normalizing relations with the international community were premature, as it could send the wrong signals to the Congolese authorities to continue waging war, thus undercutting the ongoing peace initiatives.

During the October 2000 visit, staff discussed IMF policies relevant to the circumstances of the DRC, as well as the willingness of the IMF to support a comprehensive adjustment program under the Poverty Reduction Growth Facility (PRGF) once a strong track record of policy implementation had been established and, eventually, assistance under the Heavily Indebted Poor Countries (HIPC) Initiative. To this end, the staff noted that the IMF would be willing to work with the authorities (in close collaboration with the World Bank) to help elaborate a comprehensive policy framework, which would need to be monitored by an interministerial committee. This framework could be the basis of an interim program of the government, which could be monitored by the IMF staff. At the Congolese authorities' request, the mission left a note summarizing the IMF's cooperative approach to protracted arrears cases and outlining what could be the main elements of

---

[7]UN security phase designations comprise the following: (1) phase 1—precautionary (a warning about the security situation in the country); (2) phase 2—restricted movements (a much higher level of alert and imposition of major restrictions on movement of personnel); (3) phase 3—relocation (serious security threat exists, may result in relocation of personnel, and travel strictly limited); (4) phase 4—program suspension (relocation outside the country of all nonessential personnel and travel strictly limited); and (5) phase 5—evacuation (travel to the country is cancelled).

an interim program. Such a program, if implemented steadfastly, would help the authorities establish a track record that could facilitate the normalization of relations with the international community. The possibility of renewing such relations contributed to the deepening of the debate within the government, setting in opposition those who preferred the status quo and those who were in favor of a change in the policy stance. The Congolese authorities took several important actions just after the mission left Kinshasa that showed their willingness to move forward. The actions included, notably, the repeal of a decree forbidding transactions in foreign exchange and a devaluation of the official exchange rate, with the latter action somewhat reducing the difference between the official rate and the parallel rate. The government was also reshuffled and the minister of finance was replaced.

President Kabila's First Speech to the Nation: A Clear Break From the Past

The assassination of President Laurent Kabila on January 16, 2001, could have plunged the DRC into a full-fledged war. However, his son, Joseph Kabila, was quickly nominated as the new president. On January 26, the new president, in his first speech to the nation, endorsed a political and economic agenda that represented a clear break from past policy stances. The speech, which was well received by the international community, called for (1) the achievement of peace through the reactivation of the Lusaka cease-fire agreement, which provided for the withdrawal of all foreign troops and the disarmament of rebel forces; (2) the resumption of the inter-Congolese dialogue, which should lead to the adoption of a new Transitional Constitution, the formation of a Government of National Unity and, after an interim period, the holding of free and transparent elections; and (3) the normalization of relations with the international community, the stabilization of the macroeconomic situation, and the liberalization and opening up of the economy. In addition, the speech requested the international community to help in mobilizing human and financial resources, as well as technical assistance, to support the reconstruction of the country. It was comforting to the IMF staff that all elements of the economic liberalization policies were in line with the discussions held in October 2000 with the Congolese authorities. Soon thereafter, the president made his first trip abroad, reported by the press as a success.[8] His speech and trip helped forge a growing consensus among

---

[8]The president met on January 30 with President Mbeki of South Africa, on January 31 with President Chirac of France, and on February 1 in Washington with U.S.

the international community to assist the DRC in revamping the peace process at this crucial juncture. On February 1, Mr. Köhler agreed with President Kabila that an IMF mission would visit Kinshasa as soon as possible to take stock of the situation and to initiate discussions on a comprehensive macroeconomic framework that could lay the foundation for a staff-monitored program (SMP).

IMF Multisectoral Mission Quickly Follows President's Speech

An IMF multisectoral mission headed by the African Department visited Kinshasa at the end of February 2001. The mission was relatively large, including in particular IMF technical experts in the monetary, financial, exchange rate, and fiscal areas. The early focus on technical assistance and capacity building—with involvement of all relevant IMF departments and the World Bank—allowed for a broad-based diagnosis of the economic situation, as well as the early design of a clear road map for a well-coordinated and well-targeted technical assistance strategy. The assessment shared by IMF staff and the Congolese authorities on the dire economic situation facilitated a common understanding on the design of a strategy to address the main macroeconomic disequilibria and distortions.[9] The assessment was also shared by representatives of civil society, including labor unions and the domestic and foreign private sector, which contributed early on to the design of measures. Finally, frequent contacts with the press were also key to forging a broad-based consensus and, through the pointed questions of domestic and foreign journalists, to obtaining feedback.

Openness was, therefore, crucial to the success of the new strategy that was being designed under the leadership of the president himself. The direct involvement of President Kabila and the IMF team's frequent meetings with the president avoided misunderstandings regarding the strategy being developed by the Congolese authorities. The IMF mission left with the Congolese authorities a detailed note that provided a diagnosis of the economic situation and proposed key elements of a comprehensive macroeconomic framework that could serve as the basis of an interim

---

Secretary of State Powell, President Kagame of Rwanda, Mr. Köhler, and Mr. Wolfensohn, the President of the World Bank. President Kabila also met with UN officials and Belgian authorities on his return to Kinshasa.

[9]The IMF team benefited as early as October 2000 from a good set of data that the Congolese authorities had prepared, as well as insightful discussions on the macroeconomic situation with the BCC, which was the only institution that was still functioning well. During the war, the BCC continued to collect data and produce reports of rather good quality despite the difficult operating environment.

program monitored by the IMF staff. The mission also left a list of measures that needed to be implemented immediately, including, in particular, measures aimed at regaining control of public expenditures and mobilizing fiscal revenue, reestablishing the independence of the central bank, and preparing for the adoption of a floating exchange rate system.

The multisectoral mission was followed by several IMF technical assistance missions in the areas of expenditure management, revenue mobilization, monetary and exchange rate policy, central bank management, and statistics.[10] Close collaboration with the World Bank (including several subsequent joint missions) allowed substantial progress to be made in implementing key structural reforms of macroeconomic relevance, in particular in the areas of public enterprises, the financial sector, the banking system, and the mining sector. Close coordination with bilateral donors in the field and through regular donor meetings enabled the IMF and World Bank to keep bilateral creditors informed and to stress the need for timely assistance. Finally, its observer status on the UN Planning and Management Task Force on the DRC (created at the request of the UN secretary-general in 2001) allowed IMF staff to closely follow and discuss political and military developments that had a bearing on the economic and financial situation of the country and to inform UN agencies about economic and financial developments and policies in the DRC. This cross-fertilization of information and exchange of views on the country's situation was extremely helpful to the IMF staff in forging a coherent and broad-based assessment of the rapidly evolving situation in the country.

Reaching a Common Diagnosis on the Dismal Economic Situation

On the economic front, the authorities and IMF staff agreed that the economic situation of late 2000 to early 2001 was characterized by a vicious circle of hyperinflation, a continued depreciation of the currency, increasing dollarization and financial disintermediation, a lack of saving, falling production in both agriculture and manufacturing, a deterioration of infrastructure, a generalized impoverishment of the population, an alarming spread of pandemics, and the reappearance of previously eradicated diseases, such as tuberculosis and leprosy. The lack of medical supplies further aggravated the situation. The scarcity of inputs contributed to a continued decline in production and a rise in the cost of goods and services. The government also had to contend with a serious

---

[10]See Chapters 9 and 10 for more details.

lack of office space and equipment it needed to operate adequately. It was trying by all means to obtain foreign exchange currency to finance the war. To that end, it pursued ill-advised interventionist policies, including tax harassment of the few enterprises still operating, and authorized arbitrary arrests and imprisonment by security forces, creating an environment of fear and lawlessness that pushed many operators into the parallel economy. The government compounded these actions by granting to dubious operators (including foreign armed forces) monopolies and mining concessions with tax privileges for the production and marketing of key products, notably diamonds. Multiple exchange rates and price controls generated significant distortions in relative prices and shortages of basic items and petroleum products.[11] The regulatory framework was heavy, lacked transparency, and was applied in an arbitrary fashion, engendering a climate of suspicion and economic insecurity that discouraged investment. Poor maintenance led to the rundown of infrastructure and of capital stocks. In this context, real economic growth fell by more than 40 percent over the 1995–2000 period. Output in all sectors was well below 1990 levels, and annual per capita GDP plummeted from US$224 (or about US$1 a day) in 1990 to US$85 (or US$0.23 a day) in 2000 (see Figure 2.1). Consumer prices rose at an annual average rate of 554 percent in 2000 (see Figure 2.2), and the gap between the official and parallel foreign exchange rates widened to more than 550 percent. The primary source of hyperinflation was the unbridled monetization of an uncontrolled budgetary deficit, stemming from the collapse of the expenditure system and of fiscal revenue.[12] The lack of transparency and governance also contributed to this situation. In 2000 the budget deficit (on a commitment basis) was estimated to have been equivalent to about 120 percent of government revenue. With the decline in economic activity and the shift of transactions to the nonofficial economy, the tax base shrank and budgetary revenue collapsed to less than 5 percent of GDP (the lowest in Africa; see Figure 2.3). This shrinkage was exacerbated by numerous tax exemptions, widespread fraud in the tax administration, and the diversion of revenue from the budget. Recorded budgetary expenditures were almost twice as large as revenues. Security-related payments, including military wages, were given priority while other payments were cut back. Investment outlays were negligible. The control of expenditure was weak, and extrabud-

---

[11]The DRC is a crude-oil-producing country (8.5 million barrels a year).

[12]See Chapter 8 for a discussion of the sources of hyperinflation and falling currency in the DRC.

Figure 2.1. During the War, GDP per Capita Plummeted

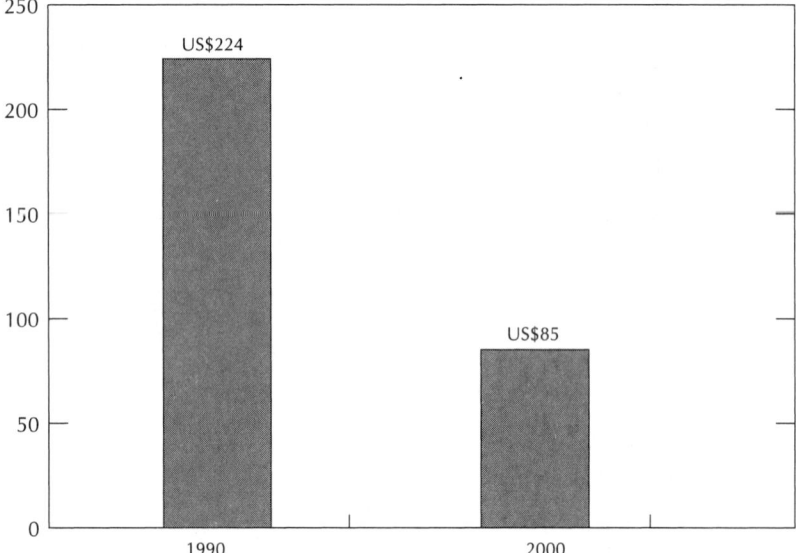

Sources: Congolese authorities; and IMF staff estimates.

Figure 2.2. During the War, Inflation Accelerated Sharply
(Average annual percent change)

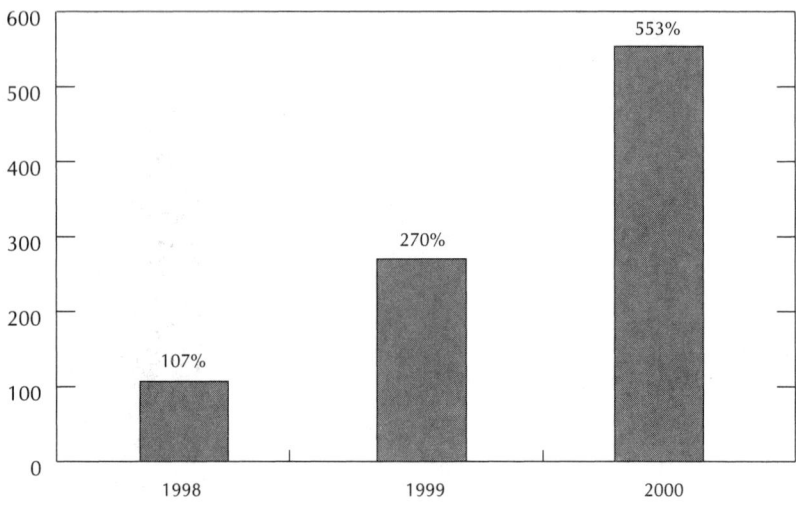

Sources: Congolese authorities; and IMF staff estimates.

Figure 2.3. During the War, the Tax Base Shrunk
(Percent of GDP)

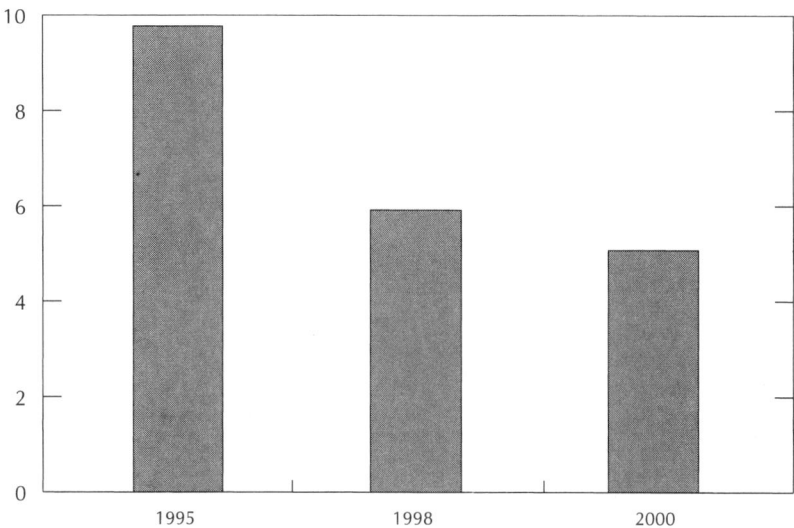

Sources: Congolese authorities; and IMF staff estimates.

Figure 2.4. During the War, Money Supply Increased with Monetization of the Fiscal Deficit
(Percent of beginning-of-period broad money)

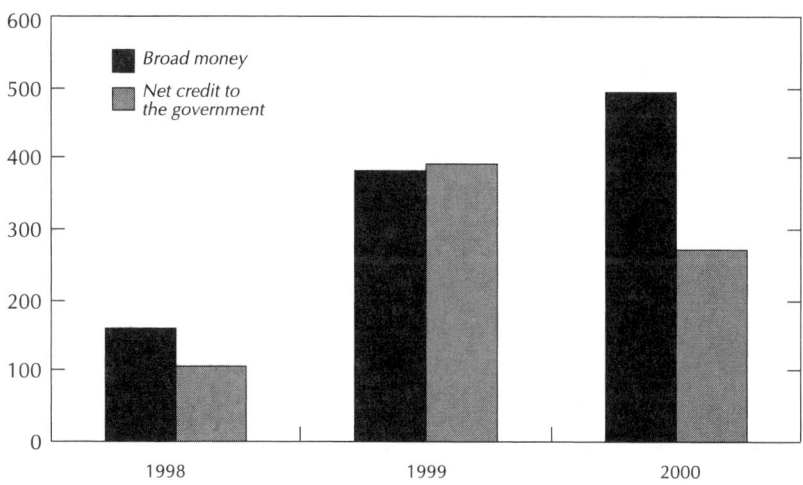

Sources: Congolese authorities; and IMF staff estimates.

getary spending, mostly related to war and sovereignty expenditure, amounted to nearly 70 percent of total revenue. The overall fiscal deficit was financed entirely by monetary expansion and through the accumulation of domestic and external arrears (see Figure 2.4). The role of the central bank was reduced to the monetization of the budgetary deficit, and it completely lost its independence in the conduct of monetary policy. The banking system was largely insolvent, and about half of the existing banks went bankrupt. The public's loss of confidence in the national currency and the banking system led to extensive dollarization and financial disintermediation.[13] The external position was extremely weak, reflecting the fiscal stance and domestic supply constraint. Foreign official reserves fell to less than two weeks of imports of goods and nonfactor services. The stock of external debt at the end of 2000 amounted to about US$13 billion (equivalent to about 900 percent of GDP), of which 80 percent constituted arrears on debt-service payments, including to the IMF and the World Bank (see Figure 2.5).

Figure 2.5. Composition of External Arrears by Creditor Type at End-December 2001
(Percent of total)

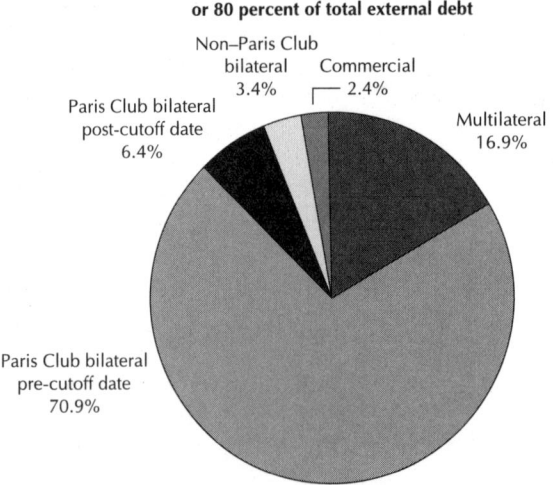

Nominal value of external arrears: US$10,646 million or 80 percent of total external debt

Non–Paris Club bilateral 3.4%

Commercial 2.4%

Paris Club bilateral post-cutoff date 6.4%

Multilateral 16.9%

Paris Club bilateral pre-cutoff date 70.9%

Sources: Congolese authorities; and IMF staff estimates.

---

[13]See Chapter 9 for a discussion of the problems of financial disintermediation.

Buttressing the Ongoing Peace Process with an Economic Pillar

The IMF multisectoral mission found that, in the face of a dismal economic situation, there had been a marked turnaround in the attitude of the Congolese authorities, and there was now a strong commitment, including at the presidential level, to address the alarming situation prevailing in the country. The main goal of the new strategy was to break the vicious circle of hyperinflation[14] and depreciation of the currency through strict budgetary and monetary policies. To reduce price distortions, a floating exchange rate would be adopted, most prices as well as interest rates liberalized, and the economic regulatory framework made more transparent and simple.[15] This attitude was underscored by the appointment of a reform-minded government on April 14, 2001. On this basis, and to ensure that the ongoing peace process on the political side would be buttressed by an economic pillar, IMF management, after consultation with the IMF Executive Board, decided to send a mission in early May 2001 (with World Bank staff participation) to negotiate an SMP and to conduct discussions for the 2001 Article IV consultation. This represented the start of the normalization of the DRC's relations with the IMF and, consequently, with the international financial community.

At the time of the multisectoral mission, the DRC had been in continuous arrears to the IMF since November 1990. On September 6, 1991, the DRC was declared ineligible to use the general resources of the IMF, and a declaration of noncooperation was issued on February 14, 1992. The voting and related rights of the DRC in the IMF were suspended on June 2, 1994. On March 18, 1998, the Executive Board decided that, at the next review of the DRC's overdue financial obligations, the IMF would consider adoption of a decision providing for the initiation of the procedure of compulsory withdrawal from the IMF unless the member resumed cooperation with the IMF. In light of the unsettled political and security situation and the limited information available on economic developments and policies, the Executive Board subsequently decided on several occasions to postpone the postsuspension review of the DRC's overdue financial obligations. In November 2000, the Executive Board once again decided to postpone the review for six months, to provide the Congolese authorities time to advance

---

[14]The Congolese authorities agreed that because hyperinflation was one of the most pernicious taxes on the population, particularly wage earners and the poor, its elimination would alleviate considerably the hardship of the population and reduce social tensions.

[15]The IMF mission left with the Congolese authorities a detailed note, along with a clear road map of the measures needed.

the peace process, improve the security situation, and design and implement appropriate economic policies. On May 2001, the Executive Board again postponed the review for six months, or to the next Article IV consultation with the DRC.

In early 2001, after years of turmoil and war, the political situation in the DRC was improving, thanks to the reactivation of the Lusaka cease-fire agreement, UN involvement, and enhanced inter-Congolese dialogue. Upon taking office, President Joseph Kabila consistently stated his commitment to restore peace and enforce the terms of the Lusaka agreement. Following the president's visit to the UN in February 2001, the UN Security Council demanded that all troops in the DRC withdraw nine miles from frontline positions within two weeks starting March 15. This was to allow UN military observers and support troops to be deployed to monitor a cease-fire. The UN confirmed later that the withdrawal of troops was broadly on schedule and the cease-fire was generally holding. A delegation of 15 members of the UN Security Council visited Kinshasa on May 18, 2001, to take stock of the situation. In late May, UN troops began reopening and policing traffic on the Congo River, a vital link in the country's transportation system. The UN Security Council hoped not only to encourage momentum for the pullback of troops but also to win approval of African governments for an international conference on the economic and political developments of the Great Lakes region.[16] At the invitation of President Kabila, the UN-appointed facilitator, Sir Ketumile Masire, former President of Botswana, visited Kinshasa to help prepare for the inter-Congolese dialogue. On May 18, 2001, a presidential decree was signed liberalizing political activities.

Section III. The Government Interim Program: A Clear Break From the Past

Content of the Program

With the above-mentioned progress on the political front, the Congolese authorities believed that the conditions were ripe for adopt-

---

[16]An important complicating factor in this respect was the continued plundering of the DRC's natural resources by foreign military forces, armed groups, some officials, and private individuals and companies (as reported in the UN Security Council in May 2001 by the Panel of Experts on the Illegal Exploitation of Natural Resources and Other Forms of Wealth of the DRC; UN, April 12, 2001, and Addendum of November 13, 2001).

ing and implementing an enhanced interim program that could be monitored by the IMF staff. The staff concurred with this assessment, but stressed that successful implementation of an SMP would critically depend on continued progress toward peace, the strengthening of government policy coordination, and the timely support of the international community. The program would be implemented in a difficult environment. In particular, the security situation, though improving, remained fragile, as political tensions had not yet subsided. Although the risks were substantial, it was worth seizing the window of opportunity. A delayed response from the IMF might have endangered the peace process, giving ammunition to the nonreformers inside and outside the country who were recklessly benefiting from the war.

The staff report on the 2001 Article IV consultation and discussions on an SMP, which was discussed by the IMF Executive Board on July 13, 2001, represented a milestone in the normalization of the DRC's relations with the IMF.[17] The Congolese authorities purposely designed, with IMF help, an ambitious macroeconomic stabilization program for the June 2001–March 2002 period to reverse the serious deterioration of the economic and financial situation. The SMP consisted of a critical mass of well-sequenced, bold, and front-loaded adjustment measures aiming principally at breaking hyperinflation, stabilizing the economic situation, and laying the foundation for a restoration of growth and reconstruction. The authorities viewed this program as a critical first step for restoring economic stability. They also saw it as the first phase of a broader strategy for postconflict reconstruction and poverty alleviation that they intended to put in place in due time. Finally, the Congolese authorities took an important action to buttress the transparency of their actions by making public the IMF staff report for the 2001 Article IV consultation and SMP.[18]

The enhanced interim program, while ambitious, duly took into account key constraints facing the DRC: (1) half of the country was still not under the control of the government, thus implying the need to ensure an appropriate level of security expenditure; (2) debt service could not be paid in the short term, given the low level of foreign reserves, and arrears on external debt service would therefore continue to accu-

---

[17]Before 2001, the IMF Executive Board last discussed a DRC Article IV consultation staff report in 1996. Article IV consultations are the main vehicle to exercise surveillance on members' economic and financial policies. Completing a consultation requires, among other things, that the member be willing to provide sufficient economic and financial information to the IMF.

[18]See Appendix 2.3 for a list of IMF staff reports since early 1990.

mulate; and (3) civil service salaries had been gravely eroded by hyper-inflation (by 60 percent in real terms in the previous two years), and there was therefore a need to substantially increase nominal salaries while ensuring that they were paid on time.[19] This realism helped in consolidating the ownership of the program, thereby furthering the chance of its successful implementation.[20]

To achieve the program's objectives, macroeconomic policies in-cluded, among other things, the following: (1) a return to a normal budgetary process[21] and a restrained budgetary policy centered on strict adherence to a monthly treasury plan; (2) a prudent monetary policy, consistent with the objective of breaking hyperinflation and buttressed by the adoption of new statutes of the central bank enshrining its in-dependence; (3) the liberalization of all prices[22] and interest rates; and (4) the adoption of a floating exchange rate system. Well-sequenced and far-reaching structural measures, designed with the help of the World Bank, were intended to pave the way for a significant reduction in price distortions, a strengthening of the banking sector, an improve-ment of governance and economic security, headway in the fight against corruption, and the liberalization of the economy. The SMP in-cluded quarterly quantitative and structural indicators to help the Congolese authorities monitor its implementation. In addition, it in-cluded quarterly reviews, which allowed IMF staff and Congolese au-thorities to adapt the program to changing circumstances and, in particular, to the weaknesses in administrative capacity, as well as the exogenous and internal shocks that were related mainly to a still un-stable security environment.

To gather early support from the international community, a meeting of donors took place in Paris in December 2001, with the participation of a Congolese delegation. The group discussed a strategic list of invest-ment projects aimed at addressing the most urgent structural and supply bottlenecks. The main goal of convening such a meeting early on was to meet near-term needs to support the government, as well as to provide

---

[19]Salaries were increased by 141 percent in May 2001. The regular payment of salaries had a positive social impact because it provided more stable financial means to house-holds (one civil servant salary finances on average the basic needs of about 10 family members).

[20]This message was conveyed by President Kabila to Mr. Köhler during his visit to Kinshasa in April 2002.

[21]With all expenditures (including military and sovereignty-related outlays) and rev-enues centralized at the treasury.

[22]Except for the prices of water, electricity, and transportation, which would be re-viewed regularly based on operating costs.

the necessary capacity for the implementation of a possible successor medium-term, PRGF-supported program. The buttressing of capacity would also help in the design of a poverty reduction strategy that could form the basis of an interim Poverty Reduction Strategy Paper (interim PRSP) endorsed in time by the IMF and the World Bank's respective Executive Boards.[23] This early support from the international financial community, and in particular from the IMF and the World Bank, sent a strong signal to the Congolese government that a satisfactory implementation of the SMP, together with further progress in consolidating the peace process and the inter-Congolese dialogue, would open the way for further support beyond humanitarian and food aid.

Progress Toward Peace and Economic Stabilization (2001 to early 2002)

On the political side, progress toward peace continued and the cease-fire generally held while the withdrawal of foreign troops started. All Namibian, most Ugandan, and some Angolan and Zimbabwean troops were leaving the country, and Burundi announced its intention to withdraw its troops. However, Rwanda, which had reportedly deployed an average of 30,000 soldiers in the eastern DRC, had not yet moved its troops, as it insisted, among other things, on the disarmament of the two Rwandese rebel groups operating in the DRC.[24] At the end of January 2002, the UN Organization Mission in the DRC (MONUC), which had deployed about 3,600 peacekeeping troops, started phase III of its operations, which provided in particular for the disarmament and demobilization of rebel groups. Following a difficult start in Ethiopia in November 2001 caused by a lack of financing, the inter-Congolese dialogue resumed on February 25, 2002, in Sun City, South Africa, and gained momentum from March to April 2002 with the hosting of a conference by President Mbeki of South Africa. The conference brought together for the first time government representatives, members of the rebel movements and the unarmed opposition, and representatives of civil society. It was expected to last for 45 days and to lead to the formation of a Government of National Unity, the adoption of a Transitional Constitution, and the holding of free and de-

---

[23]Another donors' meeting took place in June 2001 in Brussels to discuss a Multi-Country Demobilization and Reintegration Program (MDRP) for the Great Lakes region and the creation of a multidonor trust fund, to be financed jointly by the International Development Association (IDA) and other donors. The MDRP is discussed in Chapter 12.

[24]One of these rebel groups was reportedly composed of militias that had participated in the 1994 genocide in Rwanda.

mocratic elections in two years. Several commissions were constituted to deal with economic, social, and institutional matters. Although the conference ended on April 13, 2002, without a global agreement, the government did reach agreement with one of the rebel groups, the Mouvement pour la Liberation du Congo (MLC), headed by Mr. Bemba and endorsed by Uganda.[25] Under this agreement, which was supported by about 80 percent of the civil society representatives at the conference, Mr. Kabila would remain president while Mr. Bemba would become prime minister. A transitional government would be nominated in the near future. The agreement left the door open for the participation of, notably, the Rassemblement Congolais pour la Démocratie (RCD-GOMA), supported by Rwanda, which at the time rejected the agreement. With this agreement, the transitional government would control 70 percent of the DRC's territory. This partial political agreement was seen by the UN as a step forward in the inter-Congolese dialogue. However, members of the international community regretted that an all-inclusive agreement could not be reached, and they encouraged all parties to rapidly join in. A flurry of diplomatic activity took place to persuade all players, including neighboring countries, to support the formation of an all-inclusive government. Finally, just before the consideration by the IMF's Executive Board of the Congolese authorities' request for a three-year arrangement under the PRGF, a significant breakthrough was achieved on the economic front when all the delegates endorsed the new economic and social strategy presented by the DRC government (embodied in its interim PRSP). This support illustrated the ownership of the new strategy by a wide spectrum of the Congolese civil society.

On the economic side, the Congolese authorities' steadfast implementation of the SMP brought about a courageous shifting of economic policy after years of mismanagement, corruption, and civil strife. The SMP produced significant results, especially in breaking the vicious circle of hyperinflation and currency depreciation (Figure 2.6). However, although the international community was continuing to provide humanitarian aid and technical assistance, the virtual absence of foreign financial aid was causing "adjustment fatigue."[26] The macroeconomic

---

[25]The IMF staff met in Kinshasa with representatives of the MLC in February 2002. The representatives stressed that the MLC agreed with the main objectives of the economic policy of the DRC government.

[26]The report of the Security Council mission to the Great Lakes region from April 27–May 7, 2002, in paragraph 30 states: "The Security Council mission takes the strong view that further progress in the peace process take the form of economic dividends for

Figure 2.6. Selected Fiscal and Monetary Indicators, 1998–2005[1]

A. With the implementation of the SMP and the PEG, hyperinflation was broken
(Percent)

B. With the implementation of a floating exchange rate system under the SMP, the gap between the official and parallel market exchange rates became negligible
(Congo francs per U.S. dollar)

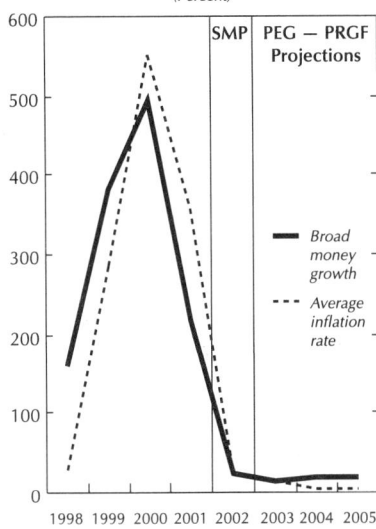

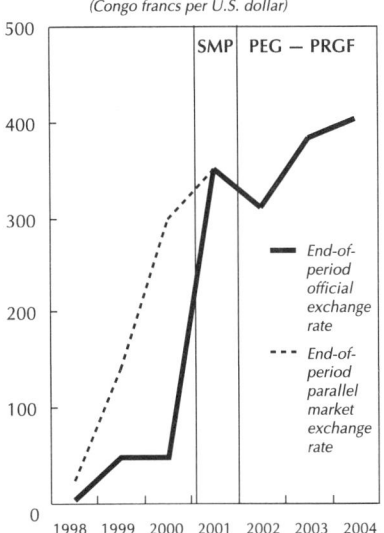

C. With the implementation of the SMP and the PEG, the fiscal situation improved and foreign-financed investment resumed during the PRGF arrangement period
(Percent of GDP)

D. With the implementation of the SMP and the PEG, the monetization of the fiscal deficit ceased
(Change in percent of beginning-of-period broad money)

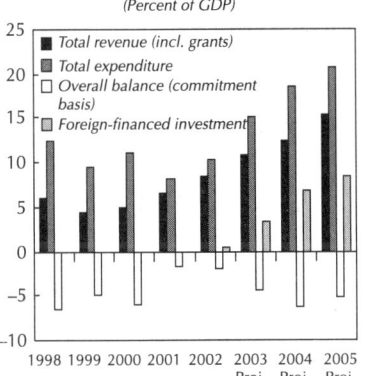

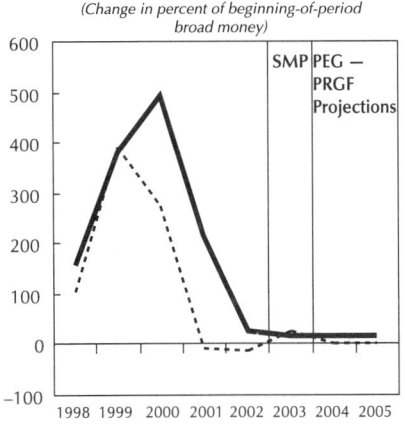

Sources: Congolese authorities; and IMF staff estimates and projections.
[1]The staff-monitored program (SMP), June 2001–March 2002. The Government Economic Program (PEG) is supported by an arrangement under the Poverty Reduction and Growth Facility (PRGF), April 2002–July 2005.

situation stabilized, following the implementation of bold and front-loaded measures. Inflation sharply decelerated from a monthly average of 18 percent during the January–May 2001 period preceding the program (an annualized rate of 632 percent) to 0.7 percent during June–December 2001 (an annualized rate of 8.8 percent). This remarkable achievement led to a stabilization of the exchange rate under the new floating exchange rate system. The difference between the official rate and the free market rate fell from the 600 percent registered before the implementation of the floating exchange rate in May 2001 to less than 1 percent at the end of December 2001. Although economic growth was negative for the year as a whole, there were some signs of recovery.[27] At the end of March 2002, all quantitative indicators of the program were met and most wage arrears had been eliminated. Important progress was made in strengthening public finances through a return to normal budgetary procedures, including the centralization of revenue and expenditure, as well as a reduction in the number of extrabudgetary channels. For the first time in many years, the budget was adopted by parliament and published. The monthly treasury cash-flow plan was strictly implemented. The monetization of the budget deficit, which was the main source of hyperinflation, ceased. Audits of four commercial banks and the internal audit of the management of the central bank were completed.

On the structural side, far-reaching and front-loaded measures were implemented. First, activities in key sectors were liberalized. The monopoly on diamond marketing was abolished in February 2001. All prices were liberalized, except those for certain public utilities (transportation, water, and electricity). Thus, in 2001, to reflect changes in their respective costs, prices of transportation were raised by 167 percent, for water by 663 percent, and for electricity by 270 percent. The prices of petroleum products, which had been heavily subsidized and maintained well below international prices, were increased by about

---

the population. The delay in achieving this risks the credibility of the process and of the international community. Accordingly, all efforts should be made to ensure that humanitarian aid, as well as longer-term economic and development assistance is provided to the DRC as soon as possible in support of the peace process. Only thus can a sound basis be created for a more durable peace." This was an important message to the donor community. IDA was the only donor at the time that was disbursing direct budgetary aid, as part of a US$50 million grant for an Emergency Early Recovery Project approved following the discussion by the IMF Executive Board of the SMP in July 2001. This grant was used for key infrastructure projects, the social sectors, and capacity building.

[27]See Chapter 6 for a discussion of the sources of growth in the DRC.

300 percent on May 2001, while a transparent and automatic price-setting mechanism was put in place. The heavy subsidies and smuggling to neighboring countries were de facto eliminated. Also, petroleum product imports were liberalized. The combined effect of these measures was to improve sharply product delivery and transportation as a whole.[28] In turn, this increased the supply of basic foodstuffs from the producing regions to the cities and lowered related prices, although progress in this regard continued to be hampered by the lack of road maintenance.

Second, to enhance economic governance and create a more transparent and predictable business environment, the legal framework underwent important changes: (1) a new investment code was published in February 2002, reflecting international best practice; (2) a new mining code was also published in July 2002 while a forestry code was being finalized, with both ensuring a transparent and competitive attribution of concessions; and (3) the judicial system was progressively strengthened, notably with the support of the European Union, including the publication of the decree creating commercial courts in July 2001. Furthermore, a labor code, clarifying the rights of employees and employers, was drafted with the help of the International Labor Organization.

Third, a good governance/anticorruption plan was in preparation. This plan included, first, the adoption of a code of ethics and good conduct applicable to all levels of the civil service. Second, the preliminary financial audits of the customs and tax departments and of most of the 114 public enterprises were completed. Following these audits, which were published in the local press, most directors of revenue-collecting agencies (*régies financières*) and public enterprises were dismissed and replaced. The directors of public enterprises, for their part, were replaced by temporary administrators, pending the restructuring, privatization, or liquidation of these enterprises. As the third part of the good governance/anticorruption plan, the audits of provincial finances led to the replacement of the governors, vice-governors, and senior staff in all but one province.

---

[28]Queuing at the gas station (sometimes for several days) ended. A few corrupt companies and individuals, including from the military, benefited from the system by buying imported petroleum products at the official prices and selling them at the parallel market prices. The increase in official prices to reflect international prices thus had a limited negative social impact.

Section IV. From Stabilization to Reconstruction and from Conflict to Reunification (2002–03)

Toward the Normalization of the DRC's Relations with the IMF

In view of the encouraging results achieved on both the political and the economic front, IMF management (after consulting with the Executive Board) decided to send a mission in February 2002 to negotiate a medium-term program (covering April 2002–July 2005) that would be supported by a three-year arrangement under the PRGF. This decision was another milestone in the normalization of the DRC's relations with the IMF and the international community. It demonstrated clearly to the Congolese authorities that progress on the economic front and the consolidation of peace could indeed yield important peace dividends to the country. In the event, negotiations were successful, and, in that context, Mr. Köhler visited Kinshasa on April 30, 2002.[29] The Congolese authorities' request for a three-year arrangement under the PRGF was presented to the IMF Executive Board on June 12, 2002, together with their interim PRSP and the preliminary document under the enhanced HIPC Initiative.[30] Significantly, President Kabila himself signed the letter of intent requesting the PRGF arrangement, as well as those letters related to the subsequent reviews every six months. In doing so, the president wanted to show the international community his willingness to exercise strong leadership in the formulation, monitoring, and implementation of the program. However, before the IMF Executive Board date of June 12, 2002, a number of hurdles needed to be overcome: (1) the modalities of arrears clearance to the IMF, the World Bank, and the African Development Bank (AfDB) Group had to be formulated; (2) an agreement in principle of financial support from the donor community, including the Paris Club creditors and other multilateral institutions, had to be reached;[31] and (3) a problem arising from a "vulture fund" had to be resolved.

---

[29]The managing director of the IMF was the first head of an international financial institution to visit the DRC since early 2001. His visit was welcomed by the population and provided a strong signal to the reformers in the DRC that the IMF supported their courageous shift in the policy stance.

[30]The submission to the Board of the PRGF-supported program was made only after implementation of a number of actions included in the authorities' program. Details on the content of the program and the modalities of its monitoring are available in the related IMF documents posted on the IMF website (http://www.imf.org) both in English and French.

[31]On January 17, 2002, in an informal session, the Paris Club creditors took note of the need for a comprehensive rescheduling of the DRC's debt in the context of a PRGF

An innovative approach was followed concerning the modalities of arrears clearance to the multilateral institutions. First, with regard to the IMF, the DRC's arrears amounted to SDR 402.2 million (or 75 percent of its current quota in the IMF). These arrears were cleared just before the IMF Executive Board's consideration of the DRC's request to use IMF resources under the PRGF through a one-day bridge loan financed by Belgium, France, South Africa, and Sweden. Taking into account the strength of the PRGF-supported program and the country's postconflict financing needs, the IMF Executive Board decided to grant the DRC total access over the period of the PRGF arrangement equivalent to SDR 580 million (or 109 percent of its current quota). Such access was above the average for first-time PRGF users (85 percent of quota), but well below the maximum limit under exceptional circumstances of 185 percent and even under the maximum access level (140 percent of quota). Excluding the amount that was used to repay the bridge loan (about SDR 405 million), access was 33 percent of quota, or 11 percent annually. The first disbursement, which was made upon Board approval, provided sufficient resources to cover the bridge loan, and subsequent disbursements of SDR 26.7 million each were to be made upon completion of six semiannual reviews. The strength of the DRC's medium-term adjustment program, coupled with debt relief—including under the enhanced HIPC Initiative—was judged sufficient to enable the DRC to meet its obligations to the IMF. To safeguard IMF resources and to avoid an interruption of IMF financial support, the Congolese authorities decided to hold sufficient SDRs in their SDR account with the IMF to cover service falling due on a six-month rolling basis.

Second, the DRC's arrears vis-à-vis the World Bank (US$331 million as of March 31, 2002) were also cleared through a bridge loan. The IMF and Bank staffs had maintained close contact with the AfDB Group and other multilateral institutions. As of the end of 2001, the DRC's arrears with the AfDB Group amounted to US$942 million. On April 24, 2002, an agreement in principle was reached to consolidate these arrears through a partial payment/partial consolidation operation.

Third, the other multilaterals all agreed that the existing arrears, totaling US$200 million as of the end of 2001, would be consolidated, with net zero transfers in the first year of the consolidation period.[32]

---

arrangement, including a deferral of post-cutoff-date arrears and capitalization of moratorium interest.

[32]This agreement was reconfirmed on May 21, 2002, at the donors' consultation meeting held in Paris. At that meeting, donors also pledged US$2.5 billion for the financing of a critical mass of investment projects defined with the help of the World Bank for the period 2003–05.

Fourth, on September 13, 2002, Paris Club creditors agreed to provide an exceptional comprehensive (flow) rescheduling of Paris Club debt on Naples terms, with the expectation of comparable treatment for the DRC's debt outstanding to non–Paris Club bilateral and commercial creditors. The Congolese authorities' medium-term program was financed with this financial support. This step represented the full normalization of the DRC's relations with the international financial community and a demonstration of the international community's confidence in the actions of the proreform-oriented government under the leadership of President Kabila. It was expected that, with the strong implementation of the PRGF-supported program and the finalization of the peace process, the country could then benefit from further debt relief under the enhanced HIPC Initiative.

New Medium-Term Strategy for Poverty Reduction

The medium-term program was designed in line with the Congolese authorities' strategy to reduce poverty, as outlined in their interim PRSP published in May 2002.[33] The DRC government's interim PRSP details the three pillars on which the strategy is based: (1) the restoration of peace and the promotion of sustainable growth; (2) macroeconomic stabilization and the achievement of equitable and sustainable growth; and (3) the promotion of community-based initiatives. At the same time, the interim PRSP distinguishes three distinct phases of economic development. The first phase was characterized by stabilization of the macroeconomic situation (i.e., breaking hyperinflation), the removal of major economic distortions, an opening of the economy, a return to a normal and transparent budgetary process (the mobilization of revenue and traceability of expenditure), the creation of an independent central bank, and the establishment of an environment conducive to private sector activity. The first phase coincided with the SMP period and, on the political side, included progress toward peace and on the inter-Congolese dialogue.

The second phase (2002–04) is defined as the transition period, which includes the normalization of relations with the international community, the achievement of peace, the nomination of an all-inclusive transitionl government, and the reunification and reconstruction of the country. This phase coincides with the medium-term program sup-

---

[33]A full and complete PRSP is expected to be finalized in 2005. It will include a revised poverty reduction strategy based particularly on an exhaustive poverty survey and will take into account recent developments, such as the impact of reunification.

ported by the IMF through the PRGF arrangement; by the World Bank through the Economic Recovery Credit, the Emergency Multisector Rehabilitation and Reconstruction Project (EMRRP), the MDRP, and the Private Sector Development and Competitiveness Project;[34] and by financial assistance from the international community, including debt relief. The PRGF-supported program includes the consolidation of macroeconomic stabilization under a floating exchange rate regime. It envisages the formulation of a propoor budget, a shift in the composition of expenditure toward social and infrastructure expenditure, and an efficient delivery of services to the poor. It also includes the implementation of far-reaching structural reforms, the redefinition of the government's role (with the expectation that it will become a supporter of the private sector rather than a competitor and predator), the establishment of the rule of law, the progressive eradication of corruption and establishment of good governance, the continued strengthening of administrative and institutional capacities, the reform of the civil service, and the restructuring of the banking system. Overall, the second phase will consolidate the basis for a sustainable rate of growth.

The third phase of economic development (2005 and beyond) will be the development phase. This phase will be achieved by increasing access to international capital markets while significantly reducing poverty levels. On the political side, free and transparent elections will be held, and a new constitution will be adopted, enshrining democracy and the unity of the national territory.

Given the initial conditions prevailing in the country, the IMF staff agreed with the Congolese authorities that poverty could be reduced only gradually. The breaking of hyperinflation already had stopped the erosion of the real incomes of the poor. In addition, with the return of peace, the end of widespread violence (torture, rapes, and killings) would benefit the most vulnerable groups, particularly the elderly, women, girls, orphans, children, and the handicapped in the occupied territories. Finally, the rehabilitation of infrastructure should improve the delivery of basic public goods and services. Nevertheless, given the current low average per capita income and high income inequality, the poverty rate is expected to diminish slowly.

In their interim PRSP, the Congolese authorities stress that it is not feasible to try to achieve the Millennium Development Goal of reducing poverty by half by 2015. Even reducing the poverty rate by one-fourth, from the current rate of 80 percent to 60 percent, would require

---

[34]See Chapter 11 for details on the World Bank activities.

an average annual rate of real growth of more than 8 percent (given the annual population growth of about 3 percent). Thus, the authorities have defined a realistic set of macroeconomic objectives and policies,[35] which include, among other things: (1) an average real GDP growth rate of about 5 percent over the period 2002–05, to allow for an average per capita increase of GDP of 2 percent; (2) a reduction in the annual inflation rate to 5 percent by 2005; and (3) a gradual increase in gross international reserves to about 9½ weeks of nonaid imports of goods and services (see Table 2.1). The projected growth patterns are similar to those observed in other postconflict countries and are predicated on three main factors: (1) the removal of major economic distortions (notably, the unification of multiple exchange rates) and the profound change in the regulatory environment will boost economic growth by improving resource allocation and supporting a better functioning of production and trading activities; (2) the substantial increase in investment, driven by international aid (Figure 2.7) and largely consisting of a rehabilitation of infrastructure, will relieve major supply bottlenecks, leading to broad-based economic expansion; and (3) the effective reunification and the restructuring of the communication, forestry, and mining sectors. In particular, the World Bank's EMRRP will boost growth in key sectors, including agriculture, transportation, and energy, which will have a strong positive impact on real exports (an increase of 11 percent annually during 2002–05). National savings are also projected to grow over the next five years. Nonetheless, macroeconomic aggregates at the end of 2005 (exports, imports, investment, saving, and real GDP) will remain well below prewar levels.[36] The medium-term scenario underlying the interim PRSP will need to be updated regularly to take into account the impact of the country's reunification and the external assistance mobilized, including external debt rescheduling.

Comprehensive Peace Agreement and Nomination of an All-Inclusive Government During the First Year of the PRGF-Supported Program

On the political front, the DRC continued to make remarkable progress during the first year of the PRGF arrangement, culminating in the agreement signed in Pretoria on December 17, 2002, that established an all-inclusive transitional government. Before that event, the

---

[35]For more details see EBS/02/76 – Requests for the Three-Year Arrangement Under the PGRF and the First Annual Program – and EBS/02/76 suppl. 1 (5/21/02).

[36]See Chapter 6 for more details on the sources of growth in the DRC.

Table 2.1. Selected Economic and Financial Indicators, 2000–06

	2000 Estimate	2001 Estimate	2002 Estimate	2003 Projected	2004 Projected	2005 Projected	2006 Projected
	(annual percentage changes)						
Output and prices							
Real GDP	−7	−2	3	5	6	7	7
Consumer prices, annual average	550	357	25	13	6	5	5
External sector							
Exports, f.o.b. (in U.S. dollar terms)	−8	−1	22	16	11	11	11
Imports, f.o.b. (in U.S. dollar terms)	48	19	35	25	27	15	11
	(percent of GDP)						
Central government finances							
Revenue (excluding grants)	5.1	6.5	7.9	8.2	9.0	10.1	11.0
Expenditure	11.1	8.2	10.3	13.2	17.6	20.2	21.5
Overall balance (commitment basis)	−6.0	−1.7	−2.0	−3.1	−4.3	−3.3	−1.7
Investment and saving							
Gross national savings	−1.2	0.4	11.3	11.1	13.3	15.8	18.9
Of which: government	−5.6	−1.6	1.3	−0.2	2.7	6.3	9.8
Gross domestic savings	4.6	3.2	4.1	5.2	5.9	7.4	9.0
Of which: government	−3.6	−0.2	1.1	1.0	1.5	2.7	4.1
Investment	3.5	5.2	9.0	12.1	17.4	20.6	22.5
Of which: government	0.5	0.1	1.0	2.6	6.9	9.6	11.5
	(millions of U.S. dollars, unless otherwise indicated)						
Gross official reserves (end of period)	51	22	75	157	272	382	479

Sources: Congolese authorities; and IMF staff estimates and projections.

DRC had signed peace agreements with Rwanda (end of July 2002) and Uganda (early September 2002). Uganda withdrew its troops, while Rwanda reportedly completed the withdrawal of its troops on October 5, 2002. Angola, Namibia, and Zimbabwe had already completed the withdrawal of their troops. On November 11, 2002, President Kabila and President Kagame of Rwanda agreed to extend the initial peace agreement period by three months to allow for the disarming and repatriation of ex-Rwandese Hutu soldiers. Meanwhile, the UN Organization Mission in the DRC (MONUC) was deploying about 5,000 peacekeeping troops and started phase III of its operation. On

Figure 2.7. Foreign-Financed Investment, 2002–06
(Percent of GDP)

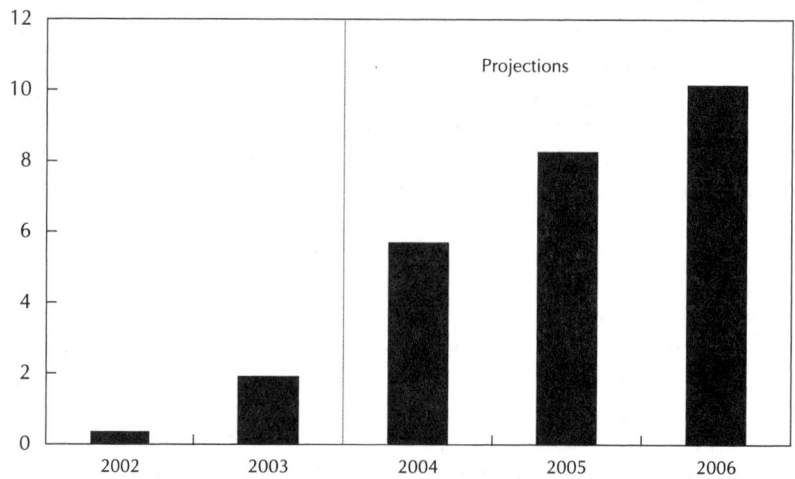

Sources: Congolese authorities; and IMF staff estimates and projections.

December 4, 2002, the UN Security Council passed Resolution 1445, raising the number of authorized peacekeeping troops assigned to MONUC from 5,500 to 8,700.

The progress made in the peace process created a renewed sense of optimism, both domestically and in the international community. Intense consultations ensued with representatives of civil society, the unarmed opposition, and all rebel movements, including the MLC, supported by Uganda, and the RCD-GOMA, supported by Rwanda. The inter-Congolese dialogue in Pretoria, hosted by South Africa's President Thabo Mbeki, and under the auspices of the UN Secretary-General's Special Envoy, Mustapha Niasse, resulted in the Pretoria agreement in December 2002 on power sharing in an all-inclusive transitional government, to assume office shortly. Meanwhile, on the basis of overall good performance under the program, the first review of the PRGF-supported program was completed by the IMF Executive Board in March 2003. At that time, the Board indicated that, with continued strong implementation of the program, as well as continued progress in the peace process and the inter-Congolese dialogue, the DRC could benefit from the enhanced HIPC Initiative in a timely manner. The new Transitional Constitution was enacted on April 4, 2003. President Kabila was sworn in as president of the DRC on April 7, 2003, for a two-year transition period, after which free and transparent elections are to be held. An all-inclusive transitional government, comprising the president, four vice-presidents, 36 ministers, and 25 vice-ministers, was nominated on June 30, 2003. The four vice-presidents are Mr. Bemba (MLC), Mr. Ruberwa (RCD-GOMA), Mr. Yerodia (the President's Party), and Mr. Z'Ahidi (unarmed political opposition). The main rebel groups were transformed into political parties. A new parliament and senate were nominated, with representatives covering the whole political spectrum. An international committee was created to monitor the transition process.

On the basis of the sustained implementation during the first year of the PRGF-supported program and the progress made in consolidating the peace process, the second review of the PRGF-supported program was completed by the IMF Executive Board on July 23, 2003. At that time, the Board also approved the DRC's reaching of the HIPC Initiative decision point. In early April 2003, Paris Club creditors provided financing assurances for the topping up of debt relief. Options for the topping up to Cologne terms of the September 2002 Agreed Minutes were discussed by the Paris Club creditors on October 8, 2003, in line with the July HIPC Initiative decision point, and an agreement was finalized in November 2003. The outstanding debt was de facto reduced by about 80 percent in net present value terms (Figure 2.8). This support from the international community, and in particular from the IMF and World Bank, once again demonstrated to the Congolese authorities that sustained progress in consolidating the peace process while simultaneously staying the course on the economic and structural reforms front was rewarding.[37]

However, the withdrawal of foreign occupying forces created a security vacuum in some parts of the country, leading to outbursts of violence, particularly in the northeast Ituri region, where rebel groups were exploiting historical rivalries between two ethnic groups (the Hema and the Lendu). This led to appalling atrocities, particularly in the town of Bunia. On May 30, 2003, the UN Security Council authorized the establishment in Bunia of an Interim Emergency Multinational Force (comprising about 700 French soldiers) until September 1, 2003. This task was subsequently handed over to MONUC, which saw its size increased and mandate broadened in October 2003. The same month, a new UN report on the illegal exploitation of natural resources was released, revealing continued intensive illegal activity in both rebel- and

---

[37]At a donors' consultation meeting held in Paris in December 2003, donors pledged US$3.9 billion for the financing of projects for the period 2004–06. A private investment forum was also held, with the participation of about 200 foreign firms.

Figure 2.8. Effect of Debt Relief in Net Present Value (NPV) Terms on NPV of Public External Debt, as of end-2002
(Millions of U.S. dollars)

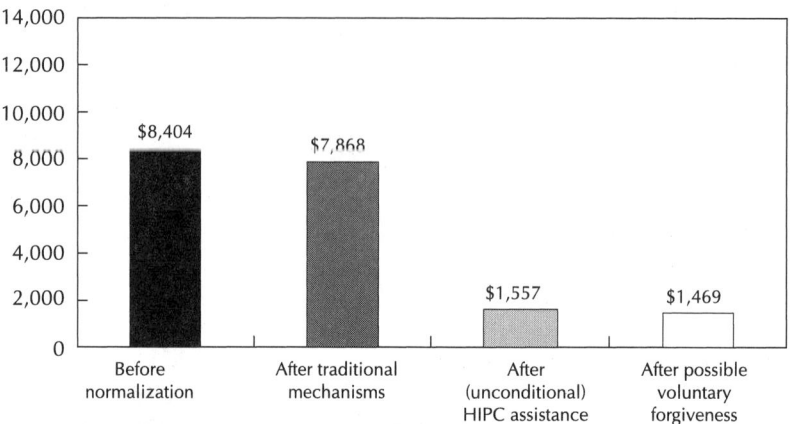

Debt-Service Ratio After HIPC, 2003–22

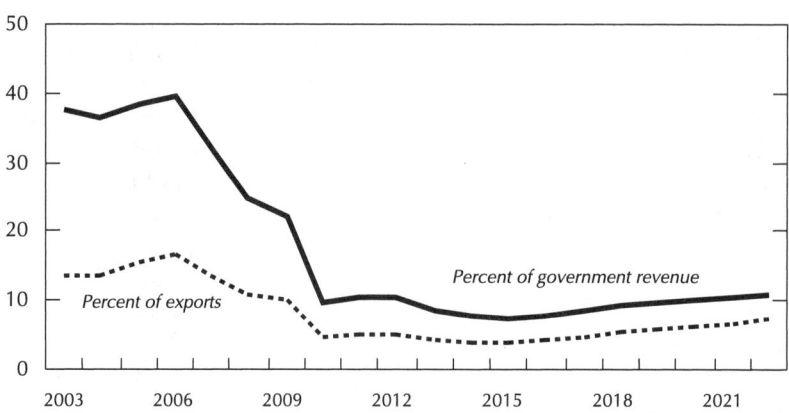

Sources: Congolese authorities; and IMF staff estimates and projections.

government-controlled areas. Achieving security for the entire territory and forcefully addressing the continued plundering of the DRC's resources remain major challenges for the new government. If these two intertwined problems are not addressed swiftly, with the help of the international community, there is a risk that they could undermine the results achieved thus far on both the economic and political fronts.

Remarkable Progress on the Economic Front

Remarkable progress was also achieved on the economic, institutional, and structural reform fronts in 2002 and 2003 under the PRGF-supported program (Figure 2.6). For the first time in 13 years, economic growth was positive, reaching 3 percent in 2002 and 5 percent in 2003. Positive growth rates were achieved in all sectors.[38] Inflation decelerated more quickly than expected. The end-period annual inflation rate, as measured by the CPI, decreased sharply from 135 percent in 2001 to 16 percent at the end of 2002, and to less than 5 percent at the end of December 2003. The Congo franc, in terms of U.S. dollars, remained stable in 2003 after depreciating by 23 percent in 2002. Gross official reserves increased from the equivalent of 1.4 weeks of non-aid-related imports in 2001 to 5 weeks in 2003.

These positive macroeconomic results were achieved through the implementation of prudent monetary and fiscal policies, together with courageous structural reforms. On the fiscal front, although the overall performance was broadly in line with the program, the anticipated shift in the composition of expenditure toward propoor spending did not fully materialize, given the shortfall in foreign-financed investment and social outlays. This outcome was compounded by higher security- and sovereignty-related expenditures both in 2002 and 2003. These higher outlays were in part explained by expenses related to the inter-Congolese dialogue and the security vacuum following the withdrawal of foreign troops, and by a noticeable weakening of expenditure control during the transition period leading to the nomination of the new government (March–June 2003). The new government subsequently put measures in place to correct for these slippages. Overall, further progress was achieved to strengthen revenue mobilization and expenditure monitoring. In particular, a new expenditure system was installed together with a new nomenclature for expenditure.[39] On the monetary side, the ending of the monetization of fiscal deficits slowed the increase in broad money as the rate decelerated from 493 percent in 2000 to 17 percent in 2003. Also, following an external audit, the BCC is implementing a comprehensive plan of action to address deficiencies in

---

[38]According to the new investment promotion agency, ANAPI (Agence Nationale pour la Promotion des Investissements), which was created to simplify administrative procedures, more than 100 investment applications from the domestic and foreign private sector, amounting to US$2.3 billion over the period 2003–07, have been approved.

[39]See Chapter 10 for a discussion on fiscal measures.

its operations and management.[40] With the good progress made on the structural side, the business environment has radically changed, creating a level playing field for private sector activity.[41] In particular, with the help of the European Union, the judiciary system for the entire territory is undergoing an audit, which should result in the formulation of a plan of action. On the external side, the DRC accepted the obligations under Article VIII, Sections 2(a), 3, and 4 of the IMF's Articles of Agreement in February 2003. With an overall rating of 3 on the IMF trade restrictiveness index (with 10 being the most restrictive), the DRC regime has become among the most liberal in Africa.

Section V. Key Lessons from the Past and Challenges for the Future

Lessons can be drawn and future challenges identified from the remarkable turnaround in the DRC's economic and financial policies.[42]

Key Lessons from the Past

In countries in conflict, it is generally recognized that the window of opportunity for the return to peace and stability tends to be small. The Congolese authorities have noted that, with regard to the DRC, the early involvement of the IMF and World Bank were key in catalyzing support for reformers inside the country and the goodwill of the international community. The quick response of the Bretton Woods institutions to the inaugural speech of President Joseph Kabila in early 2001 (which laid the basis for strengthening the peace process, the inter-Congolese dialogue, and the turnaround in economic policy) helped avoid, in their view, a possible fall back into a full-fledged war and social

---

[40]An IMF on-site safeguards assessment was conducted at the central bank in October 2002 on the basis of an external audit by a reputable international firm. As a result, a plan of action was designed to address vulnerabilities in the central bank's internal control system and its financial reporting framework. In addition, as part of the monitoring of the program, the Congolese authorities have decided that the monetary quantitative performance criteria included in their PRGF-supported program will be audited by a reputable international firm before each semiannual program review with the IMF. This represents a precedent for a country with an IMF-supported program.

[41]See Chapter 11 for a discussion on the design and implementation of structural measures.

[42]This exercise was conducted by the IMF staff and the Congolese authorities, with contributions from representatives of civil society and the international community.

chaos. Also, the Congolese authorities believed that because the Lusaka agreement had lacked an economic pillar, its effectiveness had been undermined from the outset—a lesson for future peace agreements.

Full ownership at the highest level of the new strategy ensured steady implementation of adjustment and structural reform measures, producing rapid results. Reforms were also facilitated by the creation of an interministerial committee in charge of monitoring and coordinating the program's implementation. The inter-Congolese dialogue in Sun City, South Africa, in 2002, which was attended by more than 350 representatives of civil society and all major rebel groups and political parties, was an effective forum in which to discuss and agree on the economic agenda later embodied in the interim PRSP. Timely contacts among the Bretton Woods staff, press, and civil society representatives were also key in building a wider ownership of the economic agenda.

An early assessment by the Congolese authorities, with the help of the IMF and World Bank, of the macroeconomic situation and the major structural bottlenecks facing the economy was essential to the formulation of a coherent strategy and policy mix in early 2001. The authorities stressed that early and continuous technical assistance from the Bretton Woods institutions in the budgetary, monetary, exchange rate, and structural areas was of paramount importance in drawing up a clear road map of immediate, short-term, and medium-term measures that took into account the limited administrative capacity and the specific circumstances of the country, notably the occupation of about half of the DRC by foreign forces. The early posting of four IMF technical resident experts and the opening of a resident representative office were key factors in the early strengthening of administrative capacity.

The DRC's experience shows that well-targeted and well-sequenced technical assistance is as important in postconflict settings as timely financial assistance from the international community. The Congolese authorities noted that the IMF's comprehensive assessment mission in early 2001 led to the timely formulation of an SMP even though most of the country at the time was still classified as phase 4 under the UN security system. This program helped remove major economic distortions and broke the vicious spiral of hyperinflation and currency depreciation. Given the DRC's heavy debt-service obligations, limited tax-collection capacity, and the absence of nonhumanitarian financial aid, the SMP realistically allowed for an accumulation of external payments arrears, pending the normalization of relations with the DRC's creditors. This realism helped further the chances of steady implementation of the economic agenda and clearly demonstrates that a one-size-fits-all approach is a recipe for failure.

Another important lesson is that, contingent on successful implementation, the duration of an SMP in a country emerging from conflict should not be excessively long. The end of an SMP should coincide with the launching of a PRGF-supported program to maintain the momentum of reform and to quickly mobilize external financial assistance in the form of budgetary project aid, nonproject aid, and debt relief. This view was endorsed in particular by local nongovernmental organizations (NGOs) and representatives of civil society, who stressed that quick-disbursing aid assistance could alleviate social hardship while generating peace dividends.

In a country emerging from war, such as the DRC, it is crucial that assistance comprise the right mix of humanitarian aid, project aid, budget support, and technical assistance. A judicious mix of external assistance notably increases the chances that a program will succeed and strengthen the social fabric. Humanitarian aid delivered through NGOs and religious organizations was particularly important in alleviating the suffering of the most vulnerable segments of the population, particularly in isolated areas where security and the delivery of public goods and services had collapsed. However, the absence of nonhumanitarian aid during the implementation of the SMP generated adjustment fatigue and could have led to unrest if the SMP had been prolonged. The flow of foreign aid through official channels, that is, through the central bank and the government budget, should be increased to make budgetary and monetary policies more effective. Nonproject direct budgetary aid is now needed to sustain the comprehensive reform program. Until the end of 2003, only the IMF and World Bank, among development partners, were providing financial support directly to the government and the central bank. In this regard, it is significant that the representatives of civil society have stressed the importance of closely monitoring the use of public resources, including external aid, so as to ensure the transparency and effectiveness of propoor spending.

Challenges for the Future

The strategies described in the DRC's interim PRSP and endorsed by the international community remain valid. Within the framework of the three overlapping phases—stabilization, reconstruction, and development—the DRC has moved from the stabilization phase to the reconstruction phase.

The government's principal challenge remains to consolidate macroeconomic stability while continuing far-reaching structural reforms. In light of the lessons of the recent past, and given the relatively large and heterogeneous Government of National Unity, ownership of the program remains crucially important. In addition, the reunification and related reforms will continue to demand effective interministerial coordination and well-sequenced technical assistance. Finally, timely and well-balanced external assistance will remain key to the smooth implementation of the program.

Further structural steps need to be taken to improve the business climate and to support growth, notably by cutting red tape, facilitating arbitration and legal settlements, and improving the tax regime. The DRC government is moving to join the African Trade Insurance Agency so that short-term (up to three years) transactions can be insured against political risk. The country has become a member of the Multilateral Investment Guarantee Agency. The government will need the continuous support of the international community to improve its legal and judicial systems and to publish the implementing decrees of all the codes that have been enacted. The supervision and control of the banking system will also need to be strengthened to fight money laundering and the financing of terrorism.

After decades of corruption, when the government acted more like a predator than a supporter of private sector activity, the Congolese authorities' main challenge now is to develop a culture of good governance, accountability, and respect for the rule of law and of human rights. These measures, together with the already completed withdrawal of foreign troops, should help to halt the plundering and illegal exploitation of the DRC's natural resources.

The Congolese authorities should also ensure that reunification does not jeopardize macroeconomic stability and the reform agenda. Achieving this objective will require coordinated efforts to tackle concurrently the political, security, and economic issues. Foreign assistance will need to be distributed not only to Kinshasa and the surrounding area but also to the entire country; it will also have to be scaled, sequenced, and timed in an appropriate fashion. Externally financed projects will need to continue to be monitored by the independent institution charged with coordinating this assistance (Bureau Central de Coordination) to ensure a transparent bidding process until the DRC's administrative capacity becomes adequate. The international community, including the Bretton Woods institutions, needs to continue to assist the DRC government in assessing the economic situation in all provinces, particularly in areas formerly controlled by rebels, as well as to extend the capacity-building efforts throughout the entire country. The fiscal aspects of reunification will have to be carefully monitored on both the revenue and the expenditure side. In this regard, it is important that the countrywide public service census be completed rapidly with the help of the international community.

Reunification will be strengthened by the timely implementation of the UN- and World Bank–supported regional demobilization and reintegration program. A fully accountable professional army and police force need to be created. Security for the entire territory should be implemented, and illegal activities related to the plundering of the DRC's natural resources must be addressed swiftly with the help of the international community. If actions are not taken rapidly to solve these two intertwined problems, the remarkable progress achieved so far may be gravely undermined. Finally, the elections in 2005 need to be well prepared to ensure the transparency of the process. Given the country's ethnic diversity, transparency will be key to preventing an explosion of the social fabric in the DRC.

Appendix 2.1. Political Background

1960: Independence from Belgium is attained.

1960–65: The period is marked by secessionist movements (especially in Katanga) and political instability, as well as a deep rivalry between President Kasavubu and Prime Minister Lumumba (murdered in 1961). The UN intervenes to prevent growing Soviet influence. The UN Secretary-General Hammarskjöld dies in a mysterious plane crash in 1961.

1965: A military coup is led by Colonel Mobutu, who becomes president in November 1965.

1971: The country is renamed Zaïre.

1973–75: A policy of "Zaïrianization" is followed, in which nearly all foreign-owned businesses are nationalized (including the large copper-cobalt parastatal, GECAMINES).

1978: Renewed secessionist movements in Katanga are suppressed with intervention from Belgium and France.

1990: A process of democratization is announced; social unrest grows.

1991: A national conference is convened, but soon suspended by President Mobutu; widespread demonstrations, army mutiny, and looting ensue.

1991–93: Mr. Tshisekedi is named prime minister, but relations with President Mobutu are extremely difficult. By 1993, Mobutu charges Tshisekedi with high treason, while the national conference initiates impeachment proceedings against Mobutu.

1994: A new government is established under Prime Minister Kengo.

September–October 1996: An armed rebellion begins in the Kivu region. The rebel group, Alliance des forces démocratiques pour la libération du Congo-Zaïre (AFDL) makes rapid advances.

May 1997: Kinshasa falls to the rebels, and Laurent Kabila declares himself president. The former president, Mobutu Sese Seko, flees into exile.

August 1998: Tutsi rebels backed by Rwanda and Uganda open a war against the Kabila government. Angola, Namibia, Zimbabwe, and (initially) Chad intervene to prevent a rebel takeover of Kinshasa, but rebel forces capture most of the east of the country.

July 1999: A peace agreement is concluded in Lusaka, Zambia, with the heads of state of six nations involved in the war at that time (Angola, Zimbabwe, Namibia, Rwanda, Uganda, and the DRC).

January 2000: The UN Security Council passes a resolution authorizing deployment of 500 UN military observers and 5,000 troops to support them.

June 2000: Ugandan and Rwandese troops clash in the rebel-held city of Kisangani, marking the third time that the two nominal allies fight each other in that city. At least 750 civilians are killed.

October 2000: IMF staff visit in Kinshasa.

January 2001: Laurent Kabila is assassinated in Kinshasa. His son, Joseph Kabila, is appointed president and inaugurated on January 26.

January 26, 2001: President Joseph Kabila's first speech to the nation includes a sharp turn in the political and economic agenda of the country.

February 2001: IMF multisector mission with World Bank participation in Kinshasa.

February 2001: All parties meet in Lusaka and agree to disengage to positions occupied by their forces in May 2000.

March 2001: UN troops begin deploying in government- and rebel-held areas.

July 2001: IMF Executive Board concludes the 2001 Article IV consultation and discusses the staff-monitored program (SMP).

April 2002: Peace talks among all the domestic factions—the inter-Congolese dialogue—end in an agreement under which the Congolese government, the Mouvement pour la libération du Congo (MLC), will form a transition government.

June 2002: The DRC's rehabilitation and reintegration into the international community continues apace. The IMF approves a US$750 million Poverty Reduction and Growth Facility (PRGF) arrangement in mid-year, while the World Bank approves a US$410 million credit to finance part of the country's Emergency Multisector Rehabilitation and Reconstruction project. The IMF and World Bank agreements also lead to commitment of more than US$1 billion in other donor assistance over 2002–03. The preliminary document on the enhanced HIPC Initiative together with the Interim Poverty Reduction Strategy paper are also discussed by the Executive Boards of the IMF and the World Bank.

July 2002: Talks between the Rwandan and the DRC governments result in a tentative agreement.

December 17, 2002: Agreement is reached on a final, all-inclusive settlement among all the domestic players participating in the inter-Congolese dialogue in South Africa. The agreement foresees transparent and free elections in 24 months, defines the composition of a transitional government, including vice-presidents representing the two main rebel forces, the nonarmed opposition, and the presidential party. It envisages a parliament with an assembly and a senate, and representatives of the civil society will head five commissions selected to consolidate democracy.

March 2003: The 2003 Article IV consultation and first review under the PRGF-supported program is concluded by the IMF Executive Board.

April 2, 2003: Signing of the conclusion of political negotiations by the inter-Congolese dialogue, which includes among other things, the Transitional Constitution, the memoranda on security and military issues, and the 30 decisions (*résolutions*) adopted by the participants.

April 4, 2003: The Transitional Constitution is promulgated.

April 7, 2003: President Kabila is officially sworn in as president of the transitional government.

May 2003: The four vice-presidents are nominated for the transitional government: Mr. Bemba (MLC), Mr. Ruberwa (RCD-GOMA), Mr. Yerodia (the President's Party), and Mr. Z'Ahidi (unarmed political opposition).

June 30, 2003: Nomination of members of the transitional government.

July 2003: The second review under the PRGF-supported program is concluded by the IMF Executive Board as well as the decision point under the HIPC Initiative.

July 17, 2003: The new transition government is sworn in.

December 3, 2003: The Government Action Program is delivered by President Joseph Kabila to Parliament, setting the tone for the two-year transition leading up to free and democratic elections.

December 17, 2003: At a donors' consultative group meeting in Paris, donors pledge US$3.9 billion for project financing for the program 2004–06. This is followed by a private investors' forum attended by more than 200 representatives of foreign enterprises.

Appendix 2.2. United Nations Security Council Resolutions[1]

Resolution 1234: 9 April 1999

Expresses its firm commitment to preserving the national sovereignty, territorial integrity and political independence of the DRC and all other States in the region;

Recalls that the Assembly of the Heads of State and Government of the OAU during its first ordinary session held in Cairo from 17 to 21 July 1964, adopted in its resolution AHG 16 (1) the principle of the inviolability of national frontiers of African states, as stated in paragraph 2 of the communiqué of the Central Organ of the OAU Mechanism for Conflict Prevention, Management and Resolution issued on 17 August 1998 (S/1998/774);

Concerned at reports of measures taken by forces opposing the Government in the eastern part of the DRC in violation of the national sovereignty and territorial integrity of the country;

Expresses its concerns at all violations of human rights and international humanitarian law in the territory of the DRC, including acts of and incitement to ethnic hatred and violence by all parties to the conflict;

Calls for the immediate signing of a ceasefire agreement allowing the orderly withdrawal of all foreign forces, the re-establishment of the authority of the Government of the DRC throughout its territory, and the disarmament of non-governmental armed groups in the DRC, and *stresses*, in the context of a lasting peaceful settlement, the need for the engagement of all Congolese in all-inclusive process of political dialogue with a view to achieving national reconciliation and to the holding on an early date of democratic, free and fair elections, and for the provision of arrangements for security along the relevant international borders of the DRC;

Welcomes the intention of the Government of the DRC to hold an all-inclusive national debate as a precursor to elections, and *encourages* further progress in this respect;

---

[1]http://www.un.org/documents/scres.htm

Reaffirms its readiness to consider the active involvement of the United Nations, in coordination with the OAU, including through concrete sustainable and effective measures, to assist in the implementation of an effective ceasefire agreement and in an agreed process for political settlement of the conflict.

Resolution 1258: 6 August 1999

Recognizes that the current situation in the DRC demands an urgent response by the parties to the conflict with support from the international community;

Welcomes the signing of the Ceasefire Agreement on the conflict in the DRC by the States concerned in Lusaka on 10 July 1999 (S/1999/815) which represents a viable basis for a resolution of the conflict in the DRC;

Also welcomes the signing of the Ceasefire Agreement on 1 August 1999 by the Movement of the Liberation of the Congo, expresses deep concern that the Congolese Rally for Democracy has not signed the Agreement and calls upon the latter to sign the Agreement without delay in order to bring about national reconciliation and lasting peace in the DRC.

Calls upon all parties to the conflict, in particular the rebel movements, to cease hostilities, to implement fully and without delay the provisions of the Ceasefire Agreement, to cooperate fully with the OAU and the United Nations in the implementation of the Agreement and to desist from any act that may further exacerbate the situation;

Stresses the need for a continuing process of genuine national reconciliation, and *encourages* all Congolese to participate in the national debate to be organized in accordance with the provisions of the Ceasefire Agreement;

Notes with satisfaction the prompt establishment of the Political Committee and the Joint Military Commission (JMC) by the States signatories to the Ceasefire Agreement as part of their collective effort to implement the Ceasefire Agreement for the Democratic Republic of the Congo;

Authorizes the deployment of up to 90 United Nations military liaison personnel, together with the necessary civilian, political, humanitarian and administrative staff, to the capitals of the States signatories to the Ceasefire Agreement and the provisional headquarters of the JMC, and, as security conditions permit, to the rear military headquarters of the main belligerents in the DRC and, as appropriate, to other areas the

Secretary-General may deem necessary, for a period of three months, with the following mandate:

- To establish contacts and maintain liaison with the JMC and all parties to the Agreement;
- To assist the JMC and the parties in developing modalities for the implementation of the agreement;
- To provide technical assistance, as requested to the JMC;
- To provide information to the Secretary-General regarding the situation on the ground, and to assist in refining a concept of operations for a possible further role of the United Nations in the implementation of the agreement once it is signed by all partners; and
- To secure from the parties guarantees of cooperation and assurances of security for the possible deployment in-country of military observers;

Welcomes the intention of the Secretary-General to appoint a Special Representative to serve as the Head of the United Nations presence in the sub region relating to the peace process in the DRC and to provide assistance in the implementation of the Ceasefire Agreement, and *invites* him to do so as soon as possible.

Resolution 1273: 5 November 1999

Reaffirms that the Lusaka Ceasefire Agreement (S/1999/815) represents a viable basis for a resolution of the conflict in the DRC;

Decides to extend the mandate of the United Nations military liaison personnel deployed in resolution 1258 (1999) until 15 January 2000.

Resolution 1279: 30 November 1999

Reaffirms that the Lusaka Ceasefire Agreement (S/1999/815) represents the most viable basis for a resolution of the conflict in the DRC, and notes the role it requests the United Nations to play in the implementation of the ceasefire;

Stresses the need for a continuing process of genuine national reconciliation, encourages all Congolese to participate in the national dialogue to be organized in coordination with the OAU and calls upon all Congolese parties and the OAU to finalize agreement on the facilitator for the national dialogue;

Welcomes the appointment by the Secretary-General of his Special Representative for the DRC to serve as the head of the United Nations presence in the sub region relating to the peace process in the DRC and to provide assistance in the implementation of the Ceasefire Agreement;

Decides that the personnel authorized under its resolutions 1258 (1999) and 1273 (1999), including a multidisciplinary staff of personnel in the fields of human rights, humanitarian affairs, public information, medical support, child protection, political affairs and administrative support, which will assist the Special Representative, shall constitute the MONUC until 1 March 2000;

Decides to liaise with the JMC and provide technical assistance in the implementation of its functions under the Ceasefire Agreement, including in the investigation of ceasefire personnel.

Resolution 1291: 24 February 2000

Decides to extend the mandate of MONUC until 31 August 2000;

Authorizes the expansion of MONUC to consist of up to 5,537 military personnel, including up to 500 observers, or more, provided that the Secretary-General determines that there is a need and that it can be accommodated within the overall force size and structure, and appropriate civilian support staff in the areas, inter alias, of human rights, humanitarian affairs, public information, child protection, political affairs, medical support and administrative support, and *requests* the Secretary-General to recommend immediately any additional force requirements that might become necessary to enhance force protection;

Decides that MONUC, in cooperation with the JMC, shall have the following mandate:

a) to monitor the implementation of the Ceasefire Agreement and investigate violations of the ceasefire;
b) to establish and maintain continuous liaison with the field headquarters of all the parties' military forces;
c) to develop, within 45 days of adoption of this resolution, an action plan for the overall implementation of the Ceasefire Agreement by all concerned with particular emphasis on the following key objectives: the collection and verification of military information on the parties' forces, the maintenance of the cessation of hostilities and the disengagement and redeployment of the parties' forces, the comprehensive disarmament, demobilization, resettlement and reintegration of all members of all armed groups

referred to in Annex A, Chapter 9.1 of the Ceasefire Agreement, and the orderly withdrawal of all foreign forces;

d) to work with the parties to obtain the release of all prisoners of war, military captives and remains in cooperation with international humanitarian agencies;

e) to supervise and verify the disengagement and redeployment of the parties' forces;

f) within its capabilities and areas of deployment, to monitor compliance with the provisions of the Ceasefire Agreement on the supply of ammunition, weaponry and other war-related material to the field, including to all armed groups referred to in Annex A, Chapter 9.1;

g) to facilitate humanitarian assistance and human rights monitoring, with particular attention to vulnerable groups including women, children and demobilized child soldiers, as MONUC deems within its capabilities and under acceptable security conditions, in close cooperation with other United Nations agencies, related organizations and non-governmental organizations;

h) to cooperate closely with the Facilitator of the National Dialogue, provide support and technical assistance to him, and coordinate other United Nations agencies' activities to this effect;

i) to deploy mine action experts to assess the scope of the mine and unexploded ordnance problems, coordinate the initiation of mine action activities, develop a mine action plan, and carry out emergency mine action activities as required in support of its mandate.

Resolution 1304: 16 June 2000

Reaffirms the sovereignty, territorial integrity and political independence of the DRC and all States in the region;

Reaffirms also the sovereignty of the DRC over its natural resources, and noting with concern reports of the illegal exploitation of the country's assets and the potential consequences of these actions on security conditions and the continuation of hostilities;

Expresses its deep concern at the condition of the hostilities in the country;

Expresses in particular its outrage at renewed fighting between Ugandan and Rwandan forces in Kisangani, DRC, which began on 5 June 2000, and at the failure of Uganda and Rwanda to comply with their commitment to cease hostilities and withdraw from Kisangani made in their joint statements of 8 May 2000 and of 15 May 2000 (S/2000/445), and deploring the loss of civilian lives, the threat to the civilian population and the damage to property inflicted by the forces of Uganda and Rwanda on the Congolese population;

Deplores the delays in the implementation of the Ceasefire Agreement and the 8 April 2000 Kampala disengagement plan, and stresses the need for a new momentum to ensure progress in the peace process;

Expresses its deep concern at the lack of cooperation of the Government of the DRC with the facilitator of the National Dialogue designated with the assistance of the Organization of African Unity (OAU), including the fact that the delegates were prevented from attending the Cotonou preparatory meeting on 6 June 2000.

Expresses also its alarm at the dire consequences of the prolonged conflict for the security of the civilian population throughout the territory of the DRC, and its deep concern at all violations and abuses of human rights and international humanitarian law, in particular in the eastern part of the country, especially the Kivus and Kisangani;

Acting under Chapter VII of the Charter of the United Nations,

Calls on all parties to cease hostilities throughout the territory of the DRC and to fulfill their obligations under the Ceasefire Agreement and the relevant provisions of the 8 April 2000 Kampala disengagement plan;

Further demands:
   a) That Uganda and Rwanda, which have violated the sovereignty and territorial integrity of the DRC, withdraw all their forces from the territory of the DRC without further delay, in conformity with the timetable of the Ceasefire Agreement and the 8 April 2000 Kampala disengagement plan;
   b) that each phase of withdrawal completed by Ugandan and Rwandan forces be reciprocated by the other parties in conformity with the same timetable;
   c) that all other foreign military presence and activity, direct and indirect, in the territory of the DRC be brought to an end in conformity with the provisions of the Ceasefire Agreement;

Calls on all the Congolese parties to engage in the National Dialogue process as provided for in the Ceasefire Agreement, and calls in particular on the Government of the DRC to reaffirm its full commitment to the National Dialogue, to honor its obligations in this respect and to cooperate with the Facilitator designated with the assistance of the OAU and to allow for the full participation of political opposition and civil society groups in the dialogue;

Expresses the view that the Government of Uganda and Rwanda should make reparations for the loss of life and the property damage they have inflicted on the civilian population in Kisangani, and *requests* the Secretary-General to submit an assessment of the damage as a basis for such reparations.

Resolution 1323: 13 October 2000
Decides to extend the mandate of MONUC until 15 December 2000.

Resolution 1316: 23 August 2000
Reaffirms its commitment to assisting in the implementation of the Lusaka Ceasefire Agreement (S/1999/815), and noting the results of the 7 August 2000 Summit of the Southern African Development Community and the 14 August 2000 Second Summit of Parties to the Ceasefire Agreement in the DRC;

Calls on the Government of the DRC and other parties to lift all obstacles to full MONUC deployment and operations;

Decides to extend the mandate of MONUC until 15 October 2000;

Emphasizes that this technical extension of the MONUC mandate is designed to allow time for further diplomatic activities in support of the Ceasefire Agreement and for Council reflection on the future mandate of MONUC and possible adjustments thereto.

Resolution 1332: 14 December 2000
Welcomes the agreements reached at Maputo on 27 November 2000 concerning the disengagement of forces, as well as the signing of the Harare Agreement, pursuant to the Kampala disengagement plan;

Decides to extend the mandate of MONUC until 15 June 2001;

Requests the Secretary-General to submit in that report proposals to the Security Council on ways to address the situation in the eastern provinces of the DRC, including in the areas bordering Rwanda, Uganda, and Burundi;

Expresses its readiness to support the Secretary-General, as soon as he considers that conditions allow it, in the deployment of infantry units in support of the military observers in Kisangani and Mbandaka in due course and, subject to the proposals submitted by him in above paragraph, to other areas he may deem necessary, including possibly to Goma or Bukavu;

Further requests the Secretary-General to submit to the Council, in consultation with all parties concerned, detailed proposals concerning the establishment of a permanent follow-up mechanism which could address in consultation with existing mechanisms in an integrated and coordinated manner the issues of the full withdrawal of foreign forces, the disarmament and demobilization of armed groups, the security of the borders of the DRC with Rwanda, Uganda and Burundi, the return of refugees and internally displaced persons in safety, the inter-Congolese dialogue and regional economic reconstruction and cooperation.

Resolution 1341: 22 February 2001

Determining that the situation in the DRC continues to pose a threat to international peace and security in the region,

Acting under Chapter VII of the Charter of the United Nations,

Demands once again that Ugandan and Rwandan forces and all other foreign forces withdraw from the territory of the DRC in compliance with resolution 1304 (2000) and the Lusaka Ceasefire Agreement, *urges* those forces to take the necessary steps to accelerate this withdrawal;

Demands that parties implement fully the Kampala plan and the Harare sub-plans for disengagement and redeployment of forces without reservations within the 14-day period stipulated in the Harare Agreement, starting from 15 March 2001;

Demands that all armed forces and groups concerned bring an effective end to the recruitment, training and use of children in their armed forces, *calls upon* them to extend full cooperation to MONUC, the United Nations Children's Fund, and humanitarian organizations for speedy demobilization, return and rehabilitation of such children, and requests the Secretary-General to entrust the Special Representative of the Secretary-General for Children and Armed Conflicts with pursuing these objectives on a priority basis;

Welcomes the expressed willingness of the authorities of the DRC to proceed with the inter-Congolese Dialogue under the aegis of the neutral Facilitator, Sir Ketumile Masire, and in this regard *welcomes* the announcement by the President of the DRC at the Summit in Lusaka on 15 February 2001 that the Facilitator has been invited to Kinshasa, and *calls on* all Congolese parties to take immediate concrete steps to take forward the inner-Congolese dialogue.

Resolution 1355: 15 June 2001

Demands once again that Ugandan and Rwandan forces and all other foreign forces withdraw from the territory of the DRC in compliance with resolution 1304 (2000) and the Lusaka Ceasefire Agreement, *urges* those forces to take the necessary steps to accelerate this withdrawal, and *welcomes* in this regard the decision by Ugandan authorities to start withdrawing their troops from the territory of the DRC (S/2001/461);

Condemns the massacres and atrocities committed in the territory of the DRC, *demands* once again that all the parties to the conflict put an immediate end to violations of human rights and international humanitarian law, and stresses that those responsible will be held accountable;

Calls on the international community to increase its support for humanitarian relief activities within the DRC and in neighboring countries affected by the conflict in the DRC;

Expresses its full support for the work of the Expert Panel on the illegal exploitation of natural resources and other forms of wealth in the DRC, and *notes* that the report of the Expert Panel of 12 April 2001 (S/2001/357) contains disturbing information about the illegal exploitation of Congolese resources by individuals, Governments and armed groups involved in the conflict and the link between the exploitation of the natural resources and other forms of wealth in the DRC and the continuation of the conflict;

Stresses the link between the progress in the peace process and economic recovery of the DRC , *welcomes* initial economic reforms undertaken by the Government of the DRC, and *underlines* the urgent need for international economic assistance;

Decides to extend the mandate of the MONUC until 15 June 2002, and also decides to review progress at least every four months based on reporting by the Secretary-General;

Reiterates the authorization contained in resolution 1291 (2000) for up to 5,537 MONUC military personnel, including observers as deemed necessary by the Secretary-General.

Resolution 1376: 9 November 2001

Reaffirming the obligation of all States to refrain from the use of force against the territorial integrity and political independence of any State, or in any other manner inconsistent with the purposes of the United Nations, and *reaffirming* also the political independence, the territorial integrity and the sovereignty of the DRC, including over its natural resources.

Welcomes the withdrawal of some foreign forces from the DRC, including the full Namibian contingent, as a positive step towards the full withdrawal of all foreign forces, and requests all States that have not yet done so to begin to implement, without delay, their full withdrawal in accordance with resolution 1304 (2000) of 16 June 2000.

Expresses its serious concern with regard to the humanitarian situation in the DRC and calls on the international community to increase, without delay, its support for humanitarian activities;

Emphasizes that there are links between the peace processes in Burundi and in the DRC and, welcoming the recent progress in the Burundi process, *invites* the parties to the Lusaka Ceasefire Agreement to work with the Burundian authorities to advance these two processes;

Supports the launching of phase III of the deployment of the MONUC.

Resolution 1399: 19 March 2002

Condemns the resumption of fighting in the Moliro pocket, and the capture of Moliro by RCD-Goma, and *stresses* that this is a major violation of the ceasefire;

Stresses that no party to the Lusaka Ceasefire Agreement should be allowed to make military gains while a peace process is under way and while a peacekeeping operation is deployed;

Demands that RCD-Goma troops withdraw immediately and without condition from Moliro and also demands that all parties withdraw to the defensive positions called for in the Harare disengagement subplans;

Demands also that RCD-Goma withdraw from Pweto, which it occupies in contravention of the Kampala and Harare disengagement plan, so as to permit the demilitarization of this location and that all other parties also withdraw from locations they occupy in contravention of the Kampala and Harare disengagement plan.

Resolution 1417: 14 June 2002

Calls upon Member States to contribute personnel to enable MONUC to reach its authorized strength of 5,537, including observers, within the time frame outlined in its concept of operation;

Stresses that the reduction in the number of foreign forces in the territory of the DRC is encouraging, *demands* the total and expeditious withdrawal of all foreign forces, in accordance with its previous resolutions, without which the conflict cannot be resolved, and in this regard, *reiterates* that all parties must transmit to MONUC, in accordance with the Lusaka Ceasefire Agreement and Security Council resolutions, in particular resolution 1376 (2001), the plans and timetables for the total withdrawal of their troops from the territory of the DRC;

Encourages the parties, especially the Government of the DRC and the Government of Rwanda, to address the fundamental security issues at the heart of the conflict and, in this context, to explore the scope for further confidence-building measures, such as the idea discussed during the Security Council mission to the Great Lakes region of a curtain of troops, as an interim measure aimed at ensuring border security in the final stages of withdrawal, and *encourages* the parties to follow up on their initial positive reaction and develop this idea.

Resolution 1445: 4 December 2002

Authorizes the expansion of MONUC to consist of up to 8,700 military personnel;

Welcomes the signature by the DRC and Rwanda of the Pretoria Agreement on 30 July 2002 (S/2002/914), as well as the signature by the DRC and Uganda of the Luanda Agreement on 6 September 2002 and *welcomes also* the efforts of the Republic of South Africa, Angola, and the Secretary-General, in facilitating the adoption of these agreements;

Welcomes the decision by all the foreign parties to withdraw fully their troops from the territory of the DRC, as well as progress in the implementation of these processes, in particular the withdrawal of 23,400 troops from the DRC verified on 24 October, as well as withdrawals by Uganda, Zimbabwe and Angola, and *stresses* the importance for these withdrawals to be completed in a transparent, orderly and verified manner, and in this regard *underlines* the need for the parties to facilitate the verification of these withdrawals, including through the continuous provision to MONUC of detailed information on these withdrawals and requests the Secretary-General to report to the Council on this manner;

Stresses the crucial importance of preventing the situation in the DRC from having a further destabilizing effect on the neighboring States, in particular Burundi, Rwanda, Uganda and the Central African Republic, and *calls on* all parties concerned to cooperate in good faith to that end and to facilitate in this regard the continuing observation efforts by MONUC in the areas of its deployment, including eastern DRC and border areas.

Resolution 1457: 24 January 2003

Strongly condemns the illegal exploitation of the natural resources of the DRC;

Notes with concern that the plundering of the natural resources and other forms of wealth of the DRC continues and is one of the main elements fuelling the conflict in the region, and in this regard, demands that all States concerned take immediate steps to end these illegal activities, which are perpetuating the conflict, impeding the economic development of the DRC, and exacerbating the suffering of its people;

Reiterates that the natural resources of the DRC should be exploited transparently, legally and on a fair commercial basis, to benefit the country and its people;

Stresses that the completion of the withdrawal of all foreign troops from the territory of the DRC as well as the early establishment of an all-inclusive transitional government in the country, which will ensure that central government control is reinstated and that viable administrations are empowered to protect and regulate the exploitation activities, are important steps towards ending the plundering of the natural resources of the DRC;

Takes note of the importance of the natural resources and extractive sectors for the future of the DRC, encourages States, international financial institutions, and other organizations to assist Governments in the region in efforts to create appropriate national structures and institutions to control resource exploitation, encourages also the Government of the DRC to work closely with the international financial institutions and the donor community to establish Congolese institutional capacity to ensure that these sectors are controlled and operated in a transparent and legitimate way, so that the riches of the DRC can benefit the Congolese people.

Resolution 1468: 20 March 2003

Calls on the Government of Uganda to complete the withdrawal of all its troops without further delay and, in this regard, expresses its concern that that Government's commitment to withdraw by 20 March 2003 has not been met, and, concerned also at the statement of 14 March 2003 issued by the Ministry of Foreign Affairs and Regional Cooperation of Rwanda, calls on the Government of Rwanda not to return any forces to the territory of the DRC, and stresses that any renewal of strengthening of foreign military presence on the territory of the DRC would be unacceptable and would undermine the progress achieved thus far in the peace process.

Expresses its deep concern over the heavy fighting in Bunia, demands that all parties to the conflict in Ituri immediately cease the hostilities and that all parties sign an unconditional ceasefire agreement, stresses that they must cooperate with MONUC to set up without further delay the Ituri Pacification Commission, and also stresses that the necessary steps must be taken to restore public order in Bunia, in accordance with the agreements reached among Congolese parties and within the framework of the Ituri Pacification Commission.

Resolution 1484: 30 May 2003

Authorizes the deployment until 1 September 2003 of an Interim Emergency Multinational Force in Bunia in close coordination with MONUC, in particular its contingent currently deployed in the town, to contribute to the stabilization of the security conditions and the improvement of the humanitarian situation in Bunia, to ensure the protection of the airport, the internally displaced persons in the camps in Bunia and, if the situation requires it, to contribute to the safety of the civilian population, United Nations personnel and the humanitarian presence in the town;

Strongly condemns the deliberate killing of unarmed MONUC personnel and staff of humanitarian organizations in Ituri and demands that the perpetrators be brought to justice.

Resolution 1489: 26 June 2003

Deeply concerned over the continuation of hostilities in the eastern part of the DRC, in particular in the province of North Kivu.

Resolution 1493: 28 July 2003

Acting under Chapter VII of the Charter of the United Nations, *notes with appreciation* the recommendations in the second special report of the Secretary-General and authorizes increasing the military strength of MONUC to 10,800 personnel;

Expresses satisfaction at the promulgation, on 4 April 2003, of the Transitional Constitution in the DRC and at the formation, announced on 30 June 2003, of the Government of National Unity and Transition, *encourages* the Congolese parties to take the necessary decisions in order to allow the transitional institutions to begin functioning effectively, and encourages them also in this regard to include representatives of the interim institutions that emerged from the *Ituri Pacification Commission* in the transitional institutions;

Decides to extend the mandate of MONUC until 30 July 2004;

Encourages MONUC, in coordination with other United Nations agencies, donors, and non-governmental organizations, to provide assistance, during the transition period, for the reform of the security forces, the re-establishment of a State based on the rule of law and the preparation and holding of elections, throughout the territory of the DRC, and *welcomes*, in this regard, the efforts of the Member States to support the transition and national reconciliation;

Encourages donors to support the establishment of an integrated Congolese police unit and *approves* the provision by MONUC of the additional assistance that might be needed for its training;

Decides that all States, including the DRC, shall, for an initial period of 12 months from the adoption of this resolution, take the necessary measures to prevent the direct or indirect supply, sale or transfer, from their territories or by their nationals, or using their flag vessels or aircraft, of arms and any related material, and the provision of any assistance, advice or training related to military activities, to all foreign and Congolese armed groups and militias operating in the territory of North and South Kivu of Ituri, and to groups not party to the Global and All-inclusive agreement, in the DRC;

Reaffirms that an international conference on peace, security, democracy and development in the Great Lakes region of Africa, with participation by all the Governments of the region and all the other parties concerned, should be organized at the appropriate time under the aegis of the United Nations and the African Union with a view to strengthening stability in the region and working out conditions that will enable everyone to enjoy the right to live peacefully within national borders.

Resolution 1499: 13 August 2003

Welcoming recent progress in the political process and the establishment of the transitional government in the DRC;

Noting with great concern that the plundering of natural resources of the DRC continues, especially in the eastern part of the country, and *stressing* that appropriate action should be taken with regard to those responsible for such activities.

Resolution 1501: 26 August 2003

Deeply concerned by the continuation of hostilities in the eastern part of the Democratic Republic of the Congo (DRC), particularly in the district of Ituri as well as in the provinces of North and South Kivu;

Authorizes the States members of the Interim Emergency Multinational Force, within the limits of the means at the disposal of those elements of the Force which will not yet have left Bunia before 1 September 2003, to provide assistance to the MONUC contingent deployed in the town and its immediate surroundings, if MONUC requests them to do so and if exceptional circumstances demand it, during the period of the Force's disengagement which should last until 15 September 2003 at the least.

Appendix 2.3. Selected List of IMF Staff Reports From Mid-1990 to July 2003[1]

February 1996: SM/96/34—Staff Report for the 1995 Article IV Consultation.

June 2001: EBS/01/04—Staff Report for the 2001 Article IV Consultation and Staff-Monitored Program.

July 2001: SM/01/211—Selected Issues and Statistical Appendix.

May 2002: EBS/02/76—Requests for Three-Year Arrangement Under the PRGF and the First Annual Program.

May 2002: EBS/02/88—Enhanced Initiative for Heavily Indebted Poor Countries—Preliminary Document.

May 2002: EBD/02/81—Interim Poverty Reduction Strategy Paper.

May 2002: EBD/02/82—Interim Poverty Reduction Strategy Paper—Joint Staff Assessment.

February 2003: EBS/03/12—Staff Report for the 2003 Article IV Consultation, First Review Under the PRGF, and Request for Waiver of Performance Criteria.

February 2003: SM/03/52—Selected Issues and Statistical Appendix.

July 2003: EBS/03/98—Second Review Under the PRGF and Request for Waiver of Performance Criteria.

July 2003: EBD/03/64—Interim Poverty Reduction Strategy Paper Preparation Status Report.

July 2003: EBS/03/103—Enhanced Initiative for Heavily Indebted Poor Countries—Decision Point Document.

---

[1]Since 2001, all Board documents on the DRC have been published on the IMF's external website (http://www.imf.org).

3

The Economics of Postconflict
Countries: A Survey of the Literature

Ragnar Gudmundsson

Section I. Introduction

The problems affecting countries in conflict have been the focus of increased attention in recent years, with particular emphasis on the impact of civil wars, the incidence of which is now 10 times higher than that of international wars (Collier and Hoeffler, 2002a). The issue has attracted special attention on the African continent, where a majority of civil wars have been occurring, and directly or indirectly affect more than one in three African people. Addressing the issue of conflict has thus become an essential challenge for the leaders of the continent and external partners in the context of the New Partnership for Africa's Development, as the restoration of stability to countries affected by conflict is increasingly perceived as a pillar of economic development, not only for the countries themselves, but also for neighboring countries and the region as a whole.

In confronting the problems characteristic of postconflict situations, an idea that has gained greater acceptance is that the traditional approach to development and aid policy is insufficient for war-affected countries. Those countries face specific internal problems, including limited administrative capacity, weak institutions, and poor infrastructure, which call for tailored solutions. Official development assistance efforts need to be designed in a manner whereby conflict is no longer treated as an exogenous factor, but as one of the key determinants of poor economic performance, whose causes and consequences should be taken into account in all efforts to enhance economic growth and reduce poverty.

This chapter attempts to summarize briefly some of the main findings from the most recent research on conflict and their implications for postconflict assistance, with a focus on the economic, rather than the social or political, dimensions of conflict.[1] The chapter is organized as follows: Section II examines the causes of conflict; Section III looks at the consequences of conflict; Section IV considers the role of aid, capacity building, and reconstruction; Section V examines the fiscal aspects of postconflict assistance; Section VI looks at the impact of military expenditure; Section VII considers the priorities for monetary policy and the financial sector; Section VIII looks at structural reforms and good governance; and Section IX offers conclusions.

Section II. Causes of Conflict

In a paper published in March 2002, Paul Collier and Anke Hoeffler (2002b) examine the causes of conflict on the basis of a sample of 78 civil conflicts that occurred between 1960 and 1999 and that involved at least 1,000 combat-related deaths per year. In particular, they construct a "grievance" model, where conflict is caused by inequality, political oppression, and ethnic and religious divisions, and a "greed" model, which emphasizes the role played by natural resources and other financing mechanisms in the emergence of conflict. Their empirical analysis gives little support to the hypothesis that conflicts are caused by grievances. Notably, they do not find that inequality or political oppression increase the risk of conflict. They find, however, that there is a systematically higher risk of conflict in countries where one ethnic group makes up 45–90 percent of the population.

The analysis lends stronger support to the greed model, showing that countries with abundant natural resources face a higher risk of conflict,

---

[1] The chapter, for instance, does not specifically address the debate concerning the definition of conflict—which is subject to considerable margins of interpretation—and which has important consequences for many of the empirical studies on conflict. Most of the studies currently use the definition of the Stockholm International Peace Research Institute, which considers that a country is in civil conflict in any given year if there have been at least 1,000 combat-related deaths, with more than 5 percent of deaths on each side of the conflict. Such a definition excludes conflicts of lower intensity and longer duration, even though they also cripple an economy and lead to the impoverishment of a country's population. Such a measure also leads to a bias toward countries with large populations.

and that this is also the case for countries that have large diasporas that can finance rebel movements. Exports of natural resources can increase the risk of conflict by financing rebel groups, increasing the incentive for secession, worsening corruption, and increasing exposure to shocks. In this regard, Michailof, Kostner, and Devictor (2002) observe that civil conflicts that are aimed at controlling rents and natural resources often become financially self-sustaining, making it all the harder to exert economic pressure on the warring factions. Collier and Hoeffler (2002b) point out, however, that the relationship between natural resources and conflict risk is nonlinear, because the risk of conflict diminishes when a country's dependence on natural resource incomes is very high. They suggest that in such cases, primary commodities that are taxed at high rates become a significant source of revenue for the government and that this revenue can be used to strengthen the state.

Collier and Hoeffler also find that the risk of civil war is higher in countries with a low GDP per capita, where the economic opportunity cost of rebellion is low and unemployed youths can easily be recruited into rebel movements, as well as in countries that are mountainous or have an unequally distributed population. Conversely, the risk of conflict diminishes with a higher enrollment rate in secondary education and when societies are religiously and ethnically diverse. Luckham and others (2001) argue that conflict and poverty are in a "dynamic and mutually reinforcing relationship," in which conflict becomes a key determinant of poverty, which, in turn, exacerbates the impact of conflict and makes civilians more vulnerable. Fearon and Laitin (2003) argue that low GDP per capita is in fact a proxy for state strength, and that weak states have more difficulty preventing insurgency and political tensions from escalating into civil war. Addison (2002) also highlights the role played by high levels of uncertainty and weak institutions, both in fueling conflict and magnifying its negative impacts once it has taken place. For example, he remarks that high levels of uncertainty lead the private sector to focus on commerce rather than long-term investment in production, because the latter is more vulnerable to predation. In Chapter 4 in this book, Yartey extends Collier and Hoeffler's model to include institutional quality and corruption as two additional variables explaining conflict and finds that they are highly significant, underscoring the importance of good governance and institutional development in any postconflict policy framework.

Luckham and others (2001) consider that conflicts in Africa originate in the legitimacy crises faced by colonial and postcolonial states. At the same time, they observe that the conflicts that took place in the immediate postcolonial era have transformed political, social, and economic realities, and that, as a consequence, "the factors which sustain present conflicts are not necessarily those which originally caused them." Michailof, Kostner, and Devictor (2002) suggest that the end of the cold war has led to the emergence of a new type of war on the African continent, characterized by civil conflicts increasing in intensity, and gradually involving neighboring countries and regional powers. They note that the end of the cold war led to the military disengagement of non-African powers, which had transferred up to US$4 billion a year in arms to the continent, and that this disengagement was followed by a period of rising tensions fueled by deep internal tensions, poor governance and human rights records, large and underpaid standing armies, and considerable stocks of arms and ammunitions that helped sustain the fighting when conflicts erupted. Luckham and others (2001) remark that conflicts following the cold war have been associated with the delegitimization of the state, and that warfare has become a means for armed groups to accumulate power and wealth, where, increasingly, civilians have borne the costs of war.

Michailof, Kostner, and Devictor (2002) mention other causes of recent conflicts, including (1) unprecedented demographic growth, resulting in increased pressure on land and natural resources, as well as large migrations to cities, leading to social and political instability; (2) poverty, illiteracy, and large-scale unemployment; (3) exclusion from political and economic life on regional, ethnic, or social grounds; (4) mismanagement of economic rents and struggles to maintain or gain control over those rents; (5) subregional instability, with recent research pointing to a 0.55 probability that a country neighboring a conflict will suffer the same fate; and (6) easy access to small arms from regular army stocks and the international market. As pointed out by Luckham and others (2001), new financing mechanisms for civil wars, which increasingly involve neighboring countries for the purchase of weapons and the sale of mineral resources, and do not originate primarily in the major powers, have contributed to the regional instability dimension of contemporary conflicts in Africa.

Chapter 7 in this book by Ghura and Mercereau, which looks specifically at political instability and its impact on growth in the Central African Republic (C.A.R.), shows that a low domestic revenue–GDP ratio and an adverse terms-of-trade shock significantly increase the risk of a coup d'état. In particular, the authors note that weak revenue performance undermines the government's ability to pay civil servants' wages and provide basic social services, which, in turn, feeds discontent within the population and triggers political instability.

Section III. Consequences of Conflict

As Luckham and others (2001) underscore, it is especially difficult to estimate with precision the economic impact of conflicts, not least because they are often associated with the collapse of state institutions and, consequently, the data-collection systems that are required to assess the damage caused to economic growth and poverty reduction efforts. Typically, civil wars lead to the destruction of infrastructure, the collapse of state institutions and administrative capacity, a halt to investment activities in all sectors of the economy (with a lasting negative impact on investor confidence), high inflation levels that primarily affect the poorer segments of society, a worsening of the trade balance, an increase in foreign indebtedness, and a decline in external aid flows that is followed, once the conflict is over, by a shift from development aid to humanitarian aid (see Figure 3.1 for the estimated impacts on

Figure 3.1. Real GDP Growth in Conflict Countries

(Average annual percent)

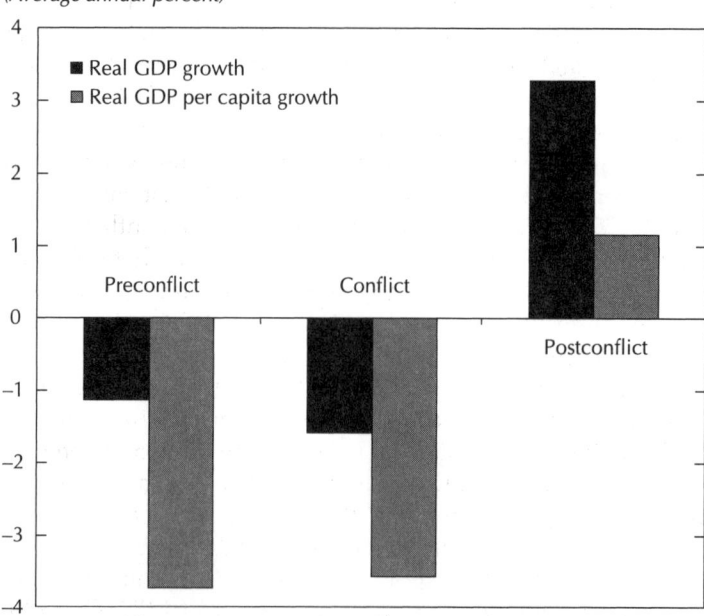

Source: Gupta and others, 2004.
Note: Based on a sample of 12 countries. The real GDP per capita growth corresponding to the preconflict, conflict, and postconflict periods is –3.7, –3.5, and 1.2 percent per annum, respectively.

GDP growth). Civil wars are also accompanied, in most countries, by a sharp decline in government revenue, not only because of the narrowing of the tax base, but also because tax collection falls as the credibility of punishment for tax evasion diminishes when a government is threatened, as pointed out by Caplan (2002).

In a study published by the World Bank, Collier and others (2003) estimate that by the end of a typical civil war, incomes are on average 15 percent lower than they otherwise would have been, and that about 30 percent more people live in absolute poverty. In addition, the authors note that many of the economic costs persist for several years after the end of the conflict, notably through high military expenditures and capital flight. Collier (1995) points out that civil wars are also different from international or liberation wars, in the sense that the latter can generate some positive effects, including the strengthening of the state, technological progress, and the mobilization of productive resources, whereas civil wars lead to the impoverishment of the population and gradual depletion of an economy's productive resources. Civil wars, from this perspective, lead only to the destruction, rather than the creation, of social capital. In that regard, research by Caplan (2002) on the impact of war on the economy shows that, although foreign wars can be associated with slightly above-average real GDP growth, domestic wars have a clear and substantial negative impact on real GDP growth.

In a draft paper on the lessons of the International Monetary Fund's involvement in 23 low-income, postconflict countries over a period totaling 30 years, Fallon and others (2004) remark that most countries that suffered conflict in the post-1990 period entered conflict with a per capita GDP that was lower than five years earlier, and that fiscal deficits in those countries had risen in the period immediately preceding the conflict because of falling revenues and buoyant defense expenditure. They also note that, while post-1990 conflicts tended to be of shorter duration (4 years on average) than pre-1990 conflicts (12 years on average), they were also characterized by more severe economic contraction, with real GDP declining to an average of 74 percent of its preconflict level. Moreover, recovery from conflict was a lengthy process, with countries emerging from conflict with output levels far below preconflict levels and in urgent need of macroeconomic stabilization.

A comparison of poverty and income trends for conflict and non-conflict countries in sub-Saharan Africa over the 1972–97 period in the October 2001 edition of the IMF's *World Economic Outlook* is also revealing with regard to the damage caused by conflict. Notably, real GDP per capita in purchasing power parity terms grew at an average annual rate of 5.5 percent in nonconflict countries, compared with 3 percent in conflict countries; the infant mortality rate for nonconflict countries fell by 36.5 percent, compared with a decline of 25.5 percent for conflict countries; life expectancy increased by 17.5 percent for nonconflict countries, compared with 9.5 percent for conflict countries; and gross primary school enrollment increased from 61 to 89 percent between 1972 and 1992 in nonconflict countries, compared with an increase from 46 to 66 percent in conflict countries.

Looking at the consequences of conflict from an African perspective, Addison (2002) observes that war "destroys the human and physical capital of the poor and undermines the family ties and relationships that are central to the livelihoods of Africa's communities." Combined with the destruction of essential services and infrastructure, he adds, these effects may weaken the poorer segments of the population to the extent that they are not able to share the benefits of recovery once the conflict is over. Referring, in particular, to the work of Ahmed (1994) on Somaliland, and Cliffe (1994) on Eritrea, Luckham and others (2001) emphasize that rural areas have been particularly affected by civil wars in the case of sub-Saharan Africa, not least because rebel movements often originate from parts of the territory over which the incumbent regime has little or no control. The impact of conflicts on rural areas includes the destruction of crops, the killing of livestock, the destruction of irrigation networks and, eventually, the dislocation of markets as farmers are compelled to leave their farms because of excessive insecurity. The displacement of rural populations to urban areas that are ill-equipped to face a surge in population adds to the political instability and the decline in living standards faced by the war-affected country. The consequences of the decline in agricultural output can also have dramatic consequences in terms of food security, as was most strikingly demonstrated by the famine suffered by the Horn of Africa region in 1983–84, when more than 2 million people are estimated to have died.

Referring to the works of Addison (1998), Bruck (1997), Collier (1995), Fitzgerald (1997), Harris (1999), and Mubarak (1997), Luckham and others (2001) note that civil wars in sub-Saharan African have led to the development of informal war economies that have created new forms of inequality and poverty. Although those parallel economies can help ensure the survival of the population during the conflict, they generally become an obstacle to the reconstruction of the economy once the conflict is over. In particular, informal war economies tend to favor activities with low productivity and short-term returns, and households tend to favor consumption rather than savings and productive investment. In addition, informal war economies lead to a significant increase in transaction costs because of the uncertainty linked to the weak legal and regulatory environment, discouraging investments in the private sector. As noted by Collier (2000), "one of the casualties of civil war is trust." Another common feature of informal war economies is the segmentation of markets, because parts of the territory are controlled by rebel groups and the main transport routes often become the target of attacks. The combination of segmented markets, rising costs, a weak regulatory environment, and reduced administrative capacity feeds the opportunistic, rent-seeking behavior of armed groups. This is especially the case for resource-rich areas that come under the control of armed groups that have a vested interest in the perpetuation of conflict, thus complicating the task of reconciliation and recovery.

The economic costs of conflict depend on the way conflict is financed. When conflicts are financed by accumulating debt, the repayment commitments mean that less financial resources will be available in the future to invest in social capital. When conflicts are financed through taxation, segments of society will suffer, and economic activity is likely to decline, especially in the formal sector. And when no additional financing is available, a country may accumulate expenditure arrears, or allocate a share of existing resources to defense expenditure. In this event, Mohammed (1999) considers that the opportunity cost of a conflict becomes the social rate of return to expenditure in any area where expenditure is reduced. This problem is exacerbated in countries where the state's ability to collect revenue has already been diminished by the conflict.

Michailof, Kostner, and Devictor (2002) underscore that the destruction of social capital and institutions poses a significant challenge to postconflict economic revival, with a 0.5 probability that countries return to war within five years of a peace agreement. They express concern about the regional economic impact of conflicts, noting that even when neighboring countries succeed in maintaining peace, the presence of a large number of refugees, the accumulation of small arms, disruptions in trade, and a heightened sense of insecurity by potential investors inevitably take a toll on their economies. The regional contagion effects of civil wars have been highlighted by Sambanis (2003), who cites the case of the African Great Lakes region, where recurrent wars and population displacements in Burundi and Rwanda helped fuel instability and conflict in the Democratic Republic of the Congo (DRC), and led to the involvement of Uganda and Zimbabwe. Sambanis's (2001) analysis of ethnic civil wars during the 1945–99 period also indicates that a country was three times as likely to face a civil war if its neighbors were undemocratic or confronted with an ethnic war of their own. In that regard, Lake and Rothschild (1998) point out that contagion can be driven "by alliances between transnational kin groups . . . or by predatory states that seek to take advantage of the internal weaknesses of others." Yartey's accompanying chapter also examines the case of the African Great Lakes region and finds that the average risk of war for the region during the 1960–99 period stood at 27 percent, far in excess of the 9 percent average for sub-Saharan Africa as a whole. Looking at the experience of the C.A.R., Ghura and Mercereau's accompanying chapter tends to confirm the regional contagion hypothesis, indicating that recent military upheavals in the country have been fueled in part by conflicts in neighboring countries, including the DRC and the Republic of Congo, which had adverse economic effects on the economy and provided politicians with military allies.

Collier and others (2003) add that civil wars impose costs at the global level, because territories are created that are outside the control of recognized government, facilitating the production and transport of hard drugs. The authors report that 95 percent of the global production of hard drugs occurs in countries with civil wars.

Section IV. Aid, Capacity Building, and Reconstruction

In a paper on the economics of postconflict aid, Demekas, McHugh, and Kosma (2002) analyze the differences between postconflict aid and conventional development aid and, in particular, their different effects on the recipient economy, including capital accumulation, growth, welfare, and resource allocation. Whereas development aid's traditional objectives are to encourage investment and growth and reduce poverty, postconflict aid has a humanitarian objective and a reconstruction objective. Reconstruction aid is aimed not only at repairing physical and capital infrastructure, but also at institution-building efforts. The two forms of aid also differ in the magnitude and timing of disbursements, postconflict aid being massive and concentrated in a short period, while conventional development aid is a relatively steady flow over time.

Demekas, McHugh, and Kosma suggest that while humanitarian aid, which is intended primarily to support basic consumption needs, can lead to the same unintended effects as conventional development aid in terms of reducing the competitiveness of export industries, through the so-called "Dutch disease" effect, this is not necessarily the case for reconstruction aid. Reconstruction aid is different in the sense that it can help ease supply bottlenecks and thus contribute to an increase in productivity in the tradable goods sector.

The analytical framework developed by the authors shows that humanitarian aid achieves its main objective, which is to enhance welfare by addressing urgent basic human needs. However, by raising permanent income, enabling the representative agent to achieve his/her desired level of consumption with a lower capital stock, it reduces capital accumulation in the long run and steady state growth. The authors do not find an unambiguous relationship between reconstruction aid and capital accumulation. While the marginal productivity of reconstruction aid tends to reduce the long-run capital stock, the impact of reconstruction aid on labor supply has an ambiguous effect, whereas the impact of reconstruction aid on savings and on the productivity of capital both tend to increase the long-run capital stock. The authors' presumption on the basis of their findings is that postconflict reconstruction aid tends to raise the equilibrium capital stock. In particular, they note that by boosting productivity in both the tradable and the nontradable goods sectors and influencing consumption decisions, reconstruction aid may result in a sustained expansion of the tradable goods sector.

Demekas, McHugh, and Kosma offer the following recommendations from their study: First, donors should sequence their aid flows. In the immediate postconflict phase, aid resources are best devoted to humanitarian aid and will have the greatest impact in terms of enhancing welfare. Second, to preserve long-term economic development, humanitarian aid should be disbursed rapidly, with modest consumption targets. The authors note that overly generous or protracted disbursement of humanitarian aid risks creating aid dependency and reducing labor supply, ultimately proving counterproductive. And third, reconstruction aid should be designed so as to stimulate the development of the tradable goods sector, with an emphasis on public services that facilitate the development of the private sector.

Collier and others (2003) also note that in postconflict cases, aid flows tend to be massive immediately following the end of the conflict, when media coverage is at its peak, but rapidly taper out. They underscore the need for more important overall aid flows in the first postconflict decade and note that those resources should be disbursed more gradually. Collier and others also find that aid flows tend to be most effective in terms of stimulating economic growth after a period of about five years, when institutions have strengthened, the infrastructure has improved, and absorptive capacity has increased. For this reason, they consider that external assistance in postconflict situations should be designed to cover a period of at least 10 years. Fallon and others (2004) also emphasize the need for improved coordination among donors regarding the magnitude and the timing of their financial support, pointing to the negative impact shortfalls in foreign financing have had on development expenditures that are essential for reconstruction and economic recovery. Based on their analysis of the regional economic implications of civil wars, Murdoch and Sandler (2003) also underscore that assessments of the effectiveness of aid flows should take into account the reduced growth rates of some recipient countries owing to their proximity to conflict areas, and that peacekeeping efforts funded by the international community have regionwide public benefits.

While noting that international actors can help in the postconflict recovery process, notably through peacekeeping, humanitarian aid, budgetary support, debt relief, and foreign direct investment, Addison (2002) emphasizes that for international assistance to work well, the capacities of national actors, encompassing communities, the private sector, and the state, must be strengthened. In addition, rather than being based on a wish list for projects, the provision of external financial assistance should focus on a set of core priorities for broad-based recovery on the basis of the needs of communities as identified from household consumption surveys or participatory poverty assessments. The author mentions that the immediate priorities in the context of a reconstruction and reform agenda include the demobilization and reintegration of former combatants, caring for refugees and displaced populations, and a timetable for multiparty elections. While acknowledging the commonly held view that economic reforms should be delayed until reconstruction is well under way, because of the need to secure peace, social stability, and political commitment in the immediate postconflict period, Addison considers such an approach to be unrealistic, because economic policymaking cannot be put on hold during the initial stages of reconstruction. In his opinion, rapid economic reforms, if they are well designed, can in fact help ensure that economic recovery will be broad based, rather than narrow, in its benefits.

Section V. Fiscal Aspects of Postconflict Assistance

Fallon and others (2004) observe that countries tended to emerge from recent conflicts with severely reduced domestic revenues and damaged tax administration. To restore macroeconomic stability it is important to increase domestic revenues by restoring the tax base and administrative capacity to collect taxes.

As in other countries, the IMF has advised governments in postconflict countries to implement a set of broad-based, equitable, and easily monitored revenue-generating instruments that can be expanded as the capacity of the country grows. In postconflict countries, limited capacity restricts the choice of instruments so that meeting revenue objectives sometimes has involved advocating a second-best option in the near term that will not impede the development of a wider and deeper revenue system in the longer term. In countries with sufficient preexisting capacity, the IMF's advice on tax-revenue instruments has focused on identifying which instruments are viable given the administrative capacity available with some modification, and on revitalizing existing administrative capacity (see also IMF, 2004, forthcoming). Where necessary, the IMF has advised that tax instruments be pared down to a realistic set that can be implemented effectively and monitored. In countries, especially those born out of conflict, with almost nonexistent capacity, the introduction of indirect taxes, especially border taxes, is typically the first step toward establishing a revenue-generating system because these taxes are paid at the source of the taxable transaction and therefore are relatively easy to implement and monitor. In that regard, the paper by Fallon and others indicates that although good tax administration is essential for successful revenue-generating systems, it is also one of the most challenging tasks in countries born out of conflict, as it involves the development of institutions from scratch, including the establishment of their legal basis, training of personnel, and the introduction of tax instruments. In addition, political factors such as lack of political will or the inability of parliaments to adopt new legislation can act as major obstacles to the reconstitution of an effective tax administration. Fallon and others note that the countries with IMF postconflict programs under review have been broadly successful in meeting their domestic revenue program targets.

Looking specifically at government revenues linked to natural resources, Collier and others (2003) underscore that such revenues are too often used inefficiently or corruptly, and that there is a need to better harness the potential growth of natural resources for economic growth. To that effect, they propose the creation of an international template for the good governance of natural resource revenues to which governments and companies could choose to adhere. The proposal would work along the following lines: National and international companies in extractive industries would report their payments to governments, governments would report their receipts from the national and international companies, the World Bank would collect the information and reconcile payments and receipts, and the IMF would integrate the net revenue figure into budgetary data and analysis. Apart from ensuring a more efficient use of such resources, the template could also be used to attract more reputable investors, according to the authors. Collier and others add that another priority is to put an end to illicit payments by extraction companies to bribe country officials, and that some progress has been made on this front, notably through new legislation in the member states of the Organization for Economic Cooperation and Development banning companies from bribing government officials.

In the area of government expenditures, Fallon and others (2004) note that postconflict countries are faced with a complex set of challenges, including the need to demobilize and reintegrate ex-combatants, resettle displaced persons, rebuild infrastructure and institutions, and improve public service delivery to create political stability. These challenges are made all the more daunting by the limited amount of resources available. The IMF's recommendations on expenditure composition have included a shift in public spending from recurrent to capital activities, higher priority to social sector spending, and a reduction or at least a freeze in the size of the civil service. Fallon and others note that although government expenditures typically increased in per capita terms following the end of the conflict, they were nevertheless well below program targets in most cases. This was due mainly to weakened implementation capacity of governments and, in some instances, to shortfalls in external financing. Fallon and others also note that the record concerning the recovery of social spending has been mixed. Even though public expenditure management systems improved during the postconflict period, fiscal institutions generally remained weak. Underscoring the limited institutional capacity of governments, the paper indicates that, in many cases, weakened civil services hindered the preparation and execution of budgets according to postconflict priorities, and that the link between public expenditures and outcome was weak, partly because of lack of fiscal accountability and transparency.

Addison (2002) emphasizes that in the immediate postconflict period, a thorough review of spending priorities and public expenditure management is required. Otherwise, there is a strong likelihood that the additional resources generated by reduced military spending and reconstruction aid will not be used efficiently. Public expenditure reform should therefore be undertaken as early as possible following the end of the conflict. In addition, Addison suggests that a fairer allocation of public spending across regions and ethnic groups is necessary to address some of the social inequalities that often characterize the prewar pattern of public infrastructure and services that may have contributed to the conflict. Figure 3.2 summarizes the evolution of the fiscal aggregates in a sample of 14 countries as they moved from the preconflict to the conflict stage, and from the conflict to the postconflict stage.

Figure 3.2. Fiscal Aggregates in Conflict Countries
(Percent of GDP)

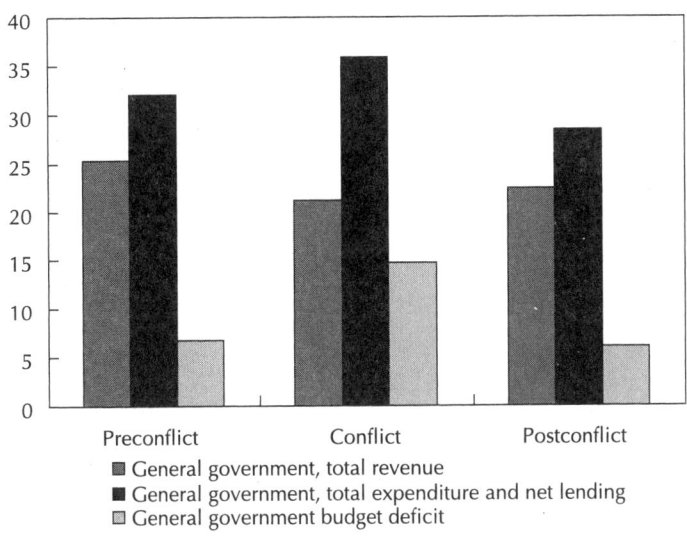

- General government, total revenue
- General government, total expenditure and net lending
- General government budget deficit

Source: Gupta and others, 2004.
Note: Based on a sample of 14 countries.

Section VI. Impact of Military Expenditures

In a paper originally published in 1996, Knight, Loayza, and Villanueva show that high levels of military spending have a negative impact on growth by reducing productive capital formation and distorting resource allocation within the economy, and that substantial cuts in military spending achieved through international peace-building efforts could significantly enhance economic growth, notably through higher expenditures on infrastructure, education, and health. According to another study by Shieh, Ching-Chong, and Wen-Ya (2002), defense expenditures can have three different impacts on the economy. First, they lead to a crowding-out effect, by reducing the resources in the economy available for private investment and public spending on sectors that have a positive impact on growth. Second, defense expenditures may lead to positive supply-side spillover effects on other sectors of the economy; however, this impact is likely to be limited in low- and middle-income countries that tend to import their armaments. And third, defense expendi-

Figure 3.3. Composition of Government Spending in Conflict Countries
(Percent of GDP)

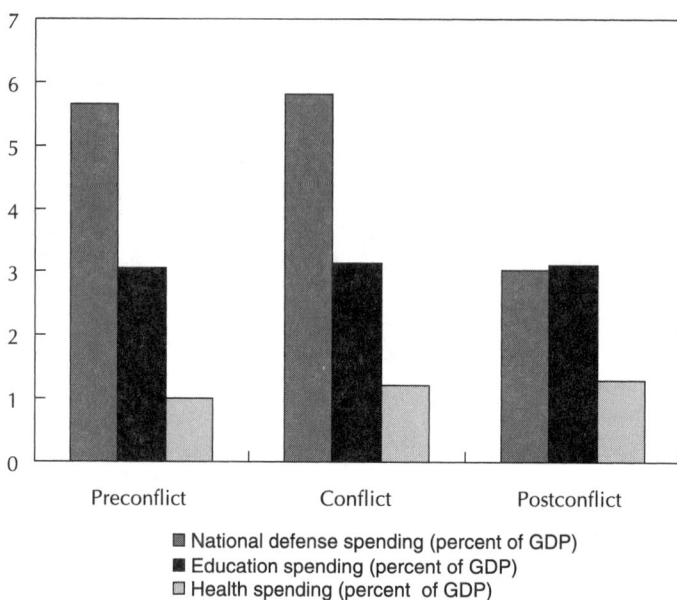

- ■ National defense spending (percent of GDP)
- ■ Education spending (percent of GDP)
- □ Health spending (percent of GDP)

Source: Gupta and others, 2004.
Note: Based on a sample of 12 countries for defense expenditure and on 6 countries each for education and health spending.

tures may lead to an increase in private savings and investment by enhancing security conditions. However, this third impact is less relevant for the analysis of countries that have already suffered from conflict.

A paper by Gupta and others (2004) uses two approaches to provide a cross-country examination of the fiscal consequences of conflict. First, the study analyzes the evolution of various macroeconomic and fiscal variables during 22 episodes of conflict and in the years immediately preceding and following the conflicts. This analysis suggests that the higher level of government expenditure on defense that takes place during conflict tends to generate greater macroeconomic instability, as reflected for example in higher budget deficits and a pickup in inflation, but does not necessarily lead to lower levels of spending on education and health as a percentage of GDP (see Figure 3.3). However, because conflict is associated with lower real GDP growth, real per capita government spending on education and health is lower during conflict periods. This is consistent with the findings of their second approach, which uses panel data for a large number of low-income countries to estimate econometrically the fiscal consequences of conflict. Their econometric results suggest that conflict has a *direct* and significant negative impact on growth, rather than an *indirect* effect through its impact on the composition of government spending. Moreover, armed conflict does not appear to have a significant impact on the government revenue–GDP ratio independent of its impact on real economic activity.

Recent research by Collier and Hoeffler (2002c) emphasizes the regional dimension of military spending, with a country's expenditure heavily influenced by expenditure in neighboring countries. In particular, they estimate an arms race multiplier effect and find that an initial exogenous increase in military spending in one country eventually leads to a doubling of expenditure in both the originating country and its neighbor. They find that, through the arms race multiplier effect, civil war leads to an increase in military expenditure by 2.9 percent of GDP in the country where conflict originates and by 1.7 percent of GDP in neighboring countries. Also, Collier and Hoeffler find that a 10 percentage point increase in the risk of civil war within a subregion, linked to the greater availability of armaments for instance, leads to an increase in military spending by 1 percent of GDP in each country.[2] In addition, the authors do not find in their regressions any offsetting positive effect of military expenditure in terms of acting as a deterrent to rebellion. Military spending by the government as a response to security concerns is ineffective, because it is matched by spending by the rebel groups, and also because it gives a signal to the population that the government's survival strategy is based on coercion rather than inclusion. In that sense, military spending might in fact become counterproductive, notably through its adverse effect on economic growth. For this reason, Collier and Hoeffler consider that military expenditure is a regional public bad, which inflicts negative externalities across borders. An important implication the authors draw from their

---

[2]In their analysis, Collier and Hoeffler also find that countries with larger populations are "potentially more secure from external threat and so have less need for military expenditure," which is difficult to reconcile with the finding in their work on the greed versus grievance model that countries with large populations face a higher risk of civil war—which would seem to point to a greater need for military expenditure. This may be due to the bias introduced by the definition of conflict to include at least 1,000 combat-related deaths per year.

analysis is that in the absence of negotiated reductions in postconflict military spending, much of the cost of a war might accrue after it is over. Therefore, the solution they advocate is for governments and regional political organizations to negotiate reciprocal reductions in military spending, and for international financial institutions that have more reliable information on military expenditure to act as an honest broker and, if necessary, to respond to increases in military budgets that breach regional agreements by reducing aid flows. In that regard, an interesting finding by Davoodi and others (2001) is that the easing of international and regional tensions accounted for up to 66 percent and 26 percent of the decline in global military spending during 1972–89 and 1990–94, respectively.

With regard to the existence of a peace dividend once the conflict is over and defense expenditures are reduced, Luckham and others (2001) underscore that this depends essentially on the capacity of states to restore their revenue base and to invest in the social sectors and infrastructure. They also emphasize that for the peace dividend to last, efforts to demobilize and reintegrate former combatants are crucial.

Section VII. Priorities for Monetary Policy and the Financial Sector

In a study published in 2000, Addison, Murshed, and Le Billon emphasize the importance of rebuilding the financial system following the end of conflict, because it plays a key role in contributing to macroeconomic stability and facilitating the resumption of investment by the private sector.

To begin with, they observe that the financial sector often plays a role in "narrow development," a development process that fails to reduce poverty and exacerbates inequalities, thus contributing to the causes of conflict. In particular, this can happen when the state banking system is used to finance private accumulation, or when weak financial regulation facilitates the accumulation of wealth by fraud. The capacity to mobilize financial resources is what enables belligerents to engage in conflicts and to prolong them, the authors note, whether through domestic financing or the mobilization of external capital inflows via commercial borrowing, official borrowing, or remittances from diasporas. Therefore, they suggest that action to cut the external financing of wars would be one way to hasten their end, while cautioning that such action, if not carefully planned, might have asymmetric effects on belligerents, leading to outcomes that might not be welfare improving. In particular, they note, as do Collier and others (2003), the need to stop the financing of wars through trade in natural resources, such as conflict diamonds, and the money-laundering activities of organized crime.[3]

Following the end of conflict, Addison, Murshed, and Le Billon (2000) note the importance of a well-functioning financial system to facilitate reconstruction and, in particular, to stimulate the investment activities of the private sector that will help recreate the market networks that were destroyed during conflict. They note that the track record of direct state control of the financial system in conflict countries has been poor, and that greater financial liberalization is generally advocated, including by allowing market mechanisms to determine the level of interest rates. Also, the fact that state banks generally need to be recapitalized often leads to their privatization, as private sector money is used to "capitalize and reinvigorate the management of former state banks." In addition, financial liberalization needs to be accompanied by measures to enhance prudential regulation and supervision by the monetary authorities. In that regard, the authors underscore the risk of "regulatory capture" in conflict and postconflict societies, when the absence of democratic institutions to impose and supervise an adequate regulatory framework leads to the abuse of the financial system for personal gain by powerful political actors. Finally, they recommend measures to stimulate the growth of domestic capital markets, so that public spending on reconstruction can be financed without resorting to monetization of the fiscal deficit.

Fallon and others (2004) note that the ability of central banks to conduct independent monetary policies and exercise their supervisory role over banks is considerably weakened by conflicts. Countries have tended to emerge from recent conflicts with increased inflation rates linked to the monetization of fiscal deficits aggravated by reduced money demand (see Figure 3.4). With the exception of countries in a monetary union, the loss of confidence in the currency and the banking system and excessive monetary expansion also led to the nominal

---

[3]An important initiative in this regard is the Kimberley Process, which was launched in May 2000 and culminated in the adoption of an international certification scheme in November 2002. This initiative involves diamond companies and trading countries and aims at preventing the trade in conflict diamonds by requiring diamond exports to be accompanied by a certificate issued by producing-country governments indicating that they are conflict free. It also requires participants to collect information on official production, import, and export data. See also website at www.kimberleyprocess.com.

Figure 3.4. Consumer Price Inflation in Conflict Countries
(Average annual percent)

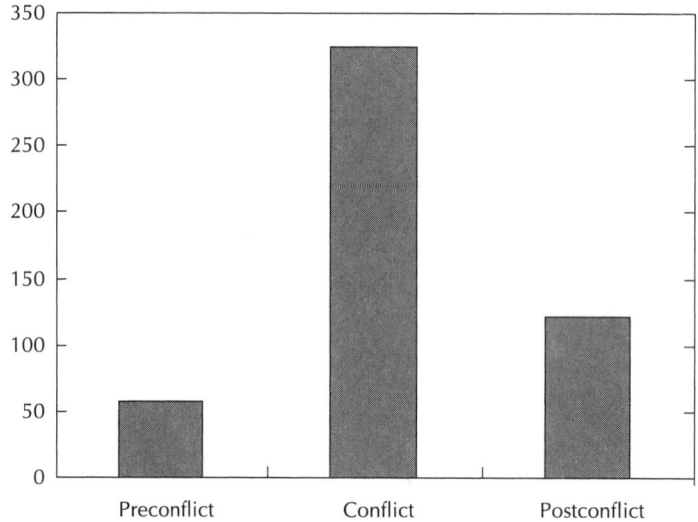

Source: Gupta and others, 2004.
Note: Based on a sample of nine countries.

depreciation of the exchange rate. The IMF's advice has generally focused on reducing inflation and rebuilding foreign reserves, through a
combination of fiscal consolidation and monetary constraint, appropriate exchange rate policies, and improvement of monetary instruments.
Fallon and others note that countries with IMF postconflict programs
under review have tended to be very successful in meeting their inflation targets. In addition, emphasis has been placed on financial restructuring, including, in particular, measures to recover overdue loans,
accelerate provisioning for risky assets, inject new capital, and transfer
nonperforming loans to special agencies, as well as promoting the establishment of a sound banking supervision system by enhancing the
legal and regulatory framework and providing training to supervision
staff at the central bank (see also IMF, 2004, forthcoming).

Section VIII. Structural Reforms and Good Governance

In the area of structural reforms, Fallon and others (2004) note
that the countries reviewed were in urgent need of structural reforms
to help the recovery process and strengthen longer-term growth.

Structural measures have been a key part of IMF postconflict programs, but have varied widely in scope and included arrears such as public sector reform, establishment or rehabilitation of fiscal and monetary institutions, and privatization. The main priorities typically have included the strengthening of good governance, privatization efforts, the rehabilitation of customs and tax administration, the implementation of an expenditure control and monitoring system, the improvement of public procurement, and the simplification of the external tariff system. There were two sets of countries with particular needs. The structural reform agenda was particularly important in those new countries born out of conflict that entirely lacked an institutional infrastructure. In these countries, the priority was to put in place new government entities to handle fiscal, monetary, and exchange rate policies. Structural reform was also important in the transition economies that needed to reorient the economy from a centralized economy to market-based economic structures. The authors conclude that countries have tended to have difficulty in implementing their structural reform agenda. The new countries were typically the most successful, followed by the transition economies. Countries whose implementation of structural reforms was the weakest were those that suffered from fragile political institutions, including dissent from entrenched political and institutional interests that favored the status quo. In addition, Fallon and others emphasize that the ambition and size of the structural reform agenda were not always realistic, with compliance on the more difficult issues waning over time, and that the lack of sufficient human resources has contributed to the difficulty of the reform process.

A similar point is made by Collier and others (2003), who underscore that in the difficult environments characteristic of postconflict countries, there is a need to resist the temptation to address too many issues simultaneously, and that structural reform efforts should be based on a sequential and selective approach, with sufficient attention given to political considerations and the need to build a constituency for reform among the population.

Addison (2002) notes that in the postconflict period, strong and sustained investment from the private sector, both domestic and foreign, is required to support the recovery process. To that effect, the state must create the right conditions for investment by providing macroeconomic stability; reforming the legal and regulatory framework so that property rights are respected; and enhancing public utilities, notably through investments in the areas of telecommunications, water, and road infrastructure. At the same time, Addison adds, the state should regulate the private sector to protect the public interest, which can be a challenging task when democratic institutions to oversee and protect the public interest are only emerging. In addition, the process of privatization needs to be carried out in a transparent and competitive manner to avoid the transfer of valuable assets to local vested interests.

Collier (2000) remarks that countries for which natural resources represent more than a quarter of GDP face a higher risk of conflict. A priority for those countries should be to generate growth and diversify their economy away from dependence on primary commodities. Key factors to achieve diversification include sound macroeconomic policy; trade liberalization; investments in human capital; improvements in the country's infrastructure, notably in the areas of water, electricity, and telecommunications; and enhanced investor confidence through a reliable judiciary system and a transparent regulatory framework. Collier also notes that, rather than playing a destructive role through their financial support to rebel groups, diasporas can play a constructive role in the development process through their skills and business connections. This points to the importance of a national reconciliation process being in place in the immediate postconflict period.

Section IX. Conclusions

From the above analysis, a few recommendations can be offered regarding the main economic areas in which to concentrate efforts to assist countries.

First, with regard to the causes of conflict, existing research by Collier and Hoeffler (2002b) shows that, in addition to poverty, a dominant economic cause of conflict has been the poor management of revenues linked to the extraction of natural resources. This situation calls not only for domestic efforts to reform extractive industries and ensure greater transparency in the management of the revenues linked to those industries, as noted by Collier and others (2003), but also international efforts to curb the trade in natural resources from conflict-affected areas.

Second, there is broad agreement that capacity building has a key role to play in a postconflict environment. Institutions and administrative capacity must be strengthened as quickly as possible, notably through the provision of technical assistance. As indicated by Fallon and others (2004), this step is essential to achieve revenue targets, conduct an independent monetary policy, ensure effective banking supervision, and facilitate the implementation of structural reforms. In this regard, it is worth emphasizing that, in light of the administrative and institutional constraints of postconflict countries, the technical assistance efforts of external partners should be coherent and consistent in their objectives.

Third, as indicated by Demekas, McHugh, and Kosma (2002), aid flows should be well sequenced and adequately coordinated among donors, with an initial focus on humanitarian aid, followed by a gradual increase in reconstruction aid as the recipient country's capacity to use that aid effectively is enhanced. External assistance requirements should be assessed more accurately, notably through closer donor involvement in program countries, as indicated by Fallon and others (2004) and Addison (2002), and they should be designed from a long-term perspective, as noted by Collier and others (2003).

Fourth, in the area of revenue generation, tax instruments should be chosen on the basis of simplicity of implementation and operation. As indicated by Fallon and others (2004), tax instruments should be reasonably nondistortionary and modified as the tax system grows. Also, tax and customs administration need to be strengthened to improve revenue collection. If revenue can be increased without augmenting the fiscal pressure, and the additional revenue is invested in propoor policies, social cohesion is likely to be enhanced as a consequence.

Fifth, with regard to government expenditures, a thorough review of public expenditure management and spending priorities is called for, as pointed out by Addison (2002), with a particular focus on the need to demobilize and reintegrate ex-combatants, rebuild infrastructure and institutions, and improve public service delivery, with a fairer allocation of public spending across ethnic groups and regions. In that context, Collier and Hoeffler (2002c) note that efforts to reduce military spending and to reorient expenditures to the social sectors should be encouraged, with increased emphasis on reciprocal reductions negotiated on a regional basis.

Sixth, in the area of monetary policy, the experience of postconflict countries shows that, with the exception of countries in a monetary union, those economies tend to suffer from high inflation levels and a depreciated exchange rate. As noted by Fallon and others (2004), recommended strategies to reduce inflation and rebuild reserves include a combination of fiscal consolidation and monetary constraint, appropriate exchange rate policies, and improvement of monetary instruments.

Seventh, measures to restore a stable banking system are an important element to stimulate the investment activities of the private sector. Enhancing prudential regulation and restoring adequate supervision of the financial sector is required not only to reassure potential investors, but also to avoid the accumulation of wealth by fraud and the financing of war by illegal means, as indicated by Addison, Murshed, and Le Billon (2000).

Finally, with regard to structural reforms, there is broad agreement that simplicity is desirable, that reform efforts should not be overly ambitious, and that the often limited administrative capacity of post-conflict countries must be taken into account. Initial reforms should focus on measures to strengthen good governance; improve expenditure management, notably in the area of public procurement; enhance the regulatory framework to attract investment; and improve public services that facilitate development of the private sector.

References

Addison, T., 1998, "Underdevelopment, Transition, and Construction in Sub-Saharan Africa," Research for Action No. 45 (Helsinki: World Institute for Development Economics Research, United Nations University).

———, 2002, "Africa's Recovery from Conflict: Making Peace Work for the Poor," Policy Brief No. 6 (Helsinki: World Institute for Development Economics Research, United Nations University).

———, S.M. Murshed, and P. Le Billon, 2000, "Finance in Conflict and Reconstruction," Working Paper Series No. 20 (November), Finance and Development Research Programme (University of Manchester: Institute for Development Policy and Management).

Ahmed, I., 1994, "Understanding Food Insecurity and Famine Conditions in Rural Somaliland" (unpublished Ph.D. dissertation; University of London, Wye College).

Bruck, T., 1997, "Macroeconomic Effects of the War in Mozambique" (Oxford: Queen Elizabeth House, University of Oxford).

Caplan, B., 2002, "How Does War Shock the Economy?" *Journal of International Money and Finance*, Vol. 21, pp. 145–62.

Cliffe, L., 1994, "The Impact of War on Food Security in Eritrea: Prospects for Recovery," in 1995, *War and Hunger: Rethinking International Responses to Complex Emergencies*, ed. by Macrae and others (London and New Jersey: Zed Books).

Collier, P., 1995, "Civil War and the Economics of the Peace Dividend," Working Paper Series, WPS/95-8 (Oxford: Centre for the Study of African Economies).

———, 2000, "Economic Causes of Civil Conflict and Their Implications for Policy," Working Paper No. 28134 (Washington: World Bank).

Collier, P., and A. Hoeffler, 2002a, "Military Expenditure: Threats, Aid and Arms Races," draft research paper presented at a Joint Bank-IMF Seminar on June 20, 2002, Washington.

————, 2002b, "Greed and Grievance in Civil War," Working Paper Series 2002-01 (Oxford: Centre for the Study of African Economies).

————, 2002c, "Military Expenditure: Threats, Aid, and Arms Races," International Monetary Fund Seminar Series No. 2002-50 (Washington: International Monetary Fund).

Collier, P., and others, 2003, *Breaking the Conflict Trap, Civil War and Development Policy* (Washington: Oxford University Press for the World Bank).

Davoodi, H., and others, 2001, "Military Spending, the Peace Dividend, and Fiscal Adjustment," *Staff Papers*, International Monetary Fund, Vol. 48, No. 2.

Demekas, D.G., J. McHugh, and T. Kosma, 2002, "The Economics of Post-Conflict Aid," IMF Working Paper WP/02/198 (Washington: International Monetary Fund).

Fallon, P., and others, 2004, *Review of Recent IMF Experience in Post Conflict Countries*, forthcoming Occasional Paper (Washington: International Monetary Fund).

Fearon, J., and D. Laitin, 2003, "Ethnicity, Insurgency, and Civil War," *American Political Science Review*, Vol. 97, No. 1, pp. 91–106.

Fitzgerald, V., 1997, "Paying for the War: Macroeconomic Stabilization in Poor Countries Under Conflict Conditions," *Oxford Development Studies*, Vol. 25, No. 1, pp. 43–65.

Gupta, S., and others, 2004, "Fiscal Consequences of Armed Conflict and Terrorism in Low- and Middle-Income Countries," *European Journal of Political Economy,* Vol. 20, No. 2, pp. 403–21.

Harris, G., 1999, *Recovery from Armed Conflict in Developing Countries: An Economic and Political Analysis* (London: Routledge).

International Monetary Fund, 2004, forthcoming, "Rebuilding Fiscal Institutions in Postconflict Countries (Washington, Fiscal Affairs Department).

————, 2004, forthcoming, "Technical Assistance to Recent Postconflict Countries" (Washington, Monetary and Financial Systems Department).

Knight, M., N. Loayza, and D. Villanueva, 1996, "The Peace Dividend—Military Spending Cuts and Economic Growth," *Staff Papers*, International Monetary Fund, Vol. 43 No. 1.

Lake, D., and D. Rothschild, eds., 1998, *The International Spread of Ethnic Conflict: Fear, Diffusion, and Escalation* (Princeton, New Jersey: Princeton University Press).

Luckham, R., and others, 2001, "Conflict and Poverty in Sub-Saharan Africa: An Assessment of the Issues and Evidence," Working Paper 128 (Brighton, England: Institute of Development Studies).

Michailof, S., M. Kostner, and X. Devictor, 2002, "Post-Conflict Recovery in Africa," Africa Region Working Paper Series No. 30 (Washington: World Bank).

Mohammed, N.A.L., 1999, "Economic Implications of Civil Wars in Sub-Saharan Africa and the Economic Policies Necessary for the Successful Transition to Peace," *Journal of African Economies*, Vol. 8, AERC supplement, pp. 107–48.

Mubarak, J., 1997, "The 'Hidden Hand' Behind the Resilience of the Stateless Economy of Somalia," *World Development*, Vol. 25, No. 12, pp. 2027–41.

Murdoch, J.C., and T. Sandler, 2003, *Civil Wars and Economic Growth: A Regional Comparison* (Washington: World Bank).

Sambanis, N., 2001, "Do Ethnic and Non-Ethnic Civil Wars Have the Same Causes? A Theoretical and Empirical Enquiry (Part 1)," *Journal of Conflict Resolution*, Vol. 45, No. 3, pp. 259–82.

———, 2003, "Using Case Studies to Expand the Theory of Civil War," CPR Working Paper No. 5 (Washington: World Bank, Conflict Prevention and Reconstruction Unit).

Shieh, J., L. Ching-Chong, and C. Wen-Ya, 2002, "Endogenous Growth and Defense Expenditures: A New Explanation of the Benoit Hypothesis," *Defense and Peace Economics*, Vol. 13, No. 3, pp. 179–86.

4

The Economics of Civil War in Sub-Saharan Africa

CHARLES AMO YARTEY

Section I. Introduction

> We have always maintained that the conflict in Sierra Leone is not about ideological, tribal or regional differences. It has nothing to do with the so-called problem of marginalized youths or, as some political commentators have characterized it, an uprising by rural poor against the urban elite. The root of the conflict is diamonds, diamonds, and diamonds.
>
> Ibrahim Kamara, Sierra Leone Ambassador
> to the United Nations[1]

Low-intensity conflicts, civil strife, and war are major threats to economic growth and sustainable development. Globally, there have been about 140 civil wars since the end of World War II. These wars have killed approximately 20 million people and displaced about 67 million (Doyle and Sambanis, 2003). In sub-Saharan Africa, about 20 countries have experienced at least one period of civil war since independence. The situation is particularly dire for countries such as Angola and Sudan, which have hardly experienced any significant period of peace since independence. While the incidence of civil war has decreased globally, the incidence and intensity of civil war in Africa have been on the rise in the past few decades. According to the *Stockholm International Peace Research Institute (SIPRI) Yearbook 2000*, of the 27

---

[1]See Crossette (2000) p. A9.

active armed conflicts going on around the world in 1999, about 41 percent were civil wars taking place in Africa.

The adverse effects of civil wars on economic growth and development can hardly be overemphasized.[2] The World Bank has labeled civil wars as "development in reverse"[3] because of the reversal effects of civil wars on economic development.[4] The risk of civil war is much higher in low-income countries than in middle-income or high-income countries. Civil wars, therefore, reflect not only a problem for development but also a failure of development (Collier and others, 2003). Between 1960 and 1999, the per capita income of countries affected by civil wars, on average, was less than that of countries that sustained peace. In addition, countries that sustained peace, on average, grew faster than countries affected by civil wars.[5]

The forces involved in these civil wars are extremely complex, each situation having its unique patterns of interests, power and powerlessness, devastation, and prosperity. Conflict prevention and peace building cannot be based on unstable solutions. Identifying the root causes of these civil wars is, therefore, crucial in any peace-building efforts. At the very basic level, internal conflicts may stem from oppression, inequality, and ethnic hatreds that manifest themselves in terms of nationalism, separatism, or fight for an ethnic identity (James and Goetze, 2001). In more complex situations, it may be rooted in greed (the desire for economic and financial gains) as opposing interests compete for resource wealth (Collier, 2000a; Grossman, 1999; Tily, 1978). The latter is referred to as the "economic theory of conflict."

Even though literature on the economics of civil war has increased understanding about economic factors that make a country prone to civil war, little attention has been paid to the specific case of sub-Saharan Africa.[6] Most of the studies on Africa are based on inferences

---

[2]For an excellent analysis of the relationship between civil wars and economic growth in sub-Saharan Africa, see Gyimah-Brempong and Corley (2001).

[3]See Foreword of Stein (2003).

[4]At the aggregate level of analysis the effect of civil wars on economic development includes the destruction of both human and nonhuman capital, the disruption of economic transactions, the distortion of the decision-making process by economic agents, and the disruption of efficient resource allocation. It has been estimated that during a war period the per capita growth rate of a country declines by 2.2 percentage points compared with the normal situation. See Collier (1999), for example.

[5]Using the Collier and Hoeffler (2002a) data set, the values for the period 1960–99 are $4,219 for no-war countries and $1,645 for war countries. The average growth rate of per capita income for war countries is 0.226 percent and that of no-war countries is 1.74 percent.

[6]Two main econometric studies have looked at the case of Africa: Collier and Hoeffler (2000b) and Elbadawi and Sambanis (2000b). Collier and Hoeffler introduced a dummy

from global samples. As Ali (2000) points out, drawing conclusions on the basis of global samples, though useful, is likely to ignore vital regional and country-specific issues that have to do with a complex interaction of socioeconomic, political, and historical legacies. This chapter takes up this challenge by looking specifically at the case of sub-Saharan Africa. The analysis applies the Collier and Hoeffler (C-H) model to sub-Saharan Africa using a panel data set of 44 countries in this region. The objective is to determine which factors are more important in explaining the risk of civil war in the region. More specifically, the chapter examines the extent to which economic growth and the development of good-quality institutions can help prevent civil wars in sub-Saharan Africa.

The C-H analysis is extended by introducing measures of institutional quality[7] and corruption. The institutional quality is introduced because many economists believe that high-quality institutions, such as rule of law, democratic accountability, and bureaucratic quality can mitigate any adverse effects of ethnic dominance or ethnic fractionalization identified by Easterly and Levine (1997). In particular, high-quality institutions can help minimize war casualties on national frontiers and even reduce the probability of genocide for any given amount of ethnic fractionalization (Easterly, 2000). The chapter investigates Rodrik's (1999) assertion that ethnic conflict is not a product of social or religious fractionalization but rather the failure of most developing countries to build institutions to mediate conflicts that arise in any society.

The remainder of the chapter is organized as follows. Section II is a theoretical and empirical discussion of the economic theory of conflict. Section III documents the trends and characteristics of civil wars in sub-Saharan Africa. Section IV presents the empirical model showing the relationship between the probability of conflict and economic, institutional, social, and demographic factors. Section V follows with the empirical results, and Section VI concludes the chapter by prescribing policy guidelines for conflict prevention and peace building in sub-Saharan Africa.

---

variable for Africa in their global model and concluded that there is no mysterious African effect. Elbadawi and Sambanis drew inferences from their global model and concluded that conflicts in Africa can be explained by the same global factors.

[7]North (1994) defines institutions as the humanly devised constraints that structure human interaction. Bardhan (1989) also defines institutions as the "social rules, conventions and other elements of the structural framework of social interactions." These institutions can be informal, such as social capital and norms, or formal legal rules such as laws ensuring individual liberties, property rights, and enforcement of contracts.

Section II. Economic Theory of Conflict

Theoretical Background

The literature on the causes of internal conflicts can be traced as far back as the nineteenth century.[8] As early as 1835, de Tocqueville considered inequality as the fundamental cause of internal conflict. Lichbach (1989) also points out that many revolutions have been based on moving away from repressive regimes and achieving egalitarian ideas.[9] Two competing models usually link inequality with the risk of violent conflict: economic discontent theory (Gurr, 1970) and political opportunity theory (Tily, 1978). According to the economic discontent theory, income inequality is the basis of all rebellions, and if economic inequality is high, violent political conflict will certainly occur. Political opportunity theory maintains that economic discontent is not as important and that political resources and opportunities determine the extent of violent political conflict within countries.

The economic theory of civil war (Collier, 2000a; Fearon and Laitin, 2000; Grossman, 1999; Tily, 1978) views civil war as the outcome of an expected utility maximization decision. Rebels are rational individuals who will evaluate the expected benefits from war against the expected costs. Rebellion is, therefore, a rational decision, and the financial viability of the rebellion is what determines whether a rebellion will be carried out. Utility is maximized by starting a rebellion if the gains from winning the war outweigh the costs of coordinating a rebellion and the likelihood that the government will be able to sustain a massive military effort to contain or put down the rebellion. Collier and Hoeffler model the demand for rebel labor as the outcome of underlying grievance and the supply of labor as the result of expected utility maximization. As per capita income rises, the government's ability to defend itself also increases, and so does the opportunity cost of the rebellion.

The upshot of Collier and Hoeffler's analysis is that wars in developing countries have become less ideological and are principally fueled not by grievance but by greed, the basic assumption of neoclassical microeconomics. Collier (1999, p. 1) argued that "group grievances beneath which inter-group hatreds lurk, often traced back through

---

[8]Ragnar Gudmundsson presents a detailed overview of the literature on alleviating poverty in postconflict countries elsewhere in Chapter 3.

[9]The main slogan in the American revolution was that "all men are created equal." In the French revolution, the slogan was "liberty, equality, fraternity." The motto of the Russian revolution was "peace, land, bread," and the Chinese communist revolution had the slogan "those who have much give much, those who have little give little."

history" are not significant factors that make a country prone to war. Instead, economic agendas and economic opportunities are far more likely than social or group grievances to cause civil wars. Collier, defending his analysis, argued that justice, revenge, and relief from grievance are public goods and are therefore subject to free-rider problems that are a disincentive for a rebellion. In addition, people are unwilling to fight for a cause unless they are convinced that the rebellion will succeed; hence, initially, rebellions face a coordination problem. Furthermore, there is a time-consistency problem in that potential recruits can recognize that a leader promising to alleviate grievances may, once in power, turn out not to deliver. However, if a rebellion is motivated by greed, it allows the participants to restrict the benefits to themselves and thereby avoid any free-rider problems.

Critics argue that there is little sense in conflicts feeding on both self-interest and concern for the public good at the same time. Furthermore, the complexity of causes and motivation for a rebellion cannot be captured adequately by the grievance variables, which, as empirically questionable measures of attributes of difference or stratification, are crude tools for capturing social relations in their diversity (Cramer, 1999). In addition, Keen (1998) suggests that some economic motivations for participating in conflict, and indeed for perpetuating and sustaining conflict, may only become paramount once a rebellion has already begun rather than being the main deciding factor in starting a rebellion.

Empirical Evidence

In the economic theory of conflict, economic motivation is paramount. Economic motivation is proxied through the measures of the primary commodities export–GDP ratio, male enrollment in secondary schools, and economic growth. Grievance is proxied by indices of social fractionalization, inequality in land ownership, and an index of political right. Using data for the period 1960–99 and probit and logit techniques, Collier and Hoeffler (2002a) find that social fractionalization, initial income, dependence on primary commodity exports, and population size are strong determinants of the probability of civil war. Collier's statistical results suggest that some countries are prone to civil war "simply because they offer more inviting economic prospects for rebellion" (Collier, 1999). Collier and Hoeffler conclude that greed is more important than grievances in explaining civil wars.

Fearon and Laitin (2000) also argue that the determinants of conflicts are mainly economic and not political. They test their theoretical model and find that nationalism and cultural cleavages are not important in explaining the prevalence and magnitude of civil wars. Their findings reveal that higher levels of economic development tend to reduce the risk of civil war. Thus, they argue further that civil war will occur when the economic opportunity costs are low and that lack of democracy and ethnic fractionalization are not significant factors in explaining the risk of civil war. Elbadawi and Sambanis (2000b) apply a variant of the Collier-Hoeffler model to analyze the case of Africa.[10] They define incidence of civil war as the sum of the probability of war initiation in a period given the presence of peace in the previous period and the probability of war in a period given the presence of war in the previous period. They confirm the Collier-Hoeffler results of the incidence of civil war.

The economic theory of civil war is supported by studies using historical data. Flanagan and Fogelman (1971) studied 65 nations from 1800 to 1960, and conclude that there is less likelihood of civil war breaking out in countries where the levels of economic development are high. Jacobsen (1996) finds no civil wars at all in the period 1945–85 in countries with high levels of economic development. A good explanation for this relationship is that more advanced countries have a higher standard of living and a more highly educated population, along with lower unemployment rates. They are less prone to civil wars because the opportunity cost of a rebellion is very high. The conclusion we infer from the studies reviewed is that a high level of economic development increases the likelihood of domestic peace.

Section III. Civil Wars in Sub-Saharan Africa
Defining Civil War

Defining what exactly constitutes civil war is difficult, especially at the level of cross-country analysis, because it is often difficult to distinguish between the beginning and the end of a period to be classified as a war period. Furthermore, all wars are not the same because their causes, intensity, geographical spread, duration, and military characteristics are different (Cramer, 1999). Consequently, there are different views about what should constitute a civil war for the purpose of empirical analysis. The definition of civil war that we adopt in this chapter is derived from

---

[10]However, Elbadawi and Sambanis (200b) examine the case of Africa by drawing inferences from a global sample. As previously mentioned, this approach ignores vital regional and historical differences. In contrast, this chapter builds on the application of a variant of the C-H model to the African data set per se.

Singer and Small's Correlates of War Project. Singer and Small (1993) define an armed conflict as a civil war if four conditions are met:
- a major battle took place entirely within the borders of a country,
- the government is a major combatant,
- effective resistance occurred on both sides, and
- at least 1,000 deaths occurred during the course of the war.

Trends and Characteristics of Civil Wars in Africa

According to SIPRI, Africa is the most conflict-ridden region of the world and the only region in which the number of armed conflicts is on the increase. The balkanization of Somalia, the implosion of Sierra Leone, ethnic genocides in Burundi and Rwanda, and the regionalization of rebellion in the Democratic Republic of the Congo (DRC) are some of the violent conflicts that have afflicted Africa since the beginning of the 1990s. Even more striking is that the incidence of war has increased in the past two decades in Africa, while it has fallen in other regions. In 1996, 14 of the 53 countries of Africa were affected by armed conflicts, accounting for more than half of all war-related deaths globally and resulting in more than 8 million refugees, returnees, and displaced people (Annan, 1998).

Table 4.1 lists Africa's major wars since 1960. Most of the wars in Africa are in the form of civil wars. Wars in Africa are relatively very short on the average and they tend to be among the bloodiest (Elbadawi and Sambanis, 2000b). For the most part, these conflicts are virtually internal conflicts, with some exceptions, including the conflict between Ethiopia and Eritrea. However, in most of these conflicts, there has been massive direct involvement of external actors (Cramer, 1999). In other situations, external involvement has been in the form of commerce and finance (Reno, 1999).

A number of factors have been identified as relevant in explaining civil wars in Africa. These factors include the historical legacies of slave trade and colonialism, the nature of the African state after independence, external intervention in the internal affairs of African countries, human rights abuses by African governments,[11] and ethnic and religious grievances.[12] The economic theory of civil war, however, sees

---

[11]The Organization of African Unity, now African Union (AU), identifies human rights violations, ethnic rivalries, and clan and other factional rivalries as relevant causal factors in explaining the incidence of civil war in Africa.

[12]Many countries in Africa are diverse ethnically, with more than 100 ethnic and language groups in Nigeria and the Democratic Republic of the Congo. Other countries,

Table 4.1. Outbreaks of Civil War, 1960–99

Country	Start of War	End of War	Previous War
Angola	Feb. 1961	Nov. 1975	No
Angola	Nov. 1975	May 1991	Yes
Angola	Sept. 1992	Ongoing	Yes
Burundi	Apr. 1972	Dec. 1973	No
Burundi	Aug. 1988	Aug. 1988	Yes
Burundi	Nov. 1991	Ongoing	Yes
Chad	Mar. 1980	Aug. 1988	No
Congo, Republic of the	1997	Oct. 1997	No
Ethiopia	July 1974	May 1991	No
Guinea Bissau	Dec. 1962	Dec. 1974	No
Liberia	Dec.1989	Nov. 1991	No
Liberia	Oct. 1992	Nov. 1996	Yes
Mozambique	Oct. 1964	Nov. 1975	No
Mozambique	July 1976	Oct. 1992	Yes
Nigeria	Jan. 1966	Jan. 1970	No
Nigeria	Dec. 1980	Aug. 1984	Yes
Rwanda	Dec. 1963	Feb. 1964	No
Rwanda	Oct. 1990	July 1994	Yes
Sierra Leone	Mar. 1991	Nov. 1996	No
Sierra Leone	May 1997	July 1999	Yes
Somalia	Apr. 1982	May 1988	No
Somalia	May 1988	Dec. 1992	Yes
Sudan	Oct. 1963	Feb. 1972	No
Sudan	July 1983	Ongoing	Yes
Uganda	May 1966	June 1966	No
Uganda	Oct. 1980	Apr. 1988	Yes
Zaïre (Congo, Democratic Republic of)	July 1960	Sep. 1965	No
Zaïre (Congo, Democratic Republic of)	Sep. 1991	Dec 1996	Yes
Zaïre (Congo, Democratic Republic of)	Sep. 1997	Sep. 1999	Yes
Zimbabwe	Dec. 1972	Dec. 1979	No

Source: Collier and Hoffler, 2002a.

civil wars in Africa as being caused by poor growth, poverty, and the abundance of natural resources such as diamonds, gold, and other precious minerals that can often be the source of much greed.

such as Burundi and Rwanda, are ethnically polarized with the Hutus comprising about 85 percent of the population and the Tutsis the remaining 15 percent.

Section IV. The Model
The Collier-Hoeffler Model

The C-H model of civil war predicts the probability that a civil war will be initiated during a five-year period. The model is based on an analytic model that is in the rational choice tradition (Collier, 2000a). The model casts the causes of civil wars in terms of utility maximization. Rebels are rational individuals who will only initiate a rebellion if the expected benefit of the rebellion is greater than the cost. Mathematically, the C-H model can be written as follows:

$$Y_{it} = \alpha + \beta X_{it} + \partial G_{it-1} + \lambda N_i + \mu_{it}, \tag{1}$$

where Y is the log of the odds ratio, or more specifically, the log odds of war.[13] The variable i stands for the ith country and t for the tth time period. The explanatory variables are either measured at the beginning of the five-year period, or during the previous five-year period, or are time invariant. The X variables are measured at the beginning of the period and include GDP per capita, primary commodity exports as a proportion of GDP, and population. The G variables are measured in the previous five-year period and include per capita income growth. The N variables change rather slowly or are time invariant and include social fractionalization.

Estimation Method

The analysis uses a panel data set of 44 sub-Saharan African countries for eight five-year periods (1960–64, 1965–69,...,1995–99) to estimate the probability that a large-scale civil war will be initiated in each five-year period using the logit regression approach. The logit is interpreted as follows: The slope coefficients measure the change in Y for a unit change in any of the explanatory variables, illustrating how the log odds change as the explanatory variables change by a unit. The predicted probability of war can be computed using the estimated coefficient for the above regression.

$$\hat{Y}_{it} = \alpha + \beta \hat{X}_{it} + \delta \hat{G}_{it-1} + \lambda \hat{N}_i. \tag{2}$$

---

[13]The odds ratio in favor of war outbreak is the ratio of the probability of a war outbreak to the probability of no war outbreak in any given five-year period. Mathematically, the odds ratio is written as $p/1-p$.

The probabilities for hypothetical observations can be calculated by first finding the average values for all explanatory variables for a subset of countries and taking this to represent a typical country within the subset. Then apply the following formula:

$$p_{it} = \frac{e^y}{1+e^y} = \frac{1}{1+e^{-y}}, \tag{3}$$

where e is the naperian log and y is the value of y [from equation (2)] using the estimated coefficients from the regression.

The Data

The dependent variable in this study is the risk of civil war (war start).[14] The war start variable takes a value of one if a civil war started during the period and zero if the country is at peace. If a war started in period t and continues in $t+1$, the value of the war-start variable is recorded as missing. As mentioned previously, a civil war is defined as an internal conflict in which at least 1,000 battle-related deaths occurred. We use mainly the data collected by Singer and Small (1993) as in Collier and Hoeffler (2002a) and according to their definitions. The general source of the data (with the exception of the institutional variables) is Collier and Hoeffler (2002a). We also introduce additional variables such as institutional quality and corruption.

Definition of explanatory variables
- *Per capita income* is the natural logarithm of per capita income. It is measured at the beginning of each subperiod.
- *Growth of per capita income* is used as a proxy for economic opportunities. It is measured in the five-year period prior to the one for which the risk of civil war is being measured.
- *Primary commodity exports/GDP* is used to proxy the abundance of natural resources. It is measured at the beginning of each subperiod.
- *(Primary commodity/GDP)2* is the square of the ratio of primary commodity exports to GDP and indicates high levels of primary commodity dependence.

---

[14]Detailed explanation of all explanatory variables as given by Collier and Hoeffler (2002a) is presented in Appendix 4.1.

- *Population* is the natural logarithm of the population and it is measured at the beginning of the period. It is included to control for the size of a country's population.
- *Social fractionalization* is the combined measure of ethnic and religious fractionalization computed by Collier and Hoeffler.
- *Ethnic dominance* is defined as occurring when the largest ethnic group constitutes between 45 and 90 percent of the population. It takes the value of one for ethnically dominant societies and zero otherwise.
- *Population dispersion* measures the geographic dispersion of the population. A value of one indicates that the total population is concentrated in one area, and a value of zero indicates that the population is evenly distributed.
- *Peace duration* measures the length of the period since the end of the previous civil war.

Measurement of institutional quality

Recent empirical analyses have typically considered three broad measures of institutions. The first is the quality of governance, including corruption, political rights, public sector efficiency, and regulatory burdens. The second is the legal protection of private property and law enforcement. The third is accountability and the limits placed on the executive and political leaders. All of these measures are subjective and are usually dependent on the perceptions and assessments of country experts or assessments made by residents responding to a survey (Edison, 2003).[15]

Using data from the *International Country Risk Guide* (PRS Group, 2003), we constructed an index of institutional quality. Because the *International Country Risk Guide*[16] has data only for 32 countries in sub-Saharan Africa, we estimate the same regression for this subset of countries this time with the inclusion of the institutional variables. We take five institutional variables from the *International Country Risk Guide* to compute an index of institutional quality. The five variables are corruption, law and order, bureaucratic quality, democratic accountability,

---

[15]The aggregate governance index is the average of six measures of institutions developed in 1999 by Kaufman, Kraay, and Zoido-Lobaton (1999). The major components are voice and accountability, political stability and absence of violence, government effectiveness, regulatory burden, and freedom from graft. Other measures of institutions focus on property rights and constraints on the executive. Our measure of institutional quality is quite similar to that of Kaufman, Kraay, and Zoido-Lobaton (1999).

[16]The definition of the component of the institutional index is from the *International Country Risk Guide*. See the *International Country Risk Guide* for a detailed explanation and the computations of the various components of our index of institutional quality.

and government stability. We average across these five measures at the beginning of each subperiod to form the overall measure of institutional quality. Then, as in Barro (1991), we use the 1984 value for the 1980–84 period under the assumption that institutional quality changes slowly. We treat the 1960s and 1970s, however, as missing observations. The higher the value of the index, the better the quality of institutions in any given country.

Our measure of institutional quality has five components: law and order, bureaucratic quality, democratic accountability, government stability, and corruption. Law and order is an assessment of the strength and impartiality of the legal system as well as the popular observance of law. It ranges from zero to six. Bureaucratic quality measures the institutional strength and quality of bureaucracy. This measure is expected to be a shock absorber that minimizes reversions of policy when government changes. High points are given to countries where the bureaucracy is autonomous from political pressure and that have an established mechanism for recruitment and training. The variable ranges from zero to four.

Democratic accountability measures how responsive the government is to its people, on the basis that the less responsive it is, the more likely it is that the government will fall, peacefully in a democratic society, but possibly violently in a nondemocratic society. It ranges from zero to six. Government stability is an assessment of both the government's ability to carry out its declared programs and its ability to stay in office. The components include government unity, legislative strength, and popular support. The variable ranges from 0 to 12. Corruption refers to corruption in the political system. The value ranges from zero to six. The higher the value of the corruption index the lower the level of corruption. In other words, countries that have a lower level of corruption have a higher value of the index and vice versa.

Section V. Regression Results

The Collier-Hoeffler Model

It is useful to begin by outlining the relevant factors that account for the initiation of civil war globally. Table 4.2, model 1 presents the results of the global model using a sample of 161 countries:[17] GDP per capita is statistically significant and negatively related to the risk of civil war.

---

[17]Using Collier and Hoeffler's data set and a pooled logit estimation technique, we reestimated their model and generated the results shown in Table 4.2, model 1. The result is similar to that of Collier and Hoeffler.

Table 4.2. The Baseline Collier-Hoeffler Results

(Global sample)

Pooled Logit Estimates
Dependent Variable: Risk of Civil War

Variable	Model 1	Model 2
Ln GDP per capita	−1.0528	−1.0529
	(−3.64)***	(−3.64)***
GDP per capita growth (t−1)	−0.1027	−0.1025
	(−2.44)***	(−2.44)***
Primary commodity exports/GDP	16.691	16.74
	(3.23)***	(3.22)***
(Primary commodity exports/GDP)2	−23.532	−23.35
	(−2.36)**	(−2.31)***
Peace duration	−0.00373	−0.0037
	(−3.76)***	(−3.74)***
Ln population	0.473	0.476
	(3.45)***	(3.38)***
Social fractionalization	−0.00022	−0.00022
	(−2.10)**	(−2.11)**
Geographic dispersion	−0.994	−0.992
	(−1.10)	(−1.09)
Ethnic dominance	0.449	0.450
	(1.36)	(1.36)
African dummy	−0.371	−0.3208
	(−0.70)	(−0.43)
Primary Africa		−0.2678
		(−0.09)
Pseudo R square	0.224	0.224
Log likelihood	−146.60	−146.60
Number of observations (N)	750	750

Source: IMF staff estimates.

Notes: Ln is the natural logarithm. All regressions include a constant. T values are in parentheses. *** and ** indicate significance at the 1 and 5 percent levels, respectively. African dummy equals one if a country is in sub-Saharan Africa and zero otherwise. Primary Africa equals the interaction between the African dummy and primary commodity exports.

Economic growth is statistically significant and negatively related to the risk of civil war. Primary commodity exports are significant and positively related to the risk of civil war. However, very high levels of primary commodity exports are negatively related to the risk of civil war. Therefore, the relationship between primary commodity exports and the risk of civil war is nonmonotonic or, more specifically, quadratic. The size of a country's population is statistically significant and positively related to the risk of civil war. Ethnic dominance is positively related to the risk of civil war but statistically insignificant. Social fractionalization is significant and negatively related to the risk of civil war. That is, more fractionalized societies have lower risk of civil war. Peace duration is statistically significant and negatively related to the risk of conflict. That is, the longer the duration of the peace period, the lower the risk of civil war.

Is There an African Effect?

We would like to extend the C-H analysis to look at the specific case of sub-Saharan Africa, to investigate whether there is any hidden African effect. To do this, we estimate the C-H model using a panel data set of 44 countries in this region. We use pooled logit estimation techniques.

Comparative statistics

First it is important to examine some comparative statistics. Table 4.3 presents comparative statistics for a sample of sub-Saharan African countries during the sample period. The data show the following:
- Countries that experienced civil wars during the period had a lower GDP per capita than those countries that sustained peace.
- Countries that experienced civil wars had a lower growth rate than countries that sustained peace.
- Countries that experienced civil wars had on average about the same primary commodity exports–GDP ratio as those countries that sustained peace.
- Countries that sustained peace had a much higher quality of institutions than those countries that had civil wars.
- Sample countries that had civil wars were more corrupt than countries that sustained peace.

It is not surprising that the main finding from this comparative analysis is that countries that had civil war(s) have a lower endowment of growth-enhancing characteristics than those countries with no civil war(s).

Descriptive statistics

Table 4.4 presents the descriptive statistics for sub-Saharan Africa collectively. Three important points are worth mentioning: (1) between 1960 and 1999, the average risk of war for sub-Saharan Africa was about 9 percent; whereas (2) the average growth rate of per capita income for the region as a whole was about 0.42 percent for the sample period; and (3) during that period, about 17.2 percent of the region's GDP was made up of the exports of primary commodities.

Correlations

At this point it is worth considering some important correlations (Table 4.5). For instance, GDP per capita is negatively correlated with

Table 4.3. Comparative Statistics

	No Civil War					Civil War				
	Mean	Standard deviation	Minimum	Maximum	N	Mean	Standard deviation	Minimum	Maximum	N
War	0	0	0	0	302	1	0	1	1	30
Ln GDP per capita	6.834	0.626	5.549	8.829	291	6.493	0.4707	5.402	7.540	28
Economic growth	0.695	3.803	−9.906	13.19	252	−1.84	3.606	−10.59	2.882	23
Primary exports/GDP	0.175	0.139	0.09	0.568	285	0.1744	0.125	0.039	0.505	30
(Primary exports/GDP)2	0.050	0.076	0.0008	0.323	285	0.046	0.066	0.0015	0.255	30
Fractionalization	3257.9	2062.4	20	6975	302	3847.6	2056.9	180	6210	30
Ethnic dominance	0.4040	0.492	0	1	302	0.233	0.430	0	1	30
Peace duration	325.86	162.26	1	592	302	198.43	166.50	1	592	30
Ln population	14.781	1.456	10.638	18.53	298	15.851	1.047	13.203	18.080	30
Geographic dispersion	0.546	0.216	0	0.858	294	0.567	0.134	0.308	0.804	30
Institutional quality	3.203	0.891	0.80	5.335	92	2.3102	0.847	0.767	3.653	28
Corruption	2.780	1.066	0	6	92	2.277	1.281	0	4	28

Source: IMF staff estimates.
Note: Ln is the natural logarithm.

Table 4.4. Descriptive Statistics

Variable	N	Mean	Standard Deviation	Minimum	Maximum
War start	332	0.0904	0.287	0	1
Ln GDP per capita	345	6.798	0.632	5.403	0.830
Growth	300	0.419	3.735	−10.49	13.189
Primary exports/GDP	347	0.172	0.136	0.009	0.568
(Primary exports/GDP)2	347	0.048	0.074	0.00008	0.323
Fractionalization	360	3369.4	2022.2	20	6975
Ethnic dominance	360	0.4	0.491	0	1
Peace duration	332	314.35	166.46	1	592
Ln population	356	15.06	1.470	10.638	18.527
Geographic dispersion	352	0.570	0.189	0	0.858
Institutional quality	120	2.995	0.956	0.757	5.335
Corruption	120	2.662	1.134	0	6

Source: IMF staff estimates.
Note: Ln is the natural logarithm.

the risk of civil war in Africa, as is economic growth. The size of a country's population is positively correlated with the risk of conflict in Africa, as is its primary commodity exports. However, very high levels of primary commodity exports are negatively correlated with the risk of civil war. The corruption index is negatively correlated with the risk of war. Low corruption (high value of the index) is negatively associated with the risk of war. Our measure of institutional quality is negatively correlated with the risk of war.

Results

Table 4.6, model 1 presents the baseline results for 44 countries in sub-Saharan Africa:
- GDP per capita is significant and negatively related to the risk of conflict. Low GDP per capita increases the risk of civil war.
- In addition, the rate of economic growth is negatively related to the risk of civil war. That is, as would be expected, higher rates of economic growth reduce the risk of civil war.
- The size of a country's population is statistically significant and positively related to the risk of civil war, so that countries with greater populations run a higher risk of civil war.
- Peace duration, or the longer a country is at peace, is statistically significant and negatively related to the risk of civil war.
- Social fractionalization is negatively related to the risk of civil war but not statistically significant.

Table 4.5. Correlations

Variable	Warsa	LnGDP	Growth	Sxp	Sxp2	Frac	Etdo4590	Peace	Lnpop	Georgia	Index	Corrupt
Warsa	1.000											
LnGDP	-0.165	1.000										
Growth	-0.179	0.260	1.000									
Sxp	0.004	0.440	0.049	1.000								
Sxp2	-0.009	0.430	0.047	0.965	1.000							
Frac	0.039	-0.077	-0.035	0.127	0.060	1.000						
Etdo4590	-0.113	0.221	0.178	0.020	0.043	-0.152	1.000					
Peace	-0.223	0.277	-0.032	0.148	0.160	-0.159	0.205	1.000				
Lnpop	0.226	-0.454	-0.223	-0.172	-0.238	0.481	-0.291	-0.264	1.000			
Georgia	0.014	-0.19	-0.158	0.014	0.004	0.064	-0.161	0.085	0.200	1.000		
Index	-0.353	0.459	0.130	-0.102	-0.089	-0.418	0.209	0.327	-0.009	0.159	1.000	
Corrupt	-0.250	0.316	0.131	-0.184	-0.186	-0.540	0.244	0.270	-0.023	0.057	0.726	1.000

Source: IMF staff estimates.
Notes: Warsa is the risk of war; Ln is the natural logarithm; LnGDP is the natural log of GDP per capita; Growth is growth of GDP per capita; Sxp is primary commodity exports/GDP; Sxp2 is the square of primary commodity exports/GDP; Frac is social fractionalization; Etdo4590 is ethnic dominance; Peace is the duration of peace period; Lnpop is the natural log of population; Georgia is geographic dispersion of population; Index is institutional quality; and Corrupt is corruption.

Table 4.6. Regression Results for Sub-Saharan Africa

Pooled Logit Estimates
Dependent Variable: Risk of Civil War

Variable	Model 1	Model 2	Model 3
Ln GDP per capita	−1.030727 (−1.80)*	−1.144799 (−1.97)**	−0.868315 (−1.72)*
GDP growth (t–1)	−0.1119062 (−1.66)*	−0.996007 (−1.45)	−0.1188602 (−1.49)
Primary commodity exports/GDP	6.71149 (0.82)	5.886767 (0.71)	7.647955 (0.92)
(Primary commodity exports/GDP)2	−4.697739 (−0.32)	−3.52968 (−0.24)	−5.723488 (−0.39)
Social fractionalization	−0.0001796 (−1.36)	−0.0001996 (−1.46)	−0.0001953 (−1.47)
Peace duration	−0.0031002 (−2.10)**	−0.0030323 (−2.04)**	−0.0028763 (−1.90)*
Ln population	0.5900376 (2.28)**	0.5914417 (2.28)**	0.5760912 (2.16)**
Ethnic dominance	−0.1260415 (−0.28)	−0.1500226 (−0.26)	0.1002307 (0.17)
Geographic dispersion	−0.4586954 (−0.28)	−0.6162363 (−0.36)	−0.2975275 (−0.19)
Diamond		0.5912055 (1.04)	
Great Lakes			0.8807 (1.35)
N	261	261	261
Pseudo R square	0.1967	0.2034	0.2081
Log likelihood	−62.517365	−63.745447	−61.629345

Source: IMF staff estimates.

Notes: All regressions include a constant. T values are in parentheses; Asterisks (** and *) indicate significance at the 5 and 10 percent levels, respectively. Great Lakes is a dummy variable for countries in the Great Lakes region. It takes a value of one if a country is in the Great Lakes region and zero otherwise. Diamond is a dummy variable for diamond-exporting countries. It takes the value one if a country exports diamonds and zero otherwise. Ln is the natural logarithm while N is the size of the sample.

- Ethnic dominance is statistically significant but negatively related to the risk of civil war.
- The dependence on a primary commodity, such as the DRC's dependence on diamonds, is positively related to the risk of civil war. However, very high levels of exports for primary commodity exports are negatively related to the risk of civil war. Neither is statistically significant.

Initial per capita income and lagged per capita income growth are both statistically significant in explaining the probability of civil war in sub-

Saharan Africa. Their level of significance improves when they are not both included in the same regression. One might wonder why the exports of a primary commodity are not significant in explaining the risk of civil war in Africa. First, compare the correlation between primary commodity exports in the global sample (0.0061) with the correlation between primary commodity exports and GDP in the African sample (0.4401), and one can see that the correlation between exports of a primary commodity and GDP in Africa is far higher than in the global sample.

Second, a cursory look at the comparative statistics reveals that those countries that experienced civil wars had on average almost the same primary commodity exports–GDP ratio as those countries that sustained peace. However, in the global sample, those countries that experienced civil wars had on average a much lower primary commodity exports–GDP ratio than countries that had experienced long periods of peace (15–17 percent). It is important to emphasize that other regions are also dependent on natural resources. However, since the relationship between natural resources and the risk of civil war is quadratic, what should be of interest is the standard deviation and not the mean (Elbadawi and Sambanis, 2000a). Our analysis shows that the standard deviation of African countries' natural resource dependence is smaller than the standard deviation of non-African countries. Therefore, more African countries are closer to the peak of natural resource dependence, a factor that maximizes the threat of civil war. If this is the case, the coefficient of primary commodity dependency should be statistically significant. To examine this hypothesis we devise a test that can be seen in the next section.

Testing for the hypothesis of equal coefficients

We test whether the coefficient of primary commodity exports is statistically the same in and outside of Africa. A basic method in applied econometric research is to introduce a dummy variable for Africa in the regression of the global sample and then interact this dummy variable with primary commodity exports to form a new variable (call it primary Africa). We then estimate the model with both the African dummy variable and the primary Africa variable in the regression.[18] A T-test on the coefficient of primary Africa is then conducted. Table 4.2, model 2 gives the results of this regression, showing that the coefficient of primary Africa is not statistically significant. Therefore, we fail to reject the null hypothesis that the coefficient of primary commodity exports in and outside of Africa is the same.

---

[18]We include both the African dummy and primary Africa variable in the regression to be sure that any rejection of the null hypothesis would not be due to the fact that the African dummy is excluded.

At this point, we test for an even stronger restriction[19]—an F-test on the null hypothesis that the coefficients of both the African dummy and the primary Africa variable are zero. This test examines the null hypothesis that not only is the coefficient of both the African dummy and the primary Africa variable the same in and outside of Africa, but also the probability of war is the same both in and outside of the continent when the full set of explanatory variables are equal. Thus, the test rejects this hypothesis.[20] A possible explanation for why the coefficient of primary commodity exports is not statistically significant in Africa is the relatively high correlation between primary commodity exports and GDP in Africa. Therefore, in subsequent versions of the C-H model we omit the growth variables to examine this hypothesis.

Diamond-exporting countries

We also investigate those countries in sub-Saharan Africa that export diamonds. We investigate whether diamond-exporting countries[21] in sub-Saharan Africa have a much higher risk of civil war.[22] Fighting over diamond deposits is believed to have been an important reason for the initiation of civil wars, their maintenance, and prolongation in Angola, the DRC, Liberia, and Sierra Leone. The Fowler report (2000) on the role of diamonds in Angola argued that rough gems are important for the ability of the National Union for the Total Independence of Angola or UNITA (Union Nacional Por La Indepencee Totale do Angola) to sustain the rebellion. Diamonds, according to the report, allow the rebels to acquire new weapons, make friends, gain external support, and serve as a store of wealth. We evaluate this probability by introducing a dummy variable (call it diamond) for countries in the region that export diamonds. We then estimate the baseline regression this time with the inclusion of the diamond variable. Table 4.6, model 2 gives the result of this regression. The coefficient of diamond is positive, indicating that diamond-exporting countries have a higher risk of civil war but the co-

---

[19]We thank an anonymous referee for suggestions on the construction of these tests.

[20]The chi-square value is 0.06 and the p value is 0.8079, thus making it possible to reject the null hypothesis at the 5 percent level of significance.

[21]The major diamond-exporting countries in sub-Saharan Africa are Angola, Botswana, Central African Republic, Congo, Côte d'Ivoire, DRC, Ghana, Guinea, Liberia, Namibia, Sierra Leone, South Africa, and Zimbabwe.

[22]This issue is investigated because of the supposed fatal role diamonds are believed to have played in several conflicts in Africa. Because of this, the United Nations has imposed sanctions on conflict diamonds originating from areas controlled by illegitimate rebel groups.

efficient is not statistically significant,[23] meaning that countries that export diamonds do not behave differently from the rest of Africa.

Institutional Quality and the Risk of Civil War

We extend the C-H analysis by looking at the role of institutions in the initiation of a war by introducing institutional quality into the C-H model while dropping the growth variables. We measure institutional quality at the beginning of each five-year period. Data represent only 32 countries in sub-Saharan Africa. However, because our measure of institutional quality is highly correlated with GDP we exclude the growth variables from models 2 and 3. We use our measure of institutional quality to represent the strength and accountability of the state. Higher values of the index represent a higher opportunity cost of rebellion because of the strength of the state. Institutions with greater quality can also represent a lower level of criticisms because they offer good opportunities for resolving grievances. The result is presented in Table 4.7. In model 1, we have the results of the C-H model for 32 countries without any institutional variables. In model 2, we introduce institutional quality. The results show that the coefficient of our measure of institutional quality is highly significant (at the 1 percent level of significance) and negatively related to the risk of civil war. This implies that the development of good-quality institutions, such as rule of law, democratic accountability, efficient bureaucracy, and government stability, can reduce the risk of civil war in sub-Saharan Africa.

In this analysis, primary commodity exports, this time, are statistically significant and have the expected positive sign. The square of primary commodity exports is also significant and has the expected negative sign. Peace duration is found to be significant with the expected negative sign, and social fractionalization has the expected negative sign but is not statistically significant. Ethnic dominance has the expected positive sign but is not statistically significant. The size of a country's population takes on a negative sign but is not statistically significant. Geographic dispersion of population is statistically insignificant and has an unexpected wrong sign.

In Table 4.7, model 3, we introduce corruption into the C-H framework. This measure of corruption, a component of the measure of institutional quality, is from the *International Country Risk Guide*. Again,

---

[23]If we exclude primary commodity exports and its square from the baseline regression, the significance of the diamond variable improves marginally (say, significant at a 20 percent level of risk).

Table 4.7. Institutions and the Risk of Civil War

Pooled Logit Estimates
Dependent Variable: Risk of Civil War

Variable	Model 1	Model 2	Model 3
Ln GDP per capita	−0.1725256		
	(−1.97)**		
GDP growth (t−1)	−1.1310005		
	(−1.65)*		
Primary commodity exports/GDP	15.03491	37.99703	29.80815
	(1.42)	(1.89)*	(1.87)*
(Primary commodity exports/GDP)2	−16.16715	−55.00197	−43.23131
	(−0.91)	(−1.67)*	(−1.65)*
Social fractionalization	−0.0001262	−0.000329	−0.0002666
	(−0.63)	(−1.02)	(−0.87)
Peace duration	−0.0042885	−0.0077776	−0.0081069
	(−2.43)**	(−2.50)**	(−2.93)***
Ln population	0.4227879	−0.026684	−0.2097021
	(1.44)	(−0.05)	(−0.52)
Ethnic dominance	0.7650991	0.5799471	0.0400845
	(1.17)	(0.56)	(0.04)
Geographic dispersion	2.837744	9.500986	7.399742
	(1.05)	(1.29)	(1.57)
Institutional quality		−1.497642	
		(-2.60)***	
Corruption			−0.7028002
			(−1.70)*
N	191	104	104
Pseudo R square	0.2335	0.4089	0.3340
Log likelihood	−45.712473	−23.1613	−26.09777

Source: IMF staff estimates.
Notes: All regressions include a constant. T values are in parentheses. Asterisks (***, **, and *) indicate significance at the 1, 5, and 10 percent level, respectively. N is the size of the sample while Ln is the natural logarithm.

because of the apparent correlation with GDP we exclude GDP from the regression. Corruption is significant at the 10 percent level of risk and has the expected negative sign. The interpretation of this variable is this: higher levels of the index (low corruption) reduce the risk of civil war. Peace duration is again statistically significant with the expected sign. Social fractionalization has the expected negative sign but is statistically not significant. Ethnic dominance has the expected positive sign but is statistically not significant. The size of the population is not statistically significant and has a negative sign. The geographic dispersion of the population is not statistically significant and has the wrong sign.

The introduction of the institutional variables (institutional quality and corruption) and the removal of the growth variables make primary commodity exports and its square significant at the 10 percent level of risk. This confirms the quadratic relationship between primary commodity exports and the risk of civil war. Primary commodity exports increase the risk of civil war, but very high levels of primary commodity exports reduce the risk of civil war. The result of this regression to some extent confirms our hypothesis that the insignificance of primary commodity exports in the baseline model is due to the strength of the relationship between primary commodity exports and GDP. The correlation between primary commodity exports and GDP is 0.44, but that of primary commodity exports and institutional quality and corruption is –0.1015 and –0.1839, respectively. Thus, there is indeed an African effect; however, this effect does not manifest itself through the outright rejection of the C-H model, but reflects in the coefficients of some important variables as we have seen in the case of primary commodity exports and GDP.

Estimation Issues: The Random-Effects Probit Model

We investigate whether the results of the chapter are affected by the choice of estimation techniques, using panel data techniques to investigate this hypothesis. Given the panel nature of our data set, the choice of any estimation technique will depend on the assumptions about the distribution of the error term (μ_{it}) and assumptions about the structure of the cross-section effects. If the μ_{it}'s are taken to be independent standard normal variables, then the panel nature of the data is irrelevant, and the pooled logit estimation method is the most appropriate (Greene, 1997). If not, then the random-effect probit estimator is more efficient because it gives us the flexibility to model cross-sectional differences that are not possible to explore using the pooled logit. The error term in a random-effects model can be specified as

$$\mu_{it} = \varepsilon_{it} + v_i, \tag{4}$$

where v_i is the individual specific effects. Both components are normally distributed with mean zero and independent of one another.[24] We assume that v_i are random because some of our explanatory variables such as social fractionalization are either time invariant or changing rather slowly. The random-effects probit model makes it possible to capture some of the unobserved heterogeneity among the cross sec-

---

[24]Full details on the estimation and inferences may be found in Butler and Moffitt (1982) and Greene (1995).

tions, and if these effects are significant then the model is more effi-cient than the pooled logit.[25] The results from the random-effects pro-bit are presented in Table 4.8. In model 1, we have the results for the baseline model (44 countries). In model 2, we include institutional quality for 32 countries. These results are statistically similar to those reached using the pooled logit. In fact, a likelihood ratio test of the cor-relation coefficient (Rho) shows that the panel variance is not signifi-cant in explaining total variance; it is correct to use the pooled logit model.[26] Therefore, we can conclude that our previous result is not based on the choice of the estimation method.[27]

Performance of the C-H Model

The C-H model predicts the risk of civil war for sub-Saharan Africa to be 8.8 percent for the period 1960–99. This prediction is done at the means of the explanatory variables. The actual risk of civil war for Africa during the sample period is 9 percent, which is close to the pre-dicted probability. Therefore, the C-H model predicts the risk of civil war in sub-Saharan Africa with considerable accuracy (see Figure 4.1). However, for individual countries, the C-H model systematically un-derpredicts the probability of war for high-risk countries and overpre-dicts the probability of civil war for low-risk countries (see Table 4.9).

So What Explains Civil Wars in Sub-Saharan Africa?

The empirical analysis performed leads us to conclude that civil wars in Africa have both economic and political undertones (see Box 4.1). Economically, Africa's high level of poverty has been a crucial causal factor in most of its civil wars. Collier and Hoeffler (2002a) interpreted low GDP per capita to mean a much lower opportunity cost of rebel-lion, encouraging rebels to launch an attack. Fearon and Laitin (2000), however, use GDP per capita to proxy the strength of the state. It is im-

---

[25]Because some of our variables are time invariant, the use of a fixed effect would cre-ate perfect multicollinearity between the nontime varying explanatory variables and the individual specific effects, forcing us to drop them from the regression. Furthermore, the logit does not lend itself well to random-effects treatment. See Greene (1997) for details.

[26]The null hypothesis is that Rho is equal to zero. The chibar2 (01) = 0.00 and the P value is 1.00 in both models 1 and 2. We therefore do not reject the null hypothesis.

[27]Collier and Hoeffler (2002a) further estimated their baseline regression using King and Zeng's (2001) rare events correction procedure. They find the difference between the rare events logit and the standard logit to be negligible.

Table 4.8. Random-Effects Probit Regression

Dependent Variable: Risk of Civil War Variable	Model 1	Model 2
Growth of GDP per capita (t–1)	–0.0685773 (–1.86)*	
GDP per capita	–0.4982207 (–1.72)*	
Primary commodity exports/GDP	2.765135 (0.68)	19.27667 (1.80)*
(Primary commodity exports/GDP)2	–1.098504 (–0.15)	–27.56934 (1.55)
Social fractionalization	–0.0000799 (–1.19)	–0.0001856 (–1.15)
Ethnic dominance	–0.0517599 (–0.18)	0.2779416 (0.49)
Ln population	0.3139633 (2.33)**	–0.0019025 (–0.01)
Peace duration	–0.0015713 (–2.04)**	–0.0039572 (–2.47)**
Geographic dispersion of population	–0.2389642 (–0.29)	5.037007 (1.09)
Institutional quality		–0.8227104 (–2.59)***
Rho	8.32e-07	8.32e-07
No. of observations	261	104
Log likelihood	–62.485802	–23.332053

Source: IMF staff estimates.
Notes: T values are in parentheses. Asterisks (***, **, *) indicate significance at the 1, 5, and 10 percent level, respectively. Ln is natural logarithm.

portant to emphasize that these two explanations are essentially the same. Higher GDP per capita implies higher strength of the state, which acts as a disincentive to rebels because they are less apt to challenge the might of the state. No matter how GDP per capita is interpreted, one important issue still remains: high GDP per capita reduces the risk of civil war.

Another important factor that explains the risk of civil war in sub-Saharan Africa is the rate of growth of GDP per capita. Africa's relatively low growth rate has been an important determinant of the strings of war on the continent. Collier and Hoeffler interpreted faster economic growth as indicating the difficulty of rebellion movements in recruiting workforce. Faster economic growth represents better life opportunities for potential rebel recruits and also lower levels of grievances. The abundance of primary commodities is also associated with

Figure 4.1. Probability of Civil War in Sub-Saharan Africa

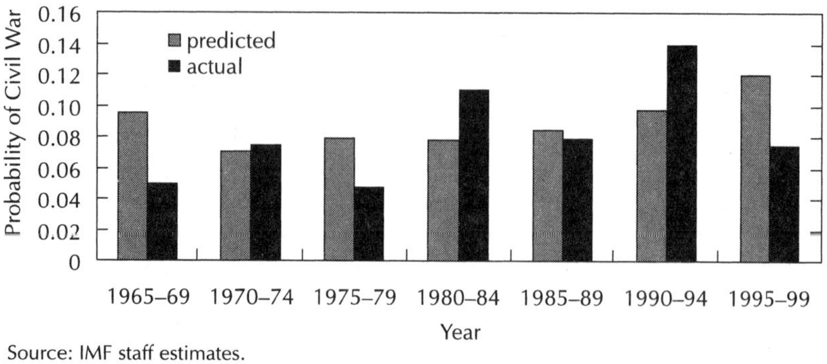

Source: IMF staff estimates.

higher risk of conflict. However, extremely abundant natural resources reduce the risk of civil war. Collier and Hoeffler define a threshold level of about 26 percent. However, very few countries are at this level. While the coefficient of primary commodity exports in Africa is not statistically significant, there is no evidence that the coefficient of primary commodity exports is statistically different in and outside of Africa.

This finding leads us to conclude that the insignificance of primary commodity exports is the result of the strength of the relationship between primary commodity exports and GDP per capita in Africa.[28] Collier and Hoeffler interpreted the abundance of primary commodities as offering an opportunity for rebels to finance themselves and thereby increase the risk of civil war. However, extremely plentiful natural resources leave the government with enough funds to defend itself. The primary commodity result should be subjected to further empirical investigations. A lot of work has to be done on the industrial organization of rebel movements before we can sufficiently say that diamonds, or other natural resources, are driving civil wars. As Herbst (2000) points out, most of the regressions reporting a relationship between resources that may be stolen and conflict may simply be picking up the fact that

[28]Using primary commodity exports as a proportion of GDP to capture the abundance of natural resources may be misleading in the African context. This ratio can also represent trade openness (if we use total exports). Because in most African countries primary commodities constitute about 60 percent of total exports, the ratio may be capturing openness rather than the abundance of natural resources.

Table 4.9. Synthetic Index of the Risk of Civil War in Sub-Saharan Africa, 1960–99

Low-Risk Countries	Actual %	Predicted %	Moderate-Risk Countries	Actual %	Predicted %	High-Risk Countries	Actual %	Predicted %
Benin	0	1.84	Congo, Rep. of	12.29	1.8	Angola	100.00	57.85
Botswana	0	0.6	Gabon	0	8.4	Burundi	42.85	23.48
Burkina Faso	0	5.8	Guinea	0	7.3	Chad	14.29	9.64
Cameroon	0	6.3	Kenya	0	8.0	Ethiopia	25.00	28.74
Cape Verde	0	1.1	Madagascar	0	11.11	Guinea Bissau	16.67	5.00
Central Africa Rep.[1]	0	2.25	Malawi	0	8.2	Liberia	28.57	6.40
Comoros	0	5.7	Mali	0	8.2	Nigeria	46.29	33.19
Djibouti	0	0.54	Mauritania	0	8.6	Rwanda	46.29	21.19
Gambia	0	3.4	Niger	0	8.6	Sierra Leone	46.29	6.40
Ghana	0	5.6	Tanzania	0	8.4	Somalia	48.80	16.67
Côte d'Ivoire	0	6.0	Zambia	0	10.19	Sudan	66.67	14.68
Lesotho	0	1.9				Uganda	28.57	16.34
Namibia	0	0.6				Zaïre (Congo, Dem. Rep. of)	42.85	34.41
Senegal	0	4.8				Zimbabwe	14.29	11.21
Seychelles	0	0.0						
South Africa	0	3.6						
Swaziland	0	1.9						
Togo	0	4.4						

Source: IMF staff estimates.

Notes: Predicted probability of civil war is calculated using the coefficients from the baseline regression and the mean values for the explanatory variables for every country and then applying the formula in equation (2). We classify a country as having low risk of civil war if the predicted and/or actual probability of civil war is less than 7 percent. If a country has between 7 and 14 percent probability of war, we classify the country as having a moderate risk of war. We classify a country to be in the high-risk category if the probability of civil war is greater than 14 percent.

[1]Even though the Central African Republic has seen some violent conflicts, these conflicts do not qualify as civil wars by the Singer-Small definition. This, among other factors, may account for its low risk of civil war.

Box 4.1. Factors Behind the Risk of Civil War in Sub-Saharan Africa

- Africa's high level of poverty,
- Africa's relatively low growth of per capita income,
- the abundance of primary commodities,
- peace duration—the longer a country is able to prolong the period of peace, the lower the risk of civil war,
- large populations,
- Africa's difficulty in developing strong institutions, and
- the high level of corruption.

---

these resources may be necessary for conflict to continue but are not the driving force of conflict.

We find peace duration to be a significant factor in explaining the probability of civil war in sub-Saharan Africa. The longer the duration of the peace period, the lower the risk of civil war and vice versa. This confirms the assertion that time is an important factor in the healing process. Population size is also important in explaining the risk of civil war in sub-Saharan Africa. The larger the population, the higher the risk of civil war and vice versa. In other words, civil wars seem more likely in countries with large populations. The theoretical argument that links population to the risk of civil war is that the larger the population, the easier it should be to find a group to challenge the government.

Moreover, Africa's difficulty in developing strong institutions can be blamed for the high incidence of civil war on the continent. As this empirical analysis shows, good-quality institutions such as rule of law, democratic accountability, government stability, efficient bureaucracy, and limited corruption are associated with a lower risk of civil war. A similar result was found by Easterly (2000),[29] who uses a measure of economic governance and shows that good-quality institutions can mitigate the negative effects of ethnic diversity on economic growth. Rodrik (1999) finds high quality of economic or political institutions to reduce the effect of ethnic diversity on persistence of economic growth following external shocks. The evidence from our analysis is consistent with the

---

[29]Easterly (2000) constructed an index of institutional quality, which is the average of Knack and Keefer's 1995 measures from the *International Country Risk Guide* of freedom from government repudiation of contracts, freedom from expropriation, rule of law, and bureaucratic quality.

evidence from the empirical literature. Good-quality institutions can support peaceful ways of resolving disputes and thereby reduce any adverse effects of ethnic dominance and social fractionalization. Indeed, countries with good-quality institutions have a lower risk of conflict.

There is no significant relationship between social fractionalization and the risk of civil war. It is important to stress that the coefficient of social fractionalization is negative, indicating that more fractionalized societies have a lower risk of civil war. This evidence provides some hope for sub-Saharan Africa whose ethnically diverse societies may have been blamed for the region's string of civil wars. Africa's ethnic diversity actually promotes peace and makes the region relatively safe. Collier and Hoeffler interpreted higher level of social fractionalization as representing the difficulty of coordinating a rebellion.

The Case of the Great Lakes Region

The Great Lakes region has witnessed some of Africa's most intense and violent conflicts. Almost all the countries in this region have seen some period or periods of violent conflict.[30] Among these violent conflicts are the genocides in Rwanda and Burundi and the regionalization of conflict in the DRC. Various conflicts that have affected the subregion have resulted in a large number of victims who have been displaced or forced to live in looted and destroyed societies. In a region in which most of the people have almost always lived very close to or below the poverty line, the continued deterioration of social, economic, and political life has resulted in the persistent uprooting and marginalization of fragile and vulnerable populations (United Nations, 1999). This empirical analysis is extended to cover countries in the Great Lakes region.

First, we compare the descriptive statistics for the Great Lakes region with that of sub-Saharan Africa. Table 4.10 presents the descriptive statistics for this subregion:

- The average risk of war for the Great Lakes region for the period from 1960 to 1999 is 27 percent. This is far higher than the risk of war for the entire continent of sub-Saharan Africa (9 percent).
- The growth of per capita income for the Great Lakes region between 1960 and 1999 was –0.58. During that period, the average growth rate for sub-Saharan Africa was 0.42 and the average for countries in Africa that experienced civil wars was –1.84.

---

[30]According to Relief Web, the countries in the Great Lakes region are Burundi, the DRC, Kenya, Rwanda, Tanzania, and Uganda. Although the United Nations excludes Kenya from the Great Lakes region, this exclusion from the analysis does not significantly change the results for the Great Lakes region.

- The average GDP per capita for the Great Lakes region is lower than the average for sub-Saharan Africa. It is also lower than the mean of countries in conflict.
- The region has a primary commodity exports–GDP ratio of 11 percent. This is lower than the average for sub-Saharan Africa (17 percent).
- The Great Lakes region has a much more fractionalized society than sub-Saharan Africa as a whole.
- Countries in the Great Lakes region have a much lower index of institutional quality than sub-Saharan Africa.
- Countries in the Great Lakes region have a much lower index of corruption and are therefore more corrupt than sub-Saharan Africa as a whole.

Second, we investigate whether the factors that explain conflict in Africa can be used to explain the higher incidence of civil war in the Great Lakes region. To do this, we introduce a dummy variable into the baseline regression for Africa. The dummy takes the value of one if a country is in the Great Lakes region and zero otherwise. We estimate the C-H model with the inclusion of the Great Lakes dummy. The result is presented in Table 4.6, model 3. Clearly, the coefficient of the Great Lakes dummy is positive, indicating that countries in the Great Lakes region have a higher probability of civil war, but this is statistically not significant. This leads us to conclude that the probability of conflict in the region could be explained by the same factors that account for civil wars in sub-Saharan Africa (economic growth, per capita income, primary commodity exports, institutional quality, and corruption). Whereas the subregion's relatively high level of social fractionalization makes this region less vulnerable to conflict, its relatively low level of economic growth and lower initial GDP makes the region more prone to civil war.

Third, we investigate the extent and accuracy to which the C-H model predicts the risk of war in this region. Figure 4.2 presents both the actual and the predicted risk of war for the Great Lakes region from 1965 to 1999. As evident from the diagram the C-H model systematically underpredicts[31] the risk of war for the region. However, for the period 1995–99 the C-H model predicted perfectly the risk of war for this region to be 33 percent (exactly the same as the actual risk of war). The average risk of war for the Great Lakes region during the sample period (1965–99) is 27 percent. The C-H model predicted the average risk of civil war for the region to be 20 percent.

---

[31]This may be because the sample size is small—consisting only of the six countries in the Great Lakes region. In larger samples, the model's predictions improve.

Table 4.10. Descriptive Statistics, Great Lakes Region

Variable	Mean	Standard Deviation	Minimum	Maximum	N
War start	0.27	0.455	0	1	29
Growth of per capita	−0.58	3.982	−10.48	7.13	28
Ln GDP per capita	6.33	0.300	5.402	6.81	32
Ln population	16.27	0.754	14.89	17.59	32
Peace duration	165.44	119.76	9	463	29
Primary exports/GDP	0.11	0.044	0.052	0.273	32
(Primary exports/GDP)2	0.014	0.013	0.0027	0.074	32
Social fractionalization	4490.7	2515	180	6210	32
Ethnic dominance	0	0	0	0	32
Geographic dispersion	0.56	0.184	0.291	0.809	32
Institutional quality	2.73	1.051	0.8	4.03	16
Corruption	1.98	1.344	0	4	16

Source: IMF staff estimates.

Section VI. Policies for Conflict Prevention and Peace Building

A peaceful and stable Africa is the wish of African countries as well as the international community. Before assessing the different policies that might help achieve permanent peace, it is important to understand the issues involved. As stated at the beginning of this chapter, conflict is complex. It does not take place just because there is greed or dissatisfaction. Neither does it occur because diamonds are abundant or because the government and social political institutions are weak. It occurs when these factors at multiple levels come together and reinforce one another. It is the result of the interaction of weak political and social institutions, deep grievances, poverty, bad governance, and global and regional geopolitics. Although most African countries are anxious for peace, they do not seem to know how to maintain it when they achieve it. As Bigombe and others (2000) point out, "civil wars always end but they usually restart," especially in Africa. The strategy then should focus on conflict prevention and the maintenance of permanent peace.[32]

For postconflict countries, the best strategy should be to prevent a new war (see Box 4.2). As this empirical analysis shows, the longer the peace period lasts, the lower the risk of further conflicts. The end of a conflict

---

[32]Globally, within the first decade of the end of a conflict, 31 percent of them have resumed. In Africa, about half of peace restorations have lasted fewer than 10 years. See Bigombe and others (2000) for details.

Figure 4.2. Probability of Civil War in the Great Lakes Region

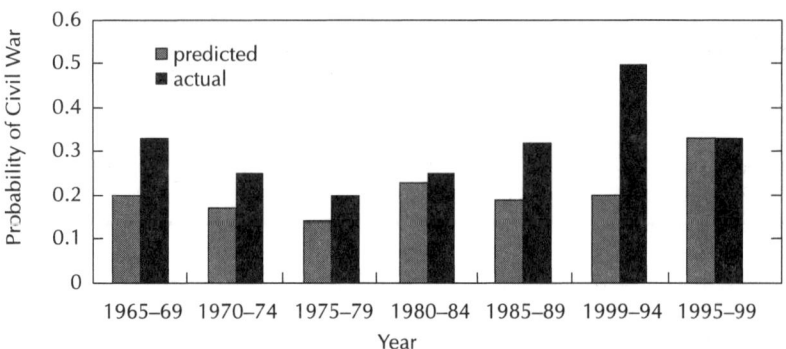

Source: IMF staff estimates.

does not suggest that the problems are over. The countries involved will face massive and onerous challenges of postwar reconstruction. Strangely enough, it is during this period that international attention shifts to other areas and regions, thereby losing valuable time in preventing a new war (Wallensteen, 2002). Thus, in a postconflict situation the priority should be to support the peace agreements that exist and to prevent the tension from reoccurring. Therefore, all planning for global development assistance should focus on observing the dangers of future war and finding means of mitigating such dangers. It is also important to entrench post-conflict peace building into global development policies. Key development projects, such as the Millennium Development Goals, should clearly and explicitly focus on reducing the risk of conflict. As a country continues to build a permanent peace, the conflict is forgotten, new concerns emerge, and the question of systematic conflict prevention becomes paramount. It is here that policies of good governance, economic growth, poverty reduction, and institutional development come in. Here, too, it is imperative to stress that every conflict situation is different. Knowing the structure of the risk factors in a specific country should provide some guidance to policy prioritization on which factors to target for policy action (Bigombe and others, 2000).

As our empirical evidence shows, some of the factors that are crucial in African conflicts are dependence on natural resources, poverty, slow growth, weak institutions, and corruption. All of these are amenable to policy alteration. It is important to emphasize that related measures are not mutually exclusive, and a good combination of them should achieve the best results. Therefore, policies for building permanent

> ## Box 4.2. Policy Implications
>
> - For postconflict countries, the best strategy should be to prevent new war. The main priority should be to support the peace agreements that exist and to prevent the tension from reoccurring.
> - It is important to entrench postconflict peace building into global development policies. Key development projects such as the Millennium Development Goals should clearly and explicitly focus on reducing the risk of conflict.
> - Postconflict economic policies should, therefore, focus on social reconciliation and reconstruction and tackle macroeconomic imbalances.
> - Policies to promote growth and reduce poverty will help in conflict prevention. The greatest gain in conflict prevention will be made in focusing development efforts on very poor countries.
> - Reducing primary commodity dependency should help prevent civil wars. In the short term, the international community should take appropriate measures to end the use of primary commodities that can be easily looted by rebel movements. This, however, will require a strong commitment from the international community.
> - In the long term, African governments should take positive steps to ensure rapid diversification of their economies. Growth, aid, and policy should help in this direction. The role of international financial institutions in the development and implementation of good and adequate economic policies becomes paramount.
> - An important approach to conflict prevention is the development of good-quality institutions such as rule of law, democratic accountability, efficient bureaucracy, government stability, and low corruption. Evidence that good-quality institutions become effective when a country reaches the middle-income level supports this policy option.

peace should be a multidimensional package. It is important to design and implement a holistic approach to conflict prevention that encompasses policies aimed at reducing all important risk factors.

The econometric evidence presented in this chapter suggests that increasing the level and the growth of per capita income should reduce the risk of civil war. Faster economic growth and lower poverty present young people with greater hopes for the future, although policies to promote growth are beyond the scope of this chapter.[33] Poverty is a factor considered by political and economic theorists as favoring rebellions. Poverty reduction increases the opportunity cost of rebellion because the poor have little to lose by joining a rebellion. At the same time,

---

[33]See Chapters 6 and 7.

poverty reduction reduces grievances against the government. The core of the approach to poverty reduction should be to reduce unemployment, because it serves to reduce the pool of potential recruits for civil war. Therefore, better employment opportunities may be an effective medium-term strategy for conflict prevention. It is important to emphasize, however, that given Africa's initial conditions, this route to conflict prevention may be a slow process.

Natural resource dependence is an important source of civil wars in sub-Saharan Africa. Primary commodity exports can increase the risk of conflict in four ways: financing rebels, worsening corruption in government, increasing the incentive for secession, and increasing exposure to shocks (Collier and others, 2003). The relationship between primary commodity exports is quadratic, implying that many African countries may reduce risk by increasing their resource dependence. However, because most African countries have primary resource dependence lower than the peak, the best policy will be to reduce the dependence on primary commodity exports. In the short term, the international community should take measures to end the use of natural resources that can be easily looted by rebel movements. This, however, will require a strong commitment on the part of the international community. In the long term, African governments should take positive steps to ensure rapid diversification of their economies. Collier and Hoeffler (2000b) find three measures that can help reduce the dependence on primary commodity exports: growth, aid, and policy. The implementation of good and adequate economic policies is of paramount interest because it advocates a role for the International Monetary Fund and the World Bank in conflict prevention.[34]

As the comparative statistics show, countries with high-quality institutions have a lower risk of civil war. An important approach for conflict prevention is the development of good-quality institutions such as rule of law, democratic accountability, efficient bureaucracy, government stability, and low corruption. In the case of sub-Saharan Africa, this calls for the reform and development of high-quality political and governance institutions. If the key to conflict prevention is the ability of the entire population to raise issues and address them in nonviolent ways through local organizations and community groups, then the establishment of formal political institutions becomes paramount. Guidelines for getting involved in political action and

---

[34]Collier and others (2003) measure the effectiveness of policy using the World Bank's Country Policy and Institutional Assessment (CPIA). They find that an improvement of one point in the CPIA (which is approximately equivalent to the difference between African and South Asian policies) would reduce the dependence on primary commodities from 15.2 percent of GDP to 13.8 percent.

how authorities relate to them become critically important—something many analysts consider as the main feature of democracy (Wallensteen, 2002). Democracy functions best as a conflict prevention strategy when the stakes of the political contests are low (Weingast, 1997). The development of political, legal, and economic institutions that help reduce the risk of war by reducing the gains to narrow interests are critical for a well-functioning democracy. Evidence that political institutions are effective once a country reaches middle-income levels strongly supports this policy option. It is equally important to develop a good-quality bureaucracy. The bureaucracy should be independent from government manipulation, and recruitment should be open to all groups and carried out in full transparency. Also, African countries should take strong measures to reduce corruption in government. The development of good-quality institutions with good checks and balances should help in this direction.

Finally, it is important to remind ourselves that conflict prevention and peace building usually require huge financial and human resources, and that African governments do not have enough resources to actually bear these costs themselves. This calls for an urgent, purposeful, and effective role for the international community (including international financial institutions) not only to end civil wars but also to ensure the sustainability of durable peace. It is important to emphasize that the performance of the international community in this direction has so far been below the expectations of African countries. This perception, according to Annan (1998, s.11), has left a "poisonous legacy that continues to undermine confidence."

Appendix 4.1. Data Definitions and Sources

The main source of data for almost all the variables that appear in this chapter is Collier and Hoeffler (2002a). The definitions of the variables are given below.

Per capita income. The variable, per capita income, is the natural logarithm of per capita income. Per capita income is measured as real purchasing power parity adjusted GDP per capita to provide reasonable comparability across countries. The primary data set is the Penn World Table 5.6 (Summers and Heston, 1991). Income data are measured at the beginning of each subperiod, 1965, 1970, ..., 1995.

Growth rate of per capita income. Using the above income per capita measure, Collier and Hoeffler calculated the average annual growth rate as a proxy for economic opportunities. This variable is measured in the five-year period prior to the one for which conflict risk is being measured.

Primary commodity exports/GDP. This is the ratio of primary commodity exports to GDP and proxies the abundance of natural resources. The data on primary commodity exports as well as GDP were obtained from the World Bank. Export and GDP data are measured in current U.S. dollars. The data are measured at the beginning of each subperiod, 1965, 1970, ..., 1995.

Population. This is the natural logarithm of the population. The data source is the World Bank's *World Development Indicators 1998*. Again, population is measured at the beginning of each subperiod—included to control for the size of the country's population. If the effect of population were neutral, then one would expect that a doubling of population would approximately double the risk of conflict. For instance, this would be the assumption if two identical neighboring countries are merged. Empirically peaceful countries have, on average, less than half the population of conflict countries, higher population density, and are more urbanized.

Social fractionalization. If intergroup hatred is a crucial factor in civil wars, then it might be expected that homogeneous societies would be considerably safer than fractionalized societies. Social fractionalization is proxied using the Collier and Hoeffler combined measure of ethnic and religious fractionalization. Ethnic fractionalization is measured by the ethno-linguistic fractionalization index. It measures the probability that two randomly drawn individuals from a given country do not speak the same language. Data are only available for 1960. Using data from Barrett (1982) on religious affiliations, Collier and Hoeffler constructed an analogous religious fractionalization index. Following Barro (1991) they aggregated the various religious affiliations into nine categories: Catholic, Protestant, Muslim, Jew, Hindu, Buddhist, eastern religions (other than Buddhist), indigenous religions, and no religious affiliation. The fractionalization indices range from 0 to 100. A value of 0 indicates that the society is completely homogeneous, whereas a value of 100 would characterize a completely heterogeneous society. Collier and Hoeffler calculated the social fractionalization index as the product of the ethno-linguistic fractionalization and the religious fractionalization index plus the ethno-linguistic or the religious fractionalization index, whichever is greater.

Ethnic dominance. Collier and Hoeffler define this as occurring where the largest ethnic group constitutes 45-90 percent of the population. Using the ethno-linguistic data from the original data source (Atlas Narodov Mira, 1964) Collier and Hoeffler calculated an indicator of ethnic dominance. This variable takes the value of one if one single ethno-linguistic group makes up 45 to 90 percent of the total population and zero otherwise. According to Collier and Hoeffler, societies characterized by ethnic dominance have about double the risk of conflict of other societies.

Population dispersion. This variable measures the geographic dispersion of the population. Collier and Hoeffler constructed a dispersion index of the population on a country-by-country basis. Based on population data for 400-square-kilometer cells, they generated a Gini coefficient of population dispersion for each country. A value of zero indicates that the population is evenly distributed across the country, and a value of one indicates that the total population is concentrated in one area. Data are available for 1990 and 1995. For years prior to 1990, we use the 1990 data.

Peace duration. This variable measures the length of the peace period since the end of the previous civil war. For countries that never experienced a civil war we measure the peace period since the end of World War II until 1962 (172 months) and add 60 peace months in each consecutive five-year period.

Bibliography

Ali, A.A.G., 2000, "The Economics of Conflicts in Africa: An Overview," *Journal of African Economies*, Vol. 9, No. 3, pp. 235–43.

Annan, K., 1998, "The Causes of Conflict and the Promotion of Durable Peace and Sustainable Development in Africa," Report of the UN Secretary General to the UN Security Council, April.

Bardhan, P., 1989, "The New Institutions Economics and Development Theory: A Brief Critical Assessment," *World Development*, Vol. 17, pp. 1389–95.

Barrett, D.B, ed., 1982, *World Christian Encyclopedia* (Oxford: Oxford University Press).

Barro, R., 1991, "Economic Growth in a Cross Section of Countries," *Quarterly Journal of Economics*, Vol. 106, No. 2, pp. 403–43.

———, 1997, *Determinants of Economic Growth* (Cambridge, Massachusetts: Massachusetts Institute of Technology).

Berdal, M., and D.M. Malone, 2000, eds., *Greed and Grievance: Economic Agendas in Civil Wars* (Boulder: Lynne Rienner Publishers).

Bigombe B., and others, 2000, "Policies for Building Post Conflict Peace," *Journal of African Economies*, Vol. 9, pp. 323–48.

Bosswell, T., and W.J. Dixon, 1990, "Dependency and Rebellion: A Crossnational Analysis," *American Sociological Review,* Vol. 55, No. 4, pp. 540–59.

Butler, J.S., and R. Moffitt, 1982, "A Computationally Efficient Quadrature Procedure for the One-Factor Multinomial Probit Model," *Econometrica*, Vol. 50, No. 3, pp. 761–64.

Collier, P., 1999, "On the Economic Consequences of Civil War," Oxford Economic Papers, Vol. 51, pp. 163–83.

———, 2000a, "Rebellion as a Quasi-Criminal Activity," *Journal of Conflict Resolution*, Vol. 44 (December), pp. 839–53.

———, 2000b, "Aid, Policy and Peace," World Bank Policy Research Working Paper (Washington: World Bank).

Collier P., and Hoeffler, A., 2002a "Greed and Grievance in Civil War," Centre for the Study of African Economies Working Paper WPS/2002–01 (Oxford).

———, 2002b, "On the Incidence of Civil War in Africa," *Journal of Conflict Resolution*, Vol. 46, No. 1, pp. 13–28.

Collier, P., and others, 2003, *Breaking the Conflict Trap: Civil War and Development Policy* (Washington: Oxford University Press for the World Bank).

Cramer, C., 1999, "The Economics and Political Economy of Conflict in Sub-Saharan Africa," CEPR Discussion Paper 1099 (London: Centre for Economic Policy Research).

Crossette, B., 2000, "Singling Out Sierra Leone, U.N. Council Sets Gem Ban," *New York Times*, July 6, 2000.

Doyle, M.W., and N. Sambanis, 2000a, "International Peace Building: A Theoretical and Quantitative Analysis" (unpublished; Princeton: Princeton University and World Bank).

———, 2000b, "Building Peace: Challenges and Strategies After Civil War" (unpublished; Princeton: Princeton University and World Bank).

———, 2003, "Alternative Measures and Estimates of Peace Building Success" (unpublished; New Haven, Connecticut: Department of Political Science, Yale University).

Dudley, R., and R.D. Miller, 1998, "Group Rebellion in the 1980s," *Journal of Conflict Resolution*, Vol. 42, No. 1, pp. 77–96.

Easterly, W., 2000, "Can Institutions Resolve Ethnic Conflict?" World Bank Policy Research Paper (Washington: The World Bank).

Easterly, R., and R. Levine, 1997, "Africa's Growth Tragedy: Policies and Ethnic Divisions," *Quarterly Journal of Economics*, Vol. 112, pp. 1203–50.

Edison, H., 2003, "Testing the Links: How Strong Are the Links Between Institutional Quality and Economic Performance?" *Finance and Development*, Vol. 40, pp. 35–37.

Elbadawi, I., and N. Sambanis, 2000a, "How Much War Will We See? Estimating the Likelihood and Amount of War in 161 Countries, 1960–1998" (unpublished; Washington: World Bank).

———, 2000b, "Why Are There So Many Civil Wars in Africa? Understanding and Preventing Violent Conflict," *Journal of African Economies*, Vol. 9, No. 3, pp. 244–69.

Fearon, J., and D. Laitin, 2000, "Ethnicity, Insurgency, and War" (unpublished; Palo Alto, California: Stanford University).

Flanagan, W.H., and E. Fogelman, 1971, "Patterns of Political Science in Comparative Historical Perspective," *Comparative Politics*, Vol. 3, No. 1, pp. 1–20.

Fowler, R.R., 2000, "Report of the Panel of Experts on Violations of Security Council Sanctions Against UNITA," United Nations Security Council, S/2000/203, March 10.

Gissinger, R., and N.P. Gleditsch, 1999, "Globalisation and Conflict: Welfare, Distribution, and Political Unrest," *Journal of World Systems Research*, Vol. 2, pp. 327–65.

Greene, W.H., 1995, *LIMDEP, Version 7.0: User Manual* (Bellport, New York: Econometric Software), pp. 234–41.

———, 1997, *Econometric Analysis* (New Jersey: Prentice Hall, 3rd ed.).

Grossman, H.I., 1991, "A General Equilibrium Model of Insurrections," *American Economic Review*, Vol. 81 (September), pp. 912–21.

———, 1999, "Kleptocracy and Revolutions," Oxford Economic Papers, Vol. 51, pp. 267–83.

Gujarati, D.N., 1995, *Basic Econometrics* (Singapore: McGraw-Hill, Inc., 3rd ed.).

Gurr, T., 1970, *Why Men Rebel* (Princeton, New Jersey: Princeton University Press).

Gyimah-Brempong, K., and M.E. Corley, 2001, "Civil Wars and Economic Growth in Sub-Saharan Africa," paper presented at the Annual ASSA Meeting, New Orleans, January 4–7.

Harff, B., and T.R. Gurr, 1996, "Victims of the State: Genocides, Politicides, and Group Repression from 1945 to 1995," in *Contemporary Genocides: Causes, Cases, Consequences* (Leiden: Netherlands PIOOM Foundation).

Hegre, H., and others, 2001, "Towards a Democratic Civil Peace?" *American Political Science Review*, Vol. 95, pp. 33–48.

Herbst, J., 2000, "Economic Incentives, Natural Resources and Conflict in Africa," *Journal of African Economies*, Vol. 9, No. 3, pp. 270–94.

Hirschleifer, J., 1995, "Theorising about Conflict" in *Handbook of Defense Economics*, Vol. 1, ed. by K. Hartley and T. Sandler (Amsterdam: North Holland).

Homer-Dixon, T., 1991, "On the Threshold: Environmental Changes as Causes of Conflict," *International Security*, Vol. 16, No. 2, pp. 76–116.

Jacobsen, M.S., 1996, "Fred og velstand eller demokratisk kaos?-en analyse av regimeendring og borgerkrig 1945–92" (Peace and Prosperity, or Democratic Chaos?), *Internasjonal Politikk*, Vol. 56, No. 2, pp. 241–50.

James, P. Westport, and D. Goetze, 2001, eds. *Evolutionary Theory and Ethnic Conflict* (Connecticut: Praeger).

Kaufman, D., A. Kraay, and P. Zoido-Lobaton, 1999, "Aggregating Governance Indicators," World Bank Policy Research Working Paper 2196 (Washington: World Bank).

Keen, D., 1998, "Economic Functions of Violence in Civil War," Adelphi Paper 320 (Oxford: Oxford University Press).

King, G., and L. Zeng, 2001, "Logistic Regression in Rare Events Data," *Political Analysis*, Vol. 9, No. 2, pp. 137–63.

Knack, S., and Keefer, P., 1995, "Institutions and Economic Performance: Cross-Country Tests Using Alternative Institutional Measures," *Economics and Politics*, Vol. 7, pp. 207–87.

Lichbach, M.I., 1989, "An Evaluation of 'Does Economic Inequality Breed Political Conflict' Studies," *World Politics*, Vol. 41, No. 4, pp. 431–70.

Muller, E., 1988, "Democracy, Economic Development, and Income Inequality," *American Sociological Review*, Vol. 53, No. 1, pp. 50–68.

Nafziger, E.W., and J. Auvinen, 1997, "War, Hunger and Displacement: An Econometric Investigation into the Sources of Humanitarian Emergencies," WIDER Working Paper No. 142 (Helsinki: World Institute for Development Economics Research).

Ngaruko, F., and J.D. Nkurunziza, 2000, "An Economic Interpretation of Conflict in Burundi," *Journal of African Economies*, Vol. 9, No. 3, pp. 370–409.

North, D.C., 1994, "Economic Performance Through Time," *American Economic Review*, Vol. 84, No. 3, pp. 359–68.

Olsson, O., 2003, "Conflict Diamond," Working Papers in Economics No. 86 (Göteborg: University of Göteborg).

PRS Group, 2003, *International Country Risk Guide*.

Reno, W., 1999, "Humanitarian Emergencies and Warlord Economies in Liberia and Sierra Leone," paper presented at a conference on "War, Hunger and Displacement: The Economics and Politics of the Prevention of Humanitarian Emergencies," Stockholm, June 15–16, United Nations University/World Institute for Development Economics Research.

Reynal-Querol, M., 2000, *Religious Conflict and Growth: Theory and Evidence* (London: London School of Economics and Political Science).

———, 2002, "Ethnicity, Political Systems, and Civil War," *Journal of Conflict Resolution*, Vol. 46, No. 1, pp. 29–54.

Rodrik, D., 1999, "Where Did All the Growth Go? External Shocks, Social Conflict, and Growth Collapses," *Journal of Economic Growth*, Vol. 4, pp. 385–412.

Sambanis, N., 2000, "Partition as a Solution to Ethnic War: An Empirical Critique of the Theoretical Literature," *World Politics*, Vol. 52, pp. 437–83.

Schock, K., 1996, "A Conjunctural Model of Political Conflict," *Journal of Conflict Resolution*, Vol. 40, No. 1, pp. 98–133.

Singer, J.D., and M. Small, 1993, *Correlates of War Project: International and Civil War Data, 1916–1992* (Ann Arbor, Michigan: Inter-University Consortium of Political Social Research).

Smith, D., 2001, "Trends and Causes of Armed Conflicts," in *Berghof Handbook for Conflict Transformation* (Berlin: Berghof Research Center for Constructive Conflict Management).

Stein, N., 2003, "Foreword," in *Breaking the Conflict Trap: Civil War and Development Policy* (Oxford: Oxford University Press for the World Bank).

Stockholm International Peace Research Institute, *Yearbook of World Armaments and Disarmaments*, various issues (Oxford: Oxford University Press).

Summers, R., and A. Heston, 1991, "The Penn World Table: An International Comparison, 1950–1988," *Quarterly Journal of Economics*, Vol. 106, No. 2, pp. 327–68.

Taylor, C.L., and M.C. Hudson, 1972, *World Handbook of Political and Social Indicators* (New Haven: Yale University Press, 2nd ed.).

Tily, C., 1978, *From Mobilization to Revolution* (New York: Random House).

Timberlake, M., and K.R. Williams, 1987, "Structural Position in the World System, Inequality, and Political Instability," *Journal of Political and Military Sociology*, Vol. 151, pp. 1–15.

Tocqueville, A.D., 1835, *Democracy in America*, Vol. II (New York: Schocken).

United Nations, 1999, *Affected Populations in the Great Lakes Region* (Nairobi, Kenya: Great Lakes Regional Office).

Wallensteen, P., 2002, Global Development Strategies for Conflict Prevention," Department of Peace and Conflict Research, Uppsala University (unpublished; Uppsala, Sweden).

Weingast, B.R., 1997, "The Political Foundations of Democracy and the Rule of Law," *American Political Science Review*, Vol. 91, No. 2, pp. 245–63.

Wolf, E., 1969, *Peasant Wars of the Twentieth Century* (New York: Harper and Row).

World Bank, 2002, *World Development Indicators* (Washington: World Bank).

5

Economic Performance Over the Conflict Cycle

NICHOLAS STAINES

Section I. Introduction

Poverty and armed conflict are closely connected, so the poorest countries face the prospect of being caught in a "conflict trap" of poverty and recurring conflict (Collier and others, 2003). One group of countries particularly at risk for conflict are those that have recently emerged from conflict. It is particularly important to help these countries ensure a quick recovery from conflict and a return to sustainable development. This effort requires an understanding of the economic features of the conflict cycle, and this chapter seeks to contribute to this topic. In particular, this chapter looks at the evolution of economic performance and the role of macroeconomic policy and aid in a selection of 24 countries as they passed through civil conflict and through the first few years of postconflict recovery. The chapter offers three main findings leading to three policy implications.

Main Findings

Shift in the key features of the conflict cycle. The first finding, developed in Section II, is that, although the economic performance of countries affected by conflict shares many features in common, the data point to a discernible and statistically significant shift in the key economic characteristics of the conflict cycle occurring at the start of the

1990s, where the conflict cycle is defined to end when real GDP per capita recovers to its preconflict level. Compared with earlier conflicts, those of the 1990s were shorter and associated with deeper economic contractions. In addition, whereas countries emerged from earlier conflicts following a prolonged period of recovery, they emerged from conflicts in the 1990s at a much earlier stage of the conflict cycle and faced significantly worse conditions. At the same time, compared with earlier conflicts, countries also generally came out of later conflicts with modestly higher growth in the first few years after conflict. This growth, although only modestly higher than after earlier conflicts, represented a significantly stronger rebound in growth from the low (negative) levels prevailing during conflict. In many cases, the conflict cycle to the recovery of output to preconflict levels remains incomplete. The chapter provides projections that suggest that the shift tended to reduce the overall length of the conflict cycle while redistributing the time spent in conflict in favor of the time spent in recovery. At the same time, it has probably also tended to reduce the overall economic cost of output foregone over the conflict cycle.

The role of macroeconomic policy. The second finding, discussed in Section III, relates to the linkages between the evolution of economic activity and macroeconomic policy. Conflict was typically accompanied by a deterioration and recovery in key macroeconomic policy variables that was much more pronounced in the conflicts of the 1990s. The changes observed over the past decade suggest that the stance of macroeconomic policy has also had a more discernible and statistically significant impact on economic activity in recent conflicts than in earlier years.[1] The chapter provides estimates that the policy stance moderated the decline and also the initial recovery in output growth in earlier conflict cycles, but accentuated it in more recent episodes. In particular, the stronger macroeconomic stabilization effort, especially with respect to inflation, has been an important factor underlying the stronger postconflict recovery of growth observed in the 1990s. Another perhaps rather surprising result also emerges. Once other factors, including policy, are taken into account, the initial impact of the start and end of hostilities on output growth was quite similar for the two sets of conflict—suggesting that, despite the different economic profiles, the same underlying "conflict process" was at work.

---

[1]Through the chapter, the policy stance is evaluated solely in terms of its estimated impact on growth and not relative to some benchmark.

The role of external assistance. The third finding, discussed in Section IV, is that these changes in part reflected a shift in donor practices following the end of the cold war that resulted in donors being less inclined to support countries during conflict but also more willing to provide assistance after conflict. Establishing linkages statistically is beyond the scope of this chapter, so the argument is only suggestive. Donors tended to increase financial assistance during pre-1990 conflicts but reduced assistance once conflict ended. In the conflicts of the 1990s, donors generally reduced assistance sharply during conflict, but also tended to increase assistance equally sharply after conflict. This difference may have contributed to more severe economic contractions and imbalances experienced by countries in these later conflicts and plausibly also contributed to their shorter duration. The greater donor willingness to provide support after recent conflicts has also contributed to stronger postconflict recoveries, which points to the potentially high productivity of aid targeted toward macroeconomic stabilization in the early postconflict recovery period.

Experience in countries receiving emergency postconflict assistance. These findings are buttressed by the experience, discussed in Section V, of six countries that have received emergency postconflict assistance (EPCA) from the International Monetary Fund since 1995.[2] The experience of these countries was broadly similar to that of other countries in the 1990s, but their performance in the first two years after conflict was generally stronger. This was arguably because their stronger commitment to sound macroeconomic policies provided the basis for the international community to provide financial support soon after conflict. In this respect, there was an important virtuous cycle in operation: Sound policy attracted external assistance that made these policies easier to implement and more fruitful.

Experience in the Democratic Republic of the Congo (DRC). These findings are again buttressed by the experience, also discussed in Section V, of the DRC (which did not receive EPCA from the IMF) where stabilization and the start of economic recovery were made more difficult by delays in official external assistance. However, although the DRC's initial postconflict growth performance was unfa-

---

[2]The IMF's experience in postconflict countries since the introduction of its EPCA policy in 1995 and especially in the six countries that received this financial assistance is discussed in *Review of Recent IMF Experience in Post-Conflict Countries"* IMF Occasional Paper, 2004, forthcoming.

vorable, the government's firm commitment to good policies was rewarded by an improvement in performance that was one of the strongest in the 1990s.

Policy Implications

The findings of this chapter point to three policy implications.

Postconflict policy priorities. First, if civil conflicts in the 1990s are representative, then compared with their earlier counterparts, countries emerging from recent conflicts face a more urgent need to restore macroeconomic stability, and the economic benefits of stabilization are also correspondingly larger. However, they also face competing political pressures that can be at odds with stabilization, including, for example, the urgent need to increase government spending to meet immediate social priorities. Nevertheless, there appears to be the need to assign a higher priority to postconflict macroeconomic stabilization than in the past.

Postconflict aid. There are possible implications for the timing and type of postconflict aid. Aid following recent conflicts has tended to peak immediately after conflict, but the ability of a country emerging from conflict to make use of aid is constrained by its political and administrative capacity. It has therefore been suggested that aid might be more effectively used if delayed until capacity was restored. This is perhaps particularly the case for project aid. In contrast, the evidence on recent conflict cases presented in this chapter indicates that the productivity of external assistance can be high in the initial postconflict period when the government is committed to following a sound macroeconomic strategy, particularly if assistance is provided to the budget in support of macroeconomic stabilization.

Aid during conflict. Finally, the findings suggest the intriguing possibility that the international community may be able, through its aid policies, to influence the economic profile of the conflict cycle, especially the trade-off between the duration and the economic severity of conflict. However, it is not clear what portion of the trade-off is preferable because, at first glance, the shift observed in the 1990s appears to have been accompanied by only a modest reduction in the short-term economic cost of conflict. Also, any evaluation would need to take into account the longer-term human and economic costs involved. This is obviously a complex issue that needs further attention.

Literature Review

Five areas of the literature of particular interest here relate to the causes of conflict, the length of conflict, the impact of conflict, the impact of macroeconomic policy, and the role of external assistance.[3]

Causes of conflict. Recent analyses have tended to downplay the traditional explanations of civil conflict revolving around the politics of grievance and have instead tended to highlight economic factors (Blomberg and Hess, 2002; Collier, 2000; Collier and Hoeffler, 1998, 2000, 2002a; Fearon and Laitin, 2002; Nafziger and Auvinen 2002). In particular, the propensity to civil conflict has been closely linked to economic stagnation and poverty, although the direction of causality is not altogether clear.

Length of conflict. The shortening of conflicts in the 1990s has been noted by Fearon (2002). No clear consensus has emerged on the factors underlying the length of conflict. It has been persuasively argued by Collier, Hoeffler, and Söderbom (2001) that the sort of factors typically used to explain the initiation of conflict have generally had little bearing on the duration of conflict. One regular feature is that, as well as being more prone to conflict, poorer countries also typically endure longer conflicts arguably because of their lower capacity to inflict damage. Fearon (2002) has also linked the length of conflict to the political nature of the conflict. For example, civil conflicts arising from coup attempts or popular revolutions or involving successful peripheral secessions have tended to be relatively brief, whereas conflicts revolving around land claims or natural resources tend to be relatively prolonged. Collier and Hoeffler (2000) have sought to explain the length of conflict by focusing on sources of financing for conflict, especially natural resources, as well as the balance of benefits to the parties involved, once conflict has started, to perpetuate conflict. The role of external assistance, especially related to military spending, in sustaining conflict has been noted in Michailof, Kostner, and Devictor (2002), and Elbadawi (2000) has also looked at the role of foreign interventions, especially in terminating conflicts.

Impact of conflict. A number of authors have looked at the cause of output losses in conflict, including Arunatilake, Jayasuriya, and Kelegama (2001), Caplan (2001), Collier (1999), Imai and Weinstein (2000), and Knight, Loayza, and Villanueva (1996). A broad consen-

---

[3]Gudmundsson in Chapter 3 provides a comprehensive survey of the literature on the economics of conflict.

sus has emerged that civil conflict reduces annual real GDP growth by about 2 percentage points. Collier (1999) also found that the negative impact of conflict persisted long after conflict. As might be expected, this work links output losses to the geographical extent of the conflict and the destruction of the human and capital stock; the disruption of government capacity to collect revenues and provide essential services; and the general disruption of commerce. A promising line of inquiry pursued by Murdoch and Sandler (2001a, b) focuses on the spillover effects from conflicts in neighboring countries and the compounding of the damage when they are part of a broader set of regional conflicts. There has been limited work on the impact of conflict on other key macroeconomic indicators. Caplan (2001) found no discernible effect of civil conflict on inflation and only a limited tendency for government spending to increase relative to GDP. Gupta and others (2002b) provide more conclusive evidence that conflict led to higher inflation, higher government spending, and higher fiscal deficits.

Impact of macroeconomic policy. The impact of macroeconomic policy on output during conflict has received very limited attention. Gupta and others (2002b), looking at experience in the 1990s, found that growth was affected by changes in the composition of government spending and the reduction in social spending in favor of military spending. Helpfully, there are a number of studies across a broad spectrum of developing countries (not necessarily in conflict) with results that can also shed light on conflict situations, especially concerning postconflict macroeconomic stabilization.

There is now a consensus that healthy fiscal balances are generally good for economic growth, but there is less agreement on the short-term impact of fiscal consolidation. The standard Keynesian conclusion that fiscal consolidation reduces growth relies on the multiplier for government spending exceeding that for tax revenues. This conclusion finds support in a survey of the empirical literature on multipliers for government spending and factor input taxes by Gerson (1998). However, Gupta and others (2002a) have shown that fiscal consolidations in the 1990s have had a positive short-term impact on growth: a reduction of 1 percentage point in the fiscal deficit-to-GDP ratio led to a short-term increase in per capita output growth of 0.5 percentage point. The impact was larger when consolidation was based on current spending cuts rather than on revenue increases or capital spending cuts and when offset by reduced domestic rather than external financing.

The linkage between fiscal deficits and inflation also remains contested, but both Catao and Terrones (2001) and Fischer, Sahay, and Vegh (2002) found strong support for a linkage when inflation is high. A 1 percentage point reduction in the fiscal deficit-to-GDP ratio reduces inflation by up to 6 percentage points. There is now strong support that even moderate inflation can damage economic growth (Brauman, 2000; Ghosh and Philips, 1998) above a threshold in developing countries of about 10 percent (Khan and Senhadji, 2000). There is less agreement on the impact of disinflation. Disinflation has a positive impact on growth when inflation is very high (Fischer, Sahay, and Vegh 2002), but may have a contractionary effect if the inflation rate is already low or if the disinflation is too severe (Ghosh and Philips, 1998).

External assistance. Michailof, Kostner, and Devictor (2002) noted the role of aid in sustaining conflict during the cold war and the changes in aid patterns since the cold war. Otherwise, discussions of the role of aid have tended to focus on the postconflict recovery period. An important strand in the literature relates to the timing and type of aid. Collier and Hoeffler (2002b) and Collier and others (2003) noted that aid tends to peak immediately after conflict and argue that aid would be more effective if it peaked about three to five years after the end of conflict when absorptive capacity is at its highest. These papers also provide evidence that, relative to other countries, aid to conflict-affected countries in support of social priorities is relatively more effective than aid in support of economic reconstruction and macroeconomic stabilization, in part because of its impact in reducing the probability of renewed hostilities. Demekas, McHugh, and Kosma (2002) have also argued that, compared with humanitarian assistance, reconstruction aid supports longer-term capital accumulation and growth but at the expense of lower current consumption.

This chapter within the literature. The chapter seeks to extend the conflict-related literature in three directions. The literature has tended to focus on the bulk of civil conflicts that started before 1990, whereas this chapter argues that there are important features that do not carry over to the more recent conflicts. A second feature of the literature is its tendency to treat conflict as a single event, while the current chapter argues that the economic phase at which a country comes out of conflict has important implications for the nature of the postconflict recovery. Finally, this chapter emphasizes the role of macroeconomic policy, and indirectly of aid, as a determinant of growth during the conflict cycle.

The Data

The chapter looks at economic developments in 24 civil conflicts in 23 countries that have taken place since 1970 (Table A5.1). This set has been pared down from a much larger set, according to data availability and whether the conflict had a discernible macroeconomic impact.[4] For example, the conflict in Vietnam was not included because of a lack of data, while India's regional conflict in Kashmir was excluded because of a lack of a discernible economic impact on India as a whole. The 24 conflicts are divided by starting date into two groups: 10 that began before 1990 and 14 that commenced after 1990.[5] In addition, performance was markedly different in four conflicts in the 1990s that arose out of dissolved federal entities (DFEs) in the Soviet Union and the Republic of Yugoslavia.

Setting beginning and end dates of conflict often requires judgment. This is especially true for internal conflicts, in which the descent into and emergence from conflict is often gradual and intermittent. For example, Sierra Leone experienced internal disturbances for several years before the coup in 1997—the date used here for this conflict. Decisions on the dates to use for analytical purposes are based on information from the Swedish International Peace Research Institute (SIPRI) and IMF staff reports.[6] The chapter uses data up to 2002 from the IMF's World Economic Outlook (WEO) database (2003). As might be expected, the quality of the data during and after conflict is weak. Data for several conflict cases are limited and are available for up to 2 years for 24 countries but are available up to 5 years for only 17.

Section II. Economic Performance over the Conflict Cycle

Profile of the Conflict Cycle

The economic cycle related to conflict is normally divided into three distinct phases that correspond to its political phases: a preconflict

---

[4]Collier (1999) as well as Sambanis (2001) have listed almost 60 conflicts that have started since 1970. Fearon (2002) listed almost 90 conflicts since 1970 with 44 civil wars outstanding in 1994.

[5]Although dividing the sample in this way creates a risk of sample selection bias, as lengthy conflicts are more likely to be excluded from the 1990s subgroups, this problem does not arise here because all conflicts that began in the 1990s had ended by 2000. Conflicts excluded from the sample because they had outlasted the 1990s (i.e., Angola and Sudan) were lengthy confrontations that commenced in earlier decades.

[6]SIPRI defines a country to be in conflict in any single year if there are more than 1,000 casualties with at least 5 percent of casualties on either side.

phase of economic deterioration, the period during conflict of reduced growth or contraction, and a postconflict phase of economic recovery. However, this perspective can be misleading if the political and economic phases of conflict are not in fact synchronized, or if there is a change in how they are synchronized. Precisely such a shift appears to have occurred in the 1990s, with important implications for the stage of the economic cycle at which countries emerged from conflict (Table 5.1, Figures 5.1 and 5.2).

Contraction. A distinguishing feature of civil conflicts, unlike cross-border conflicts, is that their onset is typically associated with a decline

Table 5.1. Length of Contraction and Recovery During Conflict
(Years)

	Total Conflict	Real GDP		Real GDP per Capita	
		Contraction[1]	In-conflict recovery	Contraction[1]	In-conflict recovery
Pre-1990	11.8	3.2	8.6	5.2	6.6
Post-1990	3.5	2.7	0.8	3.2	0.3

Source: WEO.
[1]Only includes contraction during conflict.

Figure 5.1. Real GDP
(Level, Index = 100 one year before conflict)

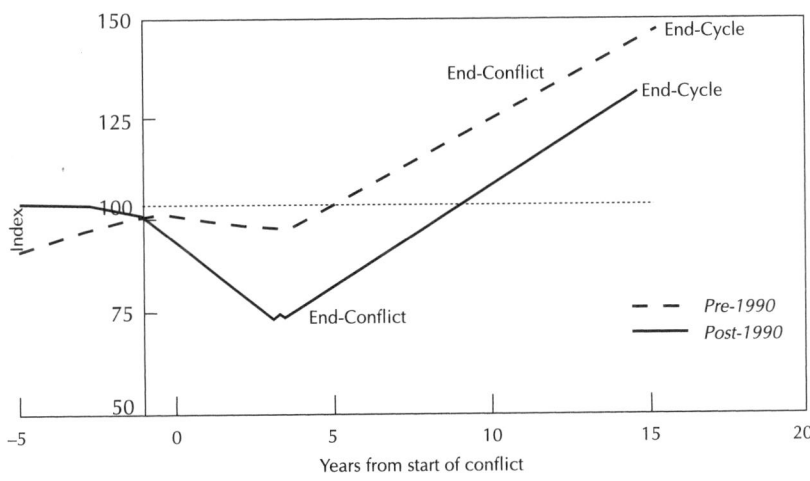

Source: WEO.

Figure 5.2. Real GDP Per Capita
(Level, Index = 100 one year before conflict)

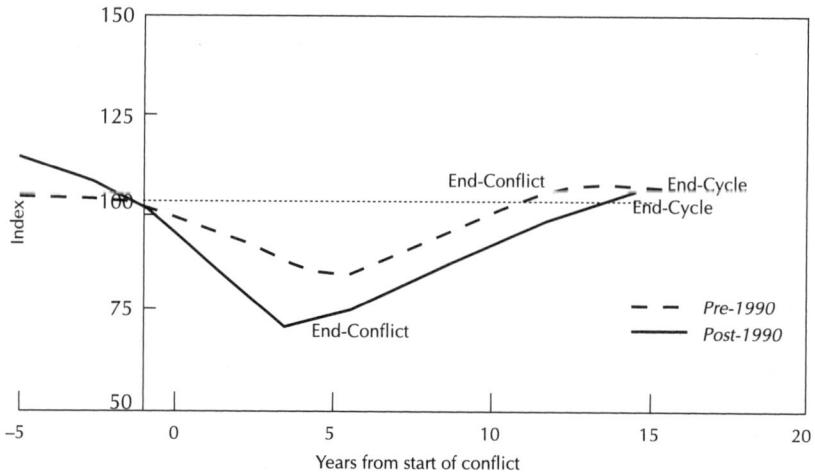

Source: WEO.

in economic performance.[7] However, in many instances, this deterioration predated the conflict: real GDP growth began to fall as much as five years before conflict, and more than half the countries (mostly in post-1990 conflicts) entered conflict with reduced GDP per capita. With the onset of conflict, most countries experienced a contraction in output that averaged about three years for all conflicts, but that was generally longer for the pre-1990 conflicts. In terms of output per capita, the contractions tended to last about a year longer. More important, the end of the contraction and the start of the economic recovery did not necessarily coincide with the end of conflict.

Recovery. A major change in the 1990s was a sharp decline in the length of conflicts, organized by starting date, which fell from an average of 12 years for pre-1990 conflicts to only 4 years for those of the 1990s.[8] In the pre-1990 conflicts, hostilities tended to end well after the

---

[7]Caplan (2001) looked at conflicts during 1950–92 and concluded that, while civil conflicts have on average *reduced* annual real GDP growth by 2 percent, international conflicts have *increased* growth by 2 percent.

[8]The conflicts are arranged here by *starting date*. By way of comparison, Fearon (2002) looked at the 122 civil wars from 1945 to the mid-1990s and estimated that the average length of civil conflict was 9 years but with a high variance so that about half in equal numbers were either less than 2 years or more than 12 years. He also noted the shortening of conflicts in the 1990s, but concluded that the average length of *outstanding* civil conflict has been steadily increasing since 1945 and reached 15 years by the mid-1990s.

start of the recovery so that there was a prolonged period of "in-conflict" recovery. In the shorter post-1990 conflicts, hostilities tended to end at about the same time as the end of the contraction (and occasionally before), and in these cases an "in-conflict" recovery period was typically absent.[9] As a result, countries emerged from these conflicts at a much earlier phase of the economic cycle than did their earlier counterparts.

Phases of recovery. Where along the economic cycle the country emerged from conflict had an important bearing on the economic conditions it faced. It is useful to distinguish three phases: a stabilization phase in which major macroeconomic imbalances were corrected along with positive output growth; a reconstruction phase, during which the security and policy environment was normalized and recovery was fully supported by donor-funded reconstruction programs; and a final development phase leading to a return to normal growth. The timing of these phases relative to the end of conflict depended, in part, on the overall length of conflict and whether there was a period of in-conflict recovery. In the pre-1990 conflicts, which typically included a lengthy in-conflict recovery period, the modest stabilization required was mostly in place by the end of conflict. In the post-1990 conflicts, where the contraction typically continued to the end of conflict, the stabilization phase only began once conflict ended and in some cases was delayed for several years after conflict.

Economic Growth

The shortening of conflicts in the 1990s was also accompanied by a marked worsening of economic performance during conflict and consequently in the conditions that countries faced as they emerged from conflict. At the same time, there was a broad improvement in economic performance in the initial years after conflict (Table 5.2). For each set of conflicts, Table 5.3 shows the difference between growth during a period extending five years before and after conflict and growth in all other periods (i.e., under normal circumstances) as well as the difference in growth between the two sets of conflicts. It also shows the statistical significance of these differences.

---

[9]For the 14 post-1990 conflicts, the contractions in real GDP and real GDP per capita ended before the end of conflict in 5 and 3 countries, respectively, and both ended after conflict in 3 countries.

Table 5.2. Evolution of Real GDP and Real GDP per Capita

	Before Conflict		During Conflict					After Conflict				
	1–5 years before	1 year before	Whole conflict	During[1] contraction	At[1] trough	During[2] recovery	End year	1 year after	2 years after	1–2 years after	3–5 years after[3]	1–5 years after[3]
Real GDP, index												
Pre-1990	96	100	111	96	94	115	130	134	139	137	153	146
Post-1990	103	100	83	81	74	85	75	80	82	81	85	85
Non-DFE	98	100	92	90	84	93	86	93	97	95	102	99
DFE	117	100	62	62	49	42	49	47	47	47	54	51
Real GDP, percent change												
Pre-1990	2.9	1.8	2.0	-3.4	-0.6	3.5	1.6	2.7	3.7	3.2	4.3	3.9
Post-1990	1.1	-1.0	-8.3	-11.5	-13.0	3.1	-9.3	5.0	3.2	4.1	5.2	4.8
Non-DFE	2.2	1.7	-4.1	-7.8	-11.7	3.4	-7.1	8.9	4.3	6.6	4.3	5.5
DFE	-1.5	-8.0	-18.9	-19.6	-16.2	1.7	-14.7	-4.7	0.3	-2.2	6.9	3.2
Real GDP per capita, index												
Pre-1990	101	100	98	88	84	100	102	102	102	102	104	103
Post-1990	108	100	79	79	71	71	71	74	75	74	74	76
Non-DFE	103	100	86	86	80	87	81	85	86	85	87	87
DFE	121	100	61	62	48	39	48	45	47	46	53	50
Real GDP per capita, percent change												
Pre-1990	0.1	-1.0	-0.4	-4.0	-3.0	2.3	-1.2	0.9	-0.2	0.4	1.3	0.9
Post-1990	-1.0	-2.9	-10.7	-12.5	-13.6	3.1	-10.2	2.0	1.1	1.6	3.0	2.4
Non-DFE	-0.4	-0.4	-7.3	-9.6	-12.5	4.2	-8.3	5.2	1.2	3.2	1.2	2.3
DFE	-2.6	-9.1	-19.1	-19.9	-16.6	0.7	-15.0	-5.9	0.9	-2.5	6.2	2.7

Source: WEO.

Note: DFE, dissolved federal entity.

[1] The contraction period and trough are defined in terms of real GDP and real GDP per capita, respectively.

[2] Not all post-1990 conflicts experienced an in-conflict recovery.

[3] Data for 3, 4, and 5 years after conflict are available for 11, 7, and 7 of 14 post-1990 conflicts, respectively.

Table 5.3. Evolution of Output over the Conflict Cycle: Differences in Growth During and Between Conflicts

	Before	During Conflict			After		
	1–5 years	Total	Contrac-tion	Recovery	1–2 years	3–5 years	1–5 years
Real GDP							
Difference from outside conflict cycle							
Pre-1990	−0.8	−1.7 ***	−7.1 ***	−0.2 ***	−0.5	0.6	0.2
Post-1990	−2.9 ***	−12.3 ***	−15.5 ***	−0.9 ***	0.1	1.2 **	0.8
Difference between conflicts	−1.8 ***	−10.3 ***	−8.1 ***	−0.4 *	0.9	0.9 *	0.9
Real GDP per capita							
Difference from outside conflict cycle							
Pre-1990	−0.8 *	−1.3 ***	−4.9 ***	1.4	−0.5	0.4	0.0
Post-1990	−2.9 **	−12.6 ***	−14.4 ***	1.2	−0.3	1.1	0.5
Difference between conflicts	−1.1	−10.3 ***	−8.5 ***	0.8	1.2	1.7	1.5

Source: WEO.
Notes: Differences evaluated using regressions allowing for serial correlation. Levels of significance at the 1, 5, and 10 percent levels are indicated by ***, **, and *, respectively.

Pre-1990 conflicts. In the pre-1990 conflicts, the pace and depth of the contractions tended to be relatively modest with an average annual decline in real GDP per capita of about 4 percent—or about 5 percentage points below normal—and a cumulative decline in real GDP per capita at its trough to about 84 percent of its preconflict level. However, since their contractions were also typically followed by lengthy recovery periods during the conflict itself, these countries emerged from conflict with a level of real GDP per capita not far below the preconflict level and real GDP significantly higher than before the conflict. As a result, over the whole conflict, output actually *increased* by an annual average of 2 percent. Also, in these countries, the end of hostilities had no immediately discernible impact on growth.

Post-1990 conflicts. The experience in the far-shorter conflicts during the 1990s was altogether different. In these conflicts, the pace and depth of the contractions were much more severe: real GDP per capita declined by about 12 percent each year—or more than 14 percentage points below normal—to about 71 percent of its preconflict level, although this was biased downward by the particularly sharp contractions in the DFEs.[10] Moreover, the contractions in the post-1990 conflicts typically continued to the end of conflict, and most countries emerged from conflict with output still far below the preconflict level. Once conflict ended, per capita output growth in the first five years was modestly higher for the later than for the earlier conflict countries, but this difference was not statistically significant. However, it is important to keep in mind that, for the later conflicts, growth after conflict was recovering from deep contractions during conflict, and the rebound was large and statistically significant. Moreover, performance in these later conflicts varied considerably because of the delayed recovery in some countries, especially in two DFEs.[11] Once the DFEs are excluded, the superior performance of the remaining post-1990 conflict countries was particularly pronounced in the initial two years after conflict when average per capita output growth in these countries was *several times* higher that in the pre-1990 conflict countries.

Length of the Overall Conflict Cycle

To assess the impact of the shifts in the 1990s, it is assumed that the return of real GDP per capita to its level the year before conflict marks the point of recovery.[12] By this measure, the recovery period after conflict was often longer than the time spent in conflict. In many instances, recovery remains incomplete. Recovery is even more prolonged, especially for conflicts in the 1990s, if the level of GDP per capita that prevailed before the preconflict deterioration is used as the benchmark. Of the 17 countries in the sample with sufficient data, only 5 had regained their preconflict level of GDP per capita within the first

---

[10]Output in the DFEs fell to 49 percent of its preconflict level during conflict and further after conflict, but much of this reflected external factors that were unrelated to conflict and also possibly related to changes in national accounting methodology. Once these factors are accounted for, the depth of the contractions in the DFEs and the post-1990 conflicts were broadly similar. By way of comparison, output for the former Soviet block countries (Commonwealth of Independent States) as a whole contracted to 62 percent of its preconflict level, suggesting that the additional impact of conflict was moderate. Also, de Melo, Denizer, and Gelb (1996) investigated the effect of civil wars in the transition economies of eastern Europe on the average growth rate over the period 1989–94 and found that civil conflict reduced the annual average growth rate during the five years by 9 percent.

[11]Contractions continued after conflict in Azerbaijan, Georgia, and the DRC, and were particularly strong in Azerbaijan.

[12]The return of real growth to "normal" is an alternative assumption employed, for example, by Collier (1999).

five years after conflict. From a different perspective, GDP per capita, which averaged 84 percent of its preconflict level at the end of the conflict, had risen to only 93 percent after five years.

Although the conflict cycles for most countries remain incomplete, WEO projections can be used to get some sense of their likely length. Using these projections, the recent developments have most probably lengthened postconflict recovery, especially in the DFEs (Table 5.4). For the most part, this is because the shift in the 1990s has redistributed the time spent in recovery from during conflict to after conflict, leaving the overall length of the conflict cycle broadly unchanged. However, once the idiosyncratic DFEs are excluded, the shift in the 1990s has probably tended to reduce the overall length of recovery, including the in-conflict recovery, and has consequently reduced the length of the conflict cycle from about 15 years to about 11 years.

The Cost of Conflict

These projections can be used to estimate the overall economic cost of conflict. This can be measured by the net present value of the output foregone, again taking the preconflict level of output per capita as the benchmark (Table 5.5). These estimates are sensitive to the discount rate and also understate the cost to the extent that, in the absence of conflict, per capita output growth would have been positive, and also because the estimates do not capture the potentially large longer-term human and economic costs.

Table 5.4. Length of the Conflict Cycle Periods

(Years)

	Conflict Contraction A[1]	In-Conflict Recovery B	Post-Conflict Recovery C[2]	Total Conflict A+B	Total Recovery B+C	Total Cycle A+B+C
Pre-1990	5.2	6.6	3.8	11.8	12.4	15.6
Post-1990	3.2	0.3	11.1	3.5	11.9	14.6
Non-DFE	3.0	0.3	7.8	3.3	8.8	11.1
DFE	3.8	0.3	19.5	4.0	19.8	23.5

Source: WEO.

Notes: Estimates are based on WEO projections (Winter 2003) up to 2008 and extrapolated beyond. DFE, dissolved federal entity.

[1] The contraction to the trough of per capita output during conflict, excluding contractions after conflict.

[2] The conflict cycle is defined to end when real GDP per capita recovers to its preconflict level.

Table 5.5. The Economic Cost of Conflict: Net Present Value in Months of Preconflict Output per Capita

	During Conflict	After Conflict	Total
5 percent discount rate			
Pre-1990	11	4	15
Post-1990	8	18	27
Non-DFE	6	8	14
DFE	16	43	59
3 percent discount rate			
Pre-1990	13	5	18
Post-1990	9	22	31
Non-DFE	6	9	15
DFE	17	53	70

Sources: WEO and IMF staff estimates.
Notes: The conflict cycle is defined to end when real GDP per capita recovers to its preconflict level. Estimates are based on WEO projections (Winter 2003) up to 2008 and extrapolated beyond. DFE, dissolved federal entities.

Subject to this qualification, the developments observed in the 1990s have reduced the average cost of the conflict period alone—the cost of the deeper contractions of the post-1990 conflicts has been more than offset by their greater brevity. However, these developments have also been accompanied by higher costs associated with the elongation of the postconflict recovery period noted above. Nevertheless, excluding the idiosyncratic DFEs, there has probably been a tendency for the overall cost of the whole conflict cycle to decline. Assuming a discount rate of 3 percent, the cost of conflict alone has declined from 13 to 6 months of preconflict economic activity, while the cost of the whole conflict cycle has declined from 18 to 15 months.[13]

Evolution of Macroeconomic Policy Indicators

The above developments have also been reflected in the evolution of policy indicators (Tables 5.6 and A5.2).

Fiscal balances. Countries typically ran fiscal deficits (including grants) before conflict that deteriorated and then recovered as they passed through the conflict cycle. These fluctuations tended to be modest relative to GDP but were much more severe relative to revenues (including grants).[14] Because of their deeper economic contractions, lower

---

[13]By way of comparison, Collier and others (2003) estimated the cost of conflict to be about seven months' output.

[14]Revenues include grants because data on tax revenues are only available for about half the countries.

Table 5.6. Macroeconomic Policy Indicators
(Period average unless otherwise indicated)

	Before		During		After			
	1–5 years	1 year	Conflict	End	1 year	2 years	1–2 years	3–5 years[1]
Fiscal balances (including grants), percent of revenues								
Pre-1990	−25	−40	−50	−56	−46	−38	−42	−30
Post-1990	−53	−37	−84	−83	−50	−33	−41	−27
Fiscal revenues (including grants), real per capita index								
Pre-1990	102	100	101	102	104	102	103	110
Post-1990	111	100	75	72	93	109	101	116
Fiscal expenditures, real per capita, index								
Pre-1990	91	100	108	107	102	97	100	101
Post-1990	114	100	92	86	93	105	99	107
Domestic financing, percent of GDP								
Pre-1990	6	0	−1	−2	0	−1	−1	−2
Post-1990	5	6	8	6	4	3	4	−2
CPI inflation, percent change, median								
Pre-1990	8	12	16	12	20	17	18	9
Post-1990	21	18	30	41	32	8	24	5

Source: WEO.
[1] Data for 3, 4, and 5 years after conflict are available for 11, 7, and 7 of 14 post-1990 conflicts, respectively.

levels of external assistance, and absence of a prolonged recovery period during conflict, countries generally emerged from post-1990 conflicts with much larger fiscal deficits than was the case in earlier conflicts.[15] However, in the initial postconflict period, the post-1990 conflict countries benefited from stronger economic growth as well as greater external assistance, so the improvement in their fiscal balances was generally more pronounced.

Revenues and expenditures. Both revenues and expenditures were initially compressed during conflict but, while revenues tended to remain low or decline, there were strong pressures to maintain or increase expenditures.[16] In the pre-1990 conflict countries, increased fiscal deficits during conflict were generally accompanied by increased revenues and expenditures whether in real terms or relative to GDP. After conflict, fiscal consolidation tended to rely more on an adjustment in expenditures than in revenues, and real spending per capita tended to decline. In the post-1990 conflicts, however, both revenues and expenditures generally remained compressed in real terms during conflict, but the compression of revenues tended to be larger. After conflict, the fiscal adjustment tended to rely more on increased revenues to accommodate increased expenditures.

Inflation. Changes in the level and composition of assistance caused financing to evolve differently from the fiscal balances.[17] In the pre-

---

[15]Important exceptions were the DFEs whose fiscal balances were stronger at the end of conflict than at the start, because these countries entered conflict with little administrative capacity to raise revenues, and this capacity had to be mobilized quickly once conflict started.

[16]Caplan (2001) looked at 66 conflicts from 1953 to 1992 and found that, during civil conflicts in low-income countries, higher military spending tended to crowd out other spending with little overall effect on total government spending. He also found that tax revenues tended to remain unchanged or declined as a share of GDP. Gupta and others (2002b) looked at 22 conflicts from 1985 to 1999 and also found evidence that military spending crowded out other spending. Smaldone (2003) looked at military spending in 42 sub-Saharan African countries in the 1990s. He found no clear difference in real military spending levels between countries that remained at peace and those affected by conflict, but found that the military's share of total government spending tended to be higher in the latter. These findings are echoed here: in the 14 countries (10 of which are post-1990) that reported data to the IMF, average military spending increased during conflict as a share of both GDP and total fiscal expenditures, but declined in real terms.

[17]Domestic financing is estimated by the financing balance after taking into account all external assistance. IMF net financing is included although it is typically routed through the central bank as balance of payments support because IMF financing also

1990 conflicts domestic financing during conflict actually declined relative to GDP but increased following conflict. In the 1990s, domestic financing increased more sharply than the fiscal deficits during conflict, but also improved more sharply following conflict. The evolution of domestic financing was reflected in CPI inflation.[18] The increase in inflation was more pronounced in the conflicts of the 1990s and, by the end of conflict, median inflation in the post-1990 conflicts (41 percent) was much higher than in the pre-1990 conflicts (12 percent).[19] Once conflict ended, inflation generally declined, but the decline was uneven. In the pre-1990 conflict countries, where domestic financing initially increased, median inflation actually accelerated in the initial two years after conflict and only fell to single digits in the fourth year. In most of the post-1990 conflict countries, where domestic financing was sharply reduced, inflation declined to single digits within two years.

External sector. External current account balances (including transfers) generally deteriorated during the conflict mainly because of reduced official transfers. The role played by the trade balance during conflict was mixed, because there were several conflicting tendencies relating to trade volumes and on the effective terms of trade, but there was probably a larger tendency toward deterioration.[20] The performance of the current account balance after conflict tended to diverge between the two sets of conflicts. The end of the pre-1990 conflicts followed a prolonged recovery that was already supported by large aid flows and robust exports and was accompanied by a surge in imports that was not supported by either stronger aid flows or export receipts so that current account balances worsened. The end of the post-1990 conflicts was also accompanied by a surge in imports, which, however, was

---

provides the resources to permit the sterilization of the monetary expansion that accompanies domestic fiscal financing and is therefore implicitly budgetary financing.

[18]The linkage between domestic financing and CPI inflation is not direct but is likely to be more closely related in countries affected by conflict where access to indirect monetary instruments is often heavily curtailed.

[19]For 66 conflicts during 1953–92, Caplan (2001) found that civil conflicts had no discernible impact on inflation. Gupta and others (2002b) found that 22 episodes of armed conflict in the 1990s had a discernible impact on inflation.

[20]The World Bank commodity price index increased in the 1970s but dropped in the 1980s and 1990s. There were important conflicting tendencies on import unit prices. In the earlier conflicts, unit prices increased (volumes dropped while expenditures rose), probably reflecting increased defense-related imports. In the later conflicts, unit prices dropped (volumes increased while expenditures declined), probably reflecting a shift in the composition of imports toward basic staples.

supported by strong increases in aid transfers as well as export receipts so that current account balances in these countries initially improved.

External debt. Countries also emerged from conflict with increased external debt that averaged 117 percent of GDP and 743 percent of exports—which was not sustainable.[21] Countries were therefore in urgent need of debt relief, and two-thirds of them subsequently became eligible for assistance under the Heavily Indebted Poor Countries Initiative. Debt-service obligations were also very high, and more than half the countries emerged from conflict with arrears, which, in some instances, posed a major hurdle to the provision of external assistance.

Section III. The Impact of Conflict and Macroeconomic Policy

The movements in output and economic indicators described above were a natural outcome of conflict. However, they were also responding to shifts in the stance of macroeconomic policy. For example, the tendency after pre-1990 conflicts for inflation to rise initially while fiscal balances were improved by reducing expenditures arguably reduced growth. In the post-1990 conflicts, the tendency for inflation to fall while fiscal balances were improved by increasing revenues to accommodate increased expenditures may have supported growth.

The Equations

These issues are assessed using equations (1) through (3), each of which contains real GDP per capita growth as the dependent variable. Equations (1) and (2) are each estimated separately for each set of conflicts while equation (3) is estimated using a panel of all conflicts.

The level of per capita real GDP growth:

$$Y_{it} = \beta_{1,75}.Y_{i75} + \beta_{1o}.d_o + {}_k\Sigma\beta_{1ok}.d_o.X_{kit} + {}_c\Sigma\beta_{1c}.d_c + {}_k\Sigma_c\Sigma \beta_{1ck}.d_c.X_{kit} + \varepsilon_{it} \qquad (1)$$

Difference between growth during and outside the conflict cycle:

$$Y_{it} = c + \beta_{2,75}.Y_{i75} + {}_k\Sigma\beta_{2k}.X_{kit} + {}_c\Sigma\beta_{2c}.d_c + {}_k\Sigma_c\Sigma\beta_{2ck}.d_c.X_{kit} + \varepsilon_{it} \qquad (2)$$

---

[21]Even allowing for an average grant element of 65 percent (comparable to International Development Association terms), this implies an average net present value of debt-to-current-exports ratio at the end of conflict of about 260 percent, well above the 150 percent threshold normally considered sustainable.

The difference between growth during the pre-1990 and post-1990 conflict cycles:

$$Y_{it} = \beta_{3,75}.Y_{i75} + \beta_{3o}.d_o + {}_k\Sigma\beta_{3ok}.d_o.X_{kit} + {}_c\Sigma\beta_{3c}.d_c. + {}_k\Sigma{}_c\Sigma\beta_{3ck}.d_c.X_{kit} + \\ \beta_{3po}.d_p.d_o + {}_k\Sigma\beta_{3pok}.d_p.d_o.X_{kit} + {}_c\Sigma\beta_{3pc}.d_p.d_c + {}_k\Sigma{}_c\Sigma\beta_{3pck}.d_p.d_c.X_{kit} + \varepsilon_{it}$$ (3)

In these equations, Y_{it} is real GDP per capita growth in country i in year t, Y_{i75} is the level of real GDP per capita in country i in 1975, X_{kit} is the value of explanatory variable k for country i in year t, ε_{it} is the error term, c is the equation constant, d_o is the dummy for period outside the conflict cycle, the d_c's are dummies for the subperiods during the conflict cycle, d_p is the dummy for post-1990 conflicts, and the β's are the coefficients to be estimated. There are no individual country-specific dummies.

For each set of conflicts and for each period in the conflict cycle, equation (1) shows the estimated growth rate as a linear combination of an "underlying" growth rate, captured by the coefficient on the dummy, plus the unit contributions of the other explanatory variables. Because there are no cross-period linkages, this equation generates the same results as would a separate equation estimated for each period.

Equation (2) compares growth during the conflict cycle with growth *outside* the conflict cycle under "normal" circumstances. Growth is estimated as the normal growth outside the conflict cycle plus a difference attributable to conflict. For each set of conflicts, the difference between growth during the conflict cycle and normal is given by the variables cross-multiplied by the conflict cycle period dummies, d_c.

Equation (3) compares growth in the two sets of conflicts. For each period, growth is given by growth in the pre-1990 conflicts plus a difference attributable to the post-1990 conflicts. For each period, the difference between the two sets of conflicts is captured by the variables cross-multiplied by the dummy for the post-1990 conflicts, d_p.

For estimation purposes only, the conflict cycle is here defined, somewhat arbitrarily, to extend five years before and after conflict. All other periods are here taken to be outside the conflict cycle. The preconflict period is included to permit the estimates for the impact of conflict to take into account the deterioration in economic performance before conflict. Defining the conflict cycle to end after only five years is solely due to data availability.

To explore the evolution of output more closely, each equation is estimated with two variants of the dummies for the conflict cycle. Variant (A) divides the conflict cycle into the five-year period before conflict, the conflict itself, and the five-year period after conflict. Variant (B) divides the conflict period into its contractionary and in-conflict recovery periods and divides the five-year postconflict period into the initial two years and the subsequent three years.[22] This permits a closer look at the more immediate impact of the start and end of hostilities on growth. For the post-1990 conflicts, only a small number of countries went through an in-conflict recovery and data availability falls off significantly in the three- to five-year period after conflict, so the results for these periods need to be interpreted cautiously.

Efforts to model output growth have typically used multiyear averaging to smooth out short-term fluctuations and have relied on a smorgasbord of explanatory variables, such as education rates, as proxies for supply-side variables. Multiyear averaging is precluded here by the focus on the short subperiods during the conflict cycle. Nor is it possible to make use of supply-side indicators, which tend to be surveyed infrequently during conflict, if at all.

Instead, output growth is modeled on the demand side and as a function of the key policy variables, which include growth in the terms of trade, growth in real per capita government spending, the change in the fiscal balance, and the CPI inflation rate.[23] The fiscal balance is expressed as a ratio to revenues (both including grants), rather than as a ratio to GDP, so as to reduce the linkage to output. The change in the fiscal balance and government per capita spending are both included so as to differentiate between changes in the size of government and pure fiscal consolidation. The terms of trade capture external effects on the assumption that exporters are price takers. Finally, to capture possible convergence effects, due to different initial conditions, the equations also include per capita output in 1975.[24]

The equations are estimated using generalized least squares with cross-section weights (WGLS) with adjustments for serial correlation and heteroskedasticity. The results are shown in Tables 5.7 and 5.8. It is important to keep in mind that equations (2) and (3) refer to differences. To ease the presentation, the tables only show the coefficients for the difference components of these equations—tagged by the conflict cycle dummies d_c in equation (2) and by the post-1990 conflict dummy d_p in equation (3).

---

[22]The contractionary and in-conflict recovery periods are here defined in terms of real GDP per capita. Also, the contraction period includes only contractions during conflict and not after conflict.

[23]Although the focus is on the impact of policy variables, CPI inflation is included instead of money growth because most of the literature focuses on the impact of inflation. Including money growth instead does not change the results significantly.

[24]There are nonlinearities at work, especially for inflation, that are not explored here.

Table 5.7. Real GDP per Capita Growth During the Conflict Cycle

(Results for equations (1–3) using variant (A) of dummies during the conflict cycle; for equations (2) and (3), only the coefficients on the difference terms are shown)

Sample period: 1967–2002	Equation 1 Pre-1990	Equation 1 Post-1990	Equation 2 Pre-1990	Equation 2 Post-1990	Equation 3 All conflicts
Real GDP p.c. in 1975, US$	0.00	0.00			0.13
Outside the conflict cycle					
Dummy	2.66 **	2.12 ***			–1.75
Terms of trade, %chg	0.04 *	0.04 **			0.00
Gvt. spending p.c., %chg	0.16 ***	0.09 ***			–0.08 **
Gvt. balance, %rev, change	0.06 ***	–0.03 *			–0.10 ***
CPI, %chg	–0.18 **	–0.06 ***			0.12 *
Conflict cycle					
1–5 years before conflict					
Dummy	1.74 **	–0.63	–1.11	–2.57 ***	–2.96 *
Terms of trade, %chg	–0.04 **	0.03	–0.08 ***	–0.02	0.06
Gvt. spending p.c., %chg	0.04	0.11 *	–0.12 ***	0.04	0.04
Gvt. balance, %rev, change	0.06 ***	0.01	0.00	0.03 *	–0.07 ***
CPI, %chg	–0.02 ***	–0.01	0.17 *	0.05 **	0.01
During conflict					
Dummy	–1.09 *	–3.95 ***	–3.92 ***	–5.51 ***	–5.27 ***
Terms of trade, %chg	–0.03 **	0.00	–0.07 ***	–0.06 **	0.05 **
Gvt. spending p.c., %chg	0.04 ***	0.05 ***	–0.12 ***	–0.02	0.00
Gvt. balance, %rev, change	0.02 *	0.10 ***	–0.04	0.12 ***	0.07 ***
CPI, %chg	0.01	–0.05 ***	0.20 **	0.01	–0.05 ***
1–5 years after conflict					
Dummy	0.91	2.35 ***	–1.73 *	0.37	1.16
Terms of trade, %chg	–0.03	–0.11 ***	–0.08 **	–0.16 ***	–0.05
Gvt. spending p.c., %chg	0.01	0.10 ***	–0.15 ***	0.03	0.07 ***
Gvt. balance, %rev, change	–0.01	0.06 ***	–0.07 ***	0.09 ***	0.08 ***
CPI, %chg	–0.01	–0.07 ***	0.18 *	–0.01	–0.06 ***
AR(1)	0.33 ***	0.06	0.32 ***	0.07	0.19 ***
F–stat	8 ***	21 ***	8 ***	21 ***	14.3 ***

Source: WEO.
Notes: Levels of significance at the 1, 5, and 10 percent levels are indicated by ***, **, and *, respectively. All estimates done by generalized least squares with cross-section weights (WGLS). Gvt., government; rev, revenue; p.c., per capita; %chg, percentage change.
All estimates done by WGLS.

The Impact of Conflict

The period dummy variables give an indication of the direct or underlying effect of the various episodes of the conflict cycle, abstracting from the impact of the policy and other variables. Table 5.9 extracts the regression results for the coefficients on these dummy variables and compares these against actual performance. For equations (2) and (3), the actual performance shown is the difference between growth during

Table 5.8. Real GDP per Capita Growth During the Conflict Cycle

(Results for equations (1–3) using variant (B) of dummies during the conflict cycle; for equations (2) and (3), only the coefficients on the difference terms are shown)

Sample period: 1967–2002	Equation 1 Pre-1990	Equation 1 Post-1990	Equation 2 Pre-1990	Equation 2 Post-1990	Equation 3 All conflicts
Real GDP p.c. in 1975, US$	0.00	0.00 *			0.15
Outside the conflict cycle					
Dummy	1.13	1.47 **			2.12
Terms of trade, %chg	0.03	0.06 ***			−0.01
Gvt. spending p.c., %chg	0.18 ***	0.09 ***			−0.08 **
Gvt. balance, %rev, change	0.08 ***	−0.02 *			−0.10 ***
CPI, %chg	−0.16 **	−0.06 ***			0.11 *
Conflict cycle					
1–5 years before conflict					
Dummy	0.37	−1.23 *	−0.76	−2.51 ***	−3.32 **
Terms of trade, %chg	−0.03	0.03	−0.07 *	−0.03	0.06
Gvt. spending p.c., %chg	0.07 ***	0.13 **	−0.10 **	0.06	0.05
Gvt. balance, %rev, change	0.09 ***	0.01	0.01	0.04 **	−0.09 ***
CPI, %chg	−0.02 ***	−0.01	0.13 **	0.05 **	0.01
Conflict contraction[1]					
Dummy	−5.19 ***	−5.28 ***	−6.32 ***	−6.53 ***	−2.44
Terms of trade, %chg	−0.01	0.01	−0.04	−0.05 *	0.03
Gvt. spending p.c., %chg	0.06 **	0.05 ***	−0.12 **	−0.02	−0.01
Gvt. balance, %rev, change	0.02	0.11 ***	−0.06	0.13 ***	0.09 ***
CPI, %chg	0.02	−0.04 ***	0.17 ***	0.01	−0.06 ***
In–conflict recovery					
Dummy	0.76	0.38	−0.37	0.62	1.95
Terms of trade, %chg	0.01	−0.08 ***	−0.02	−0.06 **	...
Gvt. spending p.c., %chg	0.01	0.13 ***	−0.17 ***	0.17 ***	...
Gvt. balance, %rev, change	0.05 ***	0.02	−0.03	0.00	...
CPI, %chg	−0.01	−0.01	0.15 **	0.01	...
1–2 years after conflict					
Dummy	0.08	0.65	−1.05	−1.05	0.72
Terms of trade, %chg	−0.05	−0.11 ***	−0.08	−0.17 ***	−0.03 **
Gvt. spending p.c., %chg	0.06	0.10 ***	−0.12 *	0.02	0.03
Gvt. balance, %rev, change	−0.03	0.07 ***	−0.10 ***	0.09 ***	0.09
CPI, %chg	−0.02 **	−0.06 ***	0.14 **	0.00	−0.06 ***
3–5 years after conflict					
Dummy	−0.54	1.45	−1.66 **	0.20	1.19 ***
Terms of trade, %chg	−0.01	−0.10 ***	−0.04	−0.14 ***	−0.07 **
Gvt. spending p.c., %chg	0.07	0.11 **	−0.11	0.06	0.13 ***
Gvt. balance, %rev, change	0.01	0.06	−0.07	0.06	0.00 ***
CPI, %chg	0.02	0.04	0.18 **	0.08	−0.06 ***
AR(1)					0.12 ***
F–stat	7 ***	16 ***	7 ***	15 ***	13.1 ***

Source: WEO.

Notes: Levels of significance at the 1, 5, and 10 percent levels are indicated by ***, **, and *, respectively. All estimates done by generalized least squares with cross-section weights (WGLS). Gvt., government; rev, revenue; p.c., per capita; %chg, percentage change. All estimates done by WGLS.

[1] The contraction period is defined in terms of real GDP per capita.

Table 5.9. Impact of Conflict on Growth

(Actual growth and regression coefficients on period dummies only; for equations (2) and (3), only the coefficients on the difference terms are shown)

	Equation 1				Equation 2				Equation 3	
	Pre-1990		Post-1990		Pre-1990		Post-1990		All Conflicts	
	Actual	Coefficient	Actual	Coefficient	Actual	Coefficient	Actual	Coefficient	Actual	Coefficient
	Variant (A)									
Outside conflict cycle	2.0	2.7 **	1.9	2.1 ***					-0.1	-1.7
Conflict cycle										
1–5 years before conflict	0.1	1.7 **	-1.0	-0.6	-1.9	-1.1	-2.9 *	-2.6 ***	-1.1	-3.0 *
During conflict	-0.4	-1.1 *	-10.7	-3.9 ***	-2.4 ***	-3.9 ***	-12.6 ***	-5.5 ***	-10.3 ***	-5.3 ***
1–5 years after conflict	0.9	0.9	2.4	2.4 ***	-1.1	-1.7 *	0.5	0.4	1.5	1.2
	Variant (B)									
Outside conflict cycle	2.0	1.1	1.9	1.5 ***					-0.1	-2.1
Conflict cycle										
1–5 years before conflict	0.1	0.4	-1.0	-1.2 *	-1.9 *	-0.8	-2.9 **	-2.5 ***	-1.1	-3.3 ***
Contractionary	-4.0	-5.2 ***	-12.5	-5.3 ***	-6.0 ***	-6.3 ***	-14.4 ***	-6.5 ***	-8.5 ***	-2.4
In-conflict recovery	2.3	0.8	3.1	0.4	0.3	-0.4	1.2	0.6	0.8	2.0
1–2 years after conflict	0.4	0.1	1.6	0.7	-1.6	-1.1	-0.3	-1.1	1.2	0.7
3–5 years after conflict	1.3	-0.5	3.0	1.5	-0.7	-1.7 **	1.1	0.2	1.7	1.2 ***

Source: WEO.

Note: Levels of significance at the 1, 5, and 10 percent levels are indicated by ***, **, and *, respectively.

the conflict cycle and normal and the difference between the two sets of conflicts, respectively.

The results support the conclusion that, compared with the earlier conflicts, countries passing through the later conflicts went through a deeper underlying deterioration before the conflict as well as a stronger underlying recovery three to five years after conflict. In addition, once allowance is made for other factors, the results for equation (2) point to a significant negative impact that persisted after the earlier, but not the later, conflicts.

The more interesting results relate to the impact of the start and end of conflict. Looking at the results for equations (1) and (2) using variant (A), the coefficients on the dummies for the conflict and for the one- to five-year postconflict period as a whole suggest that the direct negative impact of conflict on growth as well as the direct positive impact of the end of conflict were more pronounced in the later conflicts. This conclusion, however, is modified by a closer look at the subperiods of the conflict cycle using variant (B). The dummy coefficients for the contractionary period as well as for the first two years after conflict are close in magnitude for the two sets of conflicts (although, for the first two years after conflict, neither are statistically different from zero). Moreover, the results of equation (3) support the conclusion that these two coefficients are not statistically different between the two sets of conflicts.

These results using variant (B) are very much at odds with the different actual growth rates experienced by these two sets of countries. This invites the important and perhaps surprising conclusion that, once "other factors" are taken into account, the onset and ending of conflict had much the same impact on growth in both sets of conflicts. In other words, despite their different economic profiles, much the same conflict process was at work for both groups.

The Impact of Macroeconomic Policy

The conclusion that the direct impact of the onset and termination of conflict on growth was broadly similar in the two sets of conflicts leaves open the question why actual performance over the conflict cycle was so different. The results suggest that differences in macroeconomic policies may have been an important factor.

The impact of policy. Equation (1) shows how policy (and other variables) affected growth. The coefficients on government spending and inflation have the expected signs: higher government spending growth increases output growth, and higher inflation reduces growth. Although at times negative, the effect of the fiscal balance was generally positive when also statistically significant. The effect of changes in the terms of trade was generally positive outside the conflict cycle but negative during the conflict cycle.[25] The results provide no support for the presence of convergence effects. The results for equation (2) suggest that over the course of the earlier, but not the later, conflict cycles there was a decline in the magnitude and statistical significance of the impact of the policy variables.[26] The results for equation (3) suggest that once conflict started and into the postconflict period, the impact of the three policy variables was significantly larger in the later than in the earlier conflicts.

Contribution to growth. Table 5.10 shows the combined contribution made by the three policy variables to real GDP growth. A full decomposition of growth is shown in Table A5.3.[27] The policy stance was generally a detriment to growth under normal circumstances and remained a negative factor through the conflict and after conflict. However, there were important differences in the extent of the negative impact and the improvement after conflict.

In the pre-1990 conflict countries, the policy stance improved considerably with the onset of conflict—the impact turned mildly positive during the contractionary period—so that it helped moderate the reduction in growth. The policy stance deteriorated during the prolonged in-conflict recovery to become an important drag on growth in the initial two years after conflict. It was only three to five years after conflict that the policy stance was turned around to have a substantial positive impact on growth.

---

[25]This result could reflect a shift in the structure of trade (especially imports) but is also consistent with the observation that, once conflict started, rents from natural resource exports tended to prolong and arguably accentuate the depth of conflict (Collier and Hoeffler, 2000b; Collier, Hoeffler, and Söderbom, 2001).

[26]The shift in the earlier conflicts is difficult to explain, but, for example, the reduced impact of government spending arguably reflects the shift in the composition of government spending toward unproductive and more import-intensive military spending observed by Gupta and others (2002b). The only significant change in the later conflicts was for the impact of a change in the fiscal balance whose sign was reversed. This shift could also reflect the endogeneity of the policy variables. However, it is also consistent with the presence of nonlinearities on the impact of the policy variables. Estimates including the square of both the change in the fiscal balance and inflation indicate that these nonlinearities were significant, especially for inflation.

[27]The contribution of a variable in any period is the actual value of the variable multiplied by the coefficient from the WGLS regression for equation (1) in Table 5.8, taking serial correlation into account where relevant.

Table 5.10. Policy Contribution to per Capita Growth
(Percentage points, average¹)

	Pre-1990	Post-1990	
		All	Excluding DFEs
Outside conflict cycle	−1.0	−0.5	−0.6
1–5 years before conflict	−0.8	−0.8	−0.8
Conflict contraction	0.3	−4.6	−2.7
In-conflict recovery	−0.1	1.5	1.5
1–2 years after conflict	−0.8	−2.3	0.5
3–5 years after conflict	0.6	0.9	0.3

Source: WEO.

Note: DFE, dissolved federal entities.

¹ The sum of the contributions of the three policy variables is given by the generalized least squares with cross-section weights (WGLS) coefficients for equation (1) in Table 5.8 times the value of the variable.

In the post-1990 conflict countries, the policy stance deteriorated substantially once conflict started, accentuating the reduction in growth. Although it continued to diminish growth during the initial two years after conflict, the negative impact was considerably reduced from the level during conflict and this improvement was therefore supportive of the recovery. The pace of improvement was sustained so that by three to five years after conflict, the policy stance had a positive impact on growth that was also larger than in the earlier conflicts. However, policy performance in the post-1990 conflict countries was uneven and particularly poor in the idiosyncratic DFEs. Excluding the DFEs, the postconflict improvement in the policy stance was much stronger, and its contribution to growth turned positive in the first two years after conflict.[28]

Robustness

Reverse causality. As is often the case in regressions with output growth as the dependent variable, the estimates suffer from the endogeneity of the explanatory variables. This is particularly the case for inflation and government spending growth, but there is little evidence that output growth caused movements in either the growth in the terms of trade or in the change in the government balance as a percentage of revenues. The seriousness of this problem depends on the dominant direction of causality between output growth and the explanatory vari-

---

[28]This is done using the same coefficients from Table 5.8 as for the set of post-1990 conflicts as a whole.

ables.[29] To account for possible reverse causality, equations (1) and (2) are estimated by weighted two-stage least squares (WTSLS) using the lagged growth in government spending and the lagged inflation rate as instruments.[30] The results (Table A5.4) are broadly the same as before, so there is little reason to conclude that reverse causality is a significant concern.

Fixed effects. Another potential problem is the presence of unobserved country-specific effects. Depending on whether these effects are correlated with the explanatory variables, they can be estimated using a fixed-effects or a random-effects estimator. Only fixed effects can be addressed here because estimating random effects requires that the number of countries in the panel is larger than the number of coefficients, which is not the case. Because the fixed effects are not time specific and so replace the equation constant, they can only be estimated using equation (2). The results (Table A5.4) suggest little reason to conclude that there are significant unobserved country-specific effects.

Section IV. The Role of External Assistance

The lines of inquiry pursued by the conflict-related literature have been useful in accounting for key features of specific groups of conflicts. For example, the focus on the role of natural resources provides valuable insights into the conflicts in countries such as Sierra Leone and the DRC where illicit diamonds have been an important factor. Similarly, the role of spillover effects is particularly pertinent to the set of regional conflicts in West Africa and the Great Lakes region. However, they do not adequately address the sort of systemic changes in the economic profile of conflicts observed in the 1990s as outlined above.

---

[29]With respect to inflation, Fischer (1993) has argued that causality is more likely to run from inflation to growth, and studies of the impact of inflation on growth have tended to downplay the endogeneity of inflation (Catao and Terrones, 2001; Fischer, 2002; Ghosh and Phillips, 1998; Khan and Senhadji, 2000). However, in countries affected by conflict, the large swings in output could be expected to have a more discernible impact on inflation. The endogeneity of government expenditures is also difficult to ignore because of the impact of conflict on the tax revenue base. However, looking at fiscal adjustment and growth in a selection of low-income countries (not necessarily affected by conflict), Gupta and others (2002a) found little evidence of significant reverse causality between output and government expenditure growth.

[30]The set of country equations are estimated as a set of system equations with the coefficients constrained to be the same across the country equations. No single equation statistics can therefore be calculated.

The timing of the developments described above obviously suggests a linkage to the end of the cold war and to changes in the role played by the international community in low-income countries. However, establishing a statistical linkage is beyond the scope of this chapter, and the argument is therefore only suggestive.

From the early 1990s on, external assistance flows to low-income countries as a whole, and to sub-Saharan African countries in particular, declined significantly (O'Connell and Soludo, 2001). This decline was accompanied by a significant change in the profile of assistance to conflict-affected countries. On balance, the role played by the international community in the 1990s was less encumbered by geopolitical considerations and moved toward being less supportive of conflict in favor of being more supportive of the postconflict recovery effort (Tables 5.11 and A5.5).

Once conflict started there were important differences in the level and phasing of assistance, measured by net official resource inflows.[31] For the pre-1990 conflict countries, assistance increased in both real terms and relative to GDP (but not relative to population) and also tended to be front loaded, frequently spiking upward just before the conflict. The reverse occurred in the 1990s—and once conflict started the level of assistance declined, it also tended to be back loaded, frequently spiking up toward the end of conflict.

This change in the profile of assistance arguably affected both the duration and economic impact of conflict either directly through the level of material assistance provided or indirectly through the impact on macroeconomic stability.[32] By this account, the higher level and

Table 5.11. Net Official Resource Inflows

(Percent of GDP)

	Before 1–5 Years	During Conflict	After 1–2 Years	After 3–5 Years
Pre-1990	16	19	11	6
Post-1990	12	9	13	7

Source: WEO.

---

[31]Net official external resource inflows are equal to official transfers plus loans less debt service paid (after debt relief and the accumulation of arrears).

[32]The link between net resource inflows and inflation is not direct. Unless sterilized, external aid inflows lead to higher monetary growth and consequently inflation. However, by providing a source of foreign currency, the provision of external assistance also makes it easier for the central bank to sterilize domestic credit to the central government, especially when the availability of other monetary instruments has been curtailed by conflict.

front loading of assistance during the earlier conflicts provided governments with material support to conduct hostilities, as well as support for economic activity, and helped support macroeconomic stability (including low inflation). This arguably also mitigated the extent of the economic contraction—but at the expense of prolonging the conflict. Conversely, the reduced assistance during conflict in the 1990s may have accentuated the severity of the economic contraction and, together with the back loading of assistance to the end of conflict, also helped bring about a quicker termination of conflict.[33]

Once conflict ended, the pattern of assistance again differed between the two sets of conflicts. In the earlier conflicts, resource flows declined compared with their conflict levels whether in real terms or adjusted for population and GDP. Countries emerging from conflict were therefore under pressure to restrain and reduce government spending and to resort to inflationary financing, with negative implications for the recovery. In more recent conflicts, resource flows have tended to increase substantially from conflict levels, again whether in real terms or adjusted for population and GDP. Moreover, at least once adjusted for population or GDP, aid levels to these countries surpassed those to countries coming out of earlier conflicts. The higher assistance to these countries in the 1990s provided support for their stabilization efforts and permitted them to increase government spending while reducing their reliance on inflationary financing with positive implications for growth.

Section V. Performance in EPCA Countries and the DRC

Performance in the EPCA Countries

The arguments of the preceding sections are buttressed by the experience of six post-1990 conflict countries that received external financial assistance, including EPCA from the IMF, soon after the end of their conflicts.[34,35,36]

---

[33]It is difficult to distinguish whether assistance was increased at the end of the conflicts in the 1990s in anticipation of the end of conflict or whether this increased involvement itself helped bring about an earlier termination of conflict than might have otherwise occurred. However, the experience in some countries suggests that earlier and well-timed involvement of the international community can help provide the impetus for parties in conflict to reach a resolution.

[34]*Review of Recent IMF Experience in Post-Conflict Countries*, IMF Occasional Paper, 2004, forthcoming.

[35]These six countries are Albania, Guinea-Bissau, Republic of Congo, Rwanda, Sierra Leone, and Tajikistan. Three other countries have also received EPCA from the IMF

The performance of these six EPCA countries during the conflict period had many similarities to that of other post-1990 countries (Table A5.6). Like the other post-1990 conflicts, the EPCA country conflicts were generally short and accompanied by sharp contractions, so they also emerged from conflict with severe economic imbalances and needing macroeconomic stabilization. In the initial two years after conflict, the overall performance of the EPCA countries was generally stronger than that in other countries, although performance was varied and particularly weak in the Republic of Congo. Overall, real GDP per capita growth averaged 4 percent, and the inflation rate declined to single digits in all the EPCA countries (except Tajikistan). Their recovery effort in this initial period was supported by large increases in net resource inflows that exceeded inflows to other countries.

The eight other conflict countries in the 1990s (non-EPCA countries) also generally emerged from conflict with a more urgent need for macroeconomic stabilization, especially with respect to inflation. These countries also received external financial assistance after conflict, but total external assistance was generally less than to the EPCA recipients.[37] Despite substantial progress, stabilization was not reached in these countries within two years after conflict. For example, the median inflation remained high at about 50 percent, while average per capita real GDP declined 1 percent.[38] It was not until three to five years after conflict that these countries were able to reduce inflation and increase output growth to a level comparable to that of the EPCA countries.

Table 5.12 shows how the postconflict stabilization efforts in these countries affected growth (a full decomposition of growth is provided in

---

and are not included here—Burundi, Bosnia and Herzegovina, and the Federal Republic of Yugoslavia. Burundi emerged from conflict in 2000 and only received EPCA in 2002; Bosnia and Herzegovina is a new country, so no data are available before and during conflict; and the Federal Republic of Yugoslavia is not a low-income country.

[36]The IMF introduced a new policy to assist postconflict countries in 1995, and one of the policy changes was to enable the IMF to provide financial assistance to postconflict countries soon after the end of conflict and before they are ready to move to a comprehensive IMF program that could garner broader support from donors.

[37]Seven of these also received financial assistance from the IMF through vehicles other than EPCA, five of them soon after conflict.

[38]Average growth is skewed down by the particularly poor performances in Azerbaijan, Georgia, and the DRC, where output continued to contract after conflict and where inflation remained in triple digits. The median real GDP per capita growth of about 2 percent is perhaps more indicative.

Table 5.12. Contribution of Policy to per Capita Output Growth

(Percentage points, average[1])

	Post-1990			
	Sub-Saharan Africa	Emergency Postconflict Assistance	Non-EPCA	Democratic Republic of the Congo
Outside conflict cycle	−0.7	−0.6	−0.5	−1.6
1–5 years before conflict	−0.6	−0.9	−0.8	−6.2
Conflict contraction	−2.6	−6.0	−3.9	−6.8
In-conflict recovery	1.5	6.9	0.7	...
1–2 years after conflict	0.1	2.5	−5.6	−9.5
3–5 years after conflict	0.3	0.2	1.4	3.5

Source: WEO.

Note: ..., not available.

[1]The sum of the contributions of the three policy variables given by the generalized least squares with cross-section weights (WGLS) coefficients for equation (1) in Table 5.8 times the value of the variable.

Table A5.3).[39] In both sets of countries, policy deteriorated during conflict, accentuating the negative impact of conflict. However, after conflict, the EPCA countries' policy performance improved sufficiently to make a *positive* 2.5 percentage point contribution to growth. In the non-EPCA countries, policy performance *deteriorated further* and diminished growth by −5.6 in the first two years after conflict.

The relatively good performance in the EPCA countries was likely the result of a combination of factors. The circumstances of these six countries permitted the authorities to address their difficulties with greater commitment to sound macroeconomic policies. This in turn provided the basis for the international community to provide financial support to help these countries meet their policy objectives. In this respect, there was an important virtuous cycle in operation: sound policy attracted external assistance soon after conflict, which made these policies easier to implement and more fruitful and therefore also more politically acceptable.[40]

---

[39]The results in Tables 5.12 and A5.3 for these countries are derived using the same set of coefficients in Table 5.8 as for the set of post-1990 conflicts as a whole.

[40]The IMF arguably helped play a role in this virtuous cycle. On the one hand, the main role of the IMF was to help formulate a macroeconomic strategy for recovery and help rebuild administrative capacity for its implementation. On the other hand, the EPCA-supported programs played an important catalytic role in mobilizing this donor support at an early stage after conflict by signaling that the strategy was being implemented.

Performance in the DRC

The arguments of the preceding sections are also buttressed by the experience of the DRC, where stabilization and the start of economic recovery was made more difficult by delays in official external assistance. The DRC emerged from conflict in 1999, but the provision of external assistance to the government, including a comprehensive financial arrangement with the IMF, was delayed until mid-2002 following the conclusion of a peace agreement and until the DRC could clear external arrears.

The DRC emerged from conflict with real GDP per capita reduced to 80 percent of its preconflict level and hyperinflation that was above 500 percent. In 2000 inflation remained high, and the economy continued to contract. In mid-2001, the new Kabila government introduced its enhanced interim program to stabilize the economy. Despite the lack of external financial support, end-year inflation was reduced to about 135 percent in 2001, but output continued to contract. It was only in 2002 that end-year inflation was reduced to the moderate level of 16 percent and that output growth resumed.

Table 5.12 provides estimates of policy's contribution to per capita growth over the DRC's conflict cycle, and Table 5.13 provides greater detail for 1999–2002.[41] The policy stance (especially inflation) de-

Table 5.13. Democratic Republic of the Congo: Decomposition of Output Growth

(Percentage point contribution to per capita growth[1])

	1999	2000	2001	2002
Actual	−4.5	−9.5	−7.5	0.0
Dummy	−5.3	0.6	0.6	1.4
Real GDP, p.c. in 1975, level	−0.2	−0.2	−0.2	−0.2
Terms of trade, %chg	0.0	−2.2	−1.3	0.0
Policy	−8.0	−11.9	−7.1	3.5
Gvt. spending p.c., %chg	−1.7	0.6	−4.0	2.0
Gvt. balance, %rev, change	−0.3	−0.5	6.6	0.6
CPI, %chg	−5.9	−12.0	−9.7	0.9
Residual	9.0	4.1	0.4	−4.8

Source: WEO.

Notes: p.c., per capita; Gvt., government; rev, revenue, p.c., per capita; %chg, percentage change.

[1] The contribution of each variable given by the generalized least squares with cross-section weights (WGLS) coefficients for equation (1) in Table 5.8 times the value of the variable.

---

[41]The results in Table 5.13 are derived using the same set of coefficients in Table 5.8 as for the set of post-1990 conflicts as a whole.

tracted significantly from growth until 2002, but the negative impact was significantly reduced by the adjustment efforts initiated under the enhanced interim program. The improvement in the policy stance added more than 15 percentage points to growth from 2000 to 2002. However, the full impact of these efforts was not felt until 2002 when policy started to make a large positive contribution to growth.

The DRC's output performance in the first few postconflict years was one of the weakest in the 1990s. Conversely, compared with the conflict period, the DRC government's commitment to good policies after conflict was rewarded by improvement in performance that was also one of the strongest and also significantly stronger than for the post-1990 conflict or sub-Saharan Africa countries as a whole. Moreover, by the end of the postconflict period, the contribution made by policy in the DRC was significantly larger than in these other groups of countries. The policy stance added 3.5 percentage points to growth in the DRC in its third year after conflict versus not more than 1 percentage point in the post-1990 conflict countries or the sub-Saharan Africa conflict countries (Tables 5.10 and 5.12).

Section VI. Conclusions

The chapter argues that there was a shift in the key economic characteristics of conflict during the 1990s. The underlying conflict process at work has remained much the same, and this shift has probably been reflective of differences in the stance of macroeconomic policy over the conflict cycle that appear to be related to changes in donor practices toward countries affected by conflict since the end of the cold war. These findings would seem to have important implications for policy and aid priorities during and after conflict.

The chapter leaves a number of important questions unanswered. The argument linking aid patterns to these shifts has been only suggestive and needs to be explored more thoroughly. The chapter also suggests an important role for direct budgetary support in the postconflict recovery period, and further work needs to be done in exploring the effectiveness of such aid.

Appendix Tables

Table A5.1. Conflict Dates and Length   165
Table A5.2. Macroeconomic Policy Indicators   166
Table A5.3. Decomposition of Real GDP per Capita Growth   168
Table A5.4. Real GDP per Capita Growth During the
             Conflict Cycle   170
Table A5.5. Net Official Resource Inflows   172
Table A5.6. Selected Economic Indicators in EPCA Countries
             and Other Post-1990 Conflict Countries   173

Table A5.1. Conflict Dates and Length

	Start	End	Length in Years
Pre-1990 (average)	1981	1991	12
Uganda	1971	1985	15
Cambodia	1975	1992	18
Ethiopia I	1975	1990	16
Mozambique	1976	1992	17
El Salvador	1979	1992	14
Zimbabwe	1980	1987	8
Guatemala	1982	1996	15
Chad	1989	1992	4
Liberia	1989	1997	9
Nicaragua	1989	1990	2
Post-1990 (average)	1994	1997	4
Non-DFEs (average)	1996	1998	3
Rwanda	1990	1994	5
Burundi	1993	2000	8
Yemen, Rep. of	1994	1994	1
Congo, Dem. Rep. of	1996	1999	4
Albania	1997	1997	1
Congo, Rep. of	1997	1999	3
Sierra Leone	1997	1999	3
Guinea-Bissau	1998	1999	2
Eritrea	1998	2000	3
Ethiopia II	1998	2000	3
DFEs (average)	1991	1994	4
Azerbaijan	1990	1993	4
Croatia	1990	1993	4
Georgia	1992	1993	2
Tajikistan	1992	1997	6

Sources: SIPRI; and IMF staff reports.
Note: DFE, dissolved federal entities.

Table A5.2. Macroeconomic Policy Indicators
(Period average unless otherwise indicated)

	Before		During				After		
	1–5 years	1 year	Conflict	End-Year	1 year	2 years	1–2 years	3–5 years[1]	1–5 years[1]
Fiscal balances (including grants)									
Percent of GDP									
Pre-1990	-5	-7	-6	-6	-6	-5	-6	-4	-5
Post-1990	-7	-7	-14	-12	-9	-7	-8	-5	-7
Percent of revenues									
Pre-1990	-25	-40	-50	-56	-46	-38	-42	-30	-35
Post-1990	-53	-37	-84	-83	-50	-33	-41	-27	-34
Fiscal revenues (including grants)									
Real, index									
Pre-1990	97	100	120	139	142	143	142	164	155
Post-1990	106	100	83	76	100	118	109	129	118
Real, per capita, index									
Pre-1990	102	100	101	102	104	102	103	110	107
Post-1990	111	100	75	72	93	109	101	116	107
Percent of GDP									
Pre-1990	16	16	15	15	16	16	16	17	17
Post-1990	32	33	29	21	23	24	24	21	24
Fiscal expenditures									
Real, index									
Pre-1990	86	100	130	147	141	138	140	152	147
Post-1990	109	100	96	89	99	113	106	116	113
Real, per capita, index									
Pre-1990	91	100	108	107	102	97	100	101	100
Post-1990	114	100	92	86	93	105	99	107	104
Percent of GDP									
Pre-1990	21	23	21	21	22	22	22	22	22
Post-1990	39	40	43	34	33	31	32	26	31

Domestic financing, percent of GDP									
Pre-1990	6	0	−1	−2	0	−1	−1	−2	−2
Post-1990	5	6	8	6	4	3	4	−2	3
Broad money, percent change, median									
Pre-1990	14	14	17	31	26	24	24	17	18
Post-1990	23	35	31	32	44	23	26	26	27
CPI inflation, percent change, median									
Pre-1990	8	12	16	12	20	17	18	9	17
Post-1990	21	18	30	41	32	8	24	5	16
Current account balance, percent of GDP									
Pre-1990	−6	−8	−7	−6	−7	−8	−8	−8	−8
Post-1990	−6	−5	−9	−9	−7	−8	−7	−8	−8
Trade balance on goods and services, percent of GDP									
Pre-1990	−12	−21	−18	−9	−11	−12	−11	−11	−11
Post-1990	−12	−11	−15	−20	−15	−15	−15	−13	−16
Terms of trade, goods, index									
Pre-1990	101	100	111	109	114	114	114	117	116
Post-1990	120	100	79	89	88	84	86	89	88
Gross reserve, months of imports of goods and services									
Pre-1990	3.7	3.9	2.3	1.9	1.7	2.2	2.0	2.8	2.5
Post-1990	2.2	2.1	2.4	2.0	2.5	2.9	2.7	3.1	2.9
External debt, percent of current exports									
Pre-1990	353	523	720	716	828	974	901	744	807
Post-1990	613	465	669	769	713	799	756	489	711

Source: WEO.
[1] Data for 3, 4, and 5 years after conflict are available for 11, 7, and 7 of 14 post-1990 conflicts, respectively.

Table A5.3. Decomposition of Real GDP per Capita Growth

(Contribution to real GDP per capita growth, percentage points, average)[1]

	Pre-1990	Post-1990[2]					
		All	Excluding dissolved foreign entities	Sub–Saharan Africa	Emergency postconflict assistance	Non-Emergency postconflict assistance	Democratic Republic of the Congo
Outside conflict cycle							
Actual	0.9	1.9	0.9	0.6	1.4	2.3	-1.9
Dummy	1.1	1.5	1.5	1.5	1.5	1.5	1.5
Real GDP p.c. in 1975, level	1.1	0.8	0.7	0.7	0.9	0.7	-0.2
Terms of trade, %chg	-0.1	0.0	-0.1	-0.1	0.0	0.0	0.0
Policy	-1.0	-0.5	-0.6	-0.7	-0.6	-0.5	-1.6
Residual	-0.2	0.2	-0.6	-0.8	-0.4	0.6	-1.5
Conflict cycle							
1–5 years before conflict							
Actual	0.0	-1.3	-0.5	-1.2	-3.0	-0.1	-10.8
Dummy	0.4	-1.2	-1.2	-1.2	-1.2	-1.2	-1.2
Real GDP p.c. in 1975, level	1.1	0.8	0.7	0.7	0.9	0.7	-0.2
Terms of trade, %chg	0.0	-0.1	-0.1	-0.1	-0.1	0.0	0.2
Policy	-0.8	-0.8	-0.8	-0.6	-0.9	-0.8	-6.2
Residual	-0.7	0.1	0.9	0.1	-1.7	1.3	-3.4
Conflict contraction[3]							
Actual	-3.7	-9.8	-6.2	-5.9	-12.1	-8.6	-5.6
Dummy	-5.2	-5.3	-5.3	-5.3	-5.3	-5.3	-5.3
Real GDP p.c. in 1975, level	1.1	0.8	0.7	0.7	0.9	0.7	-0.2
Terms of trade, %chg	0.0	0.0	0.0	0.0	0.0	0.0	-0.1
Policy	0.3	-4.6	-2.7	-2.6	-6.0	-3.9	-6.8
Residual	0.1	-0.7	1.0	1.3	-1.7	-0.2	6.8

In-conflict recovery							
Actual	2.3	3.4	3.4	3.4	5.7	3.0	...
Dummy	0.8	0.4	0.4	0.4	0.4	0.4	...
Real GDP p.c. in 1975, level	1.1	0.8	0.7	0.7	0.9	0.7	...
Terms of trade, %chg	0.0	1.2	1.2	1.2	-0.9	1.5	...
Policy	-0.1	1.5	1.5	1.5	6.9	0.7	...
Residual	0.6	-0.5	-0.4	-0.4	-1.6	-0.2	...
1–2 years after conflict							
Actual	0.2	1.2	3.0	2.3	4.8	-1.4	-8.5
Dummy	0.1	0.6	0.6	0.6	0.6	0.6	0.6
Real GDP p.c. in 1975, level	1.1	0.8	0.7	0.7	0.9	0.7	-0.2
Terms of trade, %chg	-0.1	-0.1	-0.4	-0.5	0.2	-0.3	-1.7
Policy	-0.8	-2.3	0.5	0.1	2.5	-5.6	-9.5
Residual	-0.1	2.3	1.5	1.4	0.5	3.1	2.3
3–5 years after conflict							
Actual	1.2	3.8	1.8	0.0	3.1	4.5	0.0
Dummy	-0.5	1.4	1.4	1.4	1.4	1.4	1.4
Real GDP p.c. in 1975, level	1.1	0.8	0.7	0.7	0.9	0.7	-0.2
Terms of trade, %chg	0.0	0.2	-0.1	0.3	-0.7	0.9	0.0
Policy	0.6	0.9	0.3	0.3	0.2	1.4	3.5
Residual	0.0	0.5	-0.6	-2.6	1.2	0.1	-4.8

Source: WEO.

Note: ..., not available; p.c., per capita; %chg, percentage change.

[1] For each variable, the contribution in each period is equal to the average of the generalized least squares with cross-section weights (WGLS) regression coefficients for equation (1) from Table 5.8 times the value of the policy variable.

[2] The results for all the post-1990 subgroups make use of the same common sample coefficient estimates for the full set of post-1990 conflicts.

[3] The contraction period is defined in terms of real GDP per capita.

Table A5.4. Real GDP per Capita Growth During the Conflict Cycle
(Equations (1) and (2), adjusting for reverse causality and fixed effects; for equation (2), only the coefficients on the difference terms are shown)

Sample period: 1967–2002	Adjusting for Reverse Causality[2]				Adjusting for Fixed Effects[3]	
	Equation 1		Equation 2		Equation 2	
	Pre-1990	Post-1990	Pre-1990	Post-1990	Pre-1990	Post-1990
Real GDP p.c. in 1975, US$[1]	0.00	0.00				
Outside the conflict cycle						
Dummy	1.72	2.58 ***				
Terms of trade, %chg	0.04	0.06 ***				
Gvt. spending p.c., %chg	0.18 ***	0.03				
Gvt. balance, %rev, change	0.07 ***	-0.01				
CPI, %chg	-0.17 ***	-0.10 ***				
Conflict cycle						
1–5 years before conflict						
Dummy	0.75	-1.02	-0.97	-3.55 ***	-0.92	-2.34 ***
Terms of trade, %chg	-0.04	0.03	-0.08	-0.02	-0.04 *	0.02
Gvt. spending p.c., %chg	0.06	0.12 ***	-0.12	0.13 **	0.08 ***	0.12 **
Gvt. balance, %rev, change	0.08 *	0.01	0.01	0.02 *	0.10 ***	0.01
CPI, %chg	-0.02 *	-0.01 *	0.15 ***	0.09 ***	-0.02 **	-0.01
Conflict contraction[1]						
Dummy	-4.72 ***	-4.72 ***	-6.43 ***	-7.89 ***	-7.13 ***	-6.17 ***
Terms of trade, %chg	-0.02	0.01	-0.05 *	-0.05 *	-0.01	0.01
Gvt. spending p.c., %chg	0.05 *	0.05 ***	-0.13 ***	0.05	0.06 **	0.04 ***
Gvt. balance, %rev, change	0.01	0.11 ***	-0.06 *	0.12 ***	0.02	0.11 ***
CPI, %chg	0.01	-0.04 ***	0.18 ***	0.06 **	0.02	-0.05 ***
In-conflict recovery						
Dummy	0.74	0.36	-0.97	-1.61	-0.74	-0.06
Terms of trade, %chg	0.00	-0.09 *	-0.04	-0.06	0.00	-0.07 **
Gvt. spending p.c., %chg	0.00	0.21 ***	-0.18 ***	0.24 ***	0.02	0.13 **
Gvt. balance, %rev, change	0.05 **	0.01	-0.02	0.01	0.05 ***	0.02
CPI, %chg	0.00	-0.15	0.17 ***	0.23	-0.01	0.02

1–2 years after conflict						
Dummy	0.48	0.72	-1.23	-1.97	-1.09	-0.62
Terms of trade, %chg	-0.04	-0.12 **	-0.07	-0.17 ***	-0.08	-0.11 ***
Gvt. spending p.c., %chg	0.05	0.10 ***	-0.13 **	0.10 **	0.06	0.11 ***
Gvt. balance, %rev, change	-0.02	0.07 ***	-0.09 ***	0.08 ***	-0.03	0.07 ***
CPI, %chg	-0.02	-0.06 ***	0.15 ***	0.04	-0.02 **	-0.06 ***
3–5 years after conflict						
Dummy	0.10	1.93	-1.62	-0.66	-1.59 **	-0.15
Terms of trade, %chg	-0.02	-0.10 **	-0.06	-0.15 ***	0.00	-0.08 ***
Gvt. spending p.c., %chg	0.05	0.11	-0.13 *	0.12	0.05	0.09 *
Gvt. balance, %rev, change	0.01	0.05	-0.06	0.06	0.01	0.01
CPI, %chg	0.02	0.03	0.18 ***	0.12	0.01	0.07
AR(1)	0.18 ***		0.18 ***			

Source: WEO.

Notes: Levels of significance at the 1, 5, and 10 percent levels are indicated by ***, **, and *, respectively. p.c., per capita; Gvt., government; rev, revenue; %chg, percentage change.

[1] The contraction period is defined in terms of real GDP per capita.

[2] Estimates done by weighted two-stage least squares (WTSLS) using the lagged growth in government spending and lagged inflation as instruments.

[3] Estimates done by generalized least squares with cross-section weights (WGLS).

Table A5.5. Net Official Resource Inflows
(Period average)

	Before		During				After		
	1–5 years	1 year	Conflict	End year	1 year	2 years	1–2 years	3–5 years[1]	1–5 years
World Economic Outlook									
Constant USD, US$m									
Pre-1990	357	602	368	290	326	340	333	324	328
Post-1990	334	35	142	148	121	229	175	62	92
Constant USD, per capita									
Pre-1990	74	123	46	33	34	37	35	22	27
Post-1990	65	17	36	34	28	51	40	30	32
Percent of GDP									
Pre-1990	16	36	19	10	10	12	11	6	8
Post-1990	12	7	9	13	12	13	13	7	9
Global Development Finance									
Constant USD, US$m									
Pre-1990	272	312	430	420	496	482	489	…	…
Post-1990	276	215	141	160	210	311	293	…	…
Constant USD, per capita									
Pre-1990	60	57	58	53	58	47	53	…	…
Post-1990	44	36	22	25	40	55	52	…	…
Percent of GDP									
Pre-1990	8	11	16	16	14	14	14	…	…
Post-1990	16	14	12	16	18	13	16	…	…

Sources: WEO, Winter 2003; and Global Development Finance, 2002.
Note: …, not available.
[1]Data for 3, 4, and 5 years after conflict are available for 11, 7, and 7 of 14 post-1990 conflicts, respectively.

Table A5.6. Selected Economic Indicators in EPCA Countries and Other Post-1990 Conflict Countries
(Period averages)

	Before		During				After		
	1–5 years	1 year	Conflict	End-conflict	1 year	2 years	1–2 years	3–5 years[1]	1–5 years
Real GDP, index									
EPCA	107	100	81	72	80	84	82	91	87
Non-EPCA	101	100	84	78	79	81	80	76	83
Real GDP, percent change									
EPCA	-0.3	-1.3	-8.3	-9.8	11.7	5.4	8.5	5.2	6.9
Non-EPCA	2.2	-0.8	-8.4	-8.9	0.0	1.5	0.8	5.6	3.3
Real GDP, per capita, index									
EPCA	112	100	79	72	77	79	78	81	80
Non-EPCA	105	100	79	71	71	71	71	66	73
Real GDP, per capita, percent change									
EPCA	-2.4	-2.9	-9.4	-7.7	7.6	2.6	5.1	2.3	3.7
Non-EPCA	0.1	-2.8	-11.7	-12.1	-2.1	0.0	-1.1	4.0	1.4
Net resource inflows, % GDP									
EPCA	17.1	9.3	10.6	16.8	10.8	19.5	15.1	13.4	14.4
Non-EPCA	7.0	5.3	7.9	10.6	13.7	8.0	10.8	0.2	5.8
Fiscal balance (incl. grants), % GDP									
EPCA	-8.1	-10.1	-11.4	-8.8	-5.9	-6.8	-6.4	-6.9	-6.3
Non-EPCA	-6.6	-3.8	-15.2	-15.3	-11.7	-7.5	-9.6	-3.2	-8.3
Domestic financing, % GDP									
EPCA	2.2	6.7	5.0	1.6	1.7	-1.2	0.3	-2.2	-0.9
Non-EPCA	6.9	4.4	11.2	9.5	6.1	6.3	6.2	-2.2	5.8
CPI, percent change, median									
EPCA	28	18	24	33	15	3	8	3	6
Non-EPCA	13	33	177	178	80	29	51	8	24
Current account (incl. grants), % GDP									
EPCA	-12.4	-10.9	-11.7	-9.5	-5.4	-7.9	-6.7	-7.6	-7.2
Non-EPCA	-1.0	-1.9	-7.8	-9.9	-8.9	-8.6	-8.8	-9.6	-9.4
Gross reserves, months of imports									
EPCA	2.2	2.1	2.6	2.4	3.2	3.0	3.1	3.3	3.2
Non-EPCA	2.2	2.0	2.2	1.7	1.9	2.8	2.4	2.8	2.6

Source: WEO.

Note: EPCA, emergency postconflict assistance.

[1] Data for 3, 4, and 5 years after conflict are only available for 11, 7, and 7 of the 14 post-1990 conflicts, respectively.

Bibliography

Arunatilake, Nisha, Sisura Jayasuriya, and Saman Kelegama, 2002, "The Economic Cost of the War in Sri Lanka," *World Development*, Vol. 29, No. 9.

Brauman, Benedikt, 2000, "Real Effects of High Inflation" IMF Working Paper WP/00/85 (Washington: International Monetary Fund).

Blomberg, Brock, and Gregory Hess, 2002, "The Temporal Links between Conflict and Economic Activity" (Washington: World Bank).

Caplan, B., 2001, "How Does War Shock the Economy?" *Journal of International Money and Finance*, Vol. 21, pp. 145–62.

Catao, Luis, and Marco Terrones, 2001, "Fiscal Deficits and Inflation: A New Look at Emerging Markets," IMF Working Paper WP/01/174 (Washington: International Monetary Fund).

Collier, Paul, 1999, "On the Economic Consequences of Civil War," Oxford Economic Papers.

———, 2000, "Economic Causes of Civil Conflict and Their Implications for Policy" (Washington: World Bank).

Collier, Paul, and Anke Hoeffler, 1998, "On Economic Causes of Civil War," Oxford Economic Papers 50.

———, 2000, "Greed and Grievance in Civil Wars" (Washington: World Bank).

———, 2002a, "On the Incidence of Civil War in Africa," *Journal of Conflict Resolution*, Vol. 46, No. 1.

———, 2002b, "Aid, Policy and Growth in Post-Conflict Countries" (Washington: World Bank).

———, 2002c, "Military Expenditure: Threats, Aid and Arms Races" (Washington: World Bank).

Collier, Paul, Anke Hoeffler, and Måns Söderbom, 2001, "On the Duration of Civil War" (Washington: World Bank).

Collier, Paul, and others, 2003, *Breaking the Conflict Trap: Civil War and Development Policy* (Washington: Oxford University Press for the World Bank).

Davoodi, Hamid, and others, 1999, "Military Spending, the Peace Dividend, and Fiscal Adjustment," IMF Working Paper WP/99/87 (Washington: International Monetary Fund).

de Melo M., C. Denizer, and A. Gelb, 1996, "From Plan to Market," Policy Research Working Paper 1564 (Washington: World Bank).

Demekas, Dimitri, James McHugh, and Theodora Kosma, 2002, "The Economics of Post-Conflict Aid," IMF Working Paper 02/198 (Washington: International Monetary Fund).

Elbadawi, Ibrahim, 2000, "External Interventions and the Duration of Civil Wars" (Washington: World Bank).

Elbadawi, Ibrahim, and Nicholas Sambanis, 2000, "Why Are There So Many Civil Wars in Africa? Understanding and Preventing Violent Conflict," *Journal of African Economies* (December).

———, 2002, "How Much War Will We See? Explaining the Prevalence of Civil War" (Washington: World Bank).

Fearon, James, 2002, "Why Do Some Civil Wars Last So Much Longer Than Others?" (Washington: World Bank).

Fearon, James, and David Laitin, 2002, "Ethnicity, Insurgency and Civil Wars," *American Political Science Review*.

Fischer, Stanley, 1993, "The Role of Macroeconomic Factors in Growth"; *Journal of Monetary Economics*, Vol. 32, pp. 485–512.

Fischer, Stanley, Ratna Sahay, Carlos Vegh, 2002, "Modern Hyper and High Inflation," IMF Working Paper WP/02/197 (Washington: International Monetary Fund).

Gerson, Philip, 1998, "The Impact of Fiscal Policy Variables on Output Growth," IMF Working Paper WP/98/1 (Washington: International Monetary Fund).

Ghosh, Atish, and Steven Philips, 1998, "Inflation, Disinflation and Growth," IMF Working Paper WP/98/68 (Washington: International Monetary Fund).

Gupta, Sanjeev, and others, 2002a, "Expenditure Composition, Fiscal Adjustment and Growth in Low-Income Countries," IMF Working Paper WP/02/77 (Washington: International Monetary Fund).

———, 2002b, "Fiscal Consequences of Armed Conflict and Terrorism in Low and Middle Income Countries," IMF Working Paper WP/02/142 (Washington: International Monetary Fund).

Hemming, Richard, Michael Kell, and Selma Mahfouz, 2002, "The Effectiveness of Fiscal Policy in Stimulating Economic Activity—A Review of the Literature," IMF Working Paper WP/02/208 (Washington: International Monetary Fund).

Humphreys, Macartan, 2002, "Economics and Violent Conflict," Harvard University, Internet essay for the Program on Humanitarian Policy and Conflict Research, Conflict Prevention Initiative. Available via the Internet: www.hsph.harvard.edu/hpcr/index.htm

Imai, Kosuke, and J.M. Weinstein, 2000, "Measuring the Economic Impact of Civil War," Working Paper No. 51 (Boston, Massachusetts: Center for International Development, Harvard University).

International Monetary Fund, 2004 (forthcoming), *Review of Recent IMF Experience in Post-Conflict Countries*. IMF Occasional Paper. (Washington).

———, 2003, World Economic Outlook (Winter).

Khan, Mohsin, and Abdelhak Senhadji, 2000, "Threshold Effects in the Relationship between Inflation and Growth," IMF Working Paper WP/00/110 (Washington: International Monetary Fund).

Knight M., N. Loayza, and D. Villanueva, 1996, "The Peace Dividend: Military Spending Cuts and Economic Growth," *Staff Papers*, International Monetary Fund, Vol. 43, pp. 1–37.

Le Billon, Philippe, 2001, "The Political Ecology of War: Natural Resources and Armed Conflicts," *Political Geography* 20.

Michailof, Serge, Markus Kostner, and Xavier Devictor, 2002, "Post-Conflict Recovery in Africa: An Agenda for the Africa Region," Africa Region Working Paper Series No. 30 (Washington: World Bank).

Murdoch, James C., and Todd Sandler, 2001a, "Civil Wars and Economic Growth: A Regional Comparison (Washington: World Bank).

———, 2001b, "Economic Growth, Civil Wars, and Spatial Spillovers" (Washington: World Bank).

Nafziger E. Wayne, and Juha Auvinen, 2002, "Economic Development, Inequality, War, and State Violence," *World Development* Vol. 30, No. 2, pp. 153–63.

O'Connell, Stephen, and Charles Soludo, 2001, "Aid Intensity in Africa," *World Development*, Vol. 29, No. 9, pp. 1527–52.

Ranveig, Gissinger, Petter Gleditsch Nils, and Håvard Hegre, 2002, "Globalization and Internal Conflict," in *Globalization and Conflict*, ed. by Gerald Schneider, Katherine Barbieri, and Nils Petter Gleditsch (Boulder, Colorado: Rowman & Littlefield).

Ross, Michael L, 2002, "Oil, Drugs, and Diamonds: How Do Natural Resources Vary in Their Impact on Civil War?" (New York, New York: International Peace Academy).

Sambanis, Nicholas, 2001, "A Review of Recent Advances and Future Directions in the Quantitative Literature on Civil War" (New Haven, Connecticut: Yale University).

Smaldone, Joe, 2003, "War and Peace in Sub-Saharan Africa, 1989–1999: Does Military Spending Matter?" paper presented to 46th Annual Meeting of the African Studies Association, October 30–November 2, 2003, Boston, Massachusetts.

World Bank, 2002, *Global Development Finance: Financing the Poorest Countries* (Washington).

6

Sources of Growth in the Democratic Republic of the Congo: An Econometric Approach

BERNARDIN AKITOBY AND MATTHIAS CINYABUGUMA

Section I. Introduction

The Democratic Republic of the Congo (DRC),[1] with a large and dynamic population of more than 55 million people, is endowed with vast natural resources including perhaps the most extensive network of navigable waterways in Africa. It also has a vast hydroelectric potential that remains largely untapped. Despite its economic potential, economic activity declined drastically during the period 1960–2000. Per capita GDP fell steadily from US$380 in 1960 to US$224 in 1990 and further to US$85 (or US$0.23 a day) in 2000, making the country among the poorest in the world (see Figure 6.1). The dramatic decline in output and income has been the result of inappropriate economic and financial policies, pervasive corruption, and, especially in the past decade, political turmoil, civil strife, and full-fledged war since 1998.

However, since early 2001, the Congolese authorities started addressing the alarming economic and social situation by stabilizing the macroeconomic situation, liberalizing the economy, and opening it up to the rest of the world. With its critical mass of macroeconomic poli-

---

[1]See Chapter 2 for an overview of political and economic developments.

Figure 6.1. Real GDP per Capita
(Index 1960 = 100)

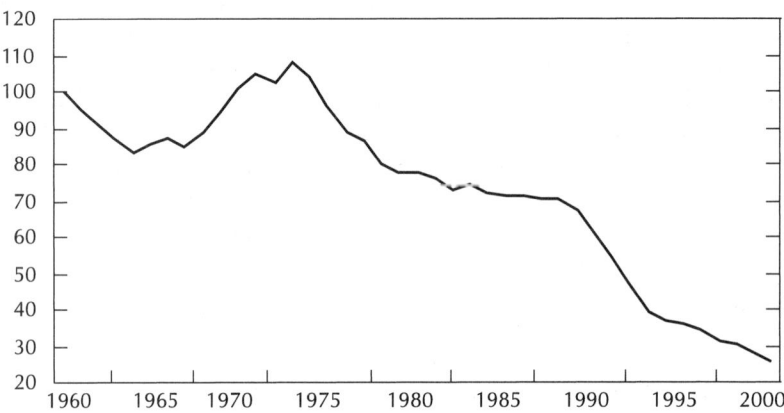

Sources: Congolese authorities; and IMF staff estimates.

cies and far-reaching structural reforms, the government's enhanced interim program, covering the period June 2001–March 2002, was a crucial first step toward stabilizing the country's economic situation and laying the foundations for reconstruction and the restoration of growth. The enhanced interim program has produced significant results, in particular, bringing hyperinflation to a halt, strengthening public finances, and laying a foundation for the resumption of growth. In 2002, for the first time in 13 years, real GDP growth was estimated to be positive, at about 3 percent. Building on these achievements, a program (covering the period April 2002–July 2005) supported by an arrangement under the International Monetary Fund's Poverty Reduction and Growth Facility (PRGF) is being implemented with the aim of reconstructing the country and reviving economic growth.

This chapter has three objectives. First, it investigates econometrically the sources of growth in the DRC and evaluates the relative importance of movements in productivity and factor accumulation. Unlike most studies on sources of growth, the analysis is extended to the key sectors of the economy: agriculture, mining, and transport. A cointegration technique is used to estimate the production function, thereby preserving the long-run information in the data. Second, the chapter assesses the DRC's medium-term growth prospects and compares them with both the postconflict growth experience to date and the growth objectives of the government's economic program. Third, based on the econometric findings, the chapter suggests a simple methodology for projecting the real GDP growth rate.

The rest of the chapter is organized as follows: Section II provides a brief background on the Congolese economy, focusing on economic performance during 1960–2000, Section III presents the theoretical framework and econometric methodology for analyzing the sources of growth, Section IV conducts the growth accounting exercise and analyzes the sources of growth, Section V reviews the recent policy reforms and assesses medium-term growth prospects, and Section VI highlights the main conclusions and their policy implications.

Section II. Economic Decline from 1960 to 2000

Focusing on the key constraints and policies that have hampered economic growth, this section analyzes both overall and sectoral growth performance. The factors constraining the DRC's economic performance have included ineffective governance and administrative bottlenecks, ill-conceived economic policies, transportation difficulties, lack of basic infrastructure, and insufficient confidence among potential local and foreign investors.

Overall Growth Performance

As mentioned previously, the DRC's overall economic performance has been extremely disappointing, notwithstanding the country's rich endowments of natural and human resources. Four decades have been lost to total mismanagement of the economy and lack of overall governance; real GDP in 2000 was below the 1960 level (see Figure 6.2). Following Maton, Schoors, and Van Bauwel (1998), the evolution in real GDP since 1960 can be usefully divided into five subperiods: (1) 1960–65: political chaos and economic disruption; (2) 1966–74: stability and growth; (3) 1975–82: economic recession and debt crisis; (4) 1983–89: adjustment supported by the IMF and stop-and-go policies; and (5) 1990–2000: hyperinflation and collapse of the economic and political system.

1960–65: Political chaos and economic disruption

This period witnessed a decline in output because of disruption in the transport network and the departure of many foreign entrepreneurs following political turmoil, civil strife, and the failed secession of Katanga Province. Real GDP declined by about 4 percent between 1960 and 1965.

Figure 6.2. Real GDP
(Index 1960 = 100)

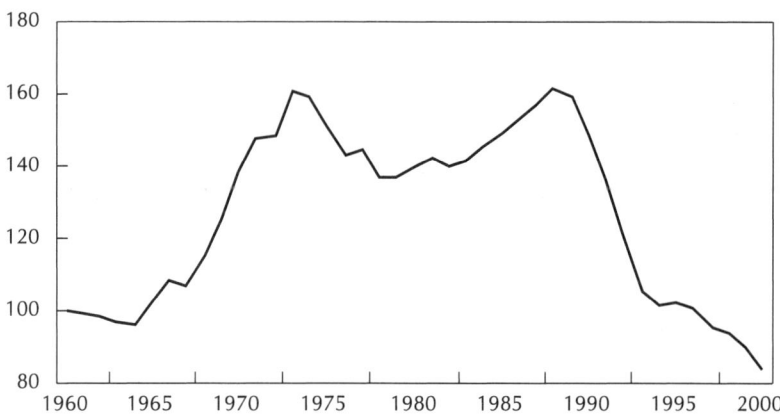

Sources: Congolese authorities; and IMF staff estimates.

1966–74: *Stability and growth*

This period was characterized by increased involvement of the state in the productive sectors of the economy. Thanks to La Politique des Grands Travaux,[2] public investment quadrupled. In 1971, the first Mobutu plan (Plan Décennal 1971–80) was launched, which aimed to raise real GDP growth to about 7 percent a year. Against this backdrop, in 1973–74 the government took steps toward the nationalization of all small, medium, and large foreign enterprises.

Increasing state control of the economy was accompanied by an impressive economic expansion, with real GDP growing at an average annual rate of 5.1 percent during 1966–74. However, following the adverse terms-of-trade shocks caused by both a reversal in copper prices and the oil crisis of 1973, the centralized economy, unable to adjust, soon revealed its severe limitations.

1975–82: *Economic recession and debt crisis*

The ill-advised economic policies and public investments of the early 1970s precipitated a debt crisis with a damaging impact on economic activity. In 1975, the country stopped servicing its debt and requested an IMF-supported program for the first time to help extricate

---

[2]La Politique des Grands Travaux was an ambitious plan for economic development aimed at implementing prestigious and large-scale projects.

the DRC from its economic crisis. Because of the overall downturn, the public investment program was grounded, capital invested in "white elephants" was lost, and the maintenance of infrastructure and productive capital was neglected or postponed indefinitely. As a result, economic activity experienced a severe decline, compounded by the invasions of Shaba Province (the heart of mining activities) in 1977 and 1978. Altogether, real GDP fell by 12 percent.

1983–89: Adjustment supported by the IMF and stop-and-go policies

To improve the economic and financial situation, and eliminate the significant distortions that had grown in the preceding period, the government started to implement in September 1983 a strong stabilization and liberalization program. This strategy had a positive impact as real GDP, which had declined by 2.2 percent in 1982, recovered with an average annual growth rate of 2.6 percent during the period 1984–86.

In 1987, with the support of the IMF and the World Bank, the government launched a structural adjustment program aimed at establishing the basis for long-term economic growth and a sustainable external financial position. The program also benefited from improved terms of trade, mostly reflecting a strong upturn in copper prices beginning in early 1987. However, with the more favorable external environment, the government all but ceased its adjustment efforts. As a result, the country's financial performance deteriorated markedly. Annual real GDP growth decelerated to 0.5 percent on average during the period 1987–89.

1990–2000: Hyperinflation and collapse of the economic and political system

In the midst of failed attempts at political liberalization, control over economic policies was lost, and the country fell into the grip of an unprecedented cycle of hyperinflation, currency depreciation, increasing dollarization and financial disintermediation, declining savings, deteriorating economic infrastructure, and broad-based output decline. The alarming economic and social situation was compounded by the full-fledged war that broke out on August 2, 1998.

In this context, a large part of the country's capital stock was destroyed, and investment was discouraged. As a result, real GDP contracted cumulatively by some 43 percent during the decade, and per capita real GDP plummeted from US$224 in 1990 to US$85 (US$0.23 a day) in 2000. Over the same period, consumer prices rose at an annual average rate of 684 percent. Government revenue fell by 80 percent, and external debt rose to about 300 percent of GDP (or almost US$13 billion).

Sectoral Growth Performance

Based on their contributions to GDP, agriculture, mining, and transport are the most important sectors.

Agriculture sector

Combined with forestry, animal husbandry, and fishing, agriculture provides direct employment to more than 75 percent of the labor force and accounts on average for about 45 percent of real GDP. Agriculture has great potential as a source of economic growth, export diversification, and gainful employment. Nevertheless, agricultural output has not recorded substantial growth (see Figure 6.3), and its contribution to exports declined continuously from about 40 percent of exports in 1960 to less than 10 percent in 2000, with some traditional export products virtually not being grown any more.[3] With regard to food crops, Maton, Schoors, and Van Bauwel (1998) have shown that food surplus for each person increased between 1965 and 1974; thereafter, a steep downward trend began, partly owing to the Zaïreanization[4] process, which undermined productivity growth.

Overall, agricultural development has been constrained by several factors. These include the deterioration of the network of rural feeder

Figure 6.3. Agricultural Real Value Added per Worker
(Index 1960 = 100)

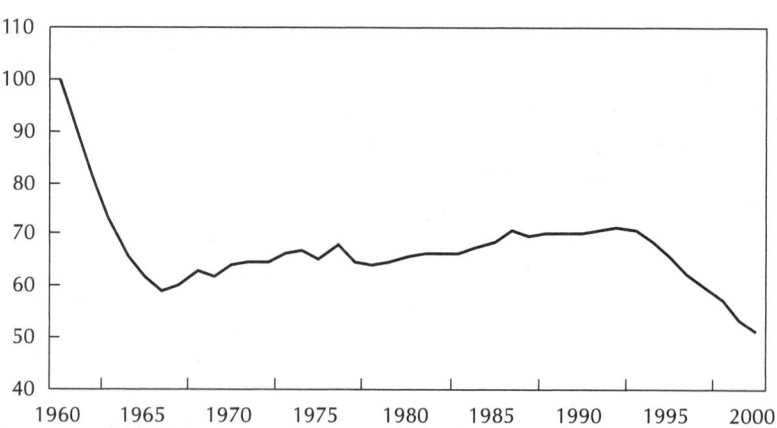

Sources: Congolese authorities; and IMF staff estimates.

---

[3]Exports mainly consist of oil products, cotton, cocoa, coffee, tea, and forestry products.

[4]The Zaïreanization process was characterized by the nationalization of a number of foreign enterprises.

roads, the dislocation caused by the Zaïreanization measures of 1973–74, inadequate credit for small-scale producers, lack of foreign exchange for essential imports, insufficient storage and other marketing facilities, and the uncertainties created by the government's pricing policies.

Mining sector

The DRC is extremely rich in mineral resources, and its mining potential remains largely untapped. Its mineral resources include copper, cobalt, diamonds, gold, zinc, uranium, tin, silver, coal, manganese, tungsten, cadmium, and crude oil. Most mining is carried out by the largest state-owned company, the Générale des Carrières et des Mines du Congo (GECAMINES), which accounts for more than 90 percent of total copper production and the entire cobalt and zinc output. In the diamond sector, while the Société Minière de Bakwanga (MIBA), partly owned by the government, is responsible for the industrial mining of diamonds, individual prospectors account for some 60 percent of total diamond production.

Beginning in the mid-1980s, the mining industry of the DRC entered a phase of steep decline (see Figure 6.4):

- By the late 1990s, copper production by GECAMINES had declined to 5 percent of the peak mid-1980s output level of more than 500,000 tons, while cobalt production had fallen by 70 percent from preconflict levels.
- Production of zinc has virtually ceased, compared with a previous capacity of 200,000 tons.
- Gold production has practically come to a halt, compared with a capacity of 6 tons per year.
- Manganese production was discontinued at the Kisenge Mining Enterprise (EMK-MN), where capacity was 360,000 tons a year during the early 1980s.
- With the sharp fall in GECAMINES's output, diamonds became the single-largest source of export earnings for the country. Because of frequent changes in marketing policies (including nationalization and the banning of foreigners from diamond-producing areas), large amounts of diamonds were exported through the parallel market. A monopoly to export artisanal diamonds granted in 2000 to a foreign company was rescinded in early 2001.

Reflecting its steep output slump, the mining sector's contributions to GDP and export earnings have been declining continuously. In the mid-1980s, mining accounted for almost one-fourth of real GDP and provided more than 70 percent of export receipts; in 2000, although the mining sector remained the main source of export earnings (owing to diamond exports), it accounted for only about 6 percent of real GDP.

Figure 6.4. Mining Real Value Added
(Index 1960 = 100)

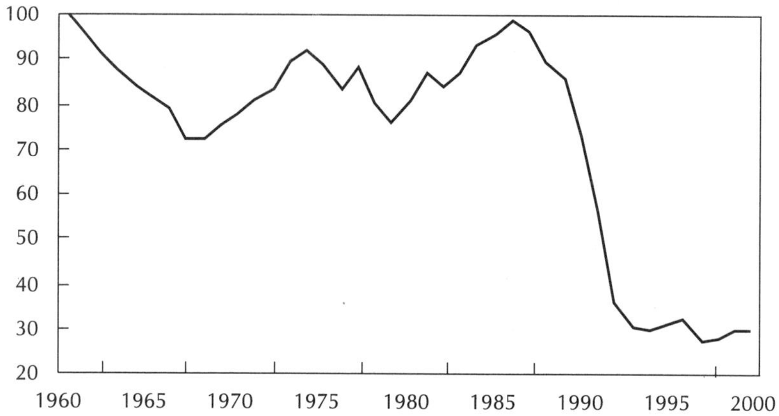

Sources: Congolese authorities; and IMF staff estimates.

The mining sector has been facing a number of problems that have constrained its development, including (1) a legal and regulatory framework not conducive to the development of the private sector; (2) serious transportation problems; and (3) chronic lack of investment.

Transport sector

When the DRC gained its independence in 1960, it inherited a comprehensive transport system, including strategically interconnecting roads, rivers, and railways. The transport sector accounted on average for about 12 percent of real GDP in the 40-year period 1960–2000. Given the large size of the country, its limited access to the sea, and the remoteness of its mineral deposits, the transport network is of vital importance to present and future economic activity. However, the sector's performance remains less than satisfactory (see Figure 6.5), and difficulties in transportation constitute a major obstacle to the realization of the DRC's immense agro-industrial and mining potential.

Three public agencies—the Société Nationale des Chemins de Fer du Congo (SNCC), the Office National des Transports (ONATRA), and the Office des Routes—play a critical role because they are responsible for operating rail and river transport and for building and maintaining the main highway network, respectively.

Since 1985, the financial situation of both ONATRA and SNCC has deteriorated sharply. Moreover, the services that they provide on

Figure 6.5. Transport Real Value Added
(Index 1960 = 100)

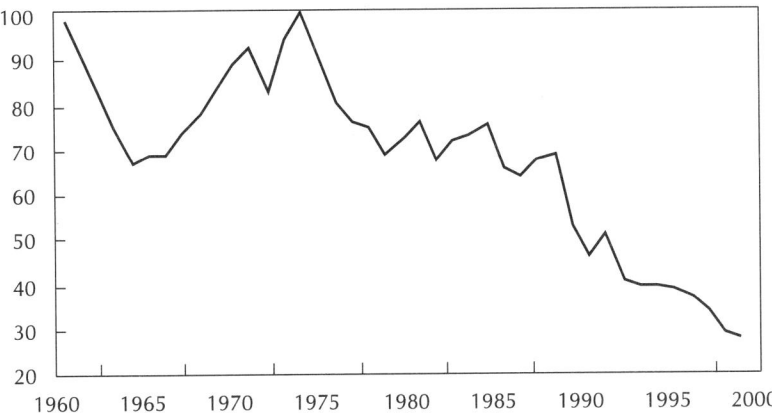

Sources: Congolese authorities; and IMF staff estimates.

the Voie Nationale, which combines the rail and water route from the Shaba mining area to the port of Matadi, have progressively declined. The poor performance of these two key agencies stems from a number of factors: the delay in adjusting tariffs in a highly inflationary environment; a decrease, or at best, stagnation in traffic; high operating costs; and chronic lack of maintenance.

In the late 1990s, the civil war took a toll on the transport sector and infrastructure collapsed. As a result, farmers have great difficulty in selling any surplus, while food prices in urban centers are high. Interregional connections are often limited to minimal air transport; as a result the country has essentially broken down into a set of economic enclaves.

Section III. Theoretical Framework and Econometric Methodology

Long-Run Production Function

The theoretical framework is a production function that relates output per worker (Y) to physical capital per worker (K):[5]

---

[5] For simplicity, the time subscripts are excluded.

$$Y = Ae^{bt} K^{\alpha}, \tag{1}$$

where t is a time index; A is the fixed component of the total factor productivity (TFP), which is assumed to improve at a rate b; and α is the long-run contribution of capital per worker to output per worker.

Taking the natural logarithm of both sides of equation (1) yields:

$$y = a + bt + \alpha k, \tag{2}$$

where the lowercase variables correspond to the logs of the uppercase variables.

Using equation (2), we estimate the long-run production function for the economy as a whole and for the key productive sectors (agriculture, mining, and transport), respectively. This allows us to analyze the sources of growth between the contributions of production factors and total factor productivity in Section IV.

Measurement of variables

Output. Output is measured by GDP at constant prices as published by the Central Bank of Congo. The sectoral output measures are given by the sectoral value added.

Labor inputs. Because employment series are not available, labor inputs are estimated by data on the economically active population (labor force) published by the International Labor Organization.[6] No adjustments for labor quality were introduced because of a lack of information on educational attainment.

Physical capital. As is the case in most developing countries, capital stock series are not readily available. Following a number of past studies,[7] we base the measure of capital on the *perpetual inventory* methodology. Having taken this route, two issues need to be dealt with: the initial capital stock and the rate of depreciation. We assume an initial capital-output ratio of 1.5 (a value of 1 was chosen for the agricultural

---

[6]The use of economically active population as labor inputs is common in most studies on developing countries.

[7]See, for instance, Bosworth; Collins, and Chen (1995); King and Levine (1994); Nehru and Dhareshwar (1993); Sacerdoti, Brunschwig, and Tang (1998); and Senhadji (1999).

sector) and the depreciation rate was set at 15 percent.[8] Based on these assumptions the capital stock dynamics is as follows:[9]

$$K_t - K_{t-1} = I_t - \delta K_{t-1}, \ K_o \text{ is given,} \tag{3}$$

where I_t is gross investment and δ is the depreciation rate.

Econometric Methodology

To estimate the long-run production function, we use the Johansen and Juselius (1990) and Johansen (1988, 1991) methodology of cointegration, interpreted as representing a long-run equilibrium relationship. The method is based on the following vector error-correction model:

$$\Delta Z_t = \sum_{i=1}^{k-1} \Gamma_i \Delta Z_{t-i} + P_0 Z_{t-1} + \mu + \varepsilon_t \tag{4}$$

$$\Gamma_i = - \sum_{j=i+1}^{k} \Pi_j \ and \ P_0 = \sum_{i=1}^{k} \Pi_i - I, \tag{5}$$

where Z_t is a $p \times 1$ vector time series, Γ_i is a $p \times p$ coefficient matrix, P_0 is a $p \times p$ matrix, μ is a $p \times 1$ vector of deterministic variables, and ε_t is a vector of Gaussian error terms.

The existence of cointegration is based on the rank of P_0:
- If rank $(P_0) = r = p$ (full rank), the vector time series is stationary and no long-run relationship exists among the variables.
- If rank $(P_0) = r = 0$, there is no cointegrating vector and a vector autoregression (VAR) based purely on the first difference of Z_t is appropriate.

---

[8]Those values for the capital-output ratio have been widely used in the literature (see, for example, Beddies, 1999; Sacerdoti, Brunschwig, and Tang, 1998; and Vera-Martin. 1999). Mankiw, Romer, and Weil (1992) found that the total capital-output ratio in developing countries is close to one. Given the relatively high rate of depreciation, the impact of the initial stock of capital decreases rapidly and vanishes in less than seven years. The high rate of depreciation mainly reflects the widespread lack of maintenance and accelerated depreciation due to several conflicts. Beddies (1999) also chose a 15 percent rate for capital depreciation, while Vera-Martin (1999) pointed out that a depreciation rate of 10 to 15 percent does not significantly alter the econometric results.

[9]Our measure of capital stock in the agricultural sector is largely underestimated, primarily because of lack of data on most investments undertaken by farmers. Therefore, the econometric results for the agricultural sector should be interpreted with caution.

- If rank $(P_0) = r < p$, then the time series are nonstationary and there exist r cointegrating vectors. Under this condition, the matrix P_0 can be expressed as the product of two $p \times r$ matrices α and β both of full column rank:

$$P_0 = \alpha\beta', \tag{6}$$

with β' being the matrix of cointegrating vectors and α representing the error-correction coefficient (which reflects the speed of adjustment to the long-run equilibrium).

Two tests are commonly used to determine the number of cointegrating vectors: the trace test and the maximum-eigenvalue test.

Unit-root test

Before turning to the tests for cointegration, one must determine the order of integration of the variables. Using the Augmented Dickey-Fuller (ADF) test, the unit-root hypothesis is tested in the level of variables as well as in their first differences. The null hypothesis is the presence of unit root. The lag length in the ADF regression is selected striking a balance between the lag length chosen by the Akaike information criterion (AIC) and the t-test of the lags. Tables 6.1 and 6.2 show the unit-root test results on the variables entering the overall and sectoral production functions. As can be seen, the null hypothesis that the level variables contain a unit root cannot be rejected at 5 percent or less.[10] All the variables were tested to be stationary in first differences. In light of these results, *we conclude that all variables are integrated of the order of one*.

Cointegration results

The presence of a unit root justifies the estimation of the production function within a cointegration framework. The Johansen's cointegration procedure starts with the determination of the length of the VAR version of equation (2). Because the cointegration test critically depends on the choice of the lag length, we base the lag selection on the likelihood ratio test of model reduction, moving from eight to four lags.[11] For the VAR estimated, different misspecification tests are re-

---

[10]The mining sectoral value added was found to have a unit root in the test with a deterministic linear time trend, but the presence of unit root was rejected at 5 percent in the test with a nonzero constant. As the graph of this variable clearly shows the presence of a linear trend, we go by the result of the first test.

[11]Because models with different lag length must be nested and estimated over the same period for the likelihood ratio test to be performed and be valid, all the VARs were estimated during the period 1968–2000, the longest time span possible for eight lags.

Table 6.1. Testing for Unit Roots (ADF Test with Constant)

Augmented Dickey-Fuller ADF(s) Test: $\Delta y = \mu + (\beta - 1)y_{t-1} + \sum\limits_{i}^{s} \gamma \Delta y_{t-1} + \varepsilon_t$

Variable	Level		Difference	
	ADF statistic	Lag length	ADF statistic	Lag length
Y	0.967	1	–2.379	0
K	–0.505	2	–1.705	1
y_a	–0.683	2	–3.947**	0
k_a	–2884	0	–4.498**	0
y_m	–3376*	0	–6.093**	0
k_m	–2.504	0	–6.824**	0
y_r	–1.307	0	–5.655**	1
k_r	–1.839	0	–4.707**	0

Source: IMF staff estimates.
Notes: The asterisks, * and ** , indicate significance at the 5 percent and 1 percent level, respectively. The critical values are –2.94 at the 5 percent significance level and –3.62 at the 1 percent significance level. The sample period is 1960–2000. Variables are as follows: output per worker (y) and physical capital per worker (k). The subscript "a" stands for agricultural sector, "m" for mining sector, and "r" for transport.

Table 6.2. Testing for Unit Roots (ADF Test with Linear Trend)

Augmented Dickey-Fuller ADF(s) Test: $\Delta y = \mu + \alpha T + (\beta - 1)y_{t-1} + \sum\limits_{i}^{s} \gamma \Delta y_{t-1} + \varepsilon_t$

Variable	Level		Difference	
	ADF statistic	Lag length	ADF statistic	Lag length
Y	–1.593	1	–3.760**	4
K	–0.465	1	–3.945**	0
y_a	–0.318	2	–3.853**	1
k_a	–2.386	0	–4.415**	0
y_m	–2.187	0	–7.227**	0
k_m	–1.236	0	–5.799**	2
y_r	–3.472*	1	–5.614**	1
k_r	–1.779	0	–4.672**	0

Source: IMF staff estimates.
Notes: The asterisks, * and **, indicate significance at the 5 percent and 1 percent level, respectively. The critical values are –2.94 at the 5 percent significance level and –3.62 at the 1 percent significance level. The sample period is 1960–2000. Variables are as follows: output per worker (y) and physical capital per worker (k). The subscript "a" stands for agricultural sector, "m" for mining sector, and "r" for transport.

ported in Table 6.3. Overall, no serious misspecification was detected, apart from the rejection of normality in one case. However, as pointed out by Gonzalo (1994) and Hubrich (1999), the Johansen procedure is not sensitive to non-normality errors.

Table 6.3. Properties of Cointegration Vector Autoregression Residuals

Diagnostic Tests	Aggregate Function		Mining Function		Transport Function	
	F-test value	P value	F-test value	P value	F-test value	P value
AR	1.710	0.129	0.892	0.532	0.685	0.700
Normality	9.386	0.052	13.862	0.007**	1.311	0.859
Autoregressive conditional heteroskedasticity	0.018	0.894	7.447	0.012*	0.249	0.624
Heteroskedasticity	0.318	0.989	0.339	0.985	——	——

Source: IMF staff estimates.

Notes: The normality property is tested with χ^2. The asterisks, * and **, denote rejection at the 5 percent and 1 percent level, respectively. There are not enough observations for the heteroskedasticity test for the mining sector.

Results for testing the number of cointegrating vectors are reported in Tables 6.4 and 6.5, with both the trace and maximum eigenvalue statistics. In the trace test, the null hypothesis is that the number of cointegating vectors is less than or equal to r ($r = 0$, 1), while in the maximum eigenvalue test, the alternative for $r = 0$ is $r = 1$. For the agricultural sector, we found no cointegrating vector (precluding any long-run relationship), while in all other cases, both tests reject the null hypothesis of no cointegration vector at 5 percent or less in favor of one cointegating vector.[12] The results yield the following long-run production functions:

Table 6.4. Cointegrating Test Results

	Overall Function		Agricultural Sector		Mining Sector		Transport Sector	
Eigenvalue	0.492	0.186	0.344	0.255	0.608	0.261	0.574	0.114
Null hypothesis on rank = r	$r = 0$	$r \leq 1$	$r = 0$	$r \leq 1$	$r = 0$	$r \leq 1$	$r = 0$	$r \leq 1$
λ_{trace}	29.22*	6.81	23.65	9.71	40.88**	9.99	32.22**	3.99
λ_{max}	22.41*	6.81	13.94	9.71	30.90**	9.99	28.24**	3.99

Source: IMF staff estimates.

Notes: The estimation period is 1968–2000, and the asterisks, * and **, denote rejection at the 5 percent and 1 percent level, respectively.

---

[12]For the mining sector, while the presence of cointegration cannot be rejected, the estimated elements of the vector are statistically insignificant (see Table 6.6). Therefore, no long-run production function was found for the mining sector.

Table 6.5. Cointegrating Vectors and Adjustment Coefficients

	Y	K	Constant	Trend
Cointegrating vectors				
Aggregate function	1	−0.34	2.43	0.03
Mining sector	1	−1.51	−3.47	−0.06
Transport sector	1	−0.33	0.65	0.05
Adjustment coefficients				
Aggregate function	−0.29	−0.11		
Mining sector	0.09	0.16		
Transport sector	−1	−0.60		

Source: IMF staff estimates.
Note: Because the capital coefficients are reported as an element of the cointegrating vector, their signs are negative.

- Overall production function

$$y = -2.43 - 0.03t + 0.34k; \text{ and} \tag{7}$$

- Transport sector production function

$$y_r = -0.65 - 0.05t + 0.33k_r. \tag{8}$$

As expected, the overall production function and the transport production function are characterized by decreasing returns to scale. Capital per worker is found to be a key determinant of long-term output per worker. The estimated coefficients for capital (0.34 for the overall function and 0.33 for the transport sector) have the right sign and are in line with the share of this factor in GDP (about 0.35 percent in developing countries). They are also consistent with the values (0.30 to 0.40) used in most growth studies. By comparison, Bosworth, Collins, and Chen (1995) obtained a coefficient of 0.4 on the capital term in the growth regression for developing countries, while Sacerdoti, Brunschwig, and Tang (1998) estimate the coefficient on physical capital at about 0.35 for West African countries.

The deterministic component of total factor productivity (TFP) growth is found to be negative (−3 percent for the overall function and −5 percent for the transport sector). This result shows, to some extent, how inappropriate economic policies implemented during the 40 years from 1960 to 2000 have negatively affected TFP. By comparison, Fischer (1993) estimates that productivity growth from 1961 to 1988 was about −5 percent a year for Haiti and Madagascar.

Table 6.6. Significance Test of Cointegration Vectors

Cointegration Vectors	$\chi^2(1)$	P Value for the Test Statistic
Aggregate production function		
Y	9.222	0.002**
K	6.015	0.014**
Trend	15.380	0.000**
Constant	8.762	0.003**
Transport production function		
y_r	21.067	0.000**
k_i	16.487	0.000**
Trend	16.675	0.000**
Constant	16.199	0.001**
Mining production function		
y_m	1.283	0.257
k_m	6.513	0.010*
Trend	1.360	0.243
Constant	1.4972	0.221

Source: IMF staff estimates.
Notes: The estimation period is 1968–2000. The asterisks, * and **, denote rejection at the 5 percent and 1 percent level, respectively.

Section IV. Sources of Growth

Having estimated the elasticity of output with respect to physical capital,[13] we now analyze the sources of growth, using a growth accounting exercise. We also investigate the policy determinants of growth.

Growth Accounting Exercise

Factor sources of growth

Table 6.7 and Figure 6.6 summarize the decomposition of the overall and sectoral outputs per worker into TFP growth and the contribution of physical capital per worker (defined as its share in output per worker multiplied by its growth rate). At the macroeconomic level, annual output per worker posted a negative average annual growth rate of –3.3 percent during 1960–2000. Negative TFP growth contributed to 60 percent of this decline, while the decline in physical capital per worker accounted for 40 percent.

---

[13]The elasticities used for agriculture and mining are 0.28 and 0.60. These values are taken from another study (Sarel, 1997), because the available data do not allow meaningful estimates of elasticity for both sectors. Therefore, the results for the mining and agriculture sectors should be interpreted with caution.

Table 6.7. Democratic Republic of the Congo: Sources of Growth by Factor Accumulation and Sector, 1960–2000

(Annual percentage change)

Period	Output per Worker	Contribution of: Physical Capital	Contribution of: Total Factor Productivity
1960–2000	–3.3	–1.3	–2.0
1960–65	–4.4	–3.7	–0.7
1966–74	2.9	1.6	1.3
1975–82	–3.8	1.0	–4.8
1983–89	–1.1	–1.9	0.8
1990–2000	–8.8	–3.9	–4.9

Period	Output per Worker	Contribution of: Agriculture	Mining	Transportation	Other
1960–2000	–0.3	0.2	–0.4	–0.4	0.3
1960–65	0.5	–2.0	–0.7	–1.3	4.5
1966–74	5.1	0.9	0.2	0.7	3.3
1975–82	–1.6	0.6	–0.2	–0.9	–1.1
1983–89	1.9	1.5	0.1	0.0	0.3
1990–2000	–5.5	–0.4	–1.0	–0.8	–3.3

Source: IMF staff estimates.

At the sectoral level, in the agricultural sector, which experienced zero average annual TFP growth during 1960–2000, negative physical capital growth explained the negative growth of output per worker of 1.7 percent over this period. In the transport sector, TFP declines accounted for 92 percent of the negative growth rate of –6 percent of output per worker during the 40 years between 1960 and 2000. The mining sector recorded some TFP growth gains, but mining output per worker fell by an average 4.1 percent per year, owing to the rapid decline in physical capital per worker.

Sectoral contributions to overall decline

The bottom panel of Table 6.7 reports the sectoral contributions to GDP. The results indicate that the mining and transport sectors account for the negative real GDP growth of 0.3 percent per year during 1960–2000. Reflecting the negative trend in their outputs, the mining and transport shares in GDP have been completely eroded. The mining sector's share in GDP fell from 20 percent in 1960 to just 6 percent in 2000, while the transport sector's share declined from 18.5 percent in 1960 to a low of 3.7 percent in 2000.

Figure 6.6. Democratic Republic of the Congo: Growth Accounting, 1960–2000

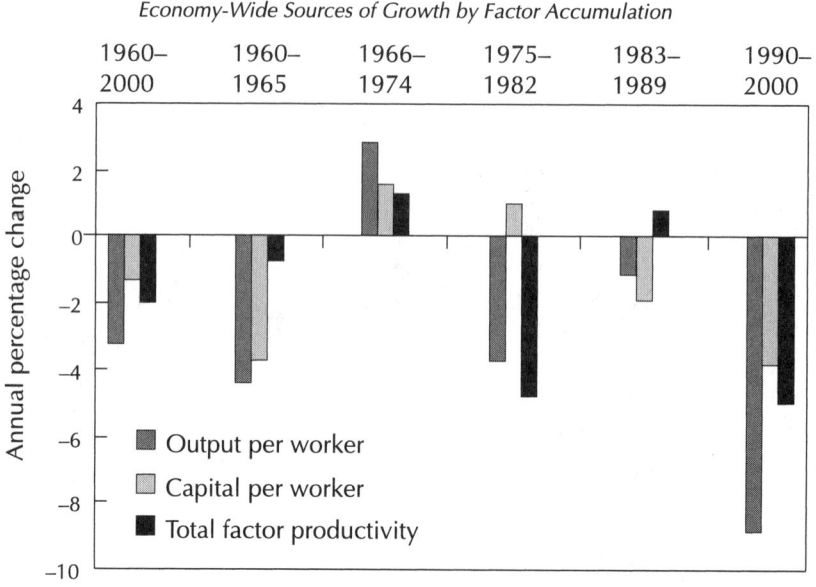

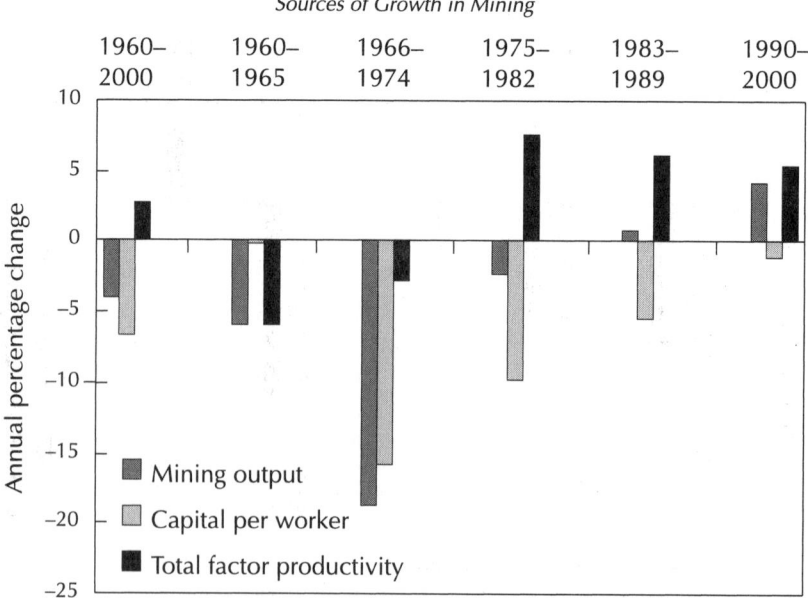

Figure 6.6. Democratic Republic of the Congo: Growth Accounting, 1960–2000 (continued)

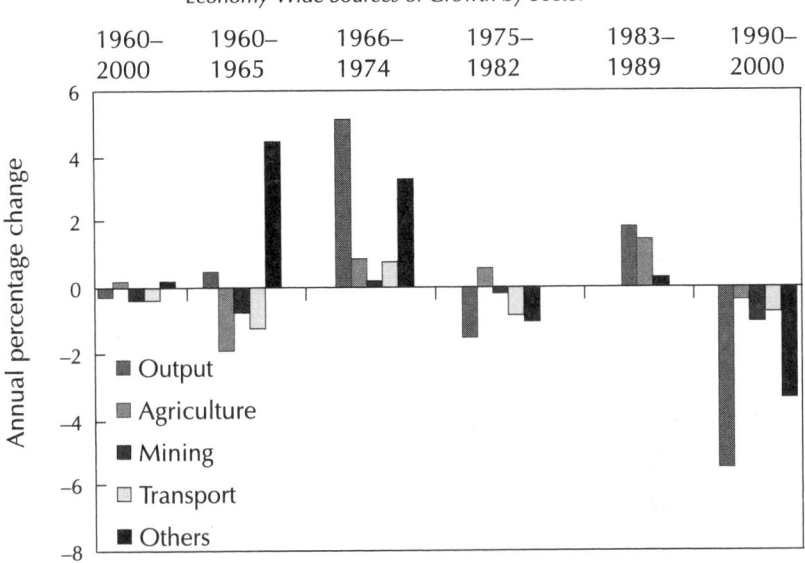

Economy-Wide Sources of Growth by Sector

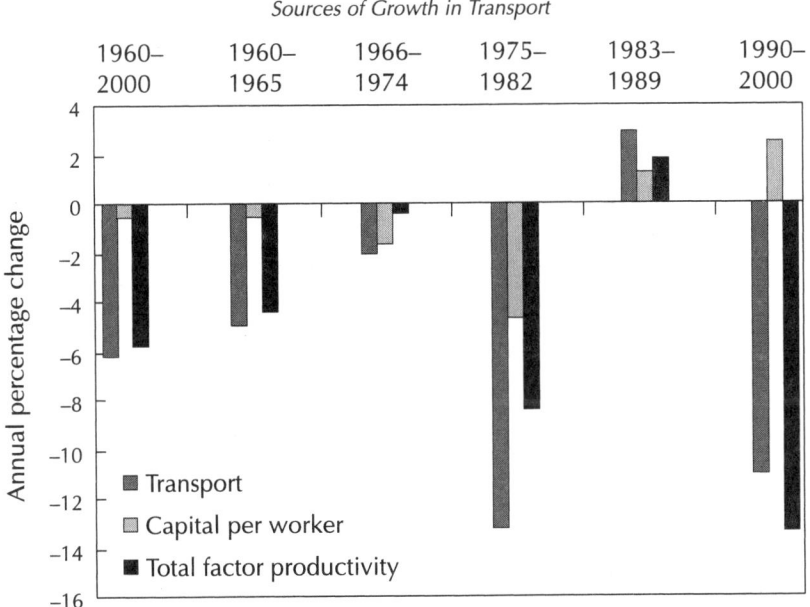

Sources of Growth in Transport

Sources: Congolese authorities; and IMF staff estimates.

Analysis across subperiods

The decomposition of sources of decline across the five subperiods (identified previously) reveals interesting patterns in the DRC's growth experience. The subperiod 1966–74 is the only one to experience a positive average growth rate, 2.9 percent, with physical capital per worker and TFP contributing equally. During the subperiod 1975–82, notwithstanding the positive contribution of physical capital per worker of 1 percentage point (the second highest of the five subperiods), output per worker still declined by 3.8 percent, reflecting the sharp drop in TFP. The reason is that a series of so-called prestigious projects (mainly white elephants) implemented during this subperiod had damaging impacts on TFP. As can be seen in Table 6.8, physical capital per worker in the key sectors of mining and transport sharply fell at the same time, as these white elephants pulled away resources from both sectors. Finally, the last subperiod (1990–2000) witnesses the largest decline in output per worker and in both physical capital and TFP, reflecting the damaging effects of hyperinflation as well as of armed conflicts (since 1998).

Table 6.8. Democratic Republic of the Congo: Sources of Growth in Agriculture, Mining, and Transport, 1960–2000

(Annual percentage change)

Sectors and Period	Output per Worker	Contribution of: Physical Capital	Contribution of: Factor Productivity
Agriculture			
1960–2000	−1.7	−1.7	0.0
1960–65	−9.6	−5.3	−4.3
1966–74	0.9	−2.8	3.7
1975–82	−0.1	−1.6	1.5
1983–89	0.8	1.1	−0.3
1990–2000	−2.9	−1.0	−1.9
Mining			
1960–2000	−4.1	−6.8	2.7
1960–65	−6.0	−0.1	−5.9
1966–74	−18.7	−15.9	−2.8
1975–82	−2.2	−9.7	7.5
1983–89	0.7	−5.3	6.0
1990–2000	4.2	−1.1	5.3
Transportation			
1960–2000	−6.2	−0.5	−5.7
1960–65	−5.0	−0.6	−4.4
1966–74	−2.1	−1.7	−0.4
1975–82	−13.2	−4.7	−8.5
1983–89	3.0	1.2	1.8
1990–2000	−11.0	2.4	−13.4

Source: IMF staff estimates.

Policy Determinants of Growth

We investigate the role of policy variables and other variables as determinants of growth, using a modified version of the neoclassical growth model applied by Ghura and Hadjimichael (1996) and Calamitsis, Basu, and Ghura (1999) to sub-Saharan Africa. The growth equation estimated takes the following form:[14]

$$\Delta y_t = \gamma_1 \, ln(I_p/Y)_t + \gamma_2 \, ln(I_g/Y)_t + \gamma_3 EXRP_t + \gamma_4 DEF_t + \gamma_5 TOT_t + \gamma_6 Dwar_t + v_t, \tag{9}$$

where Δy is the per capita output growth; I_p/Y and I_g/Y are the ratios of private and government investment to GDP; $EXRP$ is the parallel market exchange rate premium; DEF is the ratio of the central government budget deficit to GDP; TOT is the growth rate of the external terms of trade; and $Dwar$ is a dummy variable for war and conflicts.

Equation (9) is estimated using annual data for the period 1960–2000. The regression results are summarized in Table 6.9. The main results are as follows:

- The private investment–GDP ratio exerts a large positive effect on economic growth. The estimated coefficients are slightly higher than the ones reported by Calamitsis, Basu, and Ghura (1999) for sub-Saharan Africa. The impact of private investment does not change much when other variables are included in the regression.
- The effect of government investment is negative and significant in two of the three specifications, supporting the fact that public capital was mostly invested in white elephants and unproductive projects.
- The policy environment seems to have significantly influenced growth in the DRC. The estimated coefficient on the budget deficit ratio and the parallel market rate premium are negative and significant, confirming the view that hyperinflation and uncontrolled budget deficits have undermined the DRC's growth performance.
- The estimated effect of changes in the terms of trade is positive and statistically significant. The coefficient on the dummy variable indicating conflicts and wars has a negative and highly significant effect on growth, supporting the notion that political turmoil and conflicts have played a crucial role in the DRC's poor growth performance.

---

[14]Owing to data constraints, we have not included several variables found in the growth literature to have a strong influence on economic growth.

Table 6.9. Estimates of the Neoclassical Growth Equation[1,2]

	Explanatory Variables	(1)	(2)	(3)
Conventional Variables				
$Ln(I_p/Y)$	Private investment–GDP ratio	0.043[a]	0.047[a]	0.036[b]
		(2.69)	(3.35)	(2.42)
$Ln(I_G/Y)$	Government investment–GDP ratio	–0.009	–0.018[a]	–0.018[a]
		(–1.44)	(–3.10)	(–3.32)
Policy-related variables				
EXRP	Parallel market exchange rate premium		–1.6E-04[b] (–2.22)	–1.6.E-04[a] (–2.84)
DEF	Central government budget deficit		–0.004[a] (–3.17)	–0.003[a] (–3.44)
Other explanatory variables				
TOT_g	Terms-of-trade growth			7.9E-04[c] (1.89)
D_{war}	Dummy variable for conflicts and wars			–0.049[a] (–3.41)

Source: IMF staff estimates.

[1] The estimation period is 1960–2000; a, b, and c denote statistical significance at the 0.01, 0.05, and 0.10 levels, respectively. The numbers in parentheses below the estimated coefficients are the t values.

[2] The diagnostic tests for equation (3) are as follows: Testing for error autocorrelation from lags one to two $F(2, 32) = 0.3963$ [0.6760]; normality $\chi^2(2) = 3.8682$ [0.1446]; autoregressive conditional heteroskedasticity (ARCH) $F(1, 32) = 0.0291$ [0.8656]; heteroskedasticity errors $F(11,22) = 0.4578$ [0.9098].

Section V. Policy Reforms and Medium-Term Growth Prospects

A large number of theoretical and empirical studies have shown that improving macroeconomic and structural policies positively affects economic growth by increasing investment and productivity growth.[15] The DRC's medium-term growth prospects, therefore, will be assessed in light of recent policy reforms to lay the foundation for economic growth.

Macroeconomic and Structural Reforms

The implementation of bold measures under the enhanced interim program marked a turnaround in the conduct of economic policy that has produced significant results. With the restoration of the indepen-

---

[15]See, for example, Calamitsis, Basu, and Ghura (1999), Easterly and Wetzel (1989), and Ghura and Hadjimichael (1996).

dence of the central bank, the vicious circle of hyperinflation and currency depreciation has been broken. Inflation decelerated sharply from an annual rate of 511 percent in 2000 to 15 percent in 2002. The sharp decline in inflation has led to the stabilization of the exchange rate after the introduction of a floating exchange rate system at the end of May 2001. Important progress was also made in strengthening public finances via a return to normal budgetary procedures.

Far-reaching structural reforms are also being implemented, with a view to creating an environment conducive to private sector development and economic recovery. The scope of the reforms encompasses a wide range of areas, including the public sector; the financial sector; mining, agriculture, forestry, and environment; the rehabilitation of key infrastructure (transportation, telecommunications, water, and electricity); the social sectors; institutional capacity building; the judicial and regulatory environment; and the promotion of good governance and anticorruption measures.[16]

Medium-Term Growth Prospects

Sound macroeconomic policies and the ongoing far-reaching structural reforms have started to have a positive effect on growth through improved resource allocation.[17] The DRC's growth prospects are also enhanced by its untapped potential in the mining, agriculture, forestry, and energy sectors. Moreover, growth should rebound strongly and quickly (a pattern observed in other postconflict regions), because the country is starting from a very low base.

Based on the above econometric results, this section analyzes the credibility of the program's growth targets from 2002–05, discussing the feasibility of the implicit productivity growth rates underpinning these real GDP growth projections. It also assesses how fast the country can make up for the ground lost during the 40-year period from 1960 to 2000.

Assessing the credibility of the program's medium-term growth prospects

With the estimated production function derived in Section III, growth forecasts are based on projections of labor force, capital stock

---

[16]More details on the DRC's policy reform can be found in IMF country reports and the Congolese authorities' memorandum of economic and financial policy posted on the IMF's external website, www.imf.org.

[17]As pointed out in Section I, in 2002, for the first time in 13 years, real GDP growth is estimated to have been positive, at about 3 percent.

(based on investment and the perpetual inventory methodology), and productivity growth rates (reflecting ongoing economic reforms).

Using this projection methodology[18] and assuming that the labor force will grow at the population growth rate, that is, 3 percent a year, we find that a Solow residual[19] growth rate of 2.5 percent implicitly underpins the program's real GDP average growth rate of about 5 percent[20] and the average investment-GDP ratio of 16 percent from 2002–05. The whole Solow residual should not be ascribed to TFP growth, because it incorporates a "catch-up" factor that is typical for a postconflict country.[21] Unfortunately, it is not easy to estimate the latter. One indirect estimation would be to estimate the TFP growth in a normal period and argue that one would expect at least this TFP growth to be achieved in the forecast period, mainly because of policy implementation. Using this procedure, we estimate TFP growth at 1.3 percent, which implies a catch-up factor of 1.2 percent. While the 1.3 percent TFP growth is higher than those experienced in industrial, Latin American, and African countries, it is well below East Asian TFP growth rates (Table 6.10). In sum, if the actual investment rate were to fall below 16 percent of GDP over 2002–05, the average economic growth rate of 5 percent would be difficult to achieve, because it would imply unrealistic TFP growth rates.

Assessing the time required to recoup the ground lost

As indicated in Section II, output per capita and real GDP have followed a steep decline, especially since 1990. Real GDP had risen to 150 percent of its 1960 level by 1990, only to decline to about 80 percent of its 1960 level by 2001. At the same time, with 3 percent annual growth of the population, real GDP per capita fell to 60 percent of its 1960 level in 1990, and further to 25 percent of its 1960 level in 2001.

---

[18]It is expected that with the return of peace and the normal functioning of the economy, the capital depreciation rate will decline to 5 percent, beginning in 2002, from the 15 percent assumed earlier. With a 10 percent depreciation rate, the Solow residual growth will be about 1.5 percentage point higher.

[19]The Solow residual is the part of output growth that is not explained by changes in inputs.

[20]The annual economic growth rate in postconflict countries has averaged 5 percent in the five years immediately after conflict and 3 percent in per capita terms. However, the lack of data on productivity growth in postconflict countries precludes any assessment of our estimates of the Solow residual and productivity growth from a postconflict country standpoint.

[21]A significant part of the catch-up factor is due to intensified capacity utilization in the postconflict period.

Table 6.10. Democratic Republic of the Congo: Sources of Growth in Selected Countries and Regions, 1986–92

Regions/Countries	Output per Worker	Contribution of: Physical capital	Contribution of: Factor productivity
Regions			
Industrial countries	1.5	0.7	0.8
Africa	–0.4	–0.5	0.1
Latin America	–0.6	0.0	–0.6
East Asia (excluding China)	5.1	2.6	2.5
South Asia	2.9	1.2	1.7
East Asian countries			
China	6.2	3.1	3.1
Korea	6.6	3.9	2.7
Malaysia	5.4	1.9	3.5
Singapore	7.4	2.6	4.6
Thailand	8.3	3.2	4.8
Taiwan Province of China	5.9	2.8	3.1

Source: Bosworth, Collins, and Chen, 1995.

An interesting question is how many years, beginning in 2002, it would take both aggregates to reach their 1960 and 1990 levels, if the projected 5 percent real GDP growth were to continue beyond 2005 for several decades. We calculate that it would take four years for real GDP to reach its 1960 level and 13 years to return to its 1990 level. Assuming that the population continues to grow at an annual rate of 3 percent, reaching the 1960 real GDP per capita level would take 70 years, while the 1990 level would be attained in 45 years. These time frames highlight the DRC's disappointing economic performance in the 40 years from 1960 to 2000.

Section VI. Conclusions and Policy Implications

This chapter has examined the sources of growth in the DRC and assessed the medium-term growth prospects for the country. It concludes that poor economic policies and conflicts, through their effects on TFP and the investment rate, significantly hurt the country's economic performance from 1960 to 2000. However, the chapter also demonstrates that the right policies are being put in place to pave the way for growth restoration by raising the TFP growth and investment rate.

In light of the policies being implemented and investment rates envisaged under the government's economic program, an average growth rate of about 5 percent is estimated to be achievable over the next four years, 2002–05.

The main findings of the chapter can be summarized as follows:

- Using the cointegration procedure, the critical technology para-meter—the average share of physical capital per worker in output per worker—of the long-run production function is estimated at 0.34 for the whole economy and 0.33 for the transport sector. No cointegration relationship between output and capital was found for the mining and agricultural sectors.

- Using a growth accounting framework from 1960 to 2000, the findings on the TFP and factor accumulation contributions to output growth are as follows. First, at the macroeconomic level, negative TFP growth contributed to 60 percent of the negative average annual growth rate of 3.3 percent during the 40-year pe-riod from 1960 to 2000, while the decline in physical capital per worker accounted for 40 percent. Second, at the sectoral level, in the agricultural sector, which experienced zero average annual TFP growth during the period 1960–2000, negative physical cap-ital growth explained the negative growth of output per worker of 1.7 percent over this period. In the transport sector, TFP declines accounted for 92 percent of the negative 6 percent growth of out-put per worker from 1960 to 2000. The mining sector recorded some TFP growth gains, but mining output per worker fell by an average 4.1 percent per year, owing to the rapid decline in physi-cal capital per worker.

- In analyzing the determinants of the DRC's economic growth from 1960 to 2000, the regression results show that private in-vestment has had a large positive impact, whereas the effect of government investment has been negative, supporting the view that public capital was mostly invested in unproductive projects. High inflation rates (as reflected by high parallel market ex-change rate premium) and large budgetary deficits have also ex-erted a negative impact on growth. Finally, political turmoil, conflicts, and war have contributed significantly to the poor growth performance.

- In assessing the DRC's medium-term growth prospects, we note that an economic turnaround has begun, with real GDP projected to be growing by 5 percent a year over the next four years. Assuming that the population continues to grow at an annual rate of 3 percent, reaching the 1960 real GDP per capita level would take 70 years, while the 1990 level would be attained in 45 years. These estimates clearly show that the DRC has a long way to go to recoup the ground lost during the 40-year period from 1960 to

2000. The estimates also illustrate how both the creation of an enabling environment for private investment, as well as coordinated, sustained, and comprehensive foreign aid, are necessary conditions to make a real dent in the widespread poverty in the DRC.

References

Beddies, Christian H., 1999, "Investment, Capital Accumulation, and Growth: Some Evidence from Gambia 1964–98," IMF Working Paper 99/117 (Washington: International Monetary Fund).

Bosworth, Barry, Susan M. Collins, and Yu-chin Chen, 1995, "Accounting for Differences in Economic Growth," Brookings Discussion Papers in International Economics No. 115 (October), pp. 1–63.

Calamitsis, A. Evangelos, Anupam Basu, and Dhaneshwar Ghura, 1999, "Adjustment and Growth in Sub-Saharan Africa," IMF Working Paper 99/51 (Washington: International Monetary Fund).

Easterly, William R., and Deborah L. Wetzel, 1989, "Policy Determinants of Growth: Survey of Theory and Evidence," Policy, Planning, and Research Working Paper No. 343 (Washington: World Bank).

Fischer, Stanley, 1993, "The Role of Macroeconomic Factors in Growth," *Journal of Monetary Economics*, Vol. 32 (December), pp. 485–512.

Ghura, Dhaneshwar, and Michael T. Hadjimichael, 1996, "Growth in Sub-Saharan Africa," *Staff Papers*, International Monetary Fund, Vol. 43 (September), pp. 605–34.

Gonzalo, Jesus, 1994, "Five Alternative Methods of Estimating Long-Run Equilibrium Relationships," *Journal of Econometrics*, Vol. 60 (January–February), pp. 203–33.

Hubrich, Kirstin, 1999, "Estimation of a German Money Demand System: A Long-Run Analysis," *Empirical Economics*, Vol. 24 (No. 2), pp. 77–99.

Johansen, Soren, 1988, "Statistical Analysis of Cointegration Vectors," *Journal of Economic Dynamics and Control*, Vol. 12 (June–September), pp. 231–54.

———, 1991, "Estimation and Hypothesis Testing of Cointegration Vectors in Gaussian Vector Autoregressive Models," *Econometrica*, Vol. 59 (November), pp. 1551–80.

Johansen, Soren, and Katarina Juselius, 1990, "Maximum Likelihood Estimation and Inference on Cointegration—with Applications to the Demand for Money," *Oxford Bulletin of Economics and Statistics*, Vol. 52 (May), pp. 169–210.

King, Robert G., and Ross Levine, 1994, "Capitalism Fundamentalism, Economic Development, and Economic Growth," Carnegie-Rochester Conference Series on Public Policy, Vol. 40 (June), pp. 259–92.

Mankiw, N. Gregory, David Romer, and David N. Weil, 1992, "A Contribution to the Empirics of Economic Growth," *Quarterly Journal of Economic*, Vol. 107 (May), pp. 407–37.

Maton, Jef, Koen Schoors, and Annelies Van Bauwel, 1998, "Congo 1965–1997" (unpublished; Ghent: University of Ghent).

Nehru, Vikram, and Ashok Dhareshwar, 1993, "A New Database on Physical Capital Stocks: Sources, Methodology, and Results," *Revista De Analisis Economico*, Vol. 8 (June), pp. 37–59.

Sacerdoti, Emilio, Sonia Brunschwig, and Jon Tang, 1998, "The Impact of Human Capital on Growth: Evidence from West Africa," IMF Working Paper 98/162 (Washington: International Monetary Fund).

Sarel, Michael, 1997, "Growth and Productivity in ASEAN Countries," IMF Working Paper 97/97 (Washington: International Monetary Fund).

Senhadji, Abdelhak, 1999, "Sources of Economic Growth: An Extensive Growth Accounting Exercise," IMF Working Paper 99/77 (Washington: International Monetary Fund).

Vera-Martin, Mercedes, 1999, "Long-Run Growth in Mali, Niger, and Senegal" (unpublished; Washington: International Monetary Fund).

7

Political Instability and Growth in the Central African Republic, a Neighbor of the Democratic Republic of the Congo

DHANESHWAR GHURA AND BENOÎT MERCEREAU

Section I. Introduction

The Central African Republic (C.A.R.), a landlocked nation about the size of France, is one of the poorest countries in the world. It ranked 168th out of 175 countries listed in the 2003 United Nations Development Program Human Development Index. The C.A.R.'s resident population was estimated at about 3.9 million in 2002, the vast majority of whom live in rural areas and depend on food and cash crops and livestock for their livelihood. The country is endowed with considerable water and mineral resources and has untapped potential for agriculture. The economy is highly dependent on diamonds and timber. Key constraints on sustained economic growth include political instability, weak governance, a low level of human capital, inadequate infrastructure, and conflicts in neighboring countries. Progress under various attempts to set the economy on a sustainable development path has been uneven, and the country's economic performance since independence has been weak.

The political situation in the C.A.R. has been characterized by recurrent instability, with a dozen coup attempts or mutinies recorded since independence (see Table 7.1 for a chronology of key events). Such instability has undermined homegrown efforts to escape a trap revolving

205

Table 7.1. Central African Republic: Chronology of Key Events Since Independence

Independence
1960: The C.A.R. becomes independent with David Dacko as president.
1962: Dacko turns the C.A.R. into a one-party state.
1964: Dacko confirmed as president in elections in which he is the sole candidate.

Bokassa presidency
1965: Dacko ousted by the army commander, Jean-Bédel Bokassa, as the country faces bankruptcy and a threatened nationwide strike.
1972: Bokassa declares himself president for life.
1977: Bokassa proclaims himself emperor and renames the country the "Central African Empire."

Dacko and Kolingba presidency
1979: Bokassa ousted in a coup led by Dacko and backed by French troops after widespread protests in which many schoolchildren were arrested and massacred while in detention.
1981: Dacko deposed in a coup led by the army commander, André Kolingba.
1984: Amnesty declared for all political party leaders.

Transition to democracy and Patassé presidency
1991: Political parties permitted to form.
1992 October: Multiparty presidential and parliamentary elections held in which Kolingba came in last place, but are annulled by the supreme court on the grounds of widespread irregularities.
1993: Ange-Félix Patassé defeats Kolingba and Dacko in elections to become president, ending 12 years of military rule. Kolingba releases several thousand political prisoners, including Bokassa, before stepping down as president.
1996 May: Soldiers stage an uprising in the capital, Bangui, over unpaid wages.
1997 November: Soldiers stage more revolts.
1997: France begins withdrawing its forces from the republic; African peacekeepers replace French troops.
1999: Patassé reelected president.
2000 (December): Civil servants stage general strike over back pay; rally organized by 15 opposition groups that accuse President Patassé of mismanagement and corruption deteriorates into riots.
2001 (May): At least 59 killed in an abortive coup attempt by former president Kolingba. President Patassé suppresses attempt with help of Libyan and Chadian troops as well as Congolese rebels. The political upheaval increases economic instability.
2001 (November): Clashes break out as troops try to arrest sacked army chief of staff General François Bozizé who is accused of being involved in the May coup attempt. Thousands flee fighting between government troops and Bozizé's forces, while envoys from Chad, Libya, and the UN try to resolve the conflict.
2002 (May): Government lifts curfew imposed after May 2001 coup attempt to signal return of "security and peace" and anticipates return of foreign investors.
2002 (October): After six days of heavy fighting in Bangui, Libyan-backed forces and troops led by Mr. Bemba from the Democratic Republic of the Congo (DRC) help to subdue an attempt by forces loyal to dismissed army chief General Bozizé to overthrow President Patassé. Relations with neighboring Chad, accused by officials in Bangui of helping Bozizé, worsen.
2003 (February): General Bozizé's troops make a significant advance to capture key strategic cities outside Bangui in the northern part of the C.A.R.
2003 March: General Bozizé mounts a successful coup, while President Patassé is out of the country, and declares himself president.

Source: British Broadcasting Corporation (BBC) website.

around poverty and poor governance. To understand the root causes of instability would therefore be key to setting the country back on a sustainable development path. This chapter examines the following points: (1) the possible qualitative explanations of the country's political instability and poor economic performance; (2) the empirical determinants of political instability in the country; and (3) empirical factors (including political instability) that have influenced economic growth.

A number of papers have been written on the subject of conflicts.[1] Chapter 3 of this book provides an excellent survey of the literature on the causes and consequences of conflicts. In general, the empirical work finds that the risk for increased conflicts is explained primarily by economic factors (such as initial income, dependence on commodity exports, and economic growth in the preceding period), but also by noneconomic factors (such as social fractionalization). Other studies point to spillover of regional conflicts on the economic performance of a given country (e.g., Sambanis, 2003). Conflicts in neighboring countries also heighten the risk that the country itself will fall into civil war (Collier and others, 2003). The analysis in Chapter 4, focusing on data from sub-Saharan Africa, finds that conflicts in the region are caused by low economic growth and weak institutions.

The analysis in this chapter shows, first, that the propensity for political instability is increased by past low tax revenue, as well as by deteriorations in the terms of trade. Weak revenue performance undermines the ability of the government to pay the salaries of civil servants and to provide basic social services, which raises frustrations among the population and triggers political instability. Insufficient economic diversification also leaves the country vulnerable to terms-of-trade shocks, increasing not only economic but also political volatility. These results seem to suggest that efforts to enhance the country's capacity to mobilize revenue would be critical in lowering the propensity for political instability. In addition, the diversification of the C.A.R.'s economic base would not only make its economy less vulnerable to external shocks, but would also reduce the propensity of terms-of-trade shocks to fuel domestic conflict. A second conclusion from the empirical investigation is that the direct impact of political instability on growth is not significant, once an account is made of domestic investment in the C.A.R. and economic performance in neighboring countries.

The next section examines economic and political developments since 1960. Section III investigates the determinants of political insta-

---

[1]See, for example, Collier (1999), Collier and others (2003), Easterly and Levine (1997), Elbadawi and Sambanis (2000), and Sambanis (2003).

bility, Section IV analyzes the determinants of growth, and Section V offers conclusions.

Section II. Economic and Political Performance Since Independence

Summary of Economic Performance

Since gaining independence in 1960, the C.A.R.[2] economy has intermittently been adversely affected by political instability and social unrest, undermining various attempts to set the economy on a sustainable development path. Military coups, army mutinies, and extended labor disputes, combined with poor macroeconomic management and weak governance, have prevented the development of the country's rich and diverse endowment in natural resources and led to deteriorating economic and social performance. In particular, the chronic weak revenue performance has led to the accumulation of domestic wage and external debt arrears, as well as the degradation of basic social services. The country's woes have been compounded by a significant downward trend in its terms of trade since 1977. The accumulation of large arrears on and the irregular payments of wage to civil servants and military personnel have led to prolonged labor strikes and army mutinies. In spite of the C.A.R.'s efforts to pursue a democratization process in the 1990s, including the successful completion of two rounds of contested legislative and presidential elections in 1993 and 1999, the political situation was tenuous throughout the 1990s. By the late 1990s, the country was caught in a domestic and external debt trap, accentuating the dissatisfaction of the population—stemming from the wage arrears and deterioration in services—and the propensity of attempts to remove the presidency by military means.

The C.A.R. has been left behind in comparison with the group of sub-Saharan African countries (Table 7.2). During the period 1990–2000, the average economic, social, and infrastructure indicators

---

[2]The C.A.R. is a member of the French franc zone. Its currency, the *franc de la Communauté Financière Africaine* (the CFA franc), is issued by the Banque des États de l'Afrique Centrale (BEAC), and has been pegged to the euro since January 1999 at the fixed rate of €1 = CFAF 655.957. The BEAC is the central bank for six African countries—Cameroon, C.A.R., Chad, Equatorial Guinea, Gabon, and the Republic of Congo. The other members of the CFA franc zone are Benin, Burkina Faso, Côte d'Ivoire, Niger, Senegal, Togo, and, since 1984, Mali, whose common central bank is the Banque Centrale des États de l'Afrique de l'Ouest.

for the C.A.R. were weaker than the average for sub-Saharan African countries, despite receiving larger amounts of foreign aid. Life expectancy at birth, currently at about 43½ years, has been on a declining trend since 1990 and is among the lowest in sub-Saharan Africa. According to a recent report by the UN Conference on Trade and Development, about 70 percent of the population lives on less than US$1 per day (and about 86 percent lives on less than US$2 per day).

Per capita real GDP has been falling virtually continuously since 1977; notwithstanding the recent rise in output, per capita real GDP in 2002 was about two-thirds of its level in 1977. The nature of the crisis in the C.A.R. is illustrated in Figures 7.1–7.4 and is best understood by focusing on the various presidencies that ruled the country since 1960:

Table 7.2. Central African Republic and Sub-Saharan Africa: Comparative Economic and Social Performance
(Average during 1990–2000; in units indicated)

Performance Indicators	Central African Republic		Sub-Saharan Africa	
	1980s	1990s	1980s	1990s
Economic performance				
GDP per capita (constant 1995 U.S. dollars)	395.2	332	619	559
GDP growth (annual percent change)	0.9	1.4	2.2	2.1
GDP per capita growth (annual percent change)	−1.6	−0.9	−0.7	−0.5
Tax revenue (in percent of GDP)	9.3	8.0	20.2	20.9
Gross domestic savings (in percent of GDP)	−1.1	4.0	18.2	15.7
Gross domestic investment (in percent of GDP)	10.2	11.4	18.2	16.7
Trade in goods (in percent of GDP)	25.2	25.7	44.9	46.9
Cost structure				
Telephone, average cost of local call (US$ per three minutes)	...	0.71	...	0.08
External assistance				
Aid (in percent of gross national income)	14.7	13.4	4.4	5.7
Physical infrastructure/technology				
Roads, paved (in percent of total roads)	...	2.3	...	14.9
Mobile phones (per 1,000 people)	...	0.3	...	3.6
Personal computers (per 1,000 people)	...	1.4	...	8.1
Social performance				
Adult illiteracy rate (in percent of people ages 15 and above)	72.6	60.1	56.6	44.3
Primary school enrollment ratio (in percent)	72.9	57.7	78.2	75.0
Secondary school enrollment ratio (in percent)	14.8	10.1	17.5	24.6
Tertiary school enrollment ratio (in percent)	1.0	1.5	1.6	3.4
Immunization, DPT (in percent of children under 12 months)	23.8	53.6	40.5	51.5
Infant mortality rate (per 1,000 live births)	110.8	97.9	109.8	96.7
Life expectancy at birth (in years)	46.9	45.7	48.8	48.9

Sources: World Bank, social indicators database; and authorities in the Central African Republic.

- **Dacko presidency (1960–65):** Per capita real GDP fell by about 5½ percent on a cumulative basis, despite the large increase in the capital stock per person and the relative stability of the terms of trade. President Dacko was ousted by Jean-Bédel Bokassa, the army commander, in 1965 as the country faced bankruptcy and there were increasing signs of tensions from the labor unions.
- **Bokassa presidency (1965–79):** During the period 1965–77, per capita real GDP increased by about 10 percent on a cumulative basis. This was to a large extent owing to a program launched by the president (Opération Bokassa) to ensure adequate supplies of food crops, improve yields of export crops, and achieve a measure of diversification. This program received generous financial assistance from the international donor community. It appears that 1977 marked a turning point in the economic performance of the country; President Bokassa, who had already declared himself president for life in 1972, proclaimed himself emperor in 1977. The year 1977 also marks the start of a downward trend in the country's terms of trade. As the Bokassa presidency became much more repressive and brutal, foreign assistance to the country dwindled, and the country's capital stock per person started declining. By the end of this presidency, per capita real GDP also started falling, as did domestic revenue and expenditures. In 1979, Bokassa was ousted by David Dacko, the former president, after widespread protests in which many schoolchildren were massacred.
- **Dacko presidency (1979–81):** The slide in both per capita capital stock and per capita real GDP continued, with the latter falling by almost 11 percent during 1979–81. In 1981, President Dacko was deposed in a coup led by the army commander, André Kolingba.
- **Kolingba presidency (1981–93):** The country remained highly dependent on foreign aid. The slide in the capital stock on a per capita basis continued. Although the revenue-GDP ratio increased during 1981–84, it resumed its downward trend in the mid-1980s when the country's terms of trade declined sharply, reportedly compounded by the smuggling of diamonds. While an effort was made in the mid-1980s to bring the budget deficit under control, the need to jump-start the economy gave rise to an increasing expenditure-GDP ratio during 1986–91. The early 1990s was a tumultuous period for the C.A.R. as it underwent a protracted transition to democracy. Social tensions emerged in 1991 when a conflict with the labor movement led to a protracted general strike. As the public administration was paralyzed, tax collec-

Figure 7.1. Central African Republic: Per Capita Real GDP, 1960–2002
(In 1987 CFA francs; index 1960 = 100)

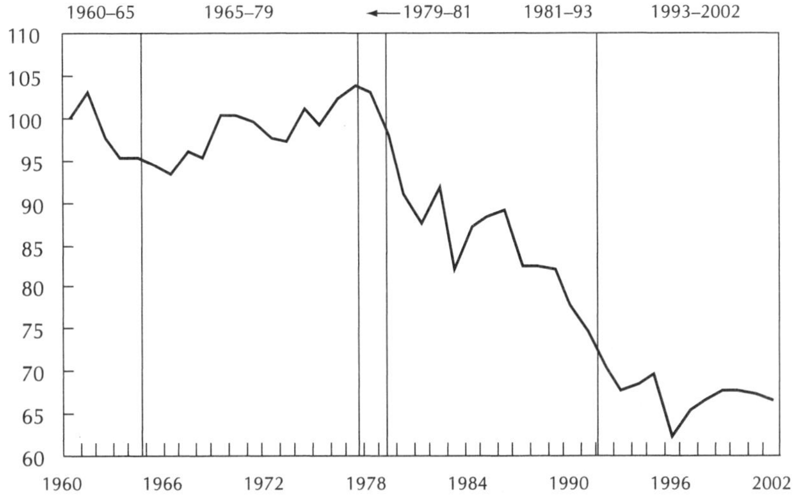

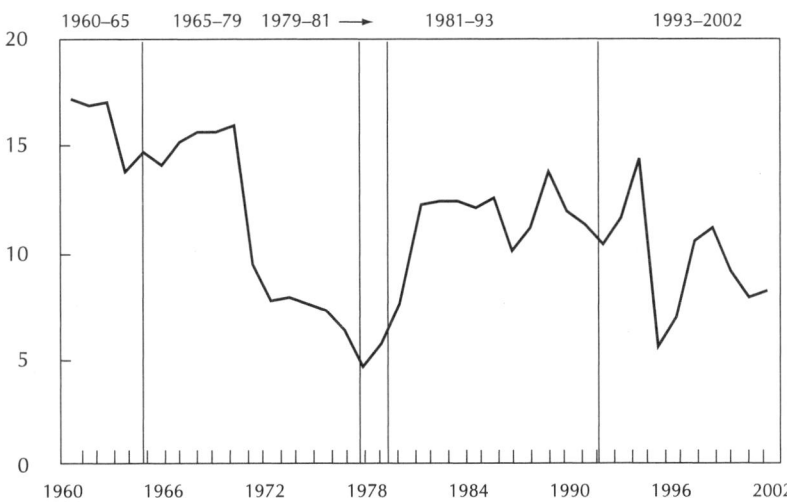

Sources: World Bank World Development Indicators; and IMF World Economic Outlook databases.

Figure 7.2. Central African Republic: Domestic Investment, 1960–2002
(In percent of GDP)

Sources: World Bank World Development Indicators; and IMF World Economic Outlook databases.

Figure 7.3. Central African Republic: Budgetary Performance, 1965–2002
(In percent of GDP)

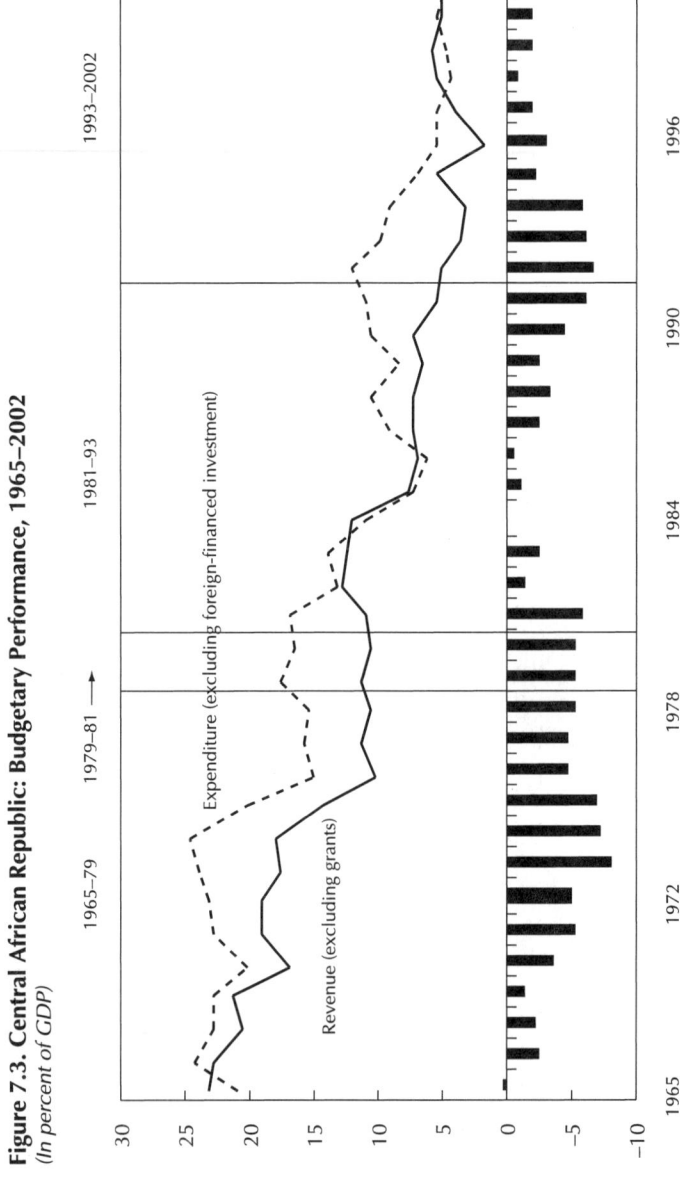

Sources: World Bank World Development Indicators; and IMF World Economic Outlook databases.

Figure 7.4. Central African Republic: Terms of Trade and Real Effective Exchange Rate, 1961–2002
(Index 1990 = 100)

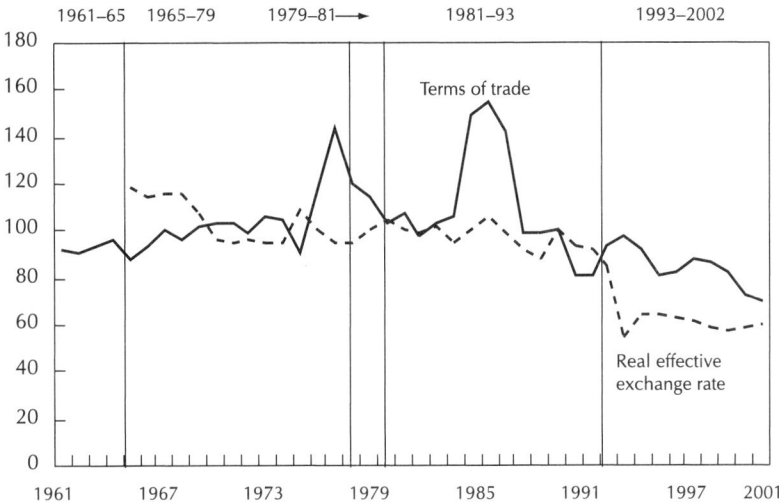

Sources: World Bank World Development Indicators; and IMF World Economic Outlook databases.

tions fell, depriving the government of the resources needed to meet domestic and external financial obligations. In particular, the government could not pay salaries on a regular basis, and arrears were accumulated. The country also suffered from an overvaluation of the CFA franc, which caused a sharp decline in the exports of coffee, cotton, and timber.

- **Patassé presidency (1993–March 2003):** Following one set of elections in 1992 that was annulled by President Kolingba on the grounds of irregularities, in 1993 Ange-Félix Patassé defeated Presidents Kolingba and Dacko to win the democratically held elections. By the time President Patassé took office, per capita real GDP was in a tailspin and the budget deficit was large. Per capita real GDP in 1993 was about two-thirds of its level in 1977. This had been accompanied by a significant decline in the per capita capital stock during the same period. Notwithstanding a number of setbacks, a series of efforts to put the economy back on track, especially as of 1998, started showing some results in terms of a slowly rising trend in revenues and fiscal consolidation. The decline in per capita real GDP was arrested in the mid-1990s, including by way of the boost provided by the devaluation of the CFA franc in 1994. Nonetheless, the propensity for attempted coups and civil disturbances was accentuated under the Patassé presidency. There was general dissatisfaction on the part of the population relating to massive wage arrears and the deterioration in services. The Patassé presidency was ended in March 2003 by a coup conducted by General Bozizé.

Qualitative Dimensions of the Crisis

Politics

An interesting feature of the C.A.R.'s political history over the past three decades or so relates to the fact that a few key personalities (Ange-Félix Patassé, François Bozizé, André Kolingba, and David Dacko) consistently have been the major players on the political scene. President Patassé was prime minister under President Bokassa in the late 1970s, and had himself staged an unsuccessful coup attempt in 1982 with General Bozizé. Mr. Kolingba seized power by force in 1981 and was President of the C.A.R. from 1981 to 1993; strong internal opposition forced this president to organize elections in the early 1990s. President Kolingba ran unsuccessfully for the presidency under democratically held elections in 1992; he was also involved in the May 2001 attempted coup. David Dacko, President of the C.A.R. during 1979–81, lost to President Patassé the democratically held elections in 1993. Mr. Bozizé, the author of the successful coup bid in March 2003, was an army general under President Bokassa in 1978, defense minister under President Dacko in 1979, and army chief under President Patassé.

A possible fundamental explanation for the rise in political instability in the C.A.R. since independence lies in the search for rents in this diamond-rich nation. Another possible reason, which became more significant in the second half of the 1990s and early 2000s, relates to the widespread dissatisfaction of the population owing to the accumulation of wage arrears and the decline in government services stemming from the lack of resources. In addition, the fact that the C.A.R. is in the midst of an unstable region has served to aggravate the inherent instability in the country. Ethnic tensions also play a role. Furthermore, the country's terms of trade have been on an almost secular downward trend since 1977.

Rent seeking

It is now well documented in the empirical literature that abundant natural resources (such as diamonds and oil) retard economic growth through political economy effects (e.g., Tornell and Lane, 1999) and increase corruption (Leite and Weidmann, 1999; Mauro, 1995). It is commonly understood that a primary channel of transmission from natural resources to poor economic performance is the fact that policymakers spend a significant amount of time on maximizing the associated rents from these resources for themselves and their associates. By implication, it also means that there may be intense competition by those close to power to access these scarce resources for personal and political gains. Collier and Hoeffler (2002) have shown that natural resources considerably increase the chances of civil conflict because the available rents can be used to finance rebellions. They estimate that countries with natural resources have a much higher probability of experiencing conflicts than those that do not.

Although it has not been formally documented, the rents available from the abundance of natural resources in the C.A.R. may have been an incentive to seize power. While diamonds (and, in recent years, timber) have been a source of wealth for the country, they have also been a source of fraud and corruption. Diamonds are valuable and easy to carry; it is well known that buyers in Antwerp, Belgium, have for years been declaring diamond imports from the C.A.R. that are higher than the country's reported exports. It is believed that this may be due to smuggling, sale of DRC or Angolan "conflict" diamonds via Bangui, and diamonds from non-African countries registered as those from the C.A.R.[3] Diamonds have allegedly been used by politicians to grease their patronage network. The abundance of natural resources also provides incentives for foreign players to get involved in the country, further complicating the security situation.

Ethnic tensions

The empirical literature has identified ethno-linguistic fractionalization (the probability that two randomly selected people from a country will not belong to the same ethnic or linguistic group) as a deterrent to growth (Sachs and Warner, 1997); these authors report that this probability is 83 percent in the C.A.R. versus an average of 64½ percent for sub-Saharan Africa. Indeed, it appears that ethnic considerations have been an aspect of the political scene in the C.A.R. in the past two decades. It is interesting to note that the first four presidents of the C.A.R. came from the south. Former President Kolingba, by naming several Yakomas to key positions, was instrumental in starting the

---

[3]See Dietrich (2002, pp. 18–23).

process of organizing a regime partially along ethnic lines. By the end of his presidency, more than two-thirds of the army soldiers were Yakomas. Former President Patassé, who comes from the north, followed this policy by appointing northerners to top jobs. By way of illustration, the top three political positions in the country (president, prime minister, and speaker of the national assembly) were all filled by people from the same region as President Patassé (Ouhan-M'pende). The organization of the presidency along ethnic lines was also apparent in the judiciary and among the managers of public companies.

Perhaps the most destabilizing aspect of the ethnic rift was the role of ethnic issues in the army. Because some soldiers put ethnic loyalty ahead of constitutional order, politicians relied on them to try to seize power by unconstitutional means. Ethnic considerations seem to have played a role in the May 2001 attempted coup. At that time, a majority of soldiers were Yakomas. It is widely believed that former President Kolingba, a Yakoma, who staged the unsuccessful coup, benefited from this ethnic connection to secure support from some soldiers. It appears, however, that the military events of late 2002 and early 2003 did not have a strong ethnic dimension. Former Army Chief of Staff François Bozizé, a Gbaya, also comes from the north.

Although ethnic considerations probably contributed to the country's problems, their importance should nevertheless not be overstated. The results of the empirical work undertaken by Collier and others (2003)—using the episodes of 52 civil wars that occurred between 1960 and 1999—show that ethnic diversity does not increase the likelihood that a country will fall into civil war. In addition, Collier and Hoeffler (2002) show that while ethnic diversity reduces the risk of conflict, there is a systematically higher risk of conflict in countries where one ethnic group represents 45–90 percent of the population.

External shocks

Diversification of the economy has been limited, and the industrialization process, which is hindered by high transportation and energy costs, remains slow. The country's high dependence on two principal export commodities (diamonds and timber) and imported oil makes the economy vulnerable to terms-of-trade shocks (Figure 7.4). Following a secular rise between 1961 and 1977, the country's terms of trade declined in an almost secular way, with the exception of the period 1985–87. The terms of trade and the per capita real GDP fell by about 52 percent and 36 percent, respectively, during 1977–2002. Thus, the sharp deterioration in the C.A.R.'s terms of trade can explain part of the severe output decline since 1979, but this explanation is mitigated by the secular depreciation in the country's real effective exchange rate since then, an outcome that counteracted part of the adverse effect of the decline in terms of trade.

Neighborhood effect

Recent research points to spillover effects of regional conflicts on the economic performance of a given country (Sambanis, 2003). Conflicts in neighboring countries also heighten the risk that the country itself will fall into civil war (Collier and others, 2003). Indeed, the C.A.R. is surrounded by Chad (on the north), Sudan (on the east), the Democratic Republic of the Congo (DRC) and the Republic of Congo (on the south), and Cameroon (on the west). Most of these countries have witnessed civil conflicts at one time or another during the period 1960–2002 (see Figure 7.5). In addition, the conflicts in neighboring countries have provided politicians with potential military allies. For example, former President Patassé received support from the Mouvement de Libération Congolais (MLC), a Congolese rebel movement led by Jean-Pierre Bemba and based in the neighboring DRC. The MLC troops helped his presidency fight off the May 2001 and October 2002 coup attempts. President Patassé also used Mr. Miskine, a Chadian rebel, as an ally. Partly as a consequence, Chad temporarily provided asylum to General Bozizé, the former C.A.R. army chief of staff who claimed responsibility for the October 2002 coup attempt and who eventually seized power in March 2003. It is also reported that the discovery of oil in Chad aggravated long-standing differences between the C.A.R. and Chad. Being a landlocked country, the C.A.R. depends on the DRC, the Republic of Congo, and Cameroon for access to ports via land or river. Conflicts in the DRC and the Republic of Congo can have serious adverse effects on the C.A.R. For example, in 2000, the civil unrest in the DRC prevented transport of goods by boat over the Congo and Oubangui Rivers, which necessitated more expensive transport by road via Cameroon.

Section III. Empirical Analysis of the Determinants of Political Instability

Leaving aside the qualitative factors noted above, this section seeks to analyze empirically the possible quantifiable factors behind the C.A.R.'s political instability. Some studies, such as that by Collier and others (2003), have found that poor economic performance raises the risk of a civil conflict. In the case of the C.A.R., this could well have

Figure 7.5. Central Africa Republic and Neighboring Countries: Per Capita GDP, 1960–2002[1]
(Index 1960 = 100)

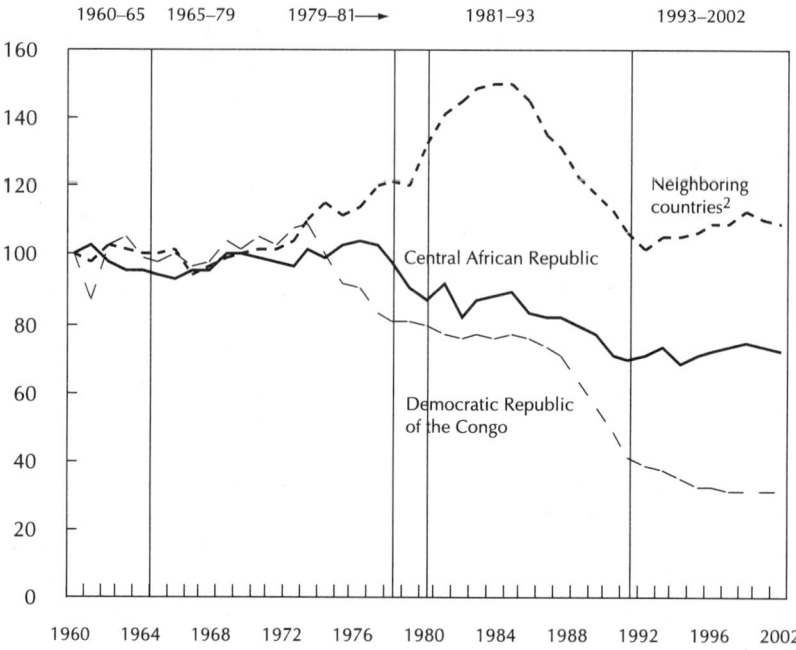

Sources: World Bank World Development Indicators; and IMF World Economic Outlook databases.
[1] Based on per capita GDP expressed in 1995 U.S. dollars.
[2] Based on weighted per capita GDP (expressed in 1995 U.S. dollars) of the DRC, Cameroon, Chad, Republic of Congo, and Sudan.

happened through the following circumstances. First, weak economic growth breeds frustration among the population, thus providing a fertile ground for a coup attempt. Second, low tax revenue, stemming from weak economic activity, may lead to the accumulation of arrears on the salaries of public employees (including especially soldiers' salaries) and create unrest and rebellions. This is often cited as a reason behind the military conflicts in the second half of the 1990s and early 2000s. Lack of resources also reduces the ability of the government to provide basic social services and security.

To test the above-mentioned hypotheses, a Probit model is estimated with data from the C.A.R. during 1967–2002. The model assesses the probability of a coup as a function of the previous year's real GDP growth rate, tax revenue (as a percentage of GDP), changes in the terms of trade, and political instability. A priori, the direction of the impact of a coup in the previous year is unclear. The model could raise the possibility of a coup in view of the destructive effect that conflicts have on the county's institutions, or it could lower the possibility in view of the end of destabilizing activities after a successful coup.

There is a potential endogeneity issue in the case of the relationship between revenue performance and political instability. It can be argued that low revenue is a consequence of political instability, not only its cause. Repeated coups undermine institutions, thus weakening the ability of the government to raise revenue. To test for this effect, we run a (two-lag) vector auto regression with revenue, GDP growth, political instability, and investment. This allows for a test of whether some of the variables used might help predict revenues. The results show that revenues are weakly exogenous to the system, suggesting that at an annual frequency political instability does not lead to low revenues.

The data were spliced from the series obtained from the International Monetary Fund World Economic Outlook and the World Bank World Development Indicators databases (see Table 7.3). The index of political instability is a dummy variable that takes a value equal to one in years during which there has been at least one attempted coup and zero otherwise. (We do not distinguish between failed and successful attempts.)

Table 7.3. Definitions and Sources of Variables

Variable	Definition
G	Real GDP growth.
g	Per capita real GDP growth.
$InvY$	Investment as a ratio to GDP (in constant terms).
$BudY$	Budget balance as a percent of GDP.
$RERg$	Rate of change of real effective exchange rate.
$TOTg$	Rate of change of the terms of trade.
PI	Dummy variable measuring political instability ($PI_t = 1$ in years in which there is an attempted coup or a rebellion; $PI_t = 0$ otherwise).
C	An indicator of possible economic or political contagion from border countries (Cameroon, Chad, Republic of Congo, the DRC, and Sudan). Measured as the growth rate of the weighted per capita real GDP of these countries expressed in 1995 constant U.S. dollars. The 1995 GDP weights are as follows: Cameroon (0.32), Chad (0.06), Republic of Congo (0.10), the DRC (0.23), and Sudan (0.29).
$Popug$	Population growth.
$revY$	Government revenue as a ratio to GDP.

Source: IMF staff estimates.

The following estimation model is used:

$$\mathrm{Prob}\big(PI_t = 1\big) = \Phi\big(ag_{t-1} + brevY_{t-1} + cTOTg_{t-1} + dPI_{t-1} + const\big), \quad (1)$$

where g is the real GDP growth rate, $revY$ is the revenue-GDP ratio, and $TOTg$ is the rate of change in terms of trade.[4]

The results of the Probit estimation are presented in Table 7.4. The impact of the revenue-GDP ratio and changes in terms of trade are statistically significant.[5] A decline of the revenue-GDP ratio by 1 percentage point raises the probability of a coup by about 3 percent. The two possible transmission channels are as follows. The accumulation of salary arrears or insufficient provision of basic social services could be a significant trigger for coup attempts.[6] However, it is also possible that low revenues reflect a more general weakening of the country's institutions, which in turn raises political instability.[7] The impact of terms-of-trade shocks, while modest, is statistically significant, in that a worsening of terms of trade by 10 percent raises the probability of a coup by about 4½ percent. Possible explanations for the role of terms-of-trade shocks include the following. First, a negative shock may weaken key economic sectors (such as cotton, diamond mining, and forestry), which might in turn trigger political instability (for example, because the incumbent is seen as unable to cope with the crisis). Second, adverse shocks can reduce the resources available for bribery. The country's main export products, diamonds and wood, are also its main sources of corruption.[8] Negative terms-of-trade shocks may lower the rent associated

---

[4]Some studies suggest that conflicts in neighboring countries can also increase the probability of a coup; unfortunately, the data do not exist to test this hypothesis. We attempted to partially control for this effect by including a dummy variable for conflicts in the DRC, constructed by Akitoby and Cynyabuguma (2004). To do so did not change the estimated coefficients, although the estimates were somewhat noisier.

[5]Given the correlation between per capita real GDP and the revenue-GDP ratio, it is possible that the latter potentially captures the impact of lower per capita real GDP on political instability. Adding per capita real GDP into the estimation leaves the coefficient on revenue virtually unchanged, although it loses its statistical significance at the 10 percent level. Per capita real GDP is also not significant at the 10 percent level when substituted for the revenue-GDP ratio in the estimation. These results suggest that revenue is an appropriate variable to include in the Probit estimation.

[6]Time series for the corresponding variables are nonexistent.

[7]The PRS Group compiles data measuring institutional quality for many countries, including some in sub-Saharan Africa. The C.A.R. is not covered. The estimation cannot directly control for institutional quality.

[8] See Dietrich (2002) on the influence of diamonds on governance in the C.A.R.

with the export of these commodities and the resources available to corrupt politicians for easing their patronage networks, thus weakening their political position. The coefficient on past real GDP growth has the expected sign (poor growth translates into more instability), but is statistically insignificant. Finally, a coup attempt in a given year is estimated to raise the probability of another coup in the next period (by about 11 percent), but this effect is not statistically significant.

Figure 7.6 plots the probability of a coup attempt predicted by our model. It shows that the latter captures the four main clusters of instability (late 1970s/early 1980s, early 1990s, mid-1990s, and early 2000s) relatively well. It does also, however, predict high probability of unrest in the late 1980s, although there was no coup attempt at that time. Overall, these results suggest that the ability of the government to raise sufficient revenues (or, possibly, to maintain institutional quality) and adverse terms-of-trade shocks played a significant role in the country's political instability.

Although these results should be treated with caution, they may have some possible policy implications. They may suggest that improving the C.A.R.'s capacity to mobilize domestic revenue, to diversify the economy (to make it less vulnerable to terms-of-trade shocks), and to fight corruption could help to reduce the recurrence of adverse political events in the country.

Section IV. Growth Determinants

This section investigates the determinants of growth in the C.A.R. and, in particular, the possible impact of political instability, using a version of the neoclassical growth model that takes the following form:

$$G_t = InvY_t + BudY_t + RERg_t + TOTg_t + C_t + PI_t + Popug_t + v_t, \qquad (2)$$

Table 7.4. C.A.R.: Probit Estimation of the Propensity of Political Instability

Variable	Coefficient	t-ratio	Slope[1]
Real GDP growth (g_{t-1})	–6.770	1.24	–1.21
Revenue-GDP ratio ($revY_{t-1}$)	–0.167	2.68**	–3.01
Political instability, previous year (PI_{t-1})	0.605	1.85	10.8
Rate of change in terms of trade ($TOTg_{t-1}$)	–4.32	3.78***	–0.46
Constant (const)	0.822	0.48	-

Source: IMF staff estimates.
Notes: *** and ** indicate significance at the 5 and 10 percents levels, respectively.
[1] The slope is the marginal effect of the variable on the probability of a coup.

Figure 7.6. Central African Republic: Predicted Probability of an Attempted Coup or Rebeliion, 1967–2002

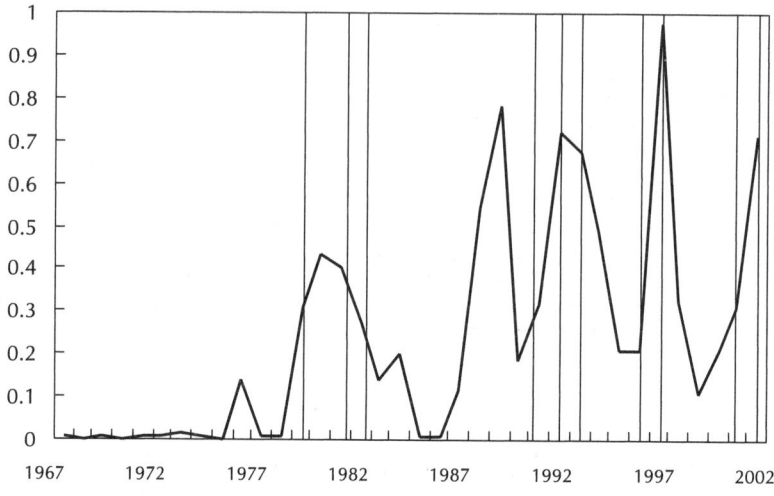

Source: IMF staff estimates.
Note: The vertical lines correspond to attempted coups or rebellion.

where G_t is real GDP growth; $InvY_t$ is the investment-GDP ratio; $BudY_t$ is the budget balance–GDP ratio; $RERg_t$ and $TOTg_t$ are the rates of change in real effective exchange rate and the terms of trade, respectively; C_t is the per capita real GDP growth in neighboring countries;[9] PI_t is a variable measuring political instability; $Popug_t$ is population growth; and v_t is a random disturbance term. Equation (2) is estimated using annual data for the period 1967–2002.

The empirical results are presented in Table 7.5. In line with previous studies[10] on sub-Saharan Africa, the impact of investment on growth in the C.A.R. is statistically significant. In addition, the C.A.R. appears particularly vulnerable to shocks from neighboring countries. A decrease by 1 percent in the weighted per capita real GDP growth rate in neighboring countries reduces per capita real GDP growth in the C.A.R. by about 0.35 percent. Changes in the real effective exchange

---

[9]These border countries are Cameroon, Chad, Republic of Congo, the DRC, and Sudan. C_t is measured as the growth rate of the weighted per capita real GDP of these countries expressed in 1995 constant U.S. dollars. 1995 GDP weights are used.

[10]See, for example, Ghura and Hadjimichael (1996) and Akitoby and Cynyabuguma (Chapter 6).

Table 7.5. Central Africa Republic: Determinants of Economic Growth, 1967–2002[1]

Variable	Coefficient	t value
Investment-GDP ratio (*InvY*)	0.2857	2.92***
Budget balance–GDP ratio (*BudY*)	0.2516	0.97
Rate of change in real exchange rate (*RERg*)	–0.0758	–1.31
Rate of change in terms of trade (*TOTg*)	0.0449	0.89
Economic contagion (*C*)	0.3688)	2.37***
Political instability (*PI*)	–0.5163	–0.38
Population growth (*Popug*)	–0.5077	–1.45

Source: IMF staff estimates.

Note: *** indicates significance at the 5 percent level.

[1] The *R*-square of the regression is 0.37. We check for serial correlation of the disturbances by running a Durbin-Watson test. The Durbin-Watson statistic is 2.88, which is greater than the 5 percent upper-bound for our parameters (1.9). We therefore cannot reject the null of no autocorrelation.

rate—an indicator of external competitiveness—and in terms of trade have the expected sign, but are not statistically significant. The dummy variable for political instability has the expected negative sign (an attempted coup reduces real GDP growth by about half a percent), but it also is not statistically significant. The latter could be due to the fact that most of the adverse military events in the C.A.R. have been relatively low in intensity, limiting the scale of immediate economic disruption. It is also possible that the impact of political instability on growth is registered indirectly through the investment channel. In any event, the frequency of political instability has created an unstable economic environment, which has discouraged investment and annihilated prospects for long-term growth.

These results are rather robust to the impact of additional variables. Fosu (2001) argues that political instability can have an impact on economic growth, not only directly but also through the efficiency with which factors of production affect growth. This hypothesis is tested by adding variables *InvY*PI* and *Popug*PI* into the regression. Both variables are statistically insignificant, and adding them in the regression does not affect the results. It is also possible that changes in the real exchange rate affect growth with a lag. With this in mind, we then add the corresponding variable into the regression and find the effect of lagged changes in real exchange rate on growth is statistically insignificant, with the result that the core results remain unchanged. Finally, we add a constant term into the regression and find that the impact of the investment ratio, while remaining positive, loses its statistical significance at conventional levels of confidence.

Section V. Conclusions

This chapter analyzes the political instability and economic growth nexus in the C.A.R. during the period 1967–2002. Since gaining independence in 1960, the C.A.R. economy has intermittently been adversely affected by political instability and social unrest. Military coups, army rebellions, and extended labor disputes, combined with poor macroeconomic management and weak governance, have prevented the development of the country's rich and diverse endowment in natural resources and have led to deteriorating economic and social performance. In particular, the chronic weak revenue performance led to the accumulation of domestic wage and external debt arrears and the degradation of basic social services. The accumulation of large arrears on and the irregular payments of wage to civil servants and military personnel led to prolonged labor strikes and army rebellions.

Empirical results first show that a low domestic revenue–GDP ratio and an adverse terms-of-trade shock significantly raise the probability of a coup. Weak revenue performance undermines the government's ability to pay civil servants' wages and to provide basic social services, which may raise frustration among the population and trigger political instability. Insufficient economic diversification and weak institutions (that allow corruption) also leave the country vulnerable to terms-of-trade shocks, which may raise political instability. Economic growth is positively influenced by increases in investment, but adversely affected by a slowdown in economic activity in neighboring countries. A second conclusion is that the direct impact of political instability on growth is not significant once account is taken of domestic investment in the C.A.R. and economic performance in neighboring countries.

These results suggest that efforts to enhance the government's capacity to mobilize revenue would lower the probability of conflicts along with bringing economic benefits on its own. In a transitional period—in which internal efforts are being made to raise domestic revenues to a level high enough for the government to pay public employee salaries and offer basic services—there is a role for the international community to play by offering budgetary support. Also, the diversification of the country's economic base would not only make its economy less vulnerable to external shocks, but would also reduce the propensity of terms-of-trade shocks to fuel political instability. Although such efforts cannot substitute for building the necessary strong and efficient institutions, they might nonetheless help the country escape the poverty and governance trap in which it has been caught for several decades.

Finally, the results indicate that efforts in neighboring countries, such as the DRC, to resolve conflicts and get their economies back on the path of sustained economic growth would be beneficial for the C.A.R.'s economic performance.

References

Collier, Paul, 1999, "On the Economic Consequences of Civil War," *Oxford Economic Papers*, Vol. 51 (January), pp. 163–83.

Collier, Paul, and Anke Hoeffler, 2002, "Greed and Grievance in African Civil Wars," CSAE Working Paper No. WPS/2002-01 (Oxford: Centre for African Economies).

Collier, Paul, and others, 2003, *Breaking the Conflict Trap: Civil War and Development Policy* (New York: Oxford University Press for the World Bank).

Dietrich, Christian, 2002, "Hard Currency: The Criminalized Diamond Economy of the Democratic Republic of Congo and its Neighbors," Occasional Paper 4 (Ottawa: Partnership Africa-Canada, International Peace Information Service, Network for Justice and Development).

Easterly, William, and Ross Levine, 1997, "Africa's Growth Tragedy: Policies and Ethnic Divisions," *Quarterly Journal of Economics*, Vol. 112 (November), pp. 1203–50.

Elbadawi, Ibrahim, and Nicholas Sambanis, 2000, "Why Are There So Many Civil Wars in Africa? Understanding and Preventing Violent Conflict," *Journal of African Economies*, Vol. 9 (October), pp. 244–69.

Fosu, Augustin Kwasi, 2001, "Political Instability and Economic Growth in Developing Economies: Some Specification Empirics," *Economics Letters*, Vol. 70 (February), pp. 289-94.

Ghura, Dhaneshwar, and Michael T. Hadjimichael, 1996, "Growth in Sub-Saharan Africa," *Staff Papers*, International Monetary Fund, Vol. 43 (September), pp. 605–34.

Leite, Carlos, and Jens Weidmann, 1999, "Does Mother Nature Corrupt? Natural Resources, Corruption and Economic Growth," IMF Working Paper WP/99/85 (Washington: International Monetary Fund).

Mauro, Paulo, 1995, "Corruption and Growth," *Quarterly Journal of Economics*, Vol. 90, pp. 681–712.

Sachs, Jeffrey, and Andrew Warner, 1997, "Sources of Slow Growth in African Economies," *Journal of African Economies*, Vol. 6, No. 3, pp. 335–76.

Sambanis, Nicholas, 2003, "Using Case Studies to Expand the Theory of Civil War," CPR Working Paper No. 5 (Washington: World Bank).

Tornell, Aaron, and Philip Lane, 1999, "Voracity Effect," *American Economic Review*, Vol. 89 (March), pp. 22–46.

8

Empirical Evidence of the Sources of Hyperinflation and Falling Currency

The Democratic Republic of the Congo (DRC) experienced hyperinflation throughout the 1990s. For instance, from October 1990 to December 1995, the cumulative increase in prices was 6.3 billion percent, while the local currency underwent a free fall on the parallel foreign exchange market. This chapter reviews the DRC's experience of hyperinflation and falling currency. Section I describes the causes and consequences of such dramatic hyperinflation and prolonged currency depreciation; Section II analyzes the theoretical and empirical bases of the policies that were implemented to break the vicious circle of hyperinflation and falling currency; and Section III highlights the main conclusions and their policy implications.

Section I. Causes and Macroeconomic Consequences of Hyperinflation in the DRC

Causes of Hyperinflation

The primary cause of hyperinflation in the DRC lay in the uncontrolled budgetary deficit financed by money creation. There was a strong correlation among the fiscal deficit (on a cash basis), net credit to the government, and the average inflation rate (as measured by the CPI). The deficit arose from the breakdown of public administration against the backdrop of political instability, governance problems, civil strife, and war. In this context, there was an extraordinary weakening of fiscal performance, as evidenced by the fall in fiscal revenue and the collapse of the expenditure control system.

Reflecting the drop in revenue and the surging of expenditure, the government cash deficit reached extremely high levels. In the absence of external borrowing options, recourse was taken to central bank credit to finance the budget.[1] As a result, the government accounted for the bulk of the increase in money, thereby completely crowding out the private sector. Broad money grew by 160 percent in 1998, 382 percent in 1999, and 493 percent in 2000, while net credit to the government surged by 104 percent, 392 percent, and 317 percent, respectively, during the same three years.

Macroeconomic Consequences of Hyperinflation

The vicious circle of hyperinflation led to a breakdown of financial intermediation, an uncontrolled spiral of exchange rate depreciation, increased dollarization, and it compounded the fall in fiscal revenue. Moreover, by creating macroeconomic instability and uncertainty, and jeopardizing the transactions role of money, hyperinflation also had a contractionary impact on key macroeconomic variables, such as investment, savings, GDP, and real wages.

Financial disintermediation

Owing to the collapse of the domestic payments system, banks ceased operating as financial institutions. Sight deposits represented less than 2 percent of broad money over the 1996–2000 period, and were largely demonetized, as checks and bank transfers were used almost exclusively for transactions with the central government, at a steep discount. A shortage of banknotes prevented banks from withdrawing excess reserves from the central bank. The excess reserves of commercial banks were equivalent to about 50 percent of their local currency deposit base. In the absence of formal financial intermediation, banking activity was confined to the brokerage of foreign exchange transactions between importers and exporters.[2]

Depreciation of the parallel market exchange rate

As a direct consequence of the hyperinflation, the parallel market exchange rate experienced a sharp depreciation. There was a strong

---

[1]The accumulation of external payments arrears with multilateral and bilateral creditors prevented the contracting of new loans.

[2]See Chapter 9 on financial intermediation.

correlation between the inflation rate and the parallel exchange rate, suggesting that the latter truly reflected the differential of inflation rates, as predicted by the theory of relative purchasing power. Since the fixing of the official exchange rate, the gap between the official and parallel exchange rates widened, rising from 44 percent at the end of 1998 to about 600 percent in May 2001.

Dollarization

As in most cases of hyperinflation, several years of hyperinflation left a trail of strong inertial inflationary expectations and an extensive dollarization of the economy,[3] based on informal institutions and arrangements centered on exchange bureaus. The dollarization was fueled both by currency substitution and asset-substitution practices. The quoting of prices in foreign currency terms (U.S. dollars and Belgian francs) was pervasive, and most people, including wage earners, relied on foreign currency as a store of value.

Decline in fiscal revenue

Hyperinflation reduced nonmining government revenue in real terms, thereby contributing to rising fiscal deficits. This adverse impact came about through two channels: (1) Because the tax system was not indexed, the usual lags in collection, combined with manipulated delays in payment, led to the erosion of real revenues. This negative effect is known as the Tanzi-Olivera effect.[4] The importance of the Tanzi-Olivera effect in the context of hyperinflation has been underscored by Dornbusch (1993). (2) With the deterioration in tax compliance, the tax yield of a given tax structure declined. Moreover, the tax base shrank as a result of the decline in economic activity and the thriving nonofficial economy.

Depressed investment and saving

As shown by Fischer (1993) and Barro (1995), hyperinflation has a negative impact on capital formation by creating macroeconomic instability and uncertainty. This negative impact on investment spending in real terms was also present in the case of the DRC. In parallel with the decline in investment, domestic saving was discouraged by interest rates that were substantially negative in real terms. In addition, as hy-

---

[3]More than 85 percent of private sector bank deposits were denominated in foreign exchange, and foreign currency circulated widely.
[4]See Olivera (1967) and Tanzi (1977, 1978).

perinflation made the holding of real balances more expensive than consumption, households consumed more and saved less.

Output contraction

The negative impact on output came about mainly through the investment channel. In the DRC, prolonged depressed investment led to a sharp decline in output.

Decline in real wages

Several years of hyperinflation all but eroded real wages in both the private and public sectors. Data compiled by the central bank show that in the private sector the real wage index declined by more than 99 percent during 1996–99. The decline could be attributed to inelastic labor supply and to an insufficiently flexible wage setting in the face of hyperinflation. In the public sector, wages also experienced a sharp decline in real terms, despite frequent wage increases. The erosion of wages depressed the consumption of wage earners (considered to have a high marginal propensity to consume), thereby contributing to output contraction.

Section II. Breaking the Vicious Circle of Hyperinflation and Falling Currency

Breaking the vicious circle of hyperinflation and falling currency in the DRC required a decisive stabilization policy, underpinned by a strong political will. The experience gained from short-lived stabilization efforts in 1995 and 1997 clearly showed how to lend credibility to the anti-inflation strategy: a substantial tightening of the fiscal stance was key to breaking the vicious circle of hyperinflation and falling currency. The anti-inflation program, therefore, included revenue-enhancing and expenditure-restraining measures. However, improving revenue collection and effectively controlling expenditure required strong political commitment. As described in Chapter 2, the new government of the DRC demonstrated its commitment in this area.

Analytical Framework for Stabilization Program

The following analytical model, which captures the specificities of the DRC's economy, shows how the recourse to money creation for financing large fiscal deficits created hyperinflation dynamics.

Consider an open economy with exogenous output (y_t).

Government deficit

The government cannot issue bonds to the public and finances its primary deficit solely through seignorage, while interest payments on foreign public debt are accumulated as arrears. The government budget in nominal terms is given by the following:

$$D_t = (g_t - \mu_t) \cdot P_t \cdot y_t, \tag{1}$$

where g_t is noninterest expenditure (as a share of nominal GDP), μ_t is government revenue (as a share of nominal GDP), and P_t is the price of output.

The financing of the deficit is given by:

$$D_t = \dot{M}_t, \tag{2}$$

where $\dot{M}_t$ is the change in nominal money stock at a given time t.

Money market equilibrium

The demand for money can be summarized by the quantity equation:

$$M_t \cdot V_t = P_t \cdot y_t, \tag{3}$$

where income velocity of money, V_t, is assumed to be variable, as is the case in a country with high inflation.

We further assume that velocity is a linear function of money growth:

$$V_t = \alpha + \beta \cdot V_{t-1} + \gamma \cdot \hat{M}_{t-1} \qquad \alpha, \beta, \text{ and } \gamma > 0; \tag{4}$$

where $\wedge$ denotes the percentage change. This specification of velocity implies that inflation expectations are adaptive.

Household decisions

We assume that the country's financial system is largely underdeveloped and the economy is highly dollarized. Accordingly, the nominal wealth of the representative household consists of nominal money stock and foreign currency (because of the extensive dollarization of the economy). The constraint on the household budget flow is given by the following:

$$\dot{M}_t + \left(\alpha{\cdot}E_t + [1-\alpha]{\cdot}E_t^p\right){\cdot}\dot{F}_t = (1-\mu_t){\cdot}P_t{\cdot}y_t - C_t, \tag{5}$$

where E_t denotes the official exchange rate, which is fixed; E_t^p the parallel market rate; F_t the stock of foreign currency; α the share of transactions carried out at the official rate; and C_t nominal consumption.

For simplicity, we assume that consumption is a share of nominal GDP ($C_t = \delta_t \cdot P_t y_t$).

Balance of payments

As is the case in the DRC, we assume that the country is faced with no external borrowing options and does not service its external debt, and therefore incurs arrears in external interest payments and amortization. Therefore, in the absence of private capital flows in the capital account, the change in foreign reserves is equal to the current account excluding interest payments:

$$X_t - IM_t = \left(\alpha{\cdot}E_t + [1-\alpha]{\cdot}E_t^p\right){\cdot}\dot{F}_t, \tag{6}$$

where X_t denotes exports, which are assumed exogenous in dollar terms ($X_t = (\alpha \cdot E_t + (1-\alpha) \cdot E_t^p) \cdot \bar{X}$), and IM_t is imports defined as a fixed share of GDP ($IM_t = m \cdot P_t y_t$).

The parallel market rate is defined by a modified version of the relative purchasing power theory:

$$\hat{E}_t^p = \lambda{\cdot}\left(\hat{P}_t - \hat{P}_t^*\right), \tag{7}$$

where P_t^* denotes the foreign price level. This equation captures the fact that in the DRC the depreciation of the parallel market rate is highly correlated with the inflation rate.

Goods market equilibrium

The above model is closed and fully determined. Combining equations (1), (2), (5), and (6) yields the market-clearing condition on the goods market:

$$P_t y_t = C_t + g_t{\cdot}P_t y_t + X_t - IM_t. \tag{8}$$

Solution of the Model: Hyperinflation Dynamics

The model can be solved to show how large fiscal deficits can generate hyperinflation dynamics, which, in turn leads to uncontrolled depreciation of the parallel market exchange rate.

The linear approximation of the percentage change of equation (3) yields the inflation rate[5]

$$\hat{P}_t = \sigma_1 \cdot \hat{M}_t + \sigma_2 \cdot \hat{V}_t, \tag{9}$$

where σ_1 and σ_2 are parameters. For simplicity, we assume that real output growth is zero.

From equation (3), M_t is given by

$$M_t = \frac{P_t \cdot y_t}{V_t}. \tag{10}$$

Equations (1) and (2) imply that

$$\frac{\dot{M}_t}{P_t} = (g_t - \mu_t) \cdot y_t. \tag{11}$$

Substituting equations (10) and (11) in (9) yields

$$\hat{P}_t = \sigma_1 \cdot (g_t - \mu_t) \cdot V_t + \sigma_2 \cdot \hat{V}_t. \tag{12}$$

Equation (12) clearly shows how uncontrolled fiscal deficits can trigger a spiral of hyperinflation and falling currency. First, past fiscal deficits financed through seignorage lead to an exponential growth in the income velocity of money, which, in turn, affects the current inflation rate. Second, the current deficit $(g_t - \mu_t)$ also has a direct impact on the current inflation rate. Through equation (7), the hyperinflation spiral will translate into a spiral of exchange rate depreciation. Thus, the only way of breaking a vicious circle of hyperinflation and falling

---

[5]For high inflation, the sum of money and velocity growth rates is no longer a good approximation of the actual inflation rate.

currency is to drastically reduce the fiscal deficit, which will lead to a decline in income velocity.

Empirical Evidence for the DRC

Exchange rate dynamics

We estimate equation (7) using monthly data over the period 1990–2000. By applying the ordinary least squares method to the data, we obtain the following results:

$$\hat{E}_t^p = -0.24 + 1.03\left(\hat{P}_t - P_t^*\right) \qquad R^2 = 0.67$$
$$(2.88) \quad (0.06) \qquad\qquad df = 129 \qquad\qquad (13)$$
$$t \ = \ (-0.085) \ (16.25) \qquad F_{1,129} = 264.24.$$

Examining the results, we observe that the estimated λ is positive, in accordance with prior expectations. The estimated value suggests that a 1 percent increase in the inflation differential will lead to 1.03 percent depreciation in the parallel market exchange rate. As to the significance of the estimated slope coefficient, the null hypothesis that there is no relationship between inflation and exchange rate depreciation can be rejected at a 0.01 percent level of significance. As the estimated intercept coefficient is not statistically different from zero, we reestimate the equation without an intercept, which gives the following results:

$$\hat{E}_t^p = 1.03\left(\hat{P}_t - P_t^*\right) \qquad R^2 = 0.67$$
$$(0.05) \qquad\qquad df = 130 \qquad\qquad (14)$$
$$t \ = \ (19.4).$$

Inflation dynamics

The data used are annual data for the period 1990–2000. Given the short span of the data, these estimates should be interpreted with caution, because the robustness of the results would need to be tested on longer data series.

We estimate the following modified version of the inflation equation:

$$\hat{P}_t = \beta_1 + \beta_2 \cdot DEFG_t + \beta_3 \cdot \hat{V}_t, \qquad\qquad (15)$$

where $DEFG_t$ is the government cash deficit as a share of GDP, and $\hat{V}_t$ is the percentage change in income velocity of money. The ordinary least squares regression's results are as follows:

$$
\begin{aligned}
\hat{P}_t &= 171.6 + 253.3\,(DEFG_t) + 27.9\,\hat{V}_t \qquad R^2 = 0.74 \\
& (844.1) \quad (114.13) \qquad\quad (5.77) \qquad\quad df = 8 \qquad (16) \\
t &= (0.20) \quad (2.22) \qquad\qquad\quad (4.83) \qquad\quad F_{2,8} = 11.89.
\end{aligned}
$$

As the estimated intercept coefficient is not statistically significant, we also run the regression without an intercept:

$$
\begin{aligned}
\hat{P}_t &= 271.4\,(DEFG_t) + 28.4\,\hat{V}_t \qquad R^2 = 0.74 \\
& (67.38) \qquad\quad (5.01) \qquad\quad df = 9 \qquad (17) \\
t &= (4.02) \qquad\qquad (5.66).
\end{aligned}
$$

Both estimated coefficients are overwhelmingly significant, and their signs are in accordance with prior expectations. The coefficient of the budget deficit is very large, implying a rapid disinflation in response to a small decline in the budget deficit ratio from its current level. Indeed, in 2001 the implementation of restrained monetary and fiscal policies, centered on strict adherence to a monthly treasury cash-flow plan, led to the breaking of hyperinflation and the stabilization of the exchange rate under the floating exchange rate system introduced in May 2001. Inflation decelerated sharply from a monthly average of 18 percent during the period January–May preceding the stabilization program (an annualized rate of 632 percent) to 0.7 percent during June–December 2001 (an annualized rate of 8.8 percent). The difference between the official exchange rate (reference rate) and the free market rate fell from about 600 percent prior to June 2001 to less than 1 percent at the end of December 2001.

Section III. Concluding Remarks

The monetization of fiscal deficits was identified as the primary source of hyperinflation in the DRC. The spiral of hyperinflation led to negative economic consequences, including a spiral of exchange rate depreciation, financial disintermediation, depressed investment and saving, and output contraction.

Based on the proposed analytical framework, a substantial tightening of fiscal policy, coupled with a money-based stabilization program, was implemented and succeeded in breaking the vicious cycle of hyperinflation in the DRC. As expected, in light of the strong relationship between inflation and the exchange rate, breaking the cycle of hyperinflation stabilized the exchange rate, while, at the same time, the parallel market exchange rate premium vanished.

References

Barro, Robert, 1995, "Inflation and Economic Growth," *Bank of England Quarterly Bulletin*, Vol. 35 (May), pp. 166–76.

Dornbusch, Rudiger, 1993, "Lessons from Experiences with High Inflation," in *Stabilization, Debt, and Reform: Policy Analysis for Developing Countries* (New York: Harvester Wheatsheaf).

Fischer, Stanley, 1993, "The Role of Macroeconomic Factors in Growth," *Journal of Monetary Economics*, Vol. 32 (December), pp. 485–512.

Olivera, J.H., 1967, "Money, Prices and Fiscal Lags: A Note on the Dynamics of Inflation," *Banca Nationale del lavoro Quarterly Review*, Vol. 20 (September), pp. 258–67.

Tanzi, Vito, 1977, "Inflation, Lags in Collection and the Real Value of Tax Revenue," *Staff Papers*, International Monetary Fund, Vol. 24, pp. 154–67.

———, 1978, "Inflation, Real Tax Revenue, and the Case for Inflationary Finance: Theory with an Application to Argentina," *Staff Papers*, International Monetary Fund, Vol. 25 (September), pp. 417–51.

9

Challenges to Financial Intermediation in the Democratic Republic of the Congo

BERNARD LAURENS AND WIM FONTEYNE

For a number of years, the financial system [including the Central Bank of the Congo or BCC (Banque Centrale du Congo)] in the Democratic Republic of the Congo (DRC) has operated with limited resources in a climate of uncertainty created by political instability, civil war, and macroeconomic mismanagement. This difficult environment has resulted in major dysfunctions and evident weaknesses. In particular, the financial system has become irrelevant in mobilizing savings and providing credit to the economy. Empowered by the promulgation of a new central bank law enshrining its independence and a new banking law, the BCC has taken measures to remedy these weaknesses and help create the preconditions for a revival of financial intermediation. Although prospects have clearly improved, the challenges ahead are enormous. Technical, financial, and human resource needs are already considerable and are likely to increase as reunification progresses. This chapter discusses the challenges the BCC faces in seeking a resumption of financial intermediation. Section I offers an overview of the situation of the financial system following several years of political instability, macroeconomic mismanagement and the resulting hyperinflation, and of the initial response of the monetary authorities. It analyzes the causes of the unique monetary experience of the DRC that has been characterized by nonfungibility between the components of base money. Section II describes the policy measures

236

that have been implemented by the monetary authorities to restore the fungibility of base money and subsequently shift to conventional monetary management, still in a context of low financial intermediation. Section III reviews the policy measures that, in the medium term, would foster reintermediation and dedollarization in the DRC context. Section IV draws some policy lessons from the DRC experience.

Section I. Developments in the Financial System

The Banking System in a Context of Disintermediation and Dollarization

Financial intermediation in the DRC has remained low, despite the significant progress made in macroeconomic stabilization since 2001, through government economic programs supported by an International Monetary Fund staff-monitored program (SMP) and a successor three-year arrangement under the Poverty Reduction and Growth Facility (PRGF). This low intermediation reflects (1) the importance of the informal, cash-based economy; (2) the continued low public confidence in the banking system—a result of, among other things, the recent experience of nonfungibility between cash and bank deposits, the poor financial health of the banks, and the lack of publicly available and reliable information on the soundness of financial institutions; (3) high fees and stringent conditions for the opening of bank accounts, in particular a requirement to maintain high minimum balances; (4) the banking system's limited coverage of the DRC's territory; and (5) certain policies that discourage bank transactions (see below). Consequently, the rate of financial penetration is very low: the DRC, with a population of about 55 million, has only 35,000 bank accounts, of which almost half are held by businesses. Congolese franc (CGF) bank deposits represent less than 15 percent of the money supply in Congolese francs, and the money supply itself (broad money, M2) amounts to only about 5 percent of GDP (see Figure 9.1). Broad money consists for almost 50 percent of currency in circulation and for 40 percent of deposits denominated in foreign exchange. The banking sector, which forms the bulk of the formal financial sector,[1] has played a limited role in the economy since the early 1990s. Its total assets only

---

[1]The financial system consists of 10 banks, 5 nonbank financial institutions, a network of credit unions, and some 110 microfinance institutions. In addition, eight banks deemed nonviable have been closed and are being liquidated. No reliable data are available on the consolidated balance sheet of the nonbank financial institutions.

Figure 9.1. Financial Aggregates in the Democratic Republic of the Congo and a Sample of Other Countries, 2001–02
(In percent of GDP)

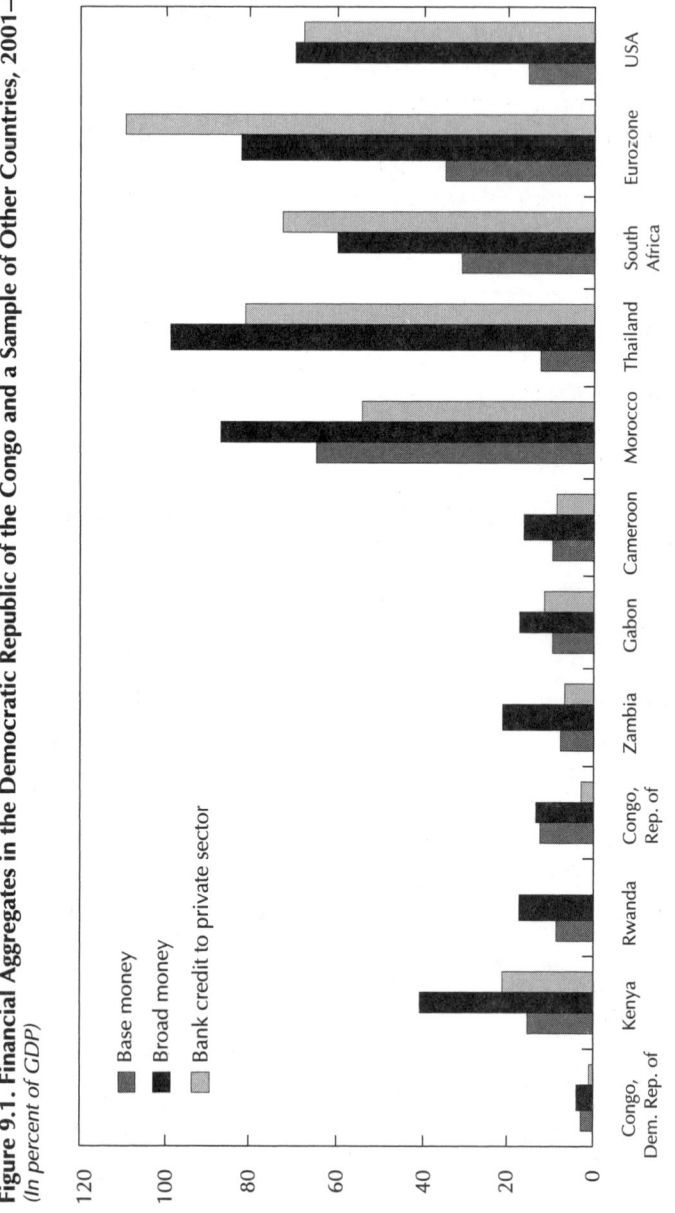

Sources: IMF; International Financial Statistics; and others to end-2002.

amount to about 5 percent of GDP (Table 9.1), and credit to the private sector is negligible, even as a share of an already low GDP. A comparison with other countries shows clearly how low financial aggregates have fallen in the DRC, even when compared with neighboring African countries (Figure 9.1).

The low level of financial intermediation is also reflected in the small contribution of the commercial banking sector (excluding the BCC) to money creation. Credit denominated in CGF accounts for just 5 percent of the aggregated balance sheet of the commercial banking system and is made up almost entirely of short-term loans to a few local enterprises. For the most part, the activity of commercial banks is limited to their role as a conduit for payments to and from the government and to the opening of letters of credit for the financing of exports. Because the commercial banks grant little or no credit to the private sector, money creation has taken place mainly through the issuance of BCC currency.

At the macro level, several years of hyperinflation accompanied by a free fall of the exchange rate, as well as continued political uncertainty, have undermined confidence in the CGF, thus creating a strong prefer-

Table 9.1. Consolidated Balance Sheet for the Commercial Banking System

| | October 18, 2002 | | | October 31, 2003 | | |
| | | Foreign | | | Foreign | |
	CGF	Exchange	Total	CGF	Exchange	Total
			(in billions of CGF)			
Assets						
BCC and interbank	**8.73**	**41.36**	**50.09**	**3.66**	**65.84**	**69.50**
Currency	2.60	7.68	10.28	1.85	13.98	15.83
Reserves at BCC	5.76	0.00	5.76	1.81	0.00	1.81
Interbank market	0.37	33.68[1]	34.05	0.00	51.86[1]	51.86
Customer operations	**8.03**	**7.13**	**15.16**	**6.08**	**10.60**	**16.67**
Credit to public sector	0.44	0.00	0.44	0.61	0.00	0.61
Credit to private sector	7.59	7.13	14.72	5.46	10.60	16.06
(nonperforming loans)	(0.51)	(0.75)	(1.26)	(0.92)	(1.05)	(1.97)
Other assets	**13.28**	**12.47**	**25.75**	**15.08**	**20.31**	**35.39**
Total assets	**30.04**	**60.96**	**91.00**	**24.81**	**96.75**	**121.56**
Liabilities						
BCC and interbank	**0.04**	**3.89**	**3.93**	**2.73**	**12.72**	**15.45**
BCC lending	0.01	1.02	1.03	2.69	0.27	2.96
Interbank market	0.03	2.87	2.90	0.04	12.45	12.49
Customer operations	**12.83**	**43.06**	**55.89**	**9.14**	**57.14**	**66.28**
Deposits by public sector	1.48	0.04	1.52	1.40	6.51	7.90
Deposits by private sector	11.35	43.02	54.37	7.74	50.63	58.37
Other liabilties and equity	**16.81**	**14.37**	**31.18**	**14.82**	**25.01**	**39.83**
Total liabilities	**29.68**	**61.32**	**91.00**	**26.69**	**94.87**	**121.56**

Source: BCC.
[1]Including balances with correspondent banks abroad.

ence for foreign exchange as a vehicle for savings. This tendency toward the use of foreign exchange is further reinforced by the absence of large-denomination banknotes in local currency (the largest banknote in CGF is equivalent to less than US$0.60), the poor quality of the banknotes in circulation, and the virtual nonexistence of functional payment systems other than cash. These circumstances have forced economic agents to use foreign exchange for the settlement of large transactions and for liquidity management. The resulting dollarization of the economy is reflected in the balance sheet of the commercial banking system, almost four-fifths of which is in foreign currency. Dollarization is even higher—and continues to rise—among private sector bank deposits, more than 85 percent of which are held in foreign exchange, up from less than 80 percent one year ago (see Table 9.1).

The domestic CGF interbank market is virtually nonexistent and dried up completely during the second half of 2003 (see Table 9.1). Almost all interbank activity is denominated in foreign currency, consisting mainly of placements with correspondent banks abroad of customer deposits in foreign exchange. Finally, bank lending is also increasingly foreign exchange based. Barely a third of outstanding credit to the private sector is now denominated in CGF, down from more than 50 percent a year ago, which implies that virtually all new loans are denominated in foreign exchange.

Financial intermediation has also suffered from institutional and policy weaknesses in the monetary area, which in turn have generated major dysfunctions in the financial system and limited the commercial banks' capacity to provide financial services to their customers. For a number of years, the BCC has not enjoyed adequate operational and financial autonomy, in part because it suffers structural operating losses caused by a balance sheet that, unlike that of the typical central bank, contains more interest-yielding liabilities than assets. As a result, the BCC has had insufficient resources to undertake the most basic central bank functions, such as maintaining the quality of currency in circulation.[2] The lack of financial resources, combined with the low level of financial intermediation, also made the use of conventional monetary policy instruments difficult and enticed the BCC to resort to unconventional tools. In particular, the BCC has frequently not allowed banks to use their free reserves to obtain currency. Although this currency rationing had initially been prompted by the apparent inability of the BCC to produce sufficient amounts of banknotes, more recently it

---

[2]The BCC has had to recirculate worn-out banknotes, because it did not have the resources to replace them.

appears to have been utilized as a substitute for conventional liquidity mopping-up operations. The rationing has resulted in the nonfungibility between the components of base money (i.e., currency in circulation and bank free reserves) and prevented the banks from being able to meet their customers' requests for deposit withdrawals, causing the emergence of a discount (*décote*) on CGF deposits in accounts with commercial banks (Figure 9.2). Using checks to transfer deposits, economic agents traded CGF bank deposits against CGF currency, at prices of up to 40 percent below par. Because the government accepted payment with deposit money, the main demand on this market came from economic agents who needed to make payments to the government.[3]

Finally, financial intermediation has been rendered difficult and costly through a number of policies outside the monetary area. The provision of credit has been discouraged by problems and uncertainties in the judicial and legal framework that make the recovery of claims difficult, as well as by a perceived antibank bias among courts. It has been hampered further by significant weaknesses in accounting and auditing and in corporate governance. Depositors have been scared away by the tax administration's heavy-handed approach toward bank clients: Banks have been compelled to provide extensive information on their depositors, and the authorities have frequently resorted to blocking and confiscating deposits, over and above the amounts of disputed tax dues.

There is, however, real potential for strengthening financial intermediation, considering the country's wealth of natural and human resources. Sustainable economic and political stabilization should stimulate both foreign and domestic investment. The financial sector should be capable of taking opportunities and participating in the financing of investments, and steps should be taken to ensure that short-term measures do not impede the long-term development of the financial sector.

Initial Steps in Strengthening Monetary Management

In the context of the SMP and the PRGF, and with the support of IMF technical assistance, rapid progress was made in strengthening the BCC's institutional framework for the conduct of monetary policy.[4] Key financial legislation reflecting international best practices—including

---

[3]In addition to the fungibility issue, commercial banks also claim that their ability to intermediate has been impeded by high fees charged by the BCC.

[4]See Appendix 9.1 for a review of IMF technical assistance to the BCC.

Figure 9.2. Décote Rate and BCC Operations on the *Décote* Market
(January 2002–August 2003)

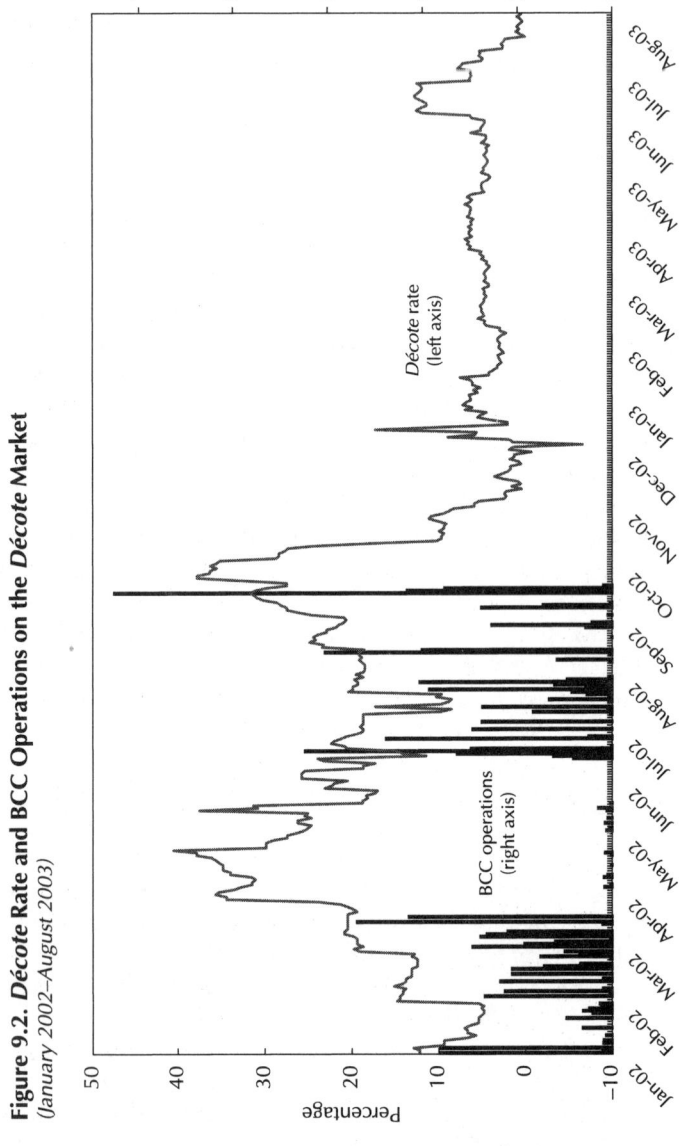

Sources: BCC; and IMF staff estimates on the basis of information provided by market sources.

new statutes for the central bank and a new banking law—was enacted during the course of 2002, although the transitional constitution approved in 2003 undid part of the central bank's freshly gained independence. Good progress was also made in strengthening the BCC's operational capacity. In particular, the BCC put in place key components of a framework to program currency issues, its net income position was consolidated in that of the government, and it established a Consultative Group on Monetary Policy to strengthen policy design and implementation.

The government's monetary program under the PRGF aims to achieve price stability by limiting the growth of broad money. To achieve that aim, the program projects a growth path for base money and puts a floor on international reserves and a ceiling on the BCC's net domestic assets. Difficulties in designing and implementing this program, however, include the instability of money demand, the high level of dollarization, and the lack of financial intermediation. As a result, the monetary program has amounted in practice to limiting the supply of CGF currency. Interest rate policy has been less essential in that effort and has been used in a more passive way, with the BCC adjusting interest rates as needed to keep them in line with declining inflation, while maintaining them at a positive level in real terms.

The currency supply itself has mainly been contained through fiscal discipline and unorthodox monetary policy measures (see above), in particular currency rationing. The resulting problem of the nonfungibility between the components of base money remained until the end of 2002. The rate of the discount (*décote*) remained volatile and at times high (up to 40 percent) in response to changes in the balance between the supply and demand for bank money. During the first six months of 2002, the BCC did not provide currency to the commercial banks, and all the currency issues were allocated to the payment of the government's expenses (Treasury outflows in Table 9.2) and those of the BCC (BCC outflows in Table 9.2). This policy was modified beginning in July 2002, under pressure from banks that could no longer ensure payment services to the government (mostly the payment of public sector salaries that have to be paid in cash), although they had excess reserves with the BCC. However, in 2003, the previous trends were exacerbated when the commercial banks became net sources of banknotes, while the treasury's needs doubled (Table 9.2).

In addition to currency rationing, the BCC relied on other unconventional instruments to regulate liquidity during the stabilization phase of 2001–2002, often at high cost to itself and/or the commercial banks and creating distortions in the process:

Table 9.2. Balance of Flows of CGF Banknotes at BCC Cashiers' Desks
(In billions of CGF)

| | Outflows | | | Inflows | |
	Jan–Dec 02	Jan–Oct 03		Jan–Dec 02	Jan–Oct 03
Treasury	15.3	29.0	*Décote* operations	5.3	0
BCC	6.1	4.0	Certificates of deposit		
Banks	4.4	–6.4	& BCC bills	–2.3	–0.1
			Foreign exchange sales	18.1	19.1
			Issues	6.1	9.1
			Other	–1.5	–1.4
Total	25.8	26.6	Total	25.8	26.6

Source: BCC.

- During 2001, certificates of deposits (CDs) were used to "buy" currency from the market.[5] However, as their remuneration was brought in line with inflation (from 25 percent a month at the beginning of the year to 0.7 percent since May 2002), demand for CDs evaporated because they no longer incorporated the implicit cost of the *décote*.[6] During 2002, BCC operations using CDs led to net repayments and the eventual retirement of the outstanding stock.
- "Special arrangements" were used during 2002 to replace CDs. They involved operations of the BCC on the *décote* market, whereby the BCC was receiving CGF notes against CGF bank money.[7] The BCC paid on average a 30 percent premium on the currency it bought, which led to a significant increase of the banks' reserves with the BCC, relative to currency in circulation, and a correlated increase in the rate of the *décote* (Figure 9.2). The rate of the *décote* dropped in July as the BCC started to "liquefy" banks' reserves at the request of the banks (see above). High volumes of BCC operations on the *décote* market in September–October led again to a sharp increase in the *décote* rate.
- Near the end of 2002, the BCC moved toward a more conventional monetary policy. In December, it introduced central bank bills (BCC bills), with which it mopped up most of the banks' free

[5]CDs were issued to finance the budget. However, they could only be purchased with cash, thus allowing the BCC, in its capacity of fiscal agent, to "buy" currency from the market that it could use for payment of the government's expenses.

[6]Because CDs were subscribed in cash, remuneration needed to incorporate the *décote* to be attractive to potential investors.

[7]The BCC's operations on the *décote* market involved purchases of foreign currency or CGF banknotes against payments in CGF bank money at a premium.

reserves. This largely contributed to the near-total disappearance of the *décote*. In July 2003, the imposition of reserve requirements on deposits in foreign exchange increased banks' liquidity requirements and further reduced the stock of free reserves (Figure 9.3). Since then, liquidity conditions have continued to tighten, requiring banks to deposit banknotes (CGF 3 billion for October alone) or have recourse to BCC refinancing. Outstanding BCC refinancing, which was close to zero at the end of June 2003, increased to just under CGF 2 billion at the end of September 2003. The tight liquidity conditions also contributed to the appreciation of the CGF in late 2003 (Figure 9.4). The BCC now operates a call money window and a window for advances in current account (Box 9.1).

Effects of the Nonfungibility of Base Money on the Financial System

The nonfungibility of base money de facto led to the creation of an additional currency in the DRC. To be able to attract banknotes, commercial banks needed to make a distinction between customer deposits made in cash (cash deposits) and customer deposits resulting from transfers through the payment system (bank money deposits), the counterpart of which consists of reserves with the BCC. Therefore, three payment instruments in local currency circulated in the DRC: currency, cash deposits, and bank money deposits. Whereas currency and cash deposits were interchangeable at par (provided that the latter were placed with a solvent bank), bank money deposits could frequently only be traded for currency at a discount (*décote*), which varied in function to the relative supply (payments in bank money made by the BCC not backed up by a willingness to issue currency) and demand for bank money deposits (capacity of taxpayers to settle their taxes in bank money).

The nonfungibility of base money also had adverse implications on financial intermediation. It acted as a barrier to the provision of payment services by the commercial banks—for instance, checks were not accepted unless the beneficiary was willing to take the risk of having to pay the *décote* to obtain currency, or was compensated for the *décote* through an increased check amount. In addition, it made bank lending virtually impossible because the banks could not provide currency to the borrowers when the latter wanted to use the loan proceeds. And it ensured that economic agents had no incentives to maintain demand deposits in the banking system. As a result, CGF-denominated demand deposits declined in absolute terms and even more so in relative terms

Figure 9.3. Changes in Bank Account Balances with the BCC

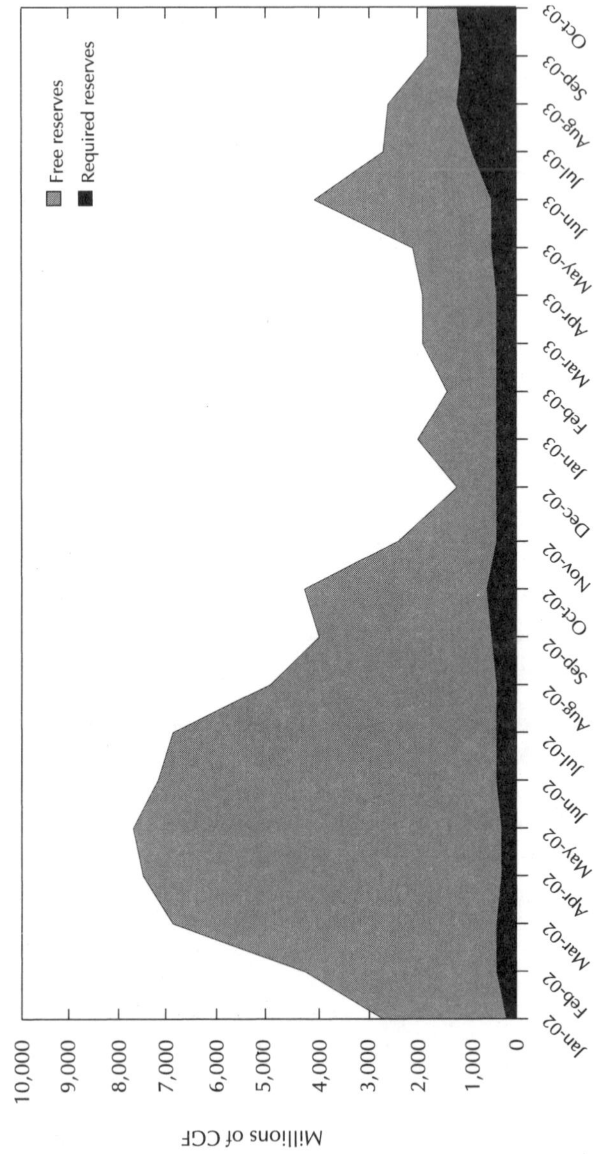

Source: BCC, Credit Directorate.

Figure 9.4. Exchange Rate Developments

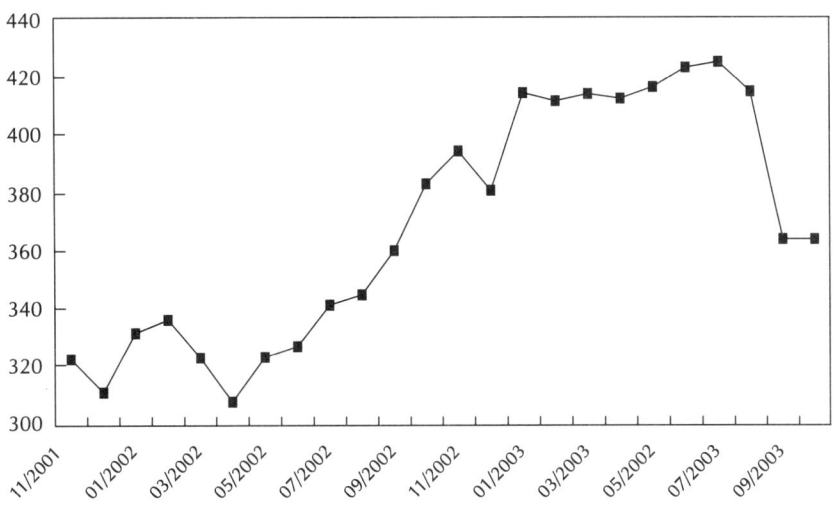

Source: BCC (DSE).

Box 9.1. DRC: Monetary Policy Instruments

Reserve Requirements

Set at 2 percent of local and foreign currency–denominated deposits; they are held in local currency.

Standing Facilities

Liquidity providing: Commercial banks may obtain rediscount credit or emergency funding from the BCC against trade bills as collateral. In view of the low quality of trade bills, the BCC is considering restricting collateral to foreign exchange.

Liquidity absorbing: Short-term BCC bills issued on demand, at a rate of remuneration that takes into account dollar interest rates and inflationary expectations.

---

vis-à-vis currency in circulation and foreign exchange deposits (Figure 9.5). However, in such a context, arbitrage between cash and bank money offered lucrative prospects for those having assets in currency and liabilities that could be settled in bank money, such as taxes.

Figure 9.5. Evolution of Currency in Circulation, Bank Deposits, and Bank Reserves, 2002–03
(In millions of Congolese francs)

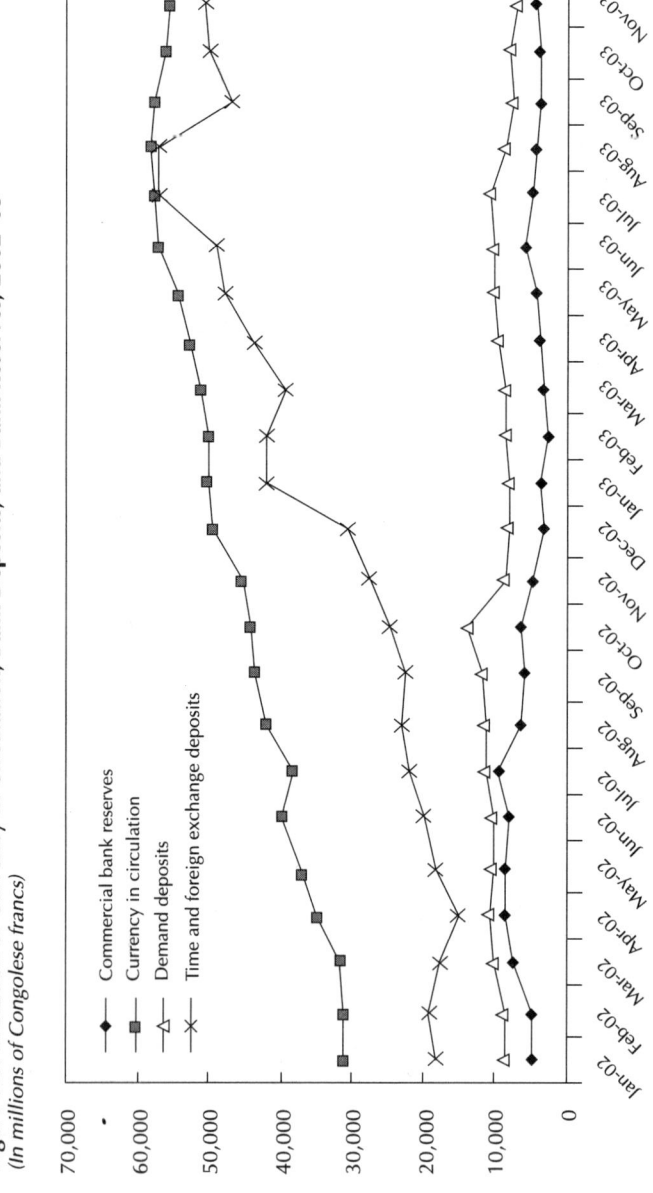

Sources: BCC and IMF staff estimates.

Section II. Restoring the Fungibility of Base Money

Fundamental Cause of the Nonfungibility of Base Money

Eventually, the nonfungibility largely confined the banks' activities to the provision of payment services related to government receipts and expenditures. In such an environment, most imbalances between the banking system's supply and demand of CGF banknotes reflected imbalances in the public sector not covered by the issuance of currency on the part of the BCC, hence the *décote*.[8] There were several potential sources of these uncovered public sector imbalances. The government budget was run using a monthly treasury cash-flow plan, which was coordinated with the BCC. The BCC was supposed to cover any projected deficits in that plan. However, imbalances were possible that were not planned or registered in the cash-flow plan, including unbudgeted payments executed by the BCC on behalf of the government; BCC operating losses that were not promptly recorded in the budget; and tax revenues retained by financial institutions to pay for unbudgeted government expenditures.[9]

In this context, the *décote* becomes an early indicator of fiscal imbalances. Indeed, if the public sector's budget were balanced, the BCC should not need to have recourse to the rationing of currency. The BCC should have been in a position to meet all payments requested by the government. However, it was not, as explained above and illustrated in Table 9.2 and in the evolution of the *décote* rate, which reached 40 percent in April–June and September–October of 2002.

Restoring the fungibility of base money is essential for a revival of financial intermediation and, indeed, the success of the reform agenda of the authorities.[10] In particular, the development of the role of the commercial banks in the payment systems is contingent on the elimination of the *décote*. In turn, better payment services through the banking system will attract deposits in the system, allowing the banks to resume the provision of credit to the economy in local currency.

---

[8]Here, "public sector" encompasses the government budget, the BCC, and all other public sector entities (including banks) that utilize the banks' payment system.

[9]The weaknesses in the information systems at the BCC, in the financial institutions, and in the public sector (*comptabilité publique*) have not permitted an assessment of the respective contributions of these potential outflows.

[10]It is important to note that financial intermediation is also conditional to a number of additional policies, including an appropriate legal framework governing contracts and efficient judicial administration, and the presence of sound and effective financial institutions. This chapter does not discuss these policies.

Corrective Measures

Durably eliminating the *décote* requires fundamental corrections to the environment that led to its appearance. In particular, it requires a refocusing of monetary policy on base money and bank reserves, rather than on currency. However, in a context where the bulk of the domestic currency transactions intermediated by the banking system are government receipts and expenditures, the government's fiscal management and the BCC's monetary management are intimately interlinked. In particular, avoiding the reappearance of the *décote* requires the BCC to be prepared at all times to provide the banks with banknotes in exchange for their free reserves in BCC accounts. However, the BCC can only do so and at the same time ensure a stable, noninflationary money supply if government budget deficits are contained and fully financed through government borrowing from economic agents other than the BCC, because, under current circumstances, the scope for the BCC to sterilize money created by monetized government budget deficits is limited. In a dollarized and cash-based economy, any injection of liquidity in the banking system caused by government expenses (i.e., expenditure in bank money rather than in cash) is most likely to result in an instantaneous demand for currency by the beneficiaries to finance their transactions or to purchase foreign exchange.

Although excess liquidity could in theory be mopped up by raising the ratio of required reserves on domestic currency deposits, or making foreign currency–denominated deposits subject to significant reserve requirements, the risk would be that banks would be unable to mobilize the necessary liquidity. The banking system as a whole could only raise CGF liquidity by collecting more deposits (thus taking currency out of circulation and returning it to the BCC), selling foreign exchange in return for CGF currency to the public or to the BCC (with the risk of generating a short foreign exchange open position), or borrowing from the BCC. To the extent that all these channels are either blocked or characterized by an inelastic supply, the risk is that such efforts would result in a resurgence of the *décote*, an unacceptably large increase in interest rates, an inability of the banking system to function, or undesirable exchange rate volatility.

It was in this context that the Congolese authorities took corrective measures at the end of 2002. On the fiscal side, these corrective measures included the freezing of nonessential expenditures, the elimination of identified "ghost" workers, and an increase in the prices of petroleum products. On the monetary side, the BCC started to issue short-term bills to mop up liquidity at positive real interest rates, starting in December 2002 (see above). Following these corrective measures, the *décote* was virtually eliminated.

Going forward, fiscal consolidation is a precondition for any program of macroeconomic stabilization to succeed. Strict adherence to the monthly treasury cash-flow plan is required to prevent the buildup of imbalances in the system because, at least until financial intermediation has deepened, the ability of monetary policy to compensate in a timely fashion for fiscal imbalances, even temporary ones, is limited. In the day-to-day implementation of monetary and fiscal policies, these limitations imply that the execution of the cash plan at the ministry of finance needs to be closely coordinated with the liquidity-forecasting exercise undertaken by the BCC.[11]

Looking to the future, a better identification and quantification of the causes of the imbalances in the public sector, along with a fundamentally improved management of the public sector's finances, will facilitate the coordination of monetary and fiscal policies, by allowing the monetary and fiscal authorities to identify deviations from the monetary program early on.

Against this background, the Congolese authorities have undertaken a number of actions:

- An action plan to strengthen the institutional capacity of the BCC was adopted and is being implemented. It includes, among other things, an overhaul of the accounting and internal audit functions, a strengthening of the monetary programming and liquidity-forecasting capacity, preliminary work to restructure its balance sheet and strengthen its financial position, and an overhaul of its information systems.
- Measures to strengthen banking supervision in order to assess potential sources of outflows through the financial institutions participating in the collection of public sector revenues.
- Measures to strengthen public accounting procedures (*comptabilité publique*) to enable the ministry of finance to more effectively monitor the government's account on the books of the BCC.

The restoration of the fungibility between the components of base money will allow a shift from the current currency programming framework to a more conventional base money programming framework. Authorities in the DRC have already taken steps to establish strong lines of communication between the BCC and the ministry of finance,

---

[11]In September 2002 the BCC created a Consultative Group on Monetary Policy to facilitate the coordination of fiscal and monetary policy (see Appendix 9.1).

which in turn have helped greatly in the coordination of monetary and fiscal policies. In particular, a computerized connection for continuous exchange of data between the BCC and the ministry of finance was established in August 2003. Progress in this area will allow the BCC to analyze the autonomous sources of demand and supply of base money and to decide on discretionary monetary operations to keep base money in line with the assumptions in the monetary program. Such a framework could also be utilized for ex post analysis of actual flows, enabling the BCC to analyze past trends and decide on corrective actions as required.

Section III. Fostering Reintermediation and Dedollarization

As noted above, past macroeconomic instability and weak BCC policies have led to a combination of a marginalized banking sector, disintermediation, and multiple forms of dollarization. Bank deposits, which represent only about 2.5 percent of GDP, are mostly denominated in foreign currencies (85 percent in September 2003).[12] At some point, total bank reserves in CGF with the BCC exceeded the level of loans in CGF. Furthermore, bank money in CGF is used mostly in the context of operations on behalf of the government, while other transactions in the economy are either executed in dollars or indexed to the dollar. As a result, any excess supply of local currency, in the face of a limited demand, leads to additional demand for foreign exchange and has a direct inflationary impact due to the high pass-through of exchange rate changes into prices. Dollarization of deposits has mainly taken the form of unremunerated foreign currency–denominated demand deposits. These deposits reflect a reluctance to hold balances in domestic currency for transaction purposes because of the recent experience of high inflation, rather than interest rate arbitrage. As these deposits are converted into Congolese francs, they can be utilized in the settlement of transactions.[13] Finally, dollarization of large transactions is encouraged by the low value of CGF banknotes. For instance, the note with the highest face value currently in circulation (CGF 200) was equivalent to less than US$0.60 when it was introduced in October 2003, whereas the CGF 100 banknote was equivalent to US$70 when it was introduced in 1998.

---

[12]At the end of 2001, average foreign currency deposits to total deposits in Africa reached 33.2 percent (see Gulde-Wolf and others, 2004).

[13]At the end of October 2002, demand deposits represented 95 percent of total bank deposits, with 80 percent of these deposits represented by demand deposits in dollars.

Fostering reintermediation and dedollarization is a long-term challenge that requires a realistic, gradual approach. An efficient financial system will not develop unless the overall business climate improves significantly, including in areas beyond the monetary authorities' responsibility. In addition, it should be noted that although dollarization has its drawbacks, it is preferable to an economy without a functional currency. In the absence of a reliable domestic currency, dollarization has facilitated the functioning of the Congolese economy. Therefore, dedollarization should be based on measures designed to restore confidence in the financial system rather than through policies aimed at discouraging—or raising the cost of—the use of foreign currency. Meanwhile, it is also important to avoid actions that might further reinforce dollarization, given the costs and risks that dollarization brings. First, dollarization reduces seignorage revenue related to the issuance of domestic currency. Second, dollarized financial systems are more vulnerable to solvency and liquidity risks. In particular, dollarization of loans to domestic borrowers could lead to increased credit risk because loans are not necessarily issued to borrowers with foreign exchange income. Dollarization also imposes limits on the central bank's lender-of-last-resort function, because the central bank cannot provide foreign exchange liquidity in the case of a run on (foreign exchange) deposits to the same extent as it could in domestic currency.

In the short term, the progress that has been achieved thus far should be consolidated, private initiative encouraged, and priorities established. The stabilization of the exchange rate, the elimination of the *décote*, and the reduction in inflation are crucial accomplishments that should be consolidated through the continued pursuit of prudent fiscal and monetary policies. To consolidate these accomplishments, the Congolese authorities must also avoid actions that might promote dollarization, impede the operation of the financial sector, or merely gain time while compromising the long-term outlook. In particular, the BCC should undertake irrevocably to guarantee the convertibility of banks' free reserves into currency and launch a communication campaign to communicate this commitment to the public.

In addition, some concrete measures need to be undertaken with high priority. Among them are the replacement of worn banknotes, the introduction of larger denomination banknotes, and the restoration of the functionality of the BCC's branch network, in coordination with the branch network strategies of the commercial banks. Regarding currency in circulation, the face value of CGF banknotes must be reevaluated with a view to ensuring a better match with the needs that arise for transaction purposes. Therefore, the BCC should have full discretion to introduce banknotes of larger denominations, although this should be done prudently, and accompanied by a communication strategy aimed at avoiding the creation of inflationary expectations.[14] These larger denominations will allow the use of the CGF in large transactions, thus reducing incentives for the use of foreign exchange. At the same time, the BCC will need to continue to provide banknotes of smaller denominations, which are still in use by a large fraction of the population, but the quality of the notes in circulation will need to be improved and permanently maintained. Finally, the BCC will need to ensure that banknotes in all denominations are available throughout the country.

Monetary policy may affect the degree of financial dollarization through the interest rate spread between currencies. The authorities should, however, resist the temptation to use their interest rate policy to prop up the exchange rate. Such a strategy could generate difficulties in the long run. In particular, it would increase the lending rate for domestic currency and encourage dollarization of loans, with unfavorable consequences for the vulnerability of the financial sector to sudden exchange rate fluctuations, as indicated above. Rather, monetary policy should continue to be guided by price stability objectives.

In the medium term, dedollarization and reintermediation will require that the authorities expand and deepen their structural reforms so as to create a favorable environment for the development of the private sector. The necessary reforms involve enhanced independence and transparency of monetary policy; a strengthening of payment systems; the putting in place of reasonable limits on the discretionary powers of the public administration, in particular the tax administration; and the establishment of a judicial and legal framework favorable to banking activity.

In low-income countries, as is the case in the DRC, most of the deposits in commercial banks are demand deposits maintained primarily for transaction purposes. Therefore, a process of reintermediation in local currency will need to be supported by the development of an efficient payments and settlement infrastructure for local currency–denominated transactions. In addition, as the DRC consolidates the gains made in stabilizing the macroeconomic framework, the demand for savings instruments in local currency is likely to rise. In such a context, the availability of a short-term instrument offered by the BCC, such as the recently in-

---

[14]In the recent past, introduction of banknotes of larger denominations was delayed because the BCC could not obtain the approval of the government. Such delays have further complicated the conduct of monetary policy, at times forcing the BCC to resort to costly monetary operations.

troduced BCC bills, will help the process of reintermediation in local currency by allowing economic agents to arbitrage between CGF and dollar instruments, thus reestablishing equilibrium between current and expected exchange rates, interest rates, and expected inflation.

Finally, it is important to recognize that the capacity to find outlets for stable demand deposits and to generate revenue will also depend on the environment in which credit activity is carried out. Therefore, the current efforts to build the pillars of sound banking activity are critical, including completion of the restructuring of the banking sector; the establishment of prudential regulation and supervision of banks in line with international standards; the completion of the reform of the public enterprise sector; the creation of a business environment conducive to the development of an efficient private sector; and the promotion of appropriate legal frameworks governing contracts and efficient judicial administration.

Section IV. Policy Lessons from the DRC Experience

The experience of the DRC with monetary policy implementation contains valuable lessons for countries sharing similar macroeconomic, institutional, and market development initial conditions for effective monetary policy, leading to low financial intermediation and high dollarization. The lessons mainly have to do with the framework for the coordination of macro policies, the desired level of institutional and operational autonomy of the central bank, and coordination of IMF operations, including technical assistance and the use of IMF resources.

The low level of financial intermediation in the DRC has imposed limits on the ability of the central bank to undertake monetary operations to sterilize excess liquidity, at times forcing the BCC to resort to unconventional, costly, and distorting instruments. This experience underlines the need for strong coordinating arrangements of monetary and fiscal policy, in particular government cash flow and central bank liquidity management. Indeed, in the extreme circumstances of low financial intermediation, monetary policy may not be effective in containing the macroeconomic effects of temporary fiscal imbalances. In such a context, implementation of the budget on a cash basis, which should incorporate any imbalances in the operating account of the central bank, has proved to be a much-needed framework to ensure macroeconomic stability. In such circumstances, fiscal discipline will be essential to the stabilization of the macroeconomic framework.

The DRC experience also shows that institutional independence for the central bank, although highly desirable, is not a sufficient condition to ensure the effectiveness of monetary policy. The central bank also needs to enjoy a sufficient degree of operational autonomy so that it can bear the cost of undertaking liquidity management operations on a timely basis and in amounts that are required for monetary policy purposes. In addition, lack of operational autonomy may undermine policy effectiveness when other governmental bodies are involved in the decision-making process and implementation of monetary policy.

The experience with monetary reforms in the DRC shows that the design of an operational framework for the conduct of monetary policy requires consideration of the nature of the constraints posed by the environment. Therefore, there are benefits from providing policy and technical advice in the context of a broad and comprehensive approach that looks at the constraints to policy implementation arising from the environment in which the instruments are implemented. The approach that was followed in the DRC, where technical assistance to the BCC started in the context of the SMP and continued under the subsequent PRGF, allowed a close coordination of technical assistance to the BCC with the work of the IMF staff for the design and negotiation of the IMF program, while also allowing technical assistance to provide inputs for the design of the program. The need for adopting a holistic approach reflects the fact that the frontier between policy formulation and policy implementation is hazy in countries where the constraints to policy implementation are high, and where the ability of the monetary authorities to implement a given monetary framework may be constrained by considerations pertaining to the sphere of policy implementation.

Appendix 9.1. Progress Accomplished in Strengthening the BCC's Operational Capacity

IMF technical assistance in the areas of monetary and exchange rate policy has been based on a multitopic diagnostic mission led by the African Department in early 2001, before the implementation of the SMP; follow-up IMF multitopic missions later in 2001, and in 2002 and 2003; the placement of IMF resident experts at the BCC; and short-term visits by experts in a wide range of central bank activities (Box A9.1).

The first multitopic mission resulted in the design of a road map of policy measures and an accompanying sequence of technical assistance, while taking into account the weak administration capacity in the DRC. This road map was updated during the review of the SMP and implementation of the successor three-year government economic program supported by an arrangement under the IMF's PRGF.

The technical assistance program began in early 2001 with a visit of an IMF short-term expert to assist the Congolese authorities in the uni-

---

Box A9.1. Overview of IMF Technical Assistance Missions

Date	Subject(s)
May and July 2001	Expert visits: foreign exchange market and operations
October 2001	IMF multitopic mission
February 2002	Expert visit: central bank accounting
February 2002	Expert visit: monetary operations
July 2002	Expert visit: foreign exchange market and operations
August 2002	Expert visit: central bank accounting
November 2002	IMF multitopic mission
April 2003	Expert visit: foreign exchange market and operations
April 2003	Expert visit: central bank accounting
April and August 2003	Expert visits: banking supervision
November 2003	IMF multitopic mission

IMF long-term resident advisors to the BCC

April 2002–December 2003	General advisor to the BCC governor
November 2003–April 2004	Internal audit
February 2003–February 2004	General advisor to the BCC governor

fication and floating of the exchange rate and the establishment of an interbank foreign exchange market, which were crucial elements of the SMP. This assistance was complemented with IMF advice provided from headquarters on new exchange legislation. The authorities subsequently proceeded to abolish the official exchange rate, which at that time was set at CGF 50 per U.S. dollar. On Friday evening, May 25, they published an indicative closing rate of CGF 315.5 per U.S. dollar. This 84 percent devaluation eradicated the difference between the official and parallel market rates, thus clearing the way for a single, market-determined exchange rate. The new unified and liberalized foreign exchange market became operational the following Monday, and the authorities allowed the exchange rate to float from that point onward. The involvement of the BCC in the determination of the exchange rate has since been limited to occasional market interventions aimed at achieving the net international reserves target, limiting excessive exchange rate volatility, and covering customer operations. In addition, the BCC calculates and publicizes a daily indicative exchange rate, which is a weighted average of the rates used in all reported transactions.

The successful unification and floating of the exchange rate, in combination with greater budgetary discipline, stabilized the macroeconomic framework sufficiently to allow a refocusing of the IMF's technical assistance efforts on capacity building. Thus, in October 2001, a new technical assistance mission visited Kinshasa to support the BCC's capacity-building efforts. At that time, exchange arrangements for international transactions had largely been liberalized. In this context, the mission concentrated on monetary management, foreign exchange operations and market functioning, and central bank accounting and audit. During the course of 2002, IMF short-term experts made several follow-up visits to assist in the implementation of earlier recommendations, and an IMF resident advisor to the BCC governor was appointed. In coordination with the IMF's efforts, the World Bank took a leading role in the restructuring of the banking sector, in particular in overseeing the liquidation of insolvent banks.

Financial Legislation

During the course of 2002, key financial legislation was enacted, including a central bank law that established the BCC's independence and a banking law that put in place frameworks for bank licensing, supervision, and liquidation. The banking law specifically gives the BCC full responsibility for the supervision of the financial sector and spells out the conditions under which credit unions can be organized and operate, and the way they are supervised. Also, a new legal framework was created for the restructuring of the banking system. The restructuring framework extended a special regime, which had been in place since 1998 but had expired on December 31, 2001.[15] The central bank law and the banking law, both of which benefited from IMF input, reflect best international practices in their respective areas and provide a sound framework for strengthening the financial sector.

Monetary Management

The October 2001 IMF technical assistance mission found that monetary management was constrained by several factors: a weak framework for liquidity forecasting, insufficient coordination between monetary management and government operations, the absence of any adjustments in official interest rates despite a downward trend in inflation, and the nonfungibility between bank reserves in account at the central bank and currency. Consistent with the recommendations of the October 2001 mission, the Congolese authorities have since implemented the following corrective measures:

- The BCC has established some of the key components of a framework to program currency issues. In particular, its treasury directorate started, at the beginning of 2002, to monitor the counterparts of currency inflows and outflows, allowing the tracking of the factors that led to net injections of currency in the system. The BCC has also already started to use this tool to forecast the net demand for currency.
- The net income position of the BCC was consolidated in the government budget to avoid the inflationary consequences of BCC losses, as had happened previously.
- In September 2002, the BCC created a Consultative Group on Monetary Policy to facilitate the coordination of fiscal and monetary policy. The group is composed of eight members (six from key BCC departments and two from the ministry of finance), meets at least twice a month, and reports to the senior management of the BCC and the minister of finance.
- The monetary authorities have brought the BCC refinance rate and the remuneration on CDs down in line with the decline in inflation,

---

[15]The new framework allows the BCC to decide to bring any institution under the regime, whereas the previous regime was voluntary. At the time of the IMF technical assistance mission, 7 of 10 active banks operated outside of the regime, and 4 private banks had been placed in liquidation.

while maintaining them at positive levels in real terms. In May 2002, the central bank refinance rate was reduced from 39 percent to 12 percent, and the monthly rate on CDs was cut from 3 to 0.7 percent.

Foreign Exchange Market

Since the unification of the multiple exchange rates and the floating of the currency in May 2001, the foreign exchange market has continued to function satisfactorily. The spread between the formal and informal markets has never exceeded 2 percent, on average; the collection and dissemination by the BCC of the market exchange rate has functioned well overall; and the published rate has become a reference rate in the market. However, the BCC's operations have suffered from the fact that the authorities used them to simultaneously pursue three objectives (reserve accumulation, limiting exchange rate volatility, and executing customer operations), without clear prioritization among them, and that no formal framework was in place for the execution of foreign exchange operations. The November 2003 technical assistance mission recommended the implementation of such a framework and the sale of foreign exchange through single-rate competitive auctions.

The October 2001 mission noted that short-term foreign exchange swaps could be used by the BCC to inject liquidity in the system given the lack of adequate collateral in domestic currency that could be used. While preliminary assistance was provided for their introduction, progress did not materialize because refinancing needs for the banking sector did not emerge at the time. When banks started to have recourse to BCC refinancing during 2003, the BCC chose to provide this financing on the basis of private paper as collateral, rather than on the basis of foreign exchange. Following the November 2003 technical assistance mission, the BCC started making arrangements for the replacement of the rediscount window by a foreign exchange swap facility.

Reserve Management

Work in the area of reserve management started with a visit by an IMF short-term expert early in 2002. The expert identified broad areas for reform, among them the need for a new organization for the reserve management function, the creation of front-office and back-office functions in the operations division, the reform of accounting practices, and the production of a procedures manual. The mission also recommended that the BCC's numerous accounts be consolidated into one main correspondent account. IMF staff involved in reserve management subsequently made a study tour to a neighboring central bank that had just reformed its reserve management function with the support of an IMF technical assistance program. Since then, significant progress has been made in all areas. In particular, a front office and back office have been set up, a draft procedure manual for the BCC trading room has been prepared, and work on the consolidation of the accounts is progressing.

Accounting Framework and Internal Control Mechanisms

The October 2001 IMF technical assistance mission and a Finance Department Safeguards Assessment mission found serious weaknesses in the accounting framework and internal control mechanisms in place at the BCC, due to a lack of human and logistical resources, disregard for internal procedures, and lapses in accounting procedures and transparency. Subsequently, the external audits of the 2000 and 2001 accounts of the BCC have been finalized, but not certified, pointing to lapses in both accounting procedures and transparency, and casting doubts on the real financial position of the BCC. In response, the BCC created an Account Restructuring Committee (Comité d'Assainissement des Comptes), with the IMF resident advisor as its chair, to clean up its balance sheet and implement transparent accounting procedures. Furthermore, in September 2002 the BCC drafted terms of reference for an overhaul of these systems by an international firm. In cooperation with the national regulatory authority on accounting, the BCC has been working toward the adoption of international accounting standards. The November 2003 mission recommended that the BCC's accounting function be organized along architecture of the type "single accounting application with decentralized input," in which decentralized units can upload their entries in a central accounting application. The mission also proposed a concrete implementation plan for the selection and putting in place of the necessary hard- and software for the new accounting system. The actions needed to modernize the BCC's accounting system will continue throughout 2004 with the assistance of an IMF expert.

Regarding the internal audit function, which had also been identified by the Safeguards Assessment and by IMF missions as a problem area requiring urgent action, the BCC issued an audit charter in September 2002 (following the establishment in 2000 of an internal audit directorate), which defined the objectives, responsibilities, powers, and methods of operation of the internal audit directorate. This measure is an important element in the BCC's efforts to implement best international practices in this area. In November 2003, an IMF expert started a six-month assignment as a resident advisor on internal audit with the BCC.

Restructuring of the Banking System

In coordination with the IMF, the World Bank has taken the lead in the restructuring of the banking system. Audits of the commercial banks by independent audit firms have revealed that only the foreign-owned banks are expected to become capable of functioning normally in the near future, while several domestically owned banks are in serious difficulties. With financial support from the World Bank, the BCC is expected to close the unviable banks and seek the restructuring of those deemed viable.

Involvement of the National Bank of Belgium

In 2003, the National Bank of Belgium set up a program of assistance to the BCC, covering a wide range of central bank operations and activities. To ensure consistency in policy advice and avoid duplication of efforts, the IMF has coordinated its program of technical assistance with the National Bank of Belgium. This has allowed the National Bank of Belgium to take over some of the capacity-building needs that had been identified by the IMF. This trend is expected to continue in the future.

Bibliography

De Boeck, Pascale, and John Leimone, 2002, "Exchange System and Exchange Measures Subject to Fund Jurisdiction under Article VIII, Sections 2 (A), 3, and 4 of the Articles of Agreement of the International Monetary Fund" (unpublished; Washington: Legal Department and Monetary and Financial Systems Department, International Monetary Fund).

Gulde-Wolf, and others, 2004, *Financial Stability in Dollarized Economies*, IMF Occasional Paper No. 230 (Washington: International Monetary Fund).

Laurens, Bernard, and others, 2001, "Capacity Building Assistance to the Central Bank of the Congo" (unpublished; Washington: Monetary and Financial Systems Department, International Monetary Fund).

Laurens, Bernard, and others, 2003, "Challenges in Developing Financial Intermediation in the Democratic Republic of the Congo" (unpublished; Washington: Monetary and Financial Systems Department, International Monetary Fund).

Laurens, Bernard, and others, 2004, "Challenges and Action Plan for Developing the Financial System in the Democratic Republic of the Congo" (unpublished; Washington: Monetary and Financial Systems Department, International Monetary Fund).

10

Rebuilding Fiscal Institutions

NICOLAS CALCOEN

Section I. Introduction

The collapse of the expenditure control system and revenue collection, and the resulting monetization of an uncontrolled budgetary deficit, were identified as the primary source of the vicious circle of hyperinflation and falling currency that plagued the Democratic Republic of the Congo (DRC) economy until the end of 2000.

A substantial tightening of the budgetary policy, through a number of revenue-enhancing and expenditure-restraining measures, was therefore a key element of the new economic strategy adopted by the government in 2001 to achieve macroeconomic stability. Measures aiming at improving governance and budget transparency were also part of the comprehensive budget reforms that were progressively implemented under a staff-monitored program (SMP) and its successor Poverty Reduction and Growth Facility (PRGF) arrangement.

In this context, rebuilding the macroeconomic management capacity was viewed as a necessary condition for the success of this strategy. Regular administrative processes within the ministry of finance, the revenue-collecting agencies, and the public administration, in general, had been impaired by years of mismanagement and the war, a lack of experience, and an absence of basic equipment. The implementation of the economic program of the government needed, therefore, to be supported by a comprehensive technical assistance program.

This chapter addresses the challenges faced in rebuilding macroeconomic institutions, focusing in particular on the fiscal area[1] and emphasizing the need for comprehensive and timely external technical assistance. Section II presents a brief description of the overall strategy for reforming fiscal institutions and providing technical assistance to that end. Sections III, IV, and V describe the reform programs designed and implemented in the areas of public expenditure management, revenue mobilization, and civil service reform, respectively. Section VI discusses the lessons learned from the experience in the DRC and the challenges facing the future reinforcement of fiscal institutions.

Section II. Overall Strategy and the Role for the International Monetary Fund and Other Donors

Contrary to some other postconflict cases, the DRC was still in conflict when it resumed its relations with the international community and radically shifted the conduct of its economic policy; consequently, many external partners were not ready to provide technical assistance from the outset. Therefore, the IMF played a leading role in assisting the DRC, not only by designing and monitoring overall reform strategies, but also by providing hands-on assistance at the early stages of implementation.

IMF assistance was initiated by a multitopic fact-finding mission fielded in March 2001, which carried out an initial diagnosis of the macroeconomic situation, proposed emergency measures, and identified technical assistance needs. It was quickly followed by specialized missions that undertook detailed assessments and designed specific road maps in all the areas of IMF expertise: monetary policy and management of the central bank, the conduct of monetary policies and production of macroeconomic statistics, as well as, in the fiscal area, revenue administration and policies and budget and expenditure management. The general approach underlying these recommendations was to distinguish between immediate priority measures, which aimed to fix the basics first and relied as much as possible on the existing systems to yield immediate results, and medium- and long-term action plans designed to strengthen and modernize in depth the country's institutional capacity. In the area of civil service reform, where the IMF has no spe-

---

[1]Reforms adopted in the area of monetary policy and the management of the central bank are presented in Chapter 9, and reforms of the legal and judiciary framework are discussed in Chapter 11.

cific expertise but which is critical for the success of reforms, the United Nations Development Program (UNDP) and the World Bank played the leading role, in coordination with other donors.

The government endorsed these strategies and was assisted in implementing the fiscal reforms and monitoring overall progress through a combination of a strong resident technical assistance program, with the posting since the beginning of 2002 of three IMF resident experts (in expenditure management, customs administration, and tax administration, respectively), and regularly scheduled specialized follow-up missions to assess the reforms undertaken, provide complementary guidance, and suggest further improvements.[2]

Although the IMF clearly had the lead on the reform and modernization of revenue and expenditure management systems, good coordination with other donors was essential to the success of this program. The World Bank provided, in particular, substantial financing to complement and support the IMF-sponsored reforms with the necessary equipment, information systems, and training. It is also providing complementary technical assistance in specialized areas, such as procurement reform and corporate taxation. The public expenditure review it undertook in 2002 was also useful in forging the links between the macroeconomic and sectoral reforms by identifying the priority sectors toward which the composition of expenditure was expected to be reallocated, and by providing an initial assessment of the capacity of the Congolese authorities to track poverty-related expenditure.

Other donors are also getting more involved in providing technical assistance, and some of them have expressed their interest in supporting the IMF-recommended reform strategies through the assignment of resident experts, to complement or replace the IMF experts.

Section III. Strengthening Budget Control and the Tracking of Expenditure

By 2000, the expenditure management system had experienced a dramatic deterioration. Basic principles of sound expenditure management were no longer being respected: there was no budget, the expenditure process had broken down, a large part of government revenue and expenditure were being carried out outside the DRC

---

[2]See Appendix 10.1 for a summary of key issues and measures in the fiscal area, Appendix 10.2 for a list of IMF technical assistance missions fielded in the fiscal area, and Appendix 10.3 for a list of technical assistance reports.

Treasury, and government expenditure was no longer being reported in an orderly fashion. Reflecting resource constraints and disturbances arising from years of civil unrest and war, a large part of the public administration was not operational. While ad hoc procedures became the norm, and the role of the Central Bank of the Congo or BCC (Banque Centrale du Congo) grew, the ministry of finance was largely deprived of its capacity to control expenditure, although the treasury did manage to some extent to monitor the financial situation of the government.

Against this background, the strategy designed in 2001 with the assistance of the IMF to rehabilitate expenditure management was based on two pillars:

- bringing the annual budget back to the center of expenditure management through the timely adoption of a comprehensive and realistic budget that reflects the priorities of the government; and
- restoring an orderly budget execution process, including the rebuilding of an effective commitment control function.

On this basis, a gradual approach was developed. The first steps, included in the SMP negotiated by the authorities with the IMF in 2001, were intended to address the most critical shortcomings in the management capacity of the government's financial operations, in particular by centralizing all revenue and expenditure in the treasury account at the central bank and under the treasury's supervision. These actions were complemented by the establishment of a medium-term strategy for the rehabilitation and modernization of the public expenditure management system, implemented with the assistance of a long-term resident expert appointed in February 2002 and of other donors.

Cash Management and Financial Planning

Immediate priority was put on restoring the capacity of the ministry of finance to record and control all revenue and expenditure. The objective was emphasized because cash planning and management are indispensable to keep expenditure within target and to prevent unanticipated borrowing that might disrupt monetary policy and trigger hyperinflation. To perform this task, the ministry of finance needs to control all public monies.

Although in theory all revenue and expenditure were covered by the budget, a large share of government revenue, coming from public enterprises and oil production and distribution, actually followed extrabudgetary channels. Amounting to one-fourth of total central government revenue (1.7 percent of GDP in 2001), this revenue financed sovereignty expenditure or fuel consumption, either through separate bank accounts in private banks or direct compensation with government expenditure. To ensure the consolidation of cash resources, avoid the fragmentation of budget revenue, and increase transparency in the management of public finance, this revenue and the corresponding expenditure were gradually reintegrated into the treasury account at the central bank by the closure of the bank accounts and the suppression of the offsetting mechanisms.

In addition, a large amount of expenditure was actually paid from the treasury account by the central bank without prior authorization (and even prior knowledge) of the ministry of finance. These outlays were gradually reduced, starting at the end of 2001, and a presidential decree, although not immediately respected, was adopted in April 2002 forbidding the financing of any government expenditure without the prior approval of the ministry of finance.

Finally, efforts are being made to reconcile on a regular basis the fiscal data of the treasury directorate and of the central bank. Two reconciliation meetings are now being held every week: one on revenue and the other on expenditure. The installation of a computerized link between the central bank and the treasury and the reorganization —expected in 2004—of the government cashier's operations within the central bank, which are currently split among five services within the BCC, should improve the quality and reliability of the data being exchanged between, and reconciled by, the two institutions.

On these bases, it is possible to improve government financial planning through the implementation of a monthly cash-flow plan. Designed with the assistance of the IMF and a key element of the program with the IMF, the monthly plan is regularly being updated by a team under the supervision of the cabinet of the ministry of finance in light of actual revenue, expenditure, and financing, and is used to program expenditure. The adoption of a commitment plan, setting expenditure limits for each ministry and institution and revised regularly in accordance with the treasury cash-flow plan, is a key element to regulate expenditure to avoid a buildup of arrears payments.

Future enhancement of cash management will include a streamlining of the numerous bank accounts held by line ministries and agencies in commercial banks, through the implementation of a plan to consolidate gradually the government's accounts in the treasury account at the BCC and reconcile permanently the remaining accounts under the treasury's authority.

Budget Formulation

Until 2001, the annual budget, if any, was adopted late in the year. By that time, it had lost its significance as a tool to allocate and prioritize expenditure, owing to the primacy of extrabudgetary or irregular procedures and to the rapidly changing context of hyperinflation and depreciation. One of the first measures of the economic program of the government, adopted in May 2001, was the preparation and adoption during the year of a budget for 2001 and the timely adoption (in early 2002) of the 2002 budget through a normal budgetary process. Efforts were made, with some assistance from the UNDP, to improve data compilation, prioritization, and coordination. Significant progress is still needed, however, to improve the construction of the macroeconomic-fiscal framework underpinning budget estimates and revenue projections; the budget preparation process, including the schedule and procedures for submissions by line ministries; the estimates for utility payments (water, electricity, etc.) based on improved control procedures; and the integration in the annual budget of externally financed projects. Only once these prerequisites for a simple annual line-item budgeting have been achieved can the development of a medium-term fiscal framework be envisaged.

In the meantime, however, some progress was made in improving the budget presentation with the adoption of a new classification system. The 1996 budget classification system was not in concordance with international standards and was not used for budget execution reporting. A new system was prepared with the assistance of the IMF resident advisor, including streamlined economic and administrative classifications, as well as a functional classification system compatible with international standards. This new classification system was introduced in the 2003 supplementary budget and the 2004 budget. On this basis, budget documentation is being streamlined and simplified to improve fiscal transparency. The new functional classification system is also being used to define and track poverty-related expenditure, in line with the sectoral priorities set out in the DRC's interim Poverty Reduction Strategy Paper.

Budget Execution

Although in theory budget execution relies on complete but rather cumbersome procedures, most expenditure was in reality executed through fast-track procedures, involving the direct submission of payment orders to the minister of finance. As a consequence, commitments were neither controlled nor recorded, paving the way for the building up of arrears, and public expenditure was poorly recorded and classified.

Against this background, reestablishing an orderly budget execution process was key to restoring effective control over expenditure and improving the transparency and tracking of spending, in particular in the context of the access of the DRC to the enhanced Heavily Indebted Poor Countries Initiative. To this end, new execution procedures, simplifying the official execution process and reinstating commitment control, were designed with the assistance of the IMF technical expert. Taking into account both the existing organization and the country's administrative capacity, the proposed procedures were based on the following principles: (1) the current system of expenditure payment and tax collection by the banking system—adopted in 1997 to end widespread corruption by public accountants—should be maintained; (2) the treasury department (Direction du Trésor et de l'Ordonnancement) should play the key role at the payment order stage of the expenditure process, as well as in the centralization and collection of financial information; and (3) the commitment stage should be reestablished beforehand.

The new procedures are supported by the implementation of a simple computerized information system, designed with IMF and World Bank assistance, and limited at first to the operations carried out by the relevant directorates of the ministries of budget and finance. It also involves reinforcement of the administrative capacity within these ministries through the equipment and partial reorganization of the main directorates involved in the budget execution chain, as well as the implementation of a training program financed by the World Bank.

Limited at first to current expenditure at the central level, the new execution system will be expanded to foreign-financed investments, which are currently managed through specific execution procedures and banking arrangements, and to the central government's operations at the local level. Special arrangements will also be necessary to take into account the specificities of the wage payment process, based on the conclusions of an audit of the payroll carried out by the French Cooperation (see Section V).

Accounting and Reporting

The implementation of the new execution procedures and of the associated computerized information system allows for the production of monthly execution reports at various stages of the execution process and in line with the economic, administrative, and functional classification system. However, the current single-entry accounting system cannot provide a full picture of the government's financial position, as it (1) cannot account for transactions such as transfers to provinces and cash advances, (2) treats assets and liability transactions as revenue or expenditure, and (3) cannot adequately track arrears. A new double-entry accounting framework will be developed in 2004, to be fully implemented in 2005.

Section IV. Enhancing Revenue Collection

Raising revenue mobilization from the very low levels collected in 2000 (5.1 percent of GDP, including off-budget revenue, one of the lowest ratios in the world) was essential to regain fiscal sustainability and finance reconstruction. With the decline in economic activity, the shift of transactions to the nonofficial economy, and the loss of control by the government of almost half of its territory,[3] the tax base had been shrinking. The poor revenue performance also resulted from the following factors: (1) the tariff and tax system was complex, owing to a plethora of taxes and other levies and to the multiplicity of rates applicable to each of them, and therefore both difficult to administer and an incentive to tax evasion; (2) the tax and customs base was narrow, owing to the numerous exemptions, deductions, and discretionary measures, particularly for public enterprises; and (3) the collecting agencies were hampered by a chaotic organizational structure, archaic procedures and systems, insufficient equipment, a lack of staff motivation, poor tax compliance, and fraud. These factors, which had resulted from years of mismanagement, only worsened during the war.

In addition to these general factors, revenue performance in recent years had been hurt because, in a context of a widening gap between the official and parallel market exchange rates, the official exchange rate had been used to assess the value of the taxable base for import and export duties, as well as for other revenues whose taxable base had been expressed in dollar terms. However, one of the first measures of the economic program adopted by the government in May 2001 was to allow the official exchange rate to float freely, thereby unifying the official and parallel market rates and generating a large positive impact on revenue collection.

Against this background, the IMF helped the authorities to design a reform program aimed both at improving revenue mobilization and facilitating economic activity by modernizing the tax system and its administration and reducing the burden on the formal economy.

---

[3]Before the beginning of the war in 1998, revenues collected from the provinces occupied by rebel movements had accounted for 10–20 percent of total government revenue.

Considering the weak initial administrative capacity, and despite the recognition of the need to reform the tariff and tax system, the IMF staff recommended that the authorities focus at first on short-term measures to strengthen the tax and customs departments before introducing policy reforms.

Strengthening the Customs and Tax Administrations

Central government revenues are collected by three main agencies: the Office des Douanes et Accises (OFIDA) collects customs duties, excises, and the turnover tax on imports; the Direction Générale des Contributions (DGC) collects domestic direct and indirect taxes; and the Direction Générale des Recettes Administratives, Judiciaires et Domaniales (DGRAD) collects nontax revenues. While measures were taken to secure the role of DGRAD in collecting nontax revenues (especially those revenues that were diverted to finance extrabudgetary expenditure and had to be centralized at the treasury), the reforms adopted by the government, in line with the IMF's recommendations and with its resident technical assistance, focused on the two main agencies: OFIDA and the DGC.

These measures included improvements in data collection, management information systems, internal management, and basic equipment; the reinvolvement of the revenue-collecting agencies in key economic sectors, such as petroleum distribution; and a stricter control of exemptions and special regimes. One of the key elements of the adopted strategy was to concentrate the efforts at first on restoring the administrative capacity to collect revenue from the main revenue sources, before extending the reforms to the whole country and to all taxpayers.

Along these lines, the first phase of the reform program—corresponding to the preliminary measures taken before the introduction of any policy measures—for tax administration (the DGC) was the creation of a large taxpayers' unit (LTU) to secure about 70 percent of total tax collections and to introduce modern organizational principles and procedures supported by computer systems. With the creation of this unit and the parallel reorganization of the DGC headquarters, modern procedures were introduced, initially for the large taxpayers (e.g., self-assessment principles for filing and payment and simplified collection procedures). A training program was implemented for the staff of the LTU, and a new information technology system was developed.

Regarding customs administration, measures adopted during the first phase of the reform strategy included the implementation of a management system providing basic statistical reports and monitoring activities of the customs offices—including a closer monitoring of exemptions—and the establishment of a pilot customs office in Matadi (the DRC's main port of entry) to develop new procedures and systems—including the Automated System for Customs Data (ASYCUDA).

In the second phase of the reform process, the objective of the modernization program is to expand the new organizational principles, procedures, and systems to cover the entire revenue administration. Relying on the new processes developed in the LTU and the pilot customs office, these programs include the following measures:

- modernization of the tax department (the DGC, which has been renamed Direction Générale des Impôts, or DGI), by strengthening the headquarters functions; restructuring the network of local offices—beginning with the establishment of specialized units (Centres des Impôts) to control medium-sized enterprises, initially in Kinshasa and eventually, by expanding this approach throughout the main cities of the country; generalizing the taxpayer numbering system; and extending the procedures and system developed for the LTU to other services (beginning with the Centres des Impôts); and

- modernization of OFIDA by simplifying the clearance process; undertaking a major reorganization of the department before the ASYCUDA system is gradually adopted; and developing selective postcontrol approaches.

Tariff and Tax Reform

Once short-term measures to strengthen the tax and customs administrations had been introduced, the Congolese authorities expressed their willingness to reform the tax system, starting with a tariff reform consistent with the DRC's commitments under regional trade agreements,[4] accompanied by domestic taxation measures to compensate for revenue losses.

In line with the IMF's November 2002 recommendations, a set of reform laws on tariff and indirect taxation was adopted by parliament in March 2003, with the overall revenue impact of the reform evaluated at about 1 percent of GDP.

The new tariff law is intended to be easier to administer, to reduce the scope for smuggling and fraud, to correct the bias of the previous tariff in favor of commercial activities, and to prepare the DRC to meet

---

[4]The DRC is member of the Southern African Development Community and the Common Market for Eastern and Southern Africa.

its commitments under regional trade agreements. The law (1) establishes a simple three-rate tariff structure (5 percent for agricultural and pharmaceutical inputs, investment goods, and raw materials; 10 percent for intermediate and essential goods; and 20 percent for other final consumption goods) in place of the previous five-rate structure; (2) eliminates the surtax that was applied to a list of specific products; and (3) precludes preferential treatment.

The reform of indirect taxation was designed to compensate for the revenue losses expected from the tariff reform while simplifying the tax system and preparing for the introduction of a value-added tax (VAT) in the future. It included the following:

- The turnover tax (*impôt sur le chiffre d'affaires*) was reformed by applying the 3 percent rate only to investment goods and agricultural inputs and the 13 percent rate to all other products, and by authorizing enterprises to deduct the turnover tax paid on their inputs. This credit mechanism, designed to limit the cascading effects of the turnover tax while preparing for the introduction of a VAT, is, for administrative capacity reasons, limited at first to the large enterprises under the responsibility of the LTU.
- The 13 percent turnover tax was extended to all the products subject to excises.
- The petroleum product price structure was simplified by increasing the excises and eliminating all parafiscal levies.

Despite some initial difficulties in drafting and implementing this reform package, it is now fully implemented and already starting to have a positive impact on overall government revenue. It will have to be complemented by strict control over all tax exemptions. This means ensuring that all new tax and customs exemptions are fully compliant with the provisions of the newly enacted investment, mining, and forestry codes,[5] and may also entail the revision of some exoneration conventions granted in the past.

On these bases, the next steps in the simplification and rationalization of the tax system should include the following:

- Measures are needed to simplify the taxes and duties (including parafiscal levies) applicable to private and public enterprises to improve the business environment, following a review of these taxes undertaken with the assistance of the World Bank. A rationalization of the taxes levied by DGRAD (including the suppression of the taxes for which there was no legal basis) is under way.

---

[5]See Chapter 11 for more details on the investment, mining, and forestry codes.

This rationalization has to be complemented by a parallel exercise for fees and duties collected by other bodies and by a reform of the corporate tax. The sectoral economic reviews undertaken with the assistance of the World Bank are providing the basis for streamlining specific taxation in key economic sectors, such as the forestry sector.

- The turnover tax should be replaced with a VAT to reduce economic distortions and to increase revenue collection. Pending the satisfactory implementation of the 2003 reform and further improvement in administrative capacity, this action could be envisaged in 2005.

Section V. Reforming the Civil Service

Although adequate control over the wage bill and efficient operation of the civil service, including within the ministry of finance and its agencies, was critical for the success of the program, the management and functioning of the civil service were hampered by the following characteristics:

- Strong uncertainties surrounded the number of civil servants, owing to the multiplicity of services involved in the payment process, the absence of an integrated payroll database, and the war, which had taken a heavy toll on the population and caused massive displacements of refugees, including civil servants. While the number of civil servants in the occupied provinces, who were not paid, was largely unknown, the number of civil servants in the provinces under the control of the government was also uncertain, despite some surveys undertaken by the authorities that had led to the elimination of some identified "ghost" workers.
- The structure of the civil service was inadequate, with a lack of skilled and well-trained staff, complex administrative structures, an aging workforce—about 70,000 staff over retirement age still in service because of the inability of the government to pay for severance allowances—and misallocation of staff resources, which remain heavily concentrated in Kinshasa.
- Wage levels, which had been largely eroded by hyperinflation, were very low, thus generating weak work incentives and increasing exposure to corruption. The wage scale (including transportation bonuses) in 2003 was between US$2 (the bottom level outside Kinshasa) and US$45 a month, with an average of less than US$15. At 1.5, the ratio of the average civil service wage per staff to GDP per capita (a measure of the well-being of the civil

service compared with that of the average individual) is the lowest in sub-Saharan Africa.

Against this background, the government developed, with the assistance of the UNDP and other donors, a strategy to reform the civil service and public administration. It includes (1) a revision of the legal framework; (2) a census of the civil service; (3) an audit of payroll procedures, to be followed by their reorganization; (4) a restructuring of all ministries, starting with pilot operations for the ministries of budget, finance, planning, and civil service; (5) a retirement program for staff over retirement age; and (6) a training program.

Considering the uncertainties surrounding the number of civil servants, the reported extent of ghost workers and workers above retirement age, and the relative size of the civil service as opposed to the very low wage levels, the effective implementation of a civil service census rapidly emerged as a priority. With World Bank assistance, the methodology for a general civil census was defined, and the census, financed by the international community, is expected to take place in 2005. The payroll system will be audited in parallel, with the assistance of the French Cooperation, with a view to establishing a new and secure system, expected to be made operational when the outcome of the census becomes available. Based on this outcome, a new effort will be made to eliminate ghost workers, a list will be compiled of active personnel eligible for the retirement program, personnel and payroll files will be created, and an in-depth civil service reform will be prepared, including a significant but progressive increase in the purchasing power of civil servants.

Section VI. Lessons and Challenges for the Future

Looking back at the progress achieved so far in rebuilding fiscal institutions and at the difficulties encountered, an important aspect of the proposed strategy is its sequencing. Based on a careful initial assessment of the problems as well as of the implementation capacity and the resource and skill constraints, the proposed strategy needs to identify the key measures necessary in the short term while drawing a clear road map for medium- and long-term reforms. The prerequisites for moving toward far-reaching measures—for example, the basic administrative requirements for introducing tax policy reforms—need to be clearly identified. In the area of civil service reform, delays in organizing the civil service census may have hampered the implementation of other key measures, although these delays will allow the census to cover the whole reunified country.

Although it is often necessary in the short run to rely on existing institutions and procedures, care should be taken to avoid consolidating inadequate organizations and processes. Regular follow-up is, therefore, critical in identifying such risks. For example, whereas the organization of the cashier operations within the central bank or the government accounting framework were not seen as priority reforms at the beginning of the process, an IMF technical assistance follow-up mission later helped to identify these measures as necessary to take full advantage of the reforms in public expenditure management already under way.

Sustained technical assistance is also essential in a context where the administrative capacity has been eroded by years of economic mismanagement and war. In postconflict countries, strategic advice will have to be supported by regular follow-up, as well as by assistance for hands-on implementation, whether undertaken by the same donor or by another one. This point can be illustrated by some difficulties encountered in implementing the tax reform during the second quarter of 2003, when the IMF tax expert had just been removed and not yet replaced. Good coordination among donors is also critical in that regard to ensure that all technical assistance or training needs are covered while avoiding overlapping assistance and contradictory advice.

However, the determining factor for success in rebuilding fiscal institutions is probably the clear recognition by the authorities of the economic problems faced by the country and their commitment to the reforms. This full ownership is necessary both from the political authorities and from top and middle managers within the administration. With a personal commitment to reforms at the highest level of the state, the appointment of reform-minded ministers, and good-faith efforts of managers in key administrative positions, the DRC offered a combination that allowed for the implementation of bold measures. On the contrary, one may notice that little progress was made during the few months of great political uncertainties that preceded the nomination of the new transitional government in June 2003. Following the new authorities' demonstration of renewed commitment to the economic program, supported by the international community, the pace of reforms resumed. Institutional resistance to reforms was encountered at times, especially when a reorganization of some departments of the ministry of finance was envisaged, but the authorities overcame this through adequate communication of the rationale and benefits of the reforms and repeated demonstrations of political commitment.

Almost three years after resuming cooperation with the international community and embarking on a vast reform program, the DRC is now at a critical point. Reforms already undertaken in the areas controlled by the government need to be consolidated and extended to the whole country, while new reform initiatives are being launched.

The Congolese authorities should continue to focus their priorities on achieving a sustainable fiscal stance by (1) improving revenue mobilization without placing an excessive burden on the formal economy—this requires continuing the modernization of the revenue administration by extending the reforms already undertaken to the whole network of the tax and customs agencies, while rationalizing the tax system—and by (2) strengthening public expenditure management capacity and budget reporting in order to restore effective control over expenditure and to improve governance and budget transparency.

Increased attention will need to be paid to capacity building to ensure the sustainability of reforms. In that regard, external assistance should, maybe more than in the past, try to identify and promote skilled counterparts within the Congolese staff and offer adequate training, in coordination with traditional technical assistance.

The reunification of the country will pose additional challenges. The reforms under way in Kinshasa and in the provinces previously under government control will have to be progressively extended to the eastern and northern provinces, where administrative capacity has been even more severely damaged by the war. In the meantime, the new political context stemming from the peace agreements is expected to lead to a process of decentralization. Fiscal relations between the central government and the provinces, including the distribution of expenditure responsibilities and tax powers, transfers from the center, and reporting arrangements, will have to be carefully designed to prevent the expected improvements in service delivery from generating additional macroeconomic risks or reducing transparency.

Appendix 10.1. Key Issues and Measures in Rebuilding Fiscal Institutions

Areas	Initial Situation	Immediate Measures	Medium-Term Measures
Public expenditure management	No budget Diversion of revenues to specific accounts outside the control of treasury and generalization of extrabudgetary expenditure Collapse of budget processes and controls Large stock of expenditure to be regularized and accumulation of arrears Only partial reporting by the treasury	Timely adoption of a realistic annual budget Centralization of revenue and expenditure in the treasury account at the central bank and elimination of off-budget expenditure Implementation of a monthly cash-flow plan	New budget classification system (2003) New expenditure procedures, reinstating and streamlining of the full expenditure chain, and partial computerization (2003) Reorganization of the cashier's function and streamlining of bank accounts (2004) Reform of government accounting framework (2004–05)
Tax system	Use of official exchange rate Numerous taxes and duties, and multiplicity of rates and cascading effects Numerous (often ad hoc) exemptions and deductions	Unification of multiple exchange rates	New investment, mining, and forestry codes (2002–03) Reform of the customs tariff and of the turnover tax and excises (2003) Introduction of VAT (2005)
Customs and tax administration	Collecting agencies poorly staffed and equipped; widespread fraud Excessively formal procedures and insufficient controls Complex administrative structures	Strengthening of DGC and OFIDA management Simplification of procedures Improvement of the management information system of the customs office	Setting up of a large enterprises' unit, using modern procedures (2002–03) Establishment of a pilot computerized customs office in Matadi (2003) Introduction of taxpayer identification number, new control procedures (2003–04) Progressive generalization of reforms (centres des impôts) for small- and medium-sized enterprises, computerization of customs offices (2004–05)
Civil service	No control over payroll; number of civil servants unknown Aging, undertrained, and misallocated staff Very low public wages	Elimination of already identified ghost workers	General civil service census (2005) Audit and reorganization of payroll procedures (2004) Retirement program (2004–05) Restructuring of civil service

Appendix 10.2. IMF Technical Assistance in the Fiscal Area (2001–03)

Subject	Date
Missions	
Multitopic fact-finding mission	February 28–March 12, 2001
Tax administration and policy	May 11–21, 2001
Expenditure management	August 4–18, 2001
Expenditure management	August 31–September 10, 2002
Tax policy	November 19–December 3, 2002
Revenue administration	December 3–17, 2002
Revenue administration	July 11–25, 2003
Expenditure management	November 11–25, 2003
Long-term resident experts	
Expenditure management	Since January 2002
Customs administration	January 2002–December 2003
Tax administration	January 2002–March 2003
	Since September 2003

Appendix 10.3. IMF Technical Assistance Reports

Benon, Olivier, and others, 2003 "République Démocratique du Congo: Modernisation de la DGC et de l'OFIDA – mise en place de la deuxième phase des réformes" (unpublished; Washington: Fiscal Affairs Department, International Monetary Fund).

Bouley, Dominique, Denis Lepage, and Hans Kwant, 2004, "République Démocratique du Congo: Pour un Renforcement de la Gestion des Finances Publiques" (unpublished; Washington: Fiscal Affairs Department, International Monetary Fund).

Corfmat, François, and Patrick Fossat, 2001, "République Démocratique du Congo: Mobilisation des recettes fiscales – Axes prioritaires des réformes et stratégie de mise en place des mesures" (unpublished; Washington: Fiscal Affairs Department, International Monetary Fund).

Geourjon, Anne-Marie, Bertrand Laporte, and Jean-Luc Schneider, 2003, "République Démocratique du Congo: Réforme de la Politique Tarifaire et Modernisation du Système Fiscal" (unpublished; Washington: Fiscal Affairs Department, International Monetary Fund).

Schiller, Christian, Jérôme Fournel, and Jean-Paul Barrier, 2001, "République Démocratique du Congo: Axes Prioritaires pour la Réhabilitation de la Gestion des Dépenses Publiques" (unpublished; Washington: Fiscal Affairs Deparment, International Monetary Fund).

11

Structural and Sectoral Policies and Their Sequencing

JACOB GONS

Section I. Introduction

As described in Chapter 2, by late 2000 the Democratic Republic of the Congo (DRC) was facing a situation of widespread conflict and war, which was compounding the negative effects of a decades-long decline in output resulting from economic mismanagement, corruption, and civil strife.[1] To reverse that trend, in early 2001 the new government decided to make a U-turn in its economic policies, including by redefining the role of the state from predator to facilitator of private sector–led activity. To achieve its goal, the government designed a well-thought-out road map of comprehensive and far-reaching structural reforms with the help of the International Monetary Fund and the World Bank; the former concentrated on macroeconomic structural measures and the latter on most other areas.[2] The IMF supported the government's measures through a staff-monitored program (SMP) that covered the period June 1, 2001–March 31, 2002 and, since July 2002, through a three-year arrangement under the Poverty Reduction and Growth Facility (PRGF). World Bank support took the form of six credits/projects, as described in Sections III and IV.

---

[1]This chapter reflects on developments through the end of 2003.

[2]Formally, the division of labor between the two institutions is set out in the Concordat.

In drawing up the road map, the authorities defined immediate measures to tackle the most egregious macroeconomic distortions, as well as the lack of accountability and poor governance. At the same time, they started to lay the foundation for a more stable and predictable business environment by defining the main building blocks of future structural reforms, including reform of the judiciary. Finally, they initiated preparations for sectoral reforms and infrastructural investment projects to alleviate major supply bottlenecks (see Box 11.1). These reforms and investments were to be extended across the nation, once reunification had been achieved. The road map was consistent with the poverty reduction strategy that was being drawn up at about the same time. This strategy, as formulated in the interim Poverty Reduction Strategy Paper (interim PRSP), distinguishes three, partly overlapping, phases: (1) a short-term stabilization phase (2001–02); (2) a medium-term reconstruction phase (2002–05); and (3) a development phase, which was expected to start in the course of 2005.

This chapter elaborates on the government's considerations in drawing up the road map of structural reforms. Section II describes the up-front measures (March–May 2001) that were taken with a view to quickly stabilizing the macroeconomic situation through a mix of exchange rate, fiscal, and monetary policies, as well as other measures of a macroeconomic nature. Section III describes the measures that were taken in the short run (June 2001–March 2002), which were aimed at laying the foundation for sustainable economic growth and reconstruction through initiation of a process of administrative and institutional strengthening. These actions focused mainly on (1) the rebuilding of public institutions; (2) financial sector reform; (3) the filling of the legal void concerning the environment for private sector activity; (4) the promotion of good governance; (5) reform of the natural resources sector; and (6) capacity building. Section IV presents the measures that were taken during the first half of the reconstruction phase (April 2002–December 2003). In addition to deepening and complementing those mentioned in Section III, these measures included the launching of sectoral reforms and the rehabilitation of infrastructure. Finally, Section V comments on the first results of the structural reforms, the lessons that can be drawn, and the challenges for the future.

Section II. Up-Front Measures (March–May 2001)

Based on the findings of a joint IMF-World Bank mission of March 2001, and consistent with its road map, the government first formulated a short-term program, the enhanced interim economic program (*programme intérimaire renforcée*) or PIR. The PIR, which covered the period June

2001–March 2002, and which was formulated with the help of, and monitored by, IMF staff,[3] consisted of a critical mass of bold and front-loaded macroeconomic measures aimed at breaking the vicious circle of currency depreciation and inflation that had been plaguing the country. These measures included the following: (1) a return to a normal budgetary process, with the centralization of all revenue and expenditure at the treasury; (2) a restrained budget policy, focusing on strict adherence to a monthly treasury cash plan, revenue mobilization, and expenditure control; (3) a prudent monetary policy, consistent with the objective of breaking hyperinflation and reinforced by the adoption of new statutes of the central bank that enshrine its independence; (4) the introduction of a floating exchange rate system and the unification of the exchange rate; (5) the elimination of price controls (except for electricity, water, and transportation); (6) the liberalization of oil imports; (7) the implementation of a transparent mechanism for the determination of petroleum prices; and (8) the abolition of the monopoly on diamond exports.[4] Through their immediate and powerful effects, these measures contributed significantly to the stabilization of the macroeconomic situation in the second half of 2001 (see Section V and Chapter 2).

Section III. Measures Taken in the Short Run (June 2001–March 2002)

The PIR also sought to lay the foundation for sustainable economic growth and reconstruction by initiating the rebuilding of public institutions[5] and the restructuring of the financial sector,[6] with assistance from the IMF and World Bank. The latter's activities took place in the context of the Emergency Early Recovery Project (EERP), which was drawn up in support of the PIR. In addition, the EERP contained a relatively limited set of structural reforms to start addressing the country's other key short-term constraints: weak institutional, administrative, and implementation capacity (see Box 11.1).[7] These reforms focused on re-

---

[3]Hence, the PIR is also referred to as the SMP.

[4]The monopoly on diamond exports, created in early 2000, was abolished in February 2001, before the official start of the SMP. The abolition allowed purchasers and private trading posts to operate without restriction in mining areas.

[5]See Chapter 10.

[6]See Chapter 9.

[7]Under the EERP, a grant of US$50 million was made available to finance, in addition to the preparation of the above-mentioned structural reform measures, the com-

Box 11.1. Structural and Sectoral Reforms and Their Sequencing

To address large-scale distortions and infrastructural disrepair resulting from decades-long economic mismanagement, corruption, civil strife and, since 1998, outright war, the government of the DRC has been preparing and implementing a wide range of structural and sectoral reform measures since early 2001. The preparation/implementation can be broken down into two phases, based on the time required to prepare/implement the measures, as well as their impact.

A. **The Stabilization Phase (2001–02),** which aimed at obtaining immediate results.

Measures taken up front (April–May 2001)
(1) introduction of a floating exchange rate system and unification of the exchange rate;
(2) elimination of price controls (except for electricity, water, and transportation);
(3) liberalization of oil imports and implementation of a transparent mechanism for the determination of petroleum prices; and
(4) abolition of the monopoly on diamond exports.

Measures taken during 2001–02
(5) removal of obstacles to the functioning of the private sector: drafting and adoption of a new investment code and a law creating commercial courts and abolishing military tribunals;
(6) drawing up and adoption of a new mining code, marking the start of the reform of the natural resources sector;
(7) capacity building, development of a transparent public procurement system, and creation of a framework for donor assistance and public investment planning;
(8) initiation of financial sector reform (Chapter 9); and
(9) strengthening of public sector management (Chapter 10).

The following measures were prepared for the reconstruction phase:
(10) on public enterprise reform, the conduct of preliminary audits of all public enterprises, publication of the results, and replacement of most of their chief executive officers;
(11) strengthening of implementation capacity through technical assistance and training in key ministries and utilities to prepare for sectoral reforms over the medium term;
(12) drawing up of the forestry code; and
(13) overall formulation of the three-year PEG.

B. The Reconstruction Phase (2002–05)

Building on A (5), a new Labor Code was approved by parliament in October 2002; a code of ethics for civil servants was enacted in November 2002; an Anti-Corruption Commission was established in August 2002; a Governance and Anticorruption Strategy and Action Plan was drawn up in late 2002; and a complete overhaul of the public procurement system was initiated in 2003.

Building on A (6)–(12), the following steps were taken:
- start of public enterprise reform and, through effective functioning of the Steering Committee on the Reform of Public Enterprises, drawing up of restructuring plans for seven key enterprises, with, in some cases, actual restructuring to start in 2004;
- continuation of reform of the natural resources sector: the new forestry code was adopted in June 2002; implementing decrees were issued concerning the mining registry, new mining regulations, and the Mining Title Validation Commission; the restructuring of GECAMINES was initiated; and audits to improve transparency in the diamond sector were being prepared;
- initiation of sectoral reforms (agriculture, health, education, and community development);
- continued restructuring of the financial sector; and
- continued strengthening of public sector management and implementation of sectoral reform.

Structural conditionality. Many of the above-mentioned measures were deemed to be so important for the success of the PIR and PEG that they were made part of the conditionality of the programs supported by the IMF or the World Bank.

moving obstacles to the functioning of the private sector and creating an environment conducive to its growth, including the promotion of good governance, as well as administrative and human capacity building. The latter implies the provision of substantial technical assistance to build program implementation and monitoring capacity, a necessary condition to secure external donor support. At the same time, because of its

bating of human immunodeficiency virus/acquired immunodeficiency syndrome (HIV/AIDS), community development, and infrastructure rehabilitation, the latter almost exclusively concerning the road between Kinshasa and the seaport of Matadi. In addition, the grant served as a conduit for assistance from other donors, either through cofinancing or parallel financing.

large potential to generate economic growth, a start was made with the reform of the natural resources sector (mining and forestry), and with preparations for the restructuring of public enterprises. The subsections below elaborate on the measures that were taken in the June 2001–March 2002 period.

Enabling the Private Sector and Supporting Good Governance[8]

Issue

During the participatory consultations conducted to prepare the interim PRSP, the population strongly expressed its belief that poor governance and rampant corruption were among the foremost causes of the widespread poverty in the country. The rule of law was almost never respected in the application and enforcement of justice. For the private sector, mutually conflicting or unwise regulations inherited from the past hampered productive economic activity and provided a vehicle for corrupt practices.[9] Economic recovery, particularly recovery leading to propoor growth, is especially difficult in such an environment.

Actions

To help the DRC move to a sound legal framework for legitimate investment, a new investment code was drawn up in line with international best practice and was approved by parliament and promulgated by the president in February 2002. The code provides a level playing field through transparent incentives for domestic and foreign investors alike and clarifies the rights and responsibilities of investors, regulatory agencies, regional governments, and the fiscal authorities.[10]

Also, an assessment was made of the legal framework, complementing activities financed by the European Union under the Justice Support Program that focused on rehabilitation of court buildings, and capacity building and awareness-raising activities concerning criminal law and the rule of law in general. In July 2001 parliament adopted a

---

[8]Efforts to improve governance in the public sector are described in Chapter 10.

[9]In the April 2003 *International Country Risk Guide*, the DRC ranked 136th out of 140 countries in terms of risk.

[10]The code also provided for the setting up of a one-stop window (*guichet unique*) for investment application/registration. This step was realized in late 2002 with the creation of the National Investment Promotion Agency or ANAPI (Agence Nationale pour la Promotion des Investissements en République Démocratique du Congo).

new law abolishing military tribunals and creating commercial courts that have the sole right to act as arbitrators in commercial disputes. Initial steps were taken to strengthen the judicial system with assistance from the European Union and bilateral donors.

Initiation of Reform of the Natural Resources Sector

Issue

The DRC contains vast forestry and mineral resources. As explained in Chapter 2, in the past these resources have been used to fuel a sad legacy of more than a century of exploitation and abuse of human rights, as well as the recent armed conflict in the Great Lakes region. The 60 million hectares of natural hardwood forest provide a source of revenue and a way of life for the country's 35 million rural people. However, in 2001, production was only 1 percent of the sustainable annual harvest of 6–10 million cubic meters. If properly exploited, the sector could generate 60,000 jobs and annual gross revenue of about US\$1 billion. Concerning minerals, annual production of diamonds fell from 26 million carats in 1988 to 16 million carats in 2000, while copper output fell from 475,000 metric tons to less than 25,000 metric tons. The public mining company, GECAMINES (Générale des Carrières et des Mines du Congo), was once the world's largest producer of cobalt and a leading producer of copper, as well as the country's largest foreign exchange earner. At the end of 2001, GECAMINES was bankrupt. However, private investors have been flocking to the DRC despite (or, in some instances, as documented in the press and by the UN Security Council, in response to) the distressed environment.[11]

Actions

A new mining code was drafted with World Bank assistance, which also included (1) discussing and disseminating the code; (2) training government officials in the implementation of the code; and (3) initiating the setting up of the mining registry (*cadastre minier*) to ensure the transparent allocation of mining rights. The mining code was published in April 2002. In the meantime, work was started to draw up a new forestry code.

---

[11]Indeed, the new mining code provides for an evaluation of existing mining rights, with a view to annulling those that are illegal.

Preparation for the Restructuring of Public Enterprises

Issue

Economic recovery is impeded by a dysfunctional public enterprise sector, comprising some 51 state-owned and 44 mixed enterprises. Through these enterprises, the state is the largest economic agent, and this situation has generated issues ranging from lack of good governance to gaps in the delivery of key social services. The legal structure governing state-owned enterprises is outdated and does not provide the necessary safeguards allowing for private sector investment.

Actions

To prepare for public enterprise reform (typically a long-term process), preliminary audits of all public enterprises were conducted in 2001 to identify major governance issues. The audit results were published in the local press, and most of the enterprises' chief executives were replaced by temporary administrators. In addition, preparations were made to set up a steering committee for public enterprise reform (see subsection on public enterprise reform in Section IV).

Capacity Building

Issue

Years of mismanagement, conflict and war, and low public sector salaries had severely eroded administrative capacity. Although elaborate procedures and controls were prescribed in existing legislation and regulations, these were generally bypassed or, if followed (e.g., the preparation of the annual budget), they were virtually meaningless for lack of effective follow-up and adequate controls. Also, there were huge logistical bottlenecks owing to the collapse of infrastructure, in particular the transport network. Because of the lack of transparency in public affairs, donors were reluctant to provide nonhumanitarian assistance.

Actions

Three main actions have been taken. First, the implementing agency for the EERP, BCECO (Bureau Central de Coordination), was strengthened, especially its procurement procedures, to ensure a transparent and competitive bidding process for public contracts, which is key for securing donor assistance. Second, feasibility studies and final design and bidding documents for priority (mainly infrastructure) projects to be financed by donors other than the World Bank were completed. Third, implementation capacity in ministries and utilities responsible for health care, roads, urban development, community-driven development, electricity, and water was strengthened through the provision of technical assistance and training in preparation for sector reforms over the medium term (see subsection on sectoral reform in Section IV), as well as to develop a framework for donor coordination and commence work on public investment planning——two activities that go hand in hand.

Section IV. Structural and Sectoral Measures Taken in 2002–03 (First Half of the Reconstruction Phase)

Based on the successful implementation of the PIR (see Chapter 2), in June 2002 the Executive Board of the IMF approved an arrangement of SDR 580 million under its PRGF in support of the three-year (2002–05) Government Economic Program or PEG (Programme Economique du Gouvernement), which had been drawn up while the SMP was being implemented, and which largely coincides with the reconstruction phase of the interim PRSP (see Section I). Under the PEG, the structural reforms that had been initiated under the PIR were to be broadened and deepened and, after the formal completion of the peace and reunification process in August 2003 (see Chapter 2), extended across the entire nation. In addition, a wide range of sectoral reforms were to be implemented. In support of these structural and sectoral reforms, the World Bank Executive Board approved two credits/projects in June–July 2002, followed in the second half of 2003 by three more.[12] Also, in December 2003, the African Development Bank approved an economic recovery and reunification support operation of about US$60 million.

---

[12]World Bank assistance was channeled through an Economic Recovery Credit of about US$450 million in support of further structural reform and, one month later, the Emergency Multisector Rehabilitation and Reconstruction Project (EMRRP) of about US$454 million and about US$1.3 billion in cofinancing, in support of, mainly, investment in infrastructure and sectoral reform. About a year later, on July 2, 2003, the Executive Board of the World Bank approved a loan of US$120 million for the Private Sector Development and Competitiveness Project (PSDCP) and, on September 11, 2003, a Post-Reunification Recovery Project of US$214 million (of which US$30 million is in grants). Both projects are in support of the ongoing structural and sector reforms. Further support from the World Bank (about US$178 million) was obtained in November 2003 in the context of the Southern African Power Market Program, mainly to upgrade the DRC's power grid to enable it to export electricity to southern Africa.

During the reconstruction period, capacity building was to continue and to be extended to the reunified provinces, with technical assistance provided by the IMF, the World Bank, and, increasingly, other donors, following the successful implementation of the PIR and several donors' meetings organized by the World Bank. Using essentially the same classification as in the previous section, the four subsections below elaborate on the measures that were taken during the first half of the reconstruction period.

Enabling the Private Sector, Improving Governance, and Fighting Corruption

Building on the progress made under the PIR, the government developed and started to implement a comprehensive strategy for further enabling the private sector, improving governance, and fighting corruption. The focus was on further strengthening the rule of law, the judiciary, and the legal and regulatory environment for private sector development and on fighting corruption in the public sector.

Actions to Date

Strengthening the rule of law and the judiciary and improving the legal and regulatory framework for private sector development

Building on its previous work in the legal area at the time of the PIR, the European Union initiated the preparation of a status report on the legal system. In the area of business law, the government started to prepare for joining the Organization for the Harmonization of Business Law in Africa or OHADA (Organisation pour l'Harmonisation en Afrique du Droit des Affaires). A status report on the taxation of enterprises was submitted to the government in January 2003 in preparation for the streamlining of the tax system to be implemented in 2004. In addition, the ANAPI, a one-stop window for investors, was established in December 2002, which, with World Bank assistance, launched a study on the administrative barriers (red tape) to private sector development. Audits of cross arrears between the government and the domestic private sector and between the government and public enterprises were completed in September 2003, and the conditions and timetable for the clearance of these arrears were to be established by the end of 2004.

To create a modern framework for labor relations, the government drew up, with World Bank and International Labor Organization assistance, a new labor code, which parliament approved in October 2002. Its main implementing decrees were to be adopted in 2004. To establish a forum for dialogue between the private sector and the government, a permanent body (le Cadre Permanent de Concertation Economique) was created.

Fighting corruption in the public sector

A multipronged strategy to address corruption in the public sector is being applied. First, a code of ethics and good conduct was enacted in November 2002 that applies to all civil servants regardless of their rank and nature of appointment. The code draws, among other things, on the model adopted by the Committee of Ministers to Member States of the Council of Europe on codes of conduct for public officials. A campaign to explain the code was launched in March 2003. The decree on the organization and operations of the code (Observatoire du Code Ethique et Professionnel) was published in April 2003, and it became operational in September 2003. On August 28, 2003, President Kabila submitted to parliament a written declaration of his wealth, and several members of the National Transitional Government have followed suit.

Second, in August 2002 the government established an Anticorruption Commission. The commission has a three-part mandate: (1) it is responsible for the investigation and prosecution of cases of corruption and related offenses; (2) it is the focal point for formulating recommendations and initiating measures to prevent corruption; and (3) it is responsible for designing and implementing a program of public awareness to help citizens combat corruption. In establishing the legal mandate of the commission, the government specified a full spectrum of corruption, criminal offenses of an economic nature, and other related offences that may be investigated and prosecuted by the commission.

Third, a Governance and Anticorruption Strategy and Action Plan was drawn up in late 2002, taking into account the conclusions of a workshop held in September of that year. Representatives of central and local government, civil society, and the private sector participated in the workshop. The action plan involves (1) creation of a legal, regulatory, and institutional framework for combating corruption; (2) reform of public institutions, including the civil service; (3) design and implementation of effective penalties for corruption; and (4) strengthening of effective partnerships among the public sector, civil society, and the international community. The action plan sets out clearly that leaders and managers in government are responsible and accountable for their actions. In the context of this action plan, a draft anticorruption law and a draft law on money laundering and the financing of transnational organized crime were to be submitted to parliament in the course of 2004. The same holds for the compendium of citizens' rights and obligations.

Fourth, a complete overhaul of public procurement procedures was initiated in July 2003, comprising (1) updating and revising procurement legislation; (2) strengthening functional structures in decision making; (3) improving contract management; (4) improving the procurement information system; and (5) training personnel. The recommendations were expected to be available by the end of April 2004, on which basis a strategy will be developed to set up a modern regulatory and institutional framework for government procurement, along with an implementation timetable. In this context, the government is to establish a list of firms and individuals prohibited from being awarded contracts. Also, the government will make available to the public information about firms (including ownership) that are eligible for government contracts.

Fifth, audits will be used to detect corrupt practices and abuse of power in tax administration, expenditure management, and procurement. As a first step, after an 18-year interruption, the audits of the 2001 and 2002 budget executions by the General Accounting Office (Cour des Comptes) were completed in the fourth quarter of 2003 and presented to parliament in December 2003 and January 2004, respectively, for their subsequent publication in the Official Journal (*Journal Officiel*).

Reform of the Natural Resources Sector

The objective of government policy in the natural resources sector is to quickly rehabilitate and develop production in the country in an economically, environmentally, and socially sustainable way and to ensure that development of the natural resources sector contributes to growth, development, and poverty reduction rather than to the wealth of a privileged elite. Thus, building on the preparations and achievements under the PIR, the specific elements of the government's strategy include (1) improving transparency and good governance in the management of mineral and forest resources; (2) increasing the participation of local communities in forest management and direct access to forest revenues; and (3) addressing the immediate constraints on the public mining company, GECAMINES.

Actions to Date

Forestry

Based on the preparatory work under the PIR, a new forestry code was drafted with World Bank assistance and approved by parliament in June 2002; most of its implementing regulations had been adopted by late 2002. Full implementation of the code, which incorporates international best practices, will ensure sustainable forestry. The code rationalizes taxation in the forestry sector by reducing the number of taxes (exceeding 60 in early 2002) and the number of authorized tax collection agencies (8 in early 2002), and it introduces market mechanisms and incentives to encourage high value-added industrialization, the equitable sharing of forestry revenues, and sustainable development. The code stipulates that 40 percent of fiscal revenues will flow directly to local communities, which will also be given the right to manage directly their own forests, thus supporting community dynamics and self-reliance of the poor—key elements of the interim PRSP. Logging concessions will be awarded through a transparent, market-based mechanism that discourages the speculative holding of property while encouraging private sector investment and exploitation, and that increases revenues accruing to government and local communities.

By April 2002, 143 concessions covering 23.4 million hectares (of 40 million hectares in 260 concessions under review) had been annulled by decree. By ministerial order, the 117 concessions that had been declared valid were published on May 24, 2003, and, also by interministerial order, the collection methods and accompanying policies for the area tax (*taxe de superficie*), which was increased from US$0.0014 to US$0.0625 per hectare (and to be raised further), were published in June 2003. The government was to publish a report on the actual collection of this tax in January 2004, and the concessions of delinquent taxpayers were to be revoked.

Mining

Revision of the legal and regulatory framework. In February 2001, the diamond sector had been liberalized. In 2003, the authorities put in place the procedures for certification of origin required to adhere to the Kimberley Accord on conflict diamonds. Recorded output and exports of diamonds have increased significantly since 2001. To further improve transparency in the sector, the government will, with external technical assistance, audit the diamond sector and it will contract an internationally reputable firm to audit the diamond mining company MIBA (Société Minière de Bakwanga).

Following publication of the new mining code in April 2002, the reform of the legal framework for the mining sector was completed in April 2003 with the publication of the decrees on the new mining regulations, the mining registry (*cadastre minier*), and the interministerial Mining Title Validation Commission. Although the new mining registry became operational in June 2003, additional strengthening is needed to bring its activities up to the level required by the new mining code.

GECAMINES will be completely restructured, a process that is complicated by the company's "quasi-state" role in the provision of social services in much of the province of Katanga, the predominant economic and social impact of the firm in that province, and its multitude of joint venture agreements, logistics contracts, and supply agreements.

The cost of terminating employment of about 11,000 candidates for voluntary departure under the collective agreement with the unions of GECAMINES—about $120 million—would pose an impossible financial burden for the bankrupt company and would set a precedent for future restructuring programs for public sector enterprises that the government would not be able to afford. Accordingly, the government has decided to put in place a voluntary retirement program, outside the existing collective bargaining agreement, which would permit a rational restructuring of the mining sector. The option of obtaining immediate payment of salary arrears instead of protracted waiting for an uncertain outcome was chosen by about 10,500 workers. The cost of the program amounts to about US$48 million and is financed by the World Bank. The program was put in place in August 2003. Departures began immediately thereafter and were completed by early 2004.

The strategy for restructuring GECAMINES is being developed: the experts to examine GECAMINES's partnership agreements with private companies are scheduled to begin their work in January 2004 and present their final reports by the end of June 2004. This should allow for the finalization of the GECAMINES restructuring strategy between July and September 2004 and its submission to parliament by the end of 2004, in the context of a law on the restructuring of GECAMINES. This law will define the action plan, as well as the implementing institution, and would authorize the sale or partnership holding of the company's assets.

Public Enterprise Reform

Based on the diagnoses made at the time of the PIR, the government formulated the following objectives for public enterprise reform: (1) to ensure that basic services are provided on a sustainable and profitable basis, (2) to reduce fiscal pressure caused by public enterprise mismanagement, and (3) to help to attract employment-generating investments through the restoration of a business environment conducive to growth. Finally, available options for private sector participation, whether fully private or through public-private partnerships, management contract, or other arrangements, will be explored. Public enterprise reform will begin in those sectors that have a direct impact on the overall competitiveness of the economy, namely, electricity, transport, and communications. These sectors, in which the quality of the services rendered is far worse than in other sub-Saharan countries, are, with mining and forestry, key for promoting economic growth.

Actions to Date

The government has started the process of building ownership, through seminars and public awareness campaigns, of the need to reform state-owned enterprises.

Following preparations during the stabilization phase, the Steering Committee on the Reform of Public Enterprises or COPIREP (Comité de Pilotage de la Réforme des Enterprises Publiques) was put in place in August 2003. It reports to an interministerial committee and has an executive secretariat.[13] COPIREP's responsibilities are to (1) undertake audits of all public enterprises; (2) define selection criteria and select those enterprises that should remain in the state portfolio and those that should be transferred out; (3) revamp the legislation governing public enterprises and establishments; (4) establish the legal framework allowing for public enterprise reform; (5) establish divestiture strategies and procedures for those companies that the state intends to divest; (6) restructure those companies that will remain in the state portfolio; and (7) define and develop appropriate social safety nets for workers made redundant by the reforms.

Sectoral working groups have been created to identify reform options for each enterprise within each sector. The Executive Secretariat of COPIREP coordinates these groups.

Based on the initial results of a diagnostic study concerning accounting practices and the functioning and operations of public enterprises undertaken in early 2003, and in the context of the World Bank's

---

[13]Before the creation of COPIREP, the responsibility for public enterprises rested with the presidency. Pending the restructuring, public enterprises, or their assets, cannot be sold by the government or the enterprises themselves without COPIREP's authorization.

PSDCP, seven key enterprises in the transport, communications, and electricity sectors have been selected for restructuring: the national railways company (Société Nationale des Chemins de Fer du Congo); the urban transportation company (Citytrain); the air traffic control system (Régie des Voies Aériennes); Congo airlines (Lignes Aériennes Congolaises); the post and telecommunications company (Office Congolais des Postes et Télécommunications); the national petroleum company (COHYDRO); and the national electricity company (Société Nationale de l'Electricité).[14]

Detailed restructuring plans are to be completed in 2004, and, in some cases, actual restructuring would also start in that year.

Sectoral Reforms

The main vehicle for sectoral reform is the World Bank's EMRRP. Its specific objectives are to help the DRC to (1) start rebuilding agricultural production and enhance food security; (2) rehabilitate and reconstruct critical infrastructure; (3) restore essential social services and build community infrastructure; and (4) strengthen the capacity of the government to formulate, implement, and manage medium- and long-term development programs.

The EMRRP is being implemented nationwide, but it initially emphasized the western part of the country, because preparations could only be made in that region. Its activities were drawn from a large, multisector program of rehabilitation and reconstruction prepared in September 2001 by the ministry of planning and reconstruction in consultation with various sector ministries (see Section III on capacity building). It comprises three main components: (1) rehabilitation and reconstruction of critical infrastructure (transport, water supply, electricity, and urban infrastructure); (2) agriculture, delivery of social services (education, health, and social protection), and community development; and (3) development of sector strategies for the medium and long term and strengthening of human and institutional capacities. The design of the EMRRP has been based on free-standing subprojects that fit within the overall program but are not integrally linked to other activities, so as to facilitate parallel financing arrangements. Over the medium term, the EMRRP projects will benefit the country through improved infrastructure, a strengthened legal and regulatory frame-

---

[14]The PSDCP also refers to the restructuring of GECAMINES, which in this chapter is discussed in the subsection on reform of the natural resources sector.

work, and more stable and effective institutions—critical conditions for better governance.

The EMRRP's main components, which by the end of 2003 were in various stages of execution, are described below.

Component A: rehabilitation and reconstruction of critical infrastructure

This component will finance the rehabilitation and reconstruction of critical transportation infrastructure, electricity services, water supplies, and urban infrastructure. The transportation subcomponent will finance activities to improve river, rail, and air transportation, including rehabilitation of ports, airports, and bridges, and the purchase of equipment for river navigation and aeronautical communications. The roads subcomponent will support rehabilitation or reconstruction of 1,200 kilometers of main roads and bridges, including Highway I (*Route nationale*), which links six provinces to the coastal ports. The electricity subcomponent will finance rehabilitation of the electricity supply networks serving major cities. The water supply subcomponent will support rehabilitation of waterworks in cities, including Kinshasa, Lubumbashi, Mbuji-Mayi, and Boma. The urban services and infrastructure subcomponent will provide support to enable selected urban centers to improve solid waste services, maintain and rehabilitate urban streets and drainage systems, and control erosion.

Component B: agriculture, delivery of social services, and community development

The agriculture subcomponent will finance rehabilitation of 5,000 kilometers of rural roads and access tracks; help establish an agricultural information system for farmers; strengthen the operations of producers' organizations, nongovernmental organizations (NGOs), and key public service providers; and support the development of a policy framework that improves the investment climate for agriculture and forestry.

The social services and community development subcomponents will finance essential services in health, education, social protection, and community development. Improving and expanding health care services is the priority among the subsectors because of the extraordinary extent to which disease is affecting the well-being and productivity of the population. The strategy for these sectors is to select modest investments that have a relatively quick and high impact. Investments in community-selected projects provide a means for rehabilitating schools and health centers that both promote community ownership of facilities and inject cash into the local economy.

The health services part will assist the government to (1) develop and disseminate laws and regulations governing the health system; (2) reinforce public-private partnerships and community participation and reestablish health planning structures; (3) rehabilitate and equip health centers and other health facilities in 100 health zones; (4) increase the number of health care workers and upgrade their skills; (5) establish central medical purchasing and distribution offices to improve the availability of medicine and other essential medical supplies throughout the country; (6) strengthen programs to prevent and treat the DRC's most serious diseases, including HIV/AIDS, malaria, tuberculosis, and sleeping sickness; and (7) provide health care services targeted to specific groups, notably mothers, children, orphans, and victims of war.

The education part will finance the rehabilitation of primary schools; the procurement of textbooks and other school supplies and equipment; and training courses for new as well as experienced teachers.

The social protection subcomponent will support pilot activities to test approaches for designing and executing programs to assist vulnerable people. Activities include informal and accelerated education for street children and programs to reintegrate child soldiers into society.

The community development subcomponent will finance small-scale projects to improve education, health, transportation, drinking water and sanitation services, energy supplies, environmental protection, and the delivery of basic social and economic services. The projects will be identified, prepared, and executed by the communities with the help of NGOs, to ensure that they reflect communities' priorities and that the communities take responsibility for maintaining the infrastructure and services.

Component C: development of medium- and long-term sector development strategies, capacity building, and institutional reform

This component will finance preparation of the development strategies for the DRC's most important sectors: agriculture, education, health, transportation (covering all modes), water and sanitation, electricity, and social protection. It will also cover costs of implementing sector and institutional reforms and of building human and institutional capacity. Finally, this component will finance the principal studies and preparatory activities for future investment programs.

Social sectors. A sectoral review of the health sector will be launched with assistance of the World Bank, with a view to preparing a comprehensive assessment as the starting point for developing the sectoral strategy by the end of 2004. Preparation of the social protection strategy will be the first stage in a program that by the end of 2004 is to set out (1) the government's actions in the area of social protection; (2) the actions of the development partners in the area of social protection; and (3) the budget and sources of financing for these activities. For the education sector, an action plan for fulfillment of the criteria of the Education for All program was completed in October 2003, whereas the sectoral strategy is to be completed by the end of 2004.

For the agricultural sector, four subsector studies (palm oil, cotton, coffee, and cocoa), as well as a study on the regulatory and tax environment for agribusinesses, will be launched by the end of December 2004. The results of these studies will be used to prepare the rural development section of the PRSP.

Infrastructure sector. In early 2004, a legal and regulatory framework and a regulatory authority will be established for the electricity sector. A water code will be finalized in 2004, as well as a new energy code.

Section V. Structural and Sectoral Reform: Results So Far, Lessons, and Challenges for the Future

By the end of 2003, the DRC had been implementing policies aimed at turning the economy around for about two-and-a-half years. Overall, the real GDP growth of 3.5 percent in 2002 (positive for the first time in 13 years), and its acceleration to 5.6 percent in 2003, along with the continued deceleration in inflation, indicate that the Congolese authorities' efforts in the areas of peace building, economic management, and structural reforms have succeeded in turning the economy around (see Chapter 2). It is difficult to determine the separate effects of these measures, especially because some of the reforms, namely public enterprise restructuring and sectoral reforms, have only just started. However, the available information indicates that structural reform did play a significant role in the turnaround of the economy. The PIR, in addition to quickly breaking the vicious circle of hyperinflation and currency depreciation, also produced significant results in structural areas. Major economic distortions were eliminated, notably via the unification of multiple exchange rates and the liberalization of the prices of goods, including the transparent and automatic mechanism for the prices of petroleum products. These actions translated into the overnight disappearance of long lines at gasoline stations, a virtual halt to smuggling, greater availability of public transportation, and an increased supply of foodstuffs because the improved transportation between consuming cities and the producing countryside led to price drops for some items.[15]

In addition, the business climate has significantly improved following the elimination of obstacles to the functioning of the private sector through the abolition of the diamond export monopoly;[16] the adoption of the new investment, mining, and forestry codes; the replacement of exceptional military courts for business and economic affairs by commercial courts; the strengthening of the judiciary; and the development of an anticorruption strategy. These developments have significantly affected investment plans of the private sector (resident as well as nonresident): in the 12 months following its inception (December 2002), ANAPI (itself the result of structural reform) approved more than 100 private sector investment projects amounting to about US$2.3 billion.[17] Although it will take time before these projects materialize, the surge in investment plans will contribute to future economic growth.

Now that the first results of the structural reforms can be determined, what conclusions and lessons can be drawn regarding the formulation and implementation of structural and sectoral reforms, and what are the challenges for the future?

The factors mentioned in Chapter 2 that determined the success of the government's programs, among other things, ownership, the appropriate sequencing of measures, the early involvement of the Bretton Woods institutions, and the early sharing of results with the donor community, were also of key importance for the successful implementation of structural reforms. This applies especially to ownership, because structural reforms tend to affect vested interests, which makes their implementation politically difficult. In addition, because most structural reforms take time to prepare and implement, their proper sequencing—taking into account the realities of the country—is key for their effective implementation. On the basis of their early diagnosis of the situation, the government and the staffs of the IMF and World Bank were able to draw up programs that distinguished clearly between immediate priority measures aiming at removing bottlenecks and stabilizing the macroeconomic situation on the one

---

[15]These macroeconomic structural reforms had an immediate and measurable impact, contrary to the effects of most other structural reforms.

[16]Declared production and exports of diamonds increased from 16,000 carats in 2000 to 27,000 carats in 2003.

[17]Recorded GDP amounted to about US$5.7 billion in 2003.

hand, and measures to be taken over the short and medium term to effect fundamental change, on the other. This sequencing was critical in creating a link early on between macroeconomic and microeconomic reform through the creation of an overall framework conducive to private sector–led growth.

Thus, in practice, the liberalization of the diamond sector and the drafting of the investment and mining codes, and, somewhat later, the forestry code, have enhanced transparency through the creation of a level playing field for private operators, eliminated bottlenecks in the functioning of the private sector, and improved the business climate. These measures were followed by the issuing of implementation decrees to give "teeth" to the just-mentioned codes, plus a wide range of measures, including the adoption of legislation, to strengthen good governance and transparency in public affairs. The early removal of structural bottlenecks was key to the revival of economic growth.

Now that the investment, mining, and forestry codes are in place, their continued proper application, including in the reunified provinces, is required to achieve their goals: the equitable treatment of economic operators and the transparent and market-based exploitation of the country's natural resources. Only then will the full confidence-building impact of these measures become apparent. This, together with the further nationwide strengthening of the judiciary, the adoption of anticorruption legislation, effective implementation of public enterprise restructuring (going well beyond the eight enterprises currently targeted to be restructured), continued financial and public sector reform (including civil service reform), and implementation of infrastructure investments and sectoral reforms supported by the World Bank and other donors, will contribute significantly to the increase in the DRC's productive capacity and, together with the continued implementation of sound macroeconomic policies, ensure a firm foundation for propoor growth.

Bibliography

Bates, Robert H., 1999, "Institutions and Economic Performance," paper delivered at the IMF Conference on Second Generation Reforms, Washington, November 8–9, 1999.

James, Harold, 1998, "From Grandmotherliness to Governance: The Evolution of IMF Conditionality," *Finance and Development*, Vol. 35, No. 4.

Rodrik, Dani, 1999, "Institutions for High-Quality Growth: What They Are and How to Acquire Them," National Bureau of Economic Research Paper W7540.

Tanzi, Vito, 1999, "The Quality of the Public Sector," paper delivered at the IMF Conference on Second Generation Reforms, Washington, November 8–9, 1999.

Thomas, Vinod, 1999, "The Quality of Growth," paper delivered at the IMF Conference on Second Generation Reforms, Washington, November 8–9, 1999.

World Bank, 2001, "Transitional Support Strategy for the Democratic Republic of Congo," World Bank Report No. 22499-ZR (Washington).

———, 2001, "Memorandum for an Emergency Early Recovery Project," World Bank Report No. P7469 ZR (Washington).

———, 2002, "Report on an Economic Recovery Credit for the DRC," World Bank Report No. P7531 (Washington).

———, 2002, "Memorandum on an Emergency Multisector Rehabilitation and Reconstruction Project," World Bank Report No. P7551 (Washington).

———, 2003, "Project Appraisal Document for a Private Sector Development and Competitiveness Project," World Bank Report No. 25707 ZR (Washington).

———, 2003, "Memorandum on an Emergency Economic and Social Reunification Support Project," World Bank Report No. P7601-ZR (Washington).

———, 2003, "Project Appraisal Document for the Southern Africa Power Market Program," World Bank Report No. 26806 (Washington).

12

The Long Road to Demilitarization: 1997–2003

MARKUS KOSTNER, ELY DIENG, AND ADRIAAN VERHEUL[1]

This chapter reviews efforts regarding the disarmament, demobiliza-tion, and reintegration (DDR) of ex-combatants in the Democratic Republic of the Congo (DRC) between 1997 and 2003. Reflecting the evolving politico-military situation and the shifting pri-orities in terms of DDR, the chapter contains the following sections. Section I analyzes the period 1997–99, from the takeover of power and the challenge of demobilizing soldiers of the army of the ousted regime to the reorientation of the DDR strategy in response to the signing of the Lusaka cease-fire agreement. Section II covers the period 1999–2001, focusing on small-scale endeavors that kept DDR on the agenda of government and the international community pending the political resolution of the Congolese conflict. Section III examines the period 2001–03 during which the international community, with an unprecedented regional approach to DDR, intensified its efforts to re-spond to the ever more complex situation until the government finally assumed principal responsibility for DDR in the country. The chapter closes with Section IV, which reflects on lessons learned from this mul-

[1]Markus Kostner was Manager of the Multi-Country Demobilization Program (MDRP) and task team leader of the World Bank's demobilization and reintegration ef-forts in Burundi, the DRC, and Rwanda. Ely Dieng was senior liaison officer at MONUC, seconded by the World Bank. Adriaan Verheul is senior demobilization and reintegration specialist at the World Bank. This chapter is based on the authors' first-hand experience and pertinent World Bank and MDRP documentation. For more in-formation, see www.mdrp.org.

tiyear process for the national DDR program in the DRC, and for similar programs elsewhere.

Section I. 1997–99: Good Efforts Coming to Naught

Startup

When the Alliance of the Democratic Forces for the Liberation of the Congo or AFDL (Alliance des forces démocratiques pour la libération du Congo) came to power in May 1997, it inherited a dysfunctional, undisciplined army. The orderly integration of the soldiers into civilian life quickly became a top priority for the new government, and a DDR program became a key element in the transition from neglect and war to peace and stability. However, the government was also acutely aware of its financial and technical limitations to successfully design and implement such a program. Consequently, only two months after acceding to power, President Laurent-Désiré Kabila requested the World Bank to assist in the demobilization and reintegration of about 75,000 soldiers of the former Armed Forces of Zaïre or FAZ (Forces Armées Zaïroises).

This decision was taken at a time when most neighboring countries were either at war (Angola, the Republic of Congo) or otherwise suffering or emerging from violent conflict (Burundi, Central African Republic, Rwanda). From the very beginning, therefore, maintaining a regional security perspective was essential for the Congolese government and its partners in the international community.

The Situation in the Aftermath of the Mobutu Regime

FAZ personnel records had by and large been destroyed before the fall of Kinshasa. It was, thus, impossible to establish the exact size of the force. The paper size of the FAZ (including police [*gendarmerie*] and the civil guard [*garde civile*], who accounted for approximately two-thirds and were under the command of the ministry of interior) was estimated at about 125,000, but estimates of the actual strength ranged from 50,000 to 90,000. Meanwhile, the AFDL never had any records. By May 1997, their strength was estimated at some 20,000, plus another 20,000 child soldiers (*kadogos*). The forces that joined the AFDL from Katanga and that had taken refuge in Angola some 30 years earlier may have reached a strength of 2,500.

The socioeconomic profile of the ex-FAZ was hardly encouraging. Many soldiers should have been retired from military service for legal, administrative, or health reasons up to 15 years earlier but were kept in the FAZ because of the risk they posed to internal security. The new government estimated that most soldiers had more than 15 years of service, had large families (with seven or more children), were undernourished, had low education and skill levels, were between 35 and 45 years of age, were poor, and had no contact with their extended families back home for a long time. Many were said to be alcoholics or mutineers, have a looting mentality, not respect civilians and the civilian administration, not want to work, and resort to violence as a form of solving conflicts.

The new government, therefore, decided to put about 55,000 ex-FAZ (army, *garde civile*, and *gendarmerie*) into two "reeducation camps" in Kitona (Bas-Congo Province; 35,000) and Kamina (Shaba Province; 20,000). These reeducation camps had a negative effect on public opinion, and many (ex-FAZ and the population at large) believed that the soldiers of the former army would not come out alive. However, there seems to have been little desire for revenge among the victorious army, and many of the ex-FAZ had been sympathetic to the AFDL in the first place. Meanwhile, possibly 5,000 to 10,000 ex-FAZ had fled to neighboring countries, whereas an unknown number had deserted to unknown locations inside the DRC.

After the takeover, each soldier (including the ex-FAZ) was supposed to receive US$100 per month as ration to cover the needs of his/her family. This US$100 would suffice to buy rice, fish, oil, salt, and some other essentials for an average family. Some soldiers seem to have received small payments, whereas others received nothing. Regular salaries, however, were not being paid.

Summer and Fall of 1997

The new authorities had planned to deploy all ex-FAZ soldiers (most of them after having passed through the reeducation camps) in units of a unified Congolese Armed Forces or FAC (Forces Armées Congolaises) before starting the demobilization process. From a DDR perspective, this decision had severe cost implications because the soldiers to be demobilized had to be transported from the two camps to the units before being discharged and then transported to their communities of settlement. However, the government strongly believed that the unification of forces and the demobilization from a unified army would go a long way toward assuring the population that the government was ready to reconcile with the former army, with an expected positive impact on security. The government thus envisaged a three-year DDR program as part of an overall effort to restructure the security apparatus of the country (i.e., military reform).

In August 1997, the government set up a working group on demobilization and rehabilitation. The key actors in this group were the ministries of defense, reconstruction and emergency planning, and interior. The working group reported directly to the *Chef du Cabinet* of President Kabila. Its first task was to draft a DDR program note for the upcoming Friends of Congo meeting and develop a work program for the DDR planning phase. The ministries of finance and planning as well as sector ministries were consulted during this process.

The working group undertook highly commendable work in sketching out the approach and elements of the Congolese program. Within a month, the program note was drafted, and the work plan for program preparation was elaborated. This work plan included a preliminary socioeconomic profile based on focal group interviews, an assessment of the opportunity structure in areas of settlement, and the design of the institutional structure and implementation plan. The core activity, however, was the identification and registration of soldiers from all forces (especially those in the reeducation camps) to establish a complete database, which was to subsequently help identify the soldiers to be demobilized.

Initially envisaged program elements included a pilot operation to test implementation arrangements; a transitional safety net for a total of 12 months to ensure coverage of a family's basic needs for at least one crop cycle; economic reintegration support measures in the area of agriculture and livestock, training and employment, and micro-projects; a focus on social reintegration including assistance to communities of settlement; and targeted support to child soldiers, disabled soldiers, and children of soldiers. Child soldiers and overage soldiers were expected to constitute the priority target for the initial phase of the DDR program.

Moreover, the working group completed a detailed organizational structure for a national DDR commission with an executive secretariat and district-level advisory councils with district cells. This structure was summarized in a draft decree submitted to the cabinet for review before being submitted for President Kabila's signature.

Building on its early technical support to the working group, and in recognition of the government's commitment vis-à-vis this program, the World Bank approved the first ever grant under its Post-Conflict Fund in the amount of US$2 million to help the government prepare the DDR program. Meanwhile, on a parallel track, the United Nations Children's Fund (UNICEF) embarked on an advocacy campaign with the aim of demobilizing child soldiers, and the United Nations Development Programme (UNDP) and the International Labor Organization (ILO) initiated a technical assistance project to assess the needs of vulnerable groups, including child soldiers and handicapped soldiers. These activities were undertaken without much coordination with the government's working group, which was supposed to have coordination responsibility over all DDR-related efforts in the country.

The Standstill of 1998

After a remarkable start, preparation for the DDR program was slowing down noticeably in early 1998, and the government's commitment was waning. Several design revisions were undertaken early in the year. In particular, the idea of a full census profile and identification was given up in favor of an initial registration (to be carried out by the FAC) and a sample socioeconomic survey. UNICEF started two pilot projects for *kadogos* in Bukavu and Goma in collaboration with provincial authorities. Given the specific roles of the authorities, the UNICEF suboffices used widely different approaches: Goma was more oriented toward psychosocial assistance, Bukavu emphasized vocational training.

However, notwithstanding the availability of funds from the World Bank, the working group essentially put on hold further program preparation pending the signature of the presidential decree establishing the National Commission for Demobilization and Rehabilitation. This policy inaction also impeded the implementation of the World Bank's grant because the commission was to manage the funds. To avoid unnecessary politicization of the technical work, the Congolese government and the World Bank tentatively agreed that a third party would execute the grant.

At the time, both UNDP and ILO indicated that they would only engage in the reintegration phase. UNICEF, meanwhile, had just signed an accord with the government on the reintegration of *kadogos* from Kapalata and was willing to facilitate the preparation of a comprehensive program (i.e., one addressing all target groups). By having UNICEF manage the grant funds on the government's behalf, the national commission would not have to be formally established at this point in time. In its place the working group proposed an informal monitoring group with representatives from all concerned ministries.

Although administrative arrangements were put in place to formally launch program preparation, and UNICEF continued its advocacy role for child soldier demobilization, the renewed outbreak of war in August 1998 put an end to any prospects of a DDR program in the foreseeable future. Notwithstanding these developments, the urgency to address the needs of overage, underage, and disabled ex-FAZ soldiers persisted, and the World Bank maintained low-level contact with the working group to facilitate reengagement as and when the situation would permit.

The Revival of Early 1999

With the de facto demarcation of the front line by early 1999, aspects of a renewed demobilization strategy for ex-FAZ soldiers emerged. The government intended to demobilize ex-FAZ soldiers as a matter of priority as reports of pillaging and other signs of indiscipline continued and as ex-FAZ soldiers, as well as other "unfit" elements, posed a growing threat to the security of the population.

Efforts aimed at the demobilization of ex-FAZ soldiers and other undisciplined elements contrasted sharply with the ongoing mobilization into the FAC. In fact, donors and agencies believed there were few ex-FAZ left to demobilize: most were thought of as having been killed during the offensive on Kinshasa in August 1998, fighting with the rebels, or having fled to neighboring countries. There was also the concern that the government's renewed interest in the DDR program was based on the dirigiste idea of a national service (*service national*) and the development brigades (*brigades de développement*), both created to absorb ex-combatants. Concerns were raised about the possibility of creating a private army or army in reserve as well as forced labor.

Meanwhile, UNICEF had initiated another working group with civilian ministries and civil society representatives to advance the issue of child soldier demobilization. Furthermore, ILO and, in principle, UNICEF were willing to collaborate with the World Bank in relaunching the preparatory phase of a comprehensive program. Given the fluid political situation and the sensitive nature of the program, a concerted effort of core international partners was seen as beneficial to all parties.

Building on the Spirit of the Lusaka Cease-Fire Agreement

With the signing of the cease-fire agreement by heads of state in Lusaka on July 11, 1999, President Kabila finally approved the start of program preparation. To respond to the new reality, the reinvigorated working group led the redesign of the overall DDR approach. The objective of the planning phase was to prepare a DDR program in two phases: one for especially vulnerable groups and the other for general demobilization. Planning activities were similar for both phases, thus maximizing limited available resources. The World Bank remained the only donor specifically having set aside funds for this activity. Other donors were ready to engage once progress was visible.

Phase I demobilization would target child soldiers, overage soldiers, chronically ill soldiers, and disabled soldiers. This phase was to commence in government-controlled areas immediately after the conclusion of the planning phase. From a security perspective, the demobilization of these groups was unlikely to affect military decision making. Hence, implementation of this phase could go ahead from a humanitarian perspective even if the second phase, general demobilization, were to be postponed.

Phase II was closely linked to the unification and restructuring of forces as envisaged in the Lusaka agreement. The launching of this phase would take place as and when the overall situation was considered opportune. This two-phased approach allowed the government to address its immediate needs while providing time for the further preparation of general demobilization.

Two other major changes were made to the original proposal of August 1997. First, identification and registration in a few central locations were no longer considered practical or cost-effective, given the by now dispersed location of troops. Second, UNICEF had initiated a partnership with the ministry of human rights to advance the issue of child soldier demobilization. Instead of duplicating this structure, phase I preparation and execution would be undertaken under joint guidance by the ministries of defense and human rights rather than by a national commission. The technical secretariat and working group already established by UNICEF would be expanded in membership and responsibility accordingly. This arrangement was to be revised for phase II.

Although this approach aimed at addressing the complex situation most comprehensively, other initiatives continued. In particular, the ministry of reconstruction started a national service, initially for youths but likely to also include ex-combatants later. In response to an urgent request by the Governor of Katanga, the United Nations Office for the Coordination of Humanitarian Affairs and UNDP provided food assistance to about 1,000 ex-combatants apparently released from prison in early July. Moreover, the commission for the reintegration of refugees was intent on including ex-combatants in its mandate.

This proliferation of activities and institutional bodies raised concerns over government ownership, including ownership of the process and program by the armed forces. Such ownership would have required significant action on the government's part, especially the signing of the presidential decree establishing the national commission that the working group had drafted two years earlier. Not surprisingly, military reform efforts, which are critical to a successful DDR program, were not visible either.

Section II. 1999–2001: Advancing on a Small Scale

A New Impetus

During the latter half of 1999, the Department of Peacekeeping Operations (DPKO) initiated planning for the deployment of the United Nations Organization Mission to the Congo (MONUC) in support of the Lusaka cease-fire agreement. Through Resolution 1279 of November 30, 1999, the UN Security Council authorized the deployment of a peacekeeping mission to the DRC. Although MONUC's mandate was to be limited to the voluntary disarmament, demobilization, and repatriation of foreign armed groups in the DRC (especially those of Rwandan origin) until mid-2003, the dynamics of DDR program planning in the DRC changed significantly.[2]

What had been an effort led by the Congolese government (with all its delays and missed opportunities) with support by the international community became more and more an activity driven by the outside with a predominantly regional rather than Congolese perspective. From the outset, the World Bank, ILO, and UNICEF were working with DPKO and MONUC to bring experiences gained to date into the new planning process. For instance, all agencies participated in DPKO-organized coordination meetings in New York. Furthermore, UNDP and the World Bank provided relevant sections for the reports of the secretary-general to the UN Security Council.

The World Bank used the new impetus to sustain the dialogue with the government and thus maintain DDR on the government's agenda even though it was understood that it would not be opportune for the government to launch a national DDR program at this time. By late 1999, after long deliberations, UNICEF finally decided not to implement the World Bank's grant because of the agency's reaffirmed sole focus on child soldiers. After ensuing discussions with UN agencies dur-

---

[2]This chapter does not review MONUC's experience regarding the disarmament, demobilization, and repatriation of foreign armed groups. For more information, see www.monuc.org.

ing the multidonor/multiagency mission to Kinshasa in November 1999 and in agreement with the government, ILO was selected as the implementing agency to manage the grant and supervise the preparation of phase I through its Kinshasa office. Consequently, the work plan and budget were revised, the strengthening of government institutions was included therein, and a new technical secretariat under the guidance of the ministries of defense and human rights was established.

Phase I was fine-tuned to consist of two parts: a six-month preparation period and a six-month pilot implementation period. This approach allowed for the implementation of a stand-alone project executed by Congolese nationals with implementation support by ILO pending the creation of a national DDR structure. It was endorsed by the government and key UN partners on the ground. Thus, the Demobilization and Reintegration Project for Vulnerable Groups (DRP-VG) was finally launched in early 2000 using the grant from the World Bank's Post-Conflict Fund.

Toward Increased Government Engagement

UNICEF continued its advocacy for the release of child combatants from the armed forces. These efforts culminated in the Kinshasa forum on child soldiers organized by the ministry of human rights in January 2000. This event benefited from technical and financial support from UNICEF and Belgium and was an important moment in the fight for the rights of children in the DRC. It raised the issue of the enrollment of children in warring factions to the international level with the participation of several advocacy groups, and called for greater involvement from partners and donors to end this phenomenon. ILO was also heavily involved in line with its Convention 182 against abusive child labor. From then on, and while fighting was still going on in the eastern DRC, there was continuing pressure on the government and, to a lesser extent, on major rebel groups to release child soldiers.[3]

The new environment created by the DRP-VG and the advocacy for child soldier demobilization by UNICEF and the ministry of human rights led to the signing of Presidential decree-law 066 of June 9, 2000, authorizing the demobilization and reintegration of vulnerable groups defined as follows: war-injured and disabled, chronically ill, widows, orphans, elderly (to be retired), and child soldiers. The ministries of de-

---

[3]Noteworthy in this respect are also a number of separate initiatives by nongovernmental organizations (NGOs) in the eastern part of the country by, among others, Save the Children UK, SOS Grands Lacs, and Don Bosco.

fense and human rights were designated to jointly execute the decree. The National Office for the Demobilization and Reintegration or BUNADER (Bureau National de Démobilisation et de Réinsertion) was subsequently created to serve as the government's interface with the World Bank and ILO regarding the DRP-VG and with UNICEF on child soldier–related issues.

Demobilization and Reintegration of Vulnerable Groups

The DRP-VG, which started in earnest in June 2000 with a tripartite agreement among the government, the World Bank, and the ILO, had three objectives: (1) undertaking preparatory studies on demobilization and reintegration and designing a technical structure for the government that could assist with the challenges of the DRP-VG; (2) strengthening Congolese capacities on DDR issues; and (3) piloting reintegration activities in three parts of the country (Kinshasa, Kananga, and Lubumbashi) with a view to drawing lessons for the future national DDR program. At the time, the security situation and political environment did not allow for engagement with rebel groups although the eventual expansion of assistance to eastern Congo was an integral part of the project.

To implement the project, ILO established a small office consisting of a project coordinator and a team of three nationals, assisted by a chief technical advisor. The office was co-located with the ministry of human rights and BUNADER. Congolese consultants carried out several studies. The World Health Organization (WHO) and UNICEF assisted with the studies on the health status of vulnerable combatants and on child soldiers, respectively. The other studies focused on social protection, the socio-economic profile of vulnerable groups within the armed forces, and economic reintegration options.

To create synergies and maximize resources among donors and agencies, arrangements were made with UNICEF to fund and closely supervise the study on child soldiers, including the organization of workshops in-country and later funding of pilot reintegration activities. Apart from efforts aimed at child soldier demobilization, however, the World Bank's grant was still the sole available resource to address demobilization and reintegration issues in the country at the time of the creation of BUNADER. The DRP-VG, therefore, also included support to the government's institution, which lacked adequate funding. DRP-VG staff operating in the three pilot provinces benefited from various training sessions during the implementation phase, while the staff of BUNADER continued to enjoy technical support from the project team in Kinshasa. Furthermore, upon its completion, the project infra-structure and capacity were to be transferred to the government in anticipation of a national DDR program.

During the latter half of 2001, the DRP-VG was moving toward its second phase of piloting reintegration projects for targeted vulnerable groups. By the time the DRP-VG was completed in September 2003, these activities benefited 800 people in all categories, except for child soldiers, who were assisted separately by UNICEF in support of BUNADER efforts.

Pilot Activities in Retrospect

The DRP-VG achieved several noteworthy results. From 1999 to 2001, the project contributed to maintaining DDR on the government's agenda and during that period served as the cement for inter-agency collaboration and cooperation related to DDR. At the institutional level, the project built a strong team of Congolese professionals with more than two years of experience in demobilization and reintegration, ready for use by the national program. The capacity-building component of the project had a positive impact on practitioners and partners through study tours and training-of-trainers sessions.

The project was able to reach a considerable number of beneficiaries from truly vulnerable groups. An evaluation of micro projects showed signs that activities were on track and might be sustainable.[4] This was mainly due to the flexible and multidimensional approach used by the project vis-à-vis the beneficiaries, a good knowledge of local realities, the variety of micro-credit livelihood activities offered, and the decentralization of project infrastructure and management through field offices. The participatory approach used for pilot activities also allowed for deepened beneficiary involvement in preparation as well as implementation, thus ensuring better targeting.

Fulfilling its initial objectives, BUNADER drafted an interim national program for demobilization and reintegration concentrated on then-government-controlled areas. This document contained several concrete case studies useful to the planning of the future national DDR program. Furthermore, the DRP-VG regularly involved various ministries (defense, human rights, social affairs, reconstruction), key UN agencies (UNICEF, UNDP, WHO), and MONUC/DPKO through ex-

---

[4]For more information, see Verhey, Beth, 2003, "Program of Demobilization and Social and Economic Reinsertion of Vulnerable Ex-Combatants," World Bank–PCF Secretariat, Preliminary Evaluation Report (Washington: World Bank).

tended working groups. These forums were essential to share information and achieve a better understanding of the challenges ahead.

Project implementation took longer than originally planned. In particular, the DRP-VG experienced a period of uncertainty with the assassination of President Laurent-Désiré Kabila in January 2001. The continuing security constraints, especially regarding extending pilot activities to the east, further complicated implementation. Moreover, owing to the complex and ever-changing political environment resulting in the slow pace of the preparation of a national DDR program, the project lacked a clear exit strategy.

Administrative procedures within the World Bank and ILO have equally had a negative impact on the speed of implementation. Reaching an agreement on ILO cost recovery was time consuming. Delays in the flow of financial resources created delays and ruptures in training and initial reintegration activities. In addition, the project suffered from uncoordinated sensitization of beneficiaries by all actors who were in contact with them, including the government and the project team.

In the end, the time was not right to inspire lasting DDR collaboration within the international community, and the DRP-VG failed in this respect. While the World Bank's grant started the preparation work for DDR activities in the country, many actors—both local and international—later joined the process, but not in a coordinated manner. At one point, more than a dozen institutions were dealing one way or another with DDR. This created confusion over the role of the project vis-à-vis BUNADER, UNICEF's child soldier demobilization efforts, such projects as the War Wounded (*Blessés de guerre*), and the national DDR program.

Building Local Capacity

Concomitant with DRP-VG implementation, the World Bank initiated a series of activities aimed at building Congolese DDR capacity. In collaboration with DPKO, the World Bank organized a DDR workshop in Washington in June 2001. Congolese participants (from BUNADER and the ministries of national defense, reintegration, and human rights) learned lessons from the DDR program team in Sierra Leone, where DDR was about to be completed.

This initiative, which was extended to rebel groups, was followed in December 2001 by a World Bank-UNICEF sponsored field trip to Sierra Leone to provide the Congolese government and NGOs an opportunity to get a first-hand appreciation of the Sierra Leonean DDR experience. The Congolese delegation visited disarmament and demobilization camps and interim care centers for children and was able to learn more about reintegration planning as well as community rehabilitation and reconstruction.

Although Sierra Leone and the DRC may seem to be quite different at first sight, there are strong similarities between the two that made this south-south exchange particularly rewarding. First, neighbors interfered in the war by supporting the rebel groups fighting forces loyal to the central government. Second, access to natural resources was fueling the war. Third, both countries had a UN presence, the UN Assistance Mission in Sierra Leone and MONUC, respectively. In addition, the World Bank and UNICEF were involved in DDR technical and financial assistance in both Sierra Leone and the DRC.

Both experiences were rewarding for the Congolese participants. The trip to Sierra Leone was a unique opportunity to witness one of the most complete DDR programs, which in turn had benefited from previous DDR programs around the world, before the launch of the DRP-VG pilot activities; these commenced in January 2002. As a result, a lessons-learned workshop was organized upon the delegation's return to Kinshasa to share the experiences with a wider group of stakeholders (NGOs, UN agencies, and other actors).

Expanding Partnerships, Inside and Across Borders

The seventh report of the Secretary General on the DRC to the UN Security Council (April 2001) stated that MONUC may be called upon to assist foreign armed elements in the DRC who may present themselves for voluntary disarmament, demobilization, and repatriation. At that time, MONUC did not have either the means (military and financial) or the formal mandate to conduct such operations should they occur. The complexity of the situation was further highlighted by a multidonor/agency mission to the DRC in May 2001, which identified five clusters of Congolese target groups with different legal frameworks: child soldiers, other vulnerable groups, Congolese armed groups, combatants of the rebel movements, and the FAC. The presence of non-Congolese armed groups (Burundi, Rwanda, Uganda) and of statutory forces of six countries (Angola, Namibia, Zimbabwe, Burundi, Rwanda, Uganda) underlined the regional dimension of the DRC conflict.

The international community was, thus, confronted with an unparalleled multitude of target groups both inside and outside the country and a multitude of Congolese and international actors in charge of various target groups, with increasing risk of overlap and competition.

Only firm government action could have introduced a methodical approach. However, other than continued political uncertainty regarding the full implementation of the Lusaka agreement, the continued lack of government leadership was considered the most critical factor endangering the long-term success of DDR efforts in the country. Hence, the call for tighter coordination among donors and UN agencies, and for nurturing government ownership.

To meet the challenge, in 2001 MONUC established a unit with more than 40 staff specifically dedicated to the disarmament, demobilization, and repatriation of foreign armed groups in the DRC. Heeding MONUC's call, and with Belgian assistance, the World Bank seconded one staff as a senior liaison officer to MONUC to contribute to the consolidation of the relationships between the two institutions.

Deepened cooperation between MONUC and the World Bank became ever more important as of July 2001, when the World Bank led the international effort to prepare, in close partnership with the Rwandan authorities, the Rwanda Demobilization and Reintegration Program (RDRP). Rwandan armed groups returning to Rwanda from the DRC are a central target group of the RDRP. Over time, coordination between the Rwandan government and MONUC helped establish procedures, in the DRC and in Rwanda, to facilitate the return of this group and their eventual reintegration into Rwandan society.

Section III. 2001–03: Toward a Concerted Effort

An Improving Political Environment

With the launch of the inter-Congolese dialogue in Addis Ababa in October 2001, as agreed upon in the Lusaka cease-fire agreement, prospects for DDR in the DRC improved. Preparation of MONUC phase 3, (i.e., the withdrawal of foreign statutory forces in the DRC and the disarmament, demobilization, and repatriation of foreign armed groups) commenced in earnest. The UN secretary-general visited the DRC and Rwanda in September 2001 to show the UN's commitment to consolidate peace in the DRC and in the Great Lakes region.

In this context, in August/September 2001, UNDP and several donors launched a mission to the region to define UNDP's role in DDR in the DRC, Burundi, Rwanda, and Uganda, as well as in small arms reduction and the demobilization of child soldiers. At about the same time, the World Bank initiated preparation of a regional, sectorwide approach to DDR covering nine countries.

A Regional Framework for Coordination and Resource Mobilization

With peace in the DRC a more realistic prospect, and in close collaboration with more than 30 multilateral and bilateral partners and the governments of participating countries,[5] the World Bank prepared a greater Great Lakes Regional Strategy for Demobilization and Reintegration, which provides the strategic framework for the Multi-Country Demobilization and Reintegration Program (MDRP). The strategy and program were approved by partners and endorsed by the World Bank's Board of Executive Directors in April 2002.

The strategy's main premise is that the DDR of ex-combatants is necessary to establish peace and restore security, which are in turn a precondition for sustainable growth and poverty reduction. The strategic objective is thus to enhance the prospects for stabilization and recovery in the region. The strategy seeks to complement and reinforce efforts by the international community in the political, security, and recovery spheres.

The program objectives are to (1) provide a comprehensive regional framework for DDR efforts for both government and irregular forces; (2) establish a single mechanism for donor coordination and resource mobilization; and (3) serve as a platform for national consultative processes that lead to the formulation of national demobilization and reintegration programs. Since early 2002, the MDRP has set the framework for DDR preparation and coordination in the DRC as well.

At the request of donors, and in consultation with participating governments, the World Bank established a US$350 million multidonor trust fund to mobilize grant resources from the donor community for the purpose of implementing the MDRP. Such a consolidated funding mechanism helps to ensure comprehensive and well-coordinated donor support to the program, facilitate the involvement of donors that might otherwise not be able to participate, minimize duplication of efforts, reduce the administrative burden on governments through the application of one set of implementation procedures, and strengthen program ownership on the part of governments. The trust fund complements an estimated US$150 million from the World Bank in support of national DDR programs in the region. The DRC, as a country participating in the MDRP, benefits from both trust fund and World Bank funding.

---

[5]The nine participating countries are Angola, Burundi, Central African Republic, DRC, Namibia, Republic of Congo, Rwanda, Uganda, and Zimbabwe. As of mid-2003, all but Namibia and Zimbabwe have been receiving support at various levels.

Furthermore, through its Technical Coordination Group of senior technical and management staff of participating countries, the MDRP helps build transparency in DDR matters across countries though information sharing on progress on DDR activities, exchanging lessons learned, exploring opportunities for technical cooperation, and building DDR capacities. The DRC has benefited extensively from these efforts.

Starting Over

Upon request by the DRC government, UNDP launched a reinvigorated effort aimed at preparing a national DDR program in August 2002. While government ownership of this process increased, the appropriate institutional set-up remained missing. Responsibility continued to be scattered among various agencies, making the interactions with the international community prone to misunderstandings.

Among the international community, commitment was high to support the government in the preparation and financing of its DDR program. However, given the multitude of target groups and local stakeholders, it was hardly surprising that the international community restarted its DDR efforts in the DRC in a rather uncoordinated manner. Because of staff changes at various UN agencies and donors there was a lack of institutional memory regarding DDR efforts between 1997 and 2001. There was also a lack of a clear and common understanding of essential DDR preparation activities, and of the MDRP framework more broadly. Coordination and communications problems reflected as much differences in the way individual donors and agencies work as differences in approaches regarding the role of government and its partners in the DDR process. Overcoming these constraints has proved to be as challenging as adapting the DDR effort to this most complex of environments.

Over time, the discipline in terms of partner cooperation that was introduced by the MDRP in the DRC and all other countries helped resolve many of the issues. MDRP partner missions visited the DRC in September 2002 and February and October 2003 to provide guidance to the international community's efforts in support of DDR and carry out the annual joint supervision of MDRP activities. The February mission also endorsed the decision that UNDP be lead agency for DDR in the DRC. To rally partners around a common vision, UNDP established a number of working groups and an interagency technical committee. In support of DDR efforts in the DRC and other countries, the MDRP Secretariat placed a senior demobilization and reintegration specialist in Kinshasa in early 2003. Furthermore, reflecting on the importance of the DDR effort in the DRC, MDRP partners held their biannual meeting in Kinshasa in November 2003.

As a result, since the MDRP framework was introduced to the DRC in mid-2002, achievements in terms of coordination have been remarkable. Activities undertaken within the framework of the MDRP by late 2003 included (1) the interim strategy and the work of UNDP and partners toward the development and implementation of technical guidelines, operational plans, technical support to government for the creation of the national DDR institutions, dialogue with government on the preparation of the national plan, and dialogue on the interlinkages between security sector reform and DDR; (2) the continued efforts of MONUC in relation to the disarmament, demobilization, and repatriation of foreign armed groups and voluntary disarmament of irregular forces; (3) the development of a strategy for demobilizing child soldiers and coordination efforts by UNICEF and child protection agencies on all issues pertaining to the care, protection, and reintegration of child soldiers; (4) ongoing activities for child soldiers by Save the Children Fund UK under the MDRP's special project window; (5) initial preparatory work by UNDP and the International Rescue Committee for the implementation of special projects; and (6) an identification mission by the World Bank for its financial contribution to the program.

· Active coordination and cooperation within the international community and the active engagement of the government by the partners have undoubtedly enhanced the effectiveness of DDR efforts and provide the best chance for the future DDR program to succeed. However, coordination—deemed by all essential for a successful national DDR program—has remained one of the most difficult challenges.

Cross-Border Efforts

On July 30, 2002, the governments of the DRC and Rwanda signed an agreement in Pretoria regarding the withdrawal of Rwandan armed forces from the DRC and the disarmament, demobilization, and repatriation of Rwandan armed groups still in the DRC to Rwanda. The first element of the agreement, the withdrawal of Rwandan armed forces, was completed in 2002. To advance the second element, technical delegations from the DRC and Rwanda met in Nairobi in September 2002 to explore opportunities to advance the technical implementation of this agreement. This meeting was facilitated by the MDRP Secretariat, which is managed by the World Bank, and was also attended by UNDP and MONUC.

After a field visit of Congolese DDR specialists to Rwanda in October/November 2002, the MDRP Secretariat, with MONUC participation, organized another meeting for technical delegations from the DRC and Rwanda in Magaliesburg, South Africa, in December that year. The two delegations elaborated a work plan for the preparation and implementation of a joint sensitization strategy that took into account the preoccupations of Rwandan armed groups still in the DRC and that also provided timely, correct, and consistent information on the DDR processes in both the DRC and Rwanda.

Both governments formally endorsed the joint strategy for cross-border communications and sensitization. Although progress was made in its implementation, including the preparation of materials for dissemination (brochures, leaflets, comic strips, etc.) and a visit to Rwanda to make a video on repatriated ex-combatants, these efforts were put on hold pending the integration of the program on the part of the DRC, under the ministry of defense as per the decree on mandates of various ministries. The Rwanda Demobilization and Reintegration Commission has been the official counterpart on the Rwandan side.

In parallel to these bilateral efforts, MONUC continued to disarm, demobilize, and repatriate foreign armed groups from the eastern DRC. By early 2004, it had repatriated 9,200 ex-combatants and dependents to Burundi, Rwanda, and Uganda; more than half of these were ex-combatants out of an estimated total of 15,000 to 20,000. Delays in this program have been attributed to various factors. Considerable suspicion and mistrust vis-à-vis the leadership of the Rwandan armed groups continued. North and South Kivu remained relatively unstable as indicated by persistent outbreaks of fighting involving multiple actors in shifting and unpredictable alliances. Furthermore, MONUC has been faced with logistical difficulties arising from the degradation of infrastructure, including roads, airstrips, and communications facilities. Moreover, a series of armed attacks carried out in early 2003 by Rassemblement Congolais pour la Démocratie (RCD-GOMA) forces resulted in the scattering into the forest of armed members who had assembled to enter MONUC's program, which seriously disrupted operations.

Target Groups and Targeted Assistance

By 2003, Congolese armed forces and movements to be disarmed and demobilized reached unprecedented numbers. These included the FAC, RCD-GOMA forces, Mouvement pour la libération du Congo (MLC) forces, RCD-K-ML forces, and the Mayi Mayi groups that are signatories to the Pretoria agreement. Members of these groups are mostly able-bodied young men familiar with weapons and warfare, thus representing a potential threat to the transition. Intertribal fighting between local armed groups severely destabilized the district of Ituri during 2002–03, making the disarmament and demobilization of these groups a special challenge. However, the military intervention by European Union troops, later replaced by MONUC units, helped stabilize the situation to a large extent. Lastly, there were still Congolese groups in other countries in need of repatriation, including approximately 4,000 ex-FAZ and FAC and their dependents in the Republic of Congo and the ex-police forces from Katanga (*ex-gendarmes katangais*) in Angola.

A key decision for DDR planning, which is ultimately political but which has enormous practical as well as financial consequences, is what criteria to apply to determine eligibility of ex-combatant access to program benefits. By the end of 2003, no clarity existed from the government or the armed groups, and it became increasingly difficult to manage the expectations of the large numbers of potential beneficiaries. Experience in Liberia at the end of 2003 has shown that this can lead to serious problems, unrest, and even loss of life.

With numbers ranging from 10,000 to 30,000, children associated with the fighting forces constituted the most important special target group, with recruitment still not fully halted in 2003. Early in 2003, UNICEF spearheaded the preparation of a national strategy for child soldier demobilization. In cooperation with various child protection agencies, UNICEF continued to advocate against the recruitment of children and to implement small-scale efforts as and when possible. At the same time, there remained a lack of a clear process by the government for the immediate demobilization of children; the existing system of issuing of demobilization papers could take up to six months.

There has been broad agreement within the international community that DDR activities, in particular reintegration, require a thorough, community-based approach. The MDRP contains the provision of such efforts through special projects pending the launch of a national program. This provision is of particular relevance to the DRC, because it also allowed the funding of targeted activities (through UN agencies and NGOs) in areas outside government control. By the end of 2003, seven such projects were approved, mainly addressing the needs of child soldiers but also providing quick support to emerging needs on the ground, the latter through a UNDP-managed rapid-response mechanism.

These special projects have suffered considerable delays in their processing. Reasons were multiple. The notion of special projects with direct contracting under a World Bank–administered trust fund represented a

novelty for the World Bank and required the elaboration of new procedures. To decentralize decision-making authority, selected MDRP partners based in Kinshasa formed a local ad hoc committee in charge of
reviewing and appraising proposals using simplified assessment tools.
Many proposals required substantial, time-consuming improvements.
Lastly, it became apparent that some recipients were interested not only
in the project they proposed to implement but also in establishing precedents that would serve them in future relations with the World Bank in
the DRC and elsewhere. As a result, some grant negotiations took inor-
dinately long. Given the overall slow political progress, however, these
delays in implementing special projects did not have any serious consequences on the situation on the ground.

A Bridge to Government Ownership

Insecurity in large parts of the country and the absence of a national
counterpart made it difficult to start comprehensive DDR planning.
Hence, the government and international partners agreed in early 2003
on the preparation of an interim DDR strategy under UNDP leadership
with technical assistance by the Department for International
Development. This strategy was based on four simultaneous approaches,
namely: (1) a dialogue between the principal political actors in the DRC
on the structure and management of a national DDR program that
should have the active support of all components of the future
Transitional Government; (2) the planning of a large and logistically
complex national DDR program; (3) the development of a rapid-response mechanism to address these issues pending the full establishment
of the national program; and (4) efforts led by UNICEF for the DDR of
child soldiers, as well as UNDP support for disabled ex-combatants,
which would later be incorporated into a national program.

The preparation of the national DDR program for the Congolese
armed groups was informed by four developments: (1) detailed discussions held by expatriate experts in Kinshasa under the auspices of
UNDP; (2) discussions among all parties on security sector reform and
the formation of an integrated, inclusive national army, and clarifica-
tion of the institutional arrangements for DDR; (3) building on relevant experience from the disarmament, demobilization, and
repatriation of foreign armed groups; and (4) the withdrawal of foreign
troops, which would open the possibility of the DDR of Congolese
armed groups. Meanwhile, the government and international partners
adopted an operational framework for spontaneous and voluntary disarmament in December 2003, which had become an urgent matter in

the prevailing situation. During that year, many groups and individuals had been coming forward wishing to disarm in the hope of benefiting from humanitarian assistance or other forms of support.

The interim strategy served as an important mechanism for the co-ordination of all technical groups established for DDR preparation. The groups soon became functional with the exception of the sensitization working group, which has been constrained by a lack of participation from various agencies. UNDP has also been regularly briefing the local donor committee on DDR that was established in early 2003.

The interim phase ended in late 2003 when the government laid out the responsibilities of the different ministries vis-à-vis demobilization and reintegration and effectively assumed the lead for DDR activities. With decrees No. 03/041, 03/042, and 03/043 of December 18, 2003, President Joseph Kabila established an interministerial DDR committee, the National Disarmament, Demobilization and Reintegration Commission or CONADER (Commission Nationale de Désarmement, Démobilisation et Réinsertion), and a committee responsible for managing DDR funds, respectively. This was a major step forward. Now, after more than six years, the international community finally had a legitimate counterpart for the planning and implementation of DDR activities in the context of a national DDR program. The government thereby removed the uncertainty associated with having to deal with manifold institutions in the DRC with different and overlapping mandates.

Aiming at Security Sector Reform

The Transitional Government, formed in June 2003 and in office since September that year, envisaged the establishment of the new Congolese armed forces in three phases: (1) sensitization and identification; (2) encampment, screening, selection for the army, and training—those not selected during this phase would be demobilized; and (3) formation of the military units and deployment. There was progress in the installation of the integrated military high command (September 4, 2003), and decisions relating to the distribution of the regional command were elaborated. One of the key priorities was to carry out an identification exercise of the current forces and also to identify sites that could be used for the screening of combatants to be integrated into the army.

A number of difficulties needed to be addressed in implementing this plan, including the question of signatories and nonsignatories, the budget, continued security problems in certain parts of the country, and a lack of expertise in reconstructing military forces. It was generally recognized by MDRP partners that DDR and security sector reform are two sides of the same coin and, thus, needed to be closely coordinated for both to be effective. The start of DDR program implementation, therefore, also depended on a final agreement on and the establishment of the future national, unified, and restructured army.

The Challenge Ahead

At the end of 2003, almost eight years after the Congolese civil war first erupted, the DRC found itself at an intersection of war and peace. The national DDR program was an integral part of this critical transition period. Three objectives have been set for the program: (1) the demobilization and reintegration into civilian life of some 90,000 to 150,000 Congolese ex-combatants; (2) the provision of reintegration assistance to the demobilized ex-combatants; and (3) special assistance to vulnerable groups. The DDR program was also expected to have a significant impact on reducing poverty in the DRC by (1) helping ex-combatants reestablish civilian livelihoods; (2) freeing national resources for investment in social and economic sectors; (3) investing in the human capital of ex-combatants; and (4) enhancing the capacity for community-based development mechanisms.

The move by the government to assume the lead for the preparation and implementation of the national DDR program coincided with the adoption by the UN Security Council of a new, firmer mandate for MONUC and much greater resources to establish security throughout the country, including for the purposes of DDR within the MDRP framework (Resolution No. 1493 of July 25, 2003). This reinforced the position of MONUC as a key partner (with UNDP) in planning and implementing the DDR program, especially in the disarmament and demobilization stages. While all necessary political, financial, and institutional conditions were largely in place by the end of 2003, much work remained to be done by the Transitional Government and its partners before the first combatant could be demobilized under a national program. If DDR was to assist in creating favorable conditions for elections in 2005, for reconciliation, peace, and economic recovery, the program needed to finally start in earnest.

Section IV. Reflections

The DDR experience in the DRC confirms a lesson drawn in many other countries, namely that without firm government commitment no DDR program can be prepared or implemented, and that DDR cannot be undertaken by the international community on behalf of the warring factions. In other words, a DDR program cannot be a substitute for a political process. In the case of the DRC, apart from the initial months in 1997, when highly commendable work was carried out, this political willingness and leadership were not forthcoming until late 2003. Conversely, the early days point to another important lesson. If political willingness exists, a government will make available high-level, competent, and empowered technical counterparts who can rapidly advance the work.

Maintaining DDR on the government's agenda over the years implied continued sensitization as to the importance of the topic and to the various issues that would eventually need to be addressed. Such sensitization is considered of value even if the pay-off is not immediate. In a similar vein, the cross-border efforts under the MDRP have helped reduce tensions and led to a better appreciation of mutual possibilities and constraints. The facilitating role of an intermediary, in this case the MDRP Secretariat, has been acknowledged by the DRC and Rwanda and testifies to the usefulness of a neutral space to discuss technical matters.

The international community exercised great patience for having accompanied the Congolese authorities in the DDR process over so many years. UNICEF has shown great perseverance advocating for and implementing child soldier demobilization at every stage of the political process. This effort has proved that child soldier demobilization is feasible even when the fighting still continues. Furthermore, the World Bank's engagement since 1997 confirms that program preparation is politically less contentious and worth undertaking, especially if done in a low-key manner that takes into account the dynamics of the situation on the ground. Even more importantly, a first-hand understanding by the World Bank of demobilization challenges and options in the DRC provided a critical impetus for assuming the regional perspective that ultimately led to the preparation of the MDRP.

A rapid response by the international community, both technically and financially, is commonly required. In the case of the DRC, UNICEF and the World Bank were able to quickly provide critical technical assistance in 1997, yet the institutional arrangements set up in 1999 were suboptimal. No other donor or agency was forthcoming at the time, preferring to await initial results before committing to support the process. When the international community finally engaged forcefully in 2002, a focus on institutional mandates rather than on issues severely hampered its effectiveness. Institutional jockeying implied the neglect of earlier experience in the DRC and the willingness to engage in prolonged contractual negotiations for special projects.

Partnerships remain central to any DDR effort in any country because no one donor or agency can handle the multitude of tasks and responsibilities. Such partnerships require a sense of discipline and a willingness to compromise and be transparent. Throughout the period 1997–2003, this remained a real challenge, and many uncoordinated efforts complicated DDR efforts enormously. Early on, international partners sent diverging signals that likely undermined national coordination efforts. Uncoordinated, piecemeal efforts also created the risk of setting precedents in terms of types and levels of assistance that might not be financed, or appropriate, for a national effort. In this respect, the introduction of the MDRP framework in late 2002 had a positive impact on donor coordination and effectiveness.

The constantly evolving situation affirmed the importance of flexibility and adaptability on the part of both the government and its partners. The conceptual shift from the comprehensive approach of 1997 to the phased approach of 1999 is testimony that on a technical level, planning parameters were regularly reviewed and adaptations made as new circumstances required. The rather unconventional approach since late 2002 with a triple focus on national program preparation, assistance to vulnerable groups (especially child and disabled soldiers), and community-based reintegration in areas outside government control was another sign of the international community's understanding of underlying parameters, and of its adaptability in terms of financial and technical assistance.

A critical factor in the country's DDR history is local capacity. Continued investments in technical staff in various government departments have created a core expertise before the launch of a national program quite unparalleled to that in other countries. The south-south exchanges with Sierra Leone and participating MDRP countries have been particularly valuable. Furthermore, continuity of staff on both the government's and the partners' sides, which in the case of the DRC was partially achieved, is deemed important. It helps build up a technical working relationship that can weather political turbulences and enable all sides to be ready for DDR planning and implementation as and when the situation permits.

The regional dimension should always be taken into account when planning and implementing a DDR program. In the case of the DRC, this need was self-evident. First, foreign powers helped put the new regime in place before changing to a strategy intent on ousting it. Second, the initial work plan and DDR policy note were literally prepared with the thunder of fighting in Brazzaville in the background. The complexity of the situation after August 1998 ultimately led to the idea of the single most ambitious DDR effort so far: the MDRP in the greater Great Lakes region. This required a conceptual shift in the approach the international community has taken to postconflict situations to date, a challenge it has lived up to with remarkable success.

Quality matters. The MDRP framework has helped partners understand this imperative, which, for instance, led to initial rejections of various special project proposals that had not been properly prepared or included unacceptably high costs. The history of DDR in the DRC, thus, confirms that to maximize the chances of success, there can be no shortcut to essential procedures, whether or not time is of the essence. Even if the sequence of program elements were altered to accommodate emerging needs, implementation capacities and sufficient funds need to be in place lest unstructured demobilization heightens reintegration problems.

Lastly, military reform is the flipside of any DDR program. There was a clear need on the part of the Congolese military authorities to come to terms with the political decision to integrate the ex-FAZ into the FAC, and later to integrate the rebel movements as stipulated in the Lusaka accord. Assistance to military reform needs to be provided through military bilateral cooperation; development agencies have neither the requisite mandate nor skills to carry out this task. Contact between DDR partners and bilaterals interested in security sector reform is important in this respect, to share information and harmonize the advice given to the authorities. Even more than DDR, however, cooperation in the reform of the security sector depends on the government's clear and continued commitment, which in the DRC had not materialized until after the establishment of the transitional government.